Politics of Religious Freedom

CW01497759

Politics of Religious Freedom

EDITED BY WINNIFRED
FALLERS SULLIVAN, ELIZABETH
SHAKMAN HURD, SABA MAHMOOD,
AND PETER G. DANCHIN

THE UNIVERSITY OF CHICAGO PRESS   CHICAGO AND LONDON

Winnifred Fallers Sullivan is professor in and chair of the Department of Religious Studies at Indiana University–Bloomington. She is also an affiliated professor of law at Indiana University–Bloomington Maurer School of Law. **Elizabeth Shakman Hurd** is associate professor in the Departments of Political Science and (by courtesy) Religious Studies at Northwestern University. **Saba Mahmood** is associate professor in the Department of Anthropology at the University of California, Berkeley. **Peter G. Danchin** is professor of law and director of the International and Comparative Law Program at the University of Maryland School of Law.

The University of Chicago Press, Chicago 60637
The University of Chicago Press, Ltd., London
© 2015 by The University of Chicago
All rights reserved. Published 2015.
Printed in the United States of America
24 23 22 21 20 19 18 17 16 15   1 2 3 4 5

ISBN-13: 978-0-226-24847-9 (cloth)
ISBN-13: 978-0-226-24850-9 (paper)
ISBN-13: 978-0-226-24864-6 (e-book)
DOI: 10.7208/chicago/9780226248646.001.0001

Library of Congress Cataloging-in-Publication Data

Politics of religious freedom / edited by Winnifred Fallers Sullivan, Elizabeth Shakman Hurd, Saba Mahmood, and Peter G. Danchin.
    pages cm
    Includes bibliographical references and index.
    ISBN 978-0-226-24847-9 (cloth : alkaline paper)—ISBN 0-226-24847-x (cloth : alkaline paper)—ISBN 978-0-226-24850-9 (paperback : alkaline paper)—ISBN 0-226-24850-x (paperback : alkaline paper)—ISBN 978-0-226-24864-6 (e-book)—ISBN 0-226-24864-x (e-book)
    1. Religion and politics. 2. Freedom of religion. I. Sullivan, Winnifred Fallers, 1950– editor. II. Hurd, Elizabeth Shakman, 1970– editor. III. Mahmood, Saba, 1962– editor. IV. Danchin, Peter, G., editor.
    BL65.P7P64235 2015
    323.44'2—dc23

                                                        2014042990

♾ This paper meets the requirements of ANSI/NISO z39.48-1992 (Permanence of Paper).

Acknowledgments

This volume is a collaborative effort in the best sense of those words, and the editors are immensely grateful to the contributors for their patience and generosity as this volume came together. The editors also wish to acknowledge the generous support of the Henry Luce Foundation, and of Toby Volkman, in particular, whose support of this project has been unstinting. We also thank Jonathan VanAntwerpen, Jessica Polebaum, and Wei Zhu at the Immanent Frame; Penelope Ismay and Neil Gali at the University of California–Berkeley; Mona Oraby at Northwestern University; Kerilyn Harkaway-Krieger at Indiana University; and Chris Rhodes and the anonymous reviewers for the University of Chicago Press.

Contents

Introduction

Winnifred Fallers Sullivan, Elizabeth Shakman Hurd,
Saba Mahmood, and Peter G. Danchin

In a remarkably short period, religious freedom has been naturalized in public discourse worldwide as an indispensable condition for peace in our time, advocated around the world and across the religious and political spectrum. Supported by a flood of reports purporting to document a rise in global religious suppression, a wide range of public and private international actors—including states, international organizations, private foundations, and nongovernmental organizations, as well as academics—have responded with laws, programs, projects, and policies designed actively to promote the right to religious freedom. Older guarantees to religious freedom built into laws and constitutions over the last few centuries are being mobilized, while such provisions are also being introduced into new legal instruments, trade agreements, constitutions, and legislation. In many legal and public policy circles today, religious freedom is being presented as *the* key to emancipating individuals and communities from violence, poverty, and oppression. Indeed, the gospel of religious freedom is often said to lead comprehensively to democracy, greater civil and political liberty, and prosperity.

Everyone seems to be for it. But what are they for? What exactly is being promoted through the discourse of religious freedom, and what is not? What is being protected under these various legal instruments? What forms of politics are enabled by these activities? How might we describe the cultural and epistemological assumptions that underlie this frenzy, and what is its longer history?

This volume brings together a collection of essays that emerged out of an edited set of blog posts on the Immanent Frame website (hosted by the Social Science Research Council) as a part of the Politics of Religious Freedom research project, a three-year effort funded by the Henry Luce Foundation to study the discourses of religious freedom in South Asia, North Africa, the Middle East, Europe, and the United States; it later was expanded to include research on sub-Saharan Africa and Brazil. The volume is divided into four sections: Religion, History, Law/Politics, and Freedom, each with a brief preface by one of the editors.

Over the course of the project, the conversation has spread out well beyond the four project leaders and editors; it has become a broad collaborative effort to describe an importantly complex phenomenon—complex well beyond our initial intuitions, one not easily reduced to a single narrative or explanatory framework. The scholars who responded to our invitations, many of whom are represented in this volume, and others who contributed to our other publications, have helped us to think through these questions in new ways. The essays collected here unsettle the assumption—so ubiquitous in policy circles—that religious freedom is easily recognized and understood, and that the only problem lies in its incomplete realization.

Our project does not take a position for or against religious freedom. Rather, we are interested in laying out the kind of work that advocacy for religious freedom has done and is doing in various times and places, and the kind of political and legal worlds it has created and is creating. Our basic assumption is that, before either championing religious freedom or rejecting it, we need to understand the complex social and legal lives of this concept. Those impatient for an improved definition of religious freedom, or those demanding a political manifesto, may be disappointed by this book. But to understand the contested historical genealogy of the concept of religious liberty, we believe it is important to grasp the ways in which this seemingly obvious and neutral right has yielded mutually contradictory and often discriminatory results. Our hope is that policy makers, academics, and others will learn, as we have, from examining this often messy story.

We have also sought to learn from cases in which religious freedom discourse is or was absent, including examining the regulation of religion in places and times distant from the present. For example, looking at the various legal regimes that coexisted in Mughal-ruled India, as Nandini Chatterjee's work has done, reveals not Muslim legal hegemony (or legal pluralism in a formal statist sense) but forum shopping and "permissive" legal centralization; not religious equality but religious multiplicity fitted into a system of religiopolitical hierarchy; not rigid faith boundaries but fluid and interpenetrating religious identities and communities, a situation that belies the common assumption that a Muslim state necessarily limits legal possibilities. Considering such examples poses crucial questions to those engaged in the promotion of religious freedom as a human right today. What is missing when religious freedom is imagined exclusively through the lexicon of liberal rights as a set of discrete freedoms claimed by individuals or groups from an assumedly neutral and secular state? What claims can and cannot be made regarding religion, personhood, and freedom? What modes of religiosity, notions of religious difference or nondifference, and idioms of social order and harmony are rendered unintelligible or incoherent?

We share a concern with others around the world today about the persistence of what is often misnamed religious persecution. But it seems to us that the reasons for persecution are varied and complex, and need to be carefully unpacked. Our research, and that of others, suggests that caution is in order in describing violence and discrimination—or, indeed, freedom or peace—as "religious" in origin or nature. While a particular group may appear to be discriminated against on the basis of an attributed identity commonly denominated as religious, it is also the case that the motivations for discrimination are multiple, complex, and often inaccessible. These essays ask whether *religious* is indeed the right modifier when discussing these situations, or whether it is advisable to open them up, making room for less certainty and more complexity regarding the context and causes of violent conflict and discrimination. Naming the causes of these events as religious while indiscriminately promoting religious freedom as the solution may exacerbate the very divisions that plague the countries and communities cited most frequently as falling short in measures of religious freedom.

Take the case of Pakistan, seen by many as a poster child for the urgency of the need for religious liberty. Violence against minorities (Ahmadis, Muslims, and Christians, in particular) has increased over the past several decades, and intolerance toward dissenters has taken root in a manner that most would not have predicted in the early years of the establishment of the postcolonial state. The key historical factors that have produced this climate of intolerance and hatred are political and economic and thus cannot be addressed through religious liberty advocacy alone. As many historians note, persecution of various kinds received its biggest boost during the ten-year military dictatorship of President

Muhammad Zia-ul-Haq (1978–88) when the rights of women, political dissidents, and minorities were brutally crushed and state persecution of political opposition was normalized. The US government supported the Zia-ul-Haq junta militarily and economically because it promised to fight a proxy war on behalf of the United States against the Soviet occupation of Afghanistan. While the Soviets were indeed pushed out of Afghanistan in 1989, in the process Pakistan was militarized to an unprecedented degree, overtaken by the mujahideen, who were supported and trained by the United States, the Pakistani military, and Saudi Arabia for over a decade. The "Pakistani Taliban" and the brutal national security agency (the Inter-Services Intelligence, or ISI) now terrorizing the majority of Pakistanis are a product of this history. The Pakistani military has made a Faustian bargain with the Taliban and Saudi Arabia on the one hand and the US government on the other in order to diminish the possibility of authentic political and economic reform. The serious problems that Pakistan now faces require political and economic solutions—most notably the curtailment of military power and the ISI. Foregrounding religious freedom as *the* key to understanding Pakistan's problems today blinds us to the political and economic pathologies of Pakistan.

The blind spots produced by a politics of religious freedom and persecution can also be seen in the recent history of Myanmar, where a population of roughly 800,000 Rohingya have been categorized by the government as "Bengali immigrants" and denied Burmese citizenship. Though most Rohingya have lived in Rakhine in northern Myanmar for generations, with many having been forcibly relocated from Bangladesh in the early nineteenth century, when Britain annexed Myanmar as a province of British India and brought in migrant Muslim laborers, the current government has for decades subjected this population to official and unofficial persecution and discrimination, including massive government-sponsored repression, crackdowns with names such as Operation Dragon King (1978) and Operation Clean and Beautiful Nation (1991). State-sanctioned violence has intensified in recent years, and as of summer 2013 many Rohingya had been driven from their villages and were subsisting in squalid refugee camps far from home. Many fled to other countries and are living in dire conditions; many are stateless. Despite this complex and messy reality, government commissions, journalists, and academics insist on identifying the Rohingya as simply victims of a lack of religious freedom. Discrimination against the Rohingya is ethnic, racial, political, economic, and national; it is difficult to say which of these factors "causes" the violence. Indeed it is always difficult to pinpoint the causes of such violence. A prominent Buddhist monks' organization, 969, led informally by a monk named U Wirathu, insists on their comprehensive exclusion from Burmese society through violent removal, if necessary. Claiming to work on behalf of the "religious rights and freedoms" of the majority Buddhist population, Wirathu's group reportedly enjoys support from senior government officials, establishment monks, and even some members of the opposition National League for Democracy—the political party of Nobel Peace Prize laureate Aung San Suu Kyi. Promoting religious rights for the Rohingya arguably plays directly into the hands of 969, which depends on the perception of hard and fast lines of Muslim/Buddhist difference and immutable ties among majoritarian (Buddhist) religion, race, and Burmese national identity. For the international community to single out religion as the operative marker of social difference in these circumstances is descriptively inaccurate and does more harm than good.

It is time to step back from the seductively over-simplified diagnosis licensed by religious freedom advocacy.

*   *   *

The essays in this volume trace several genealogies of the concept of religious freedom in a variety of contexts. They show that religious liberty is not a single, stable principle existing outside of history or spatial geographies but is an inescapably context-bound, polyvalent concept unfolding within divergent histories in differing political orders. They also provincialize all talk of West versus non-West. Consistent with much critical scholarship in the history of ideas today, the present volume explicitly challenges reigning teleological narratives that advance the simultaneous neutrality and universality of the right to religious freedom, providing a more nuanced assessment of its multiple histories and genealogies.

One oft-told origin story pictures religious liberty as emerging in a very specific early modern European context, establishing the foundation of political secularism by separating religion from politics and making the state indifferent or, in today's vernacular, "neutral" toward claims of religious truth. On this view, religious liberty, since its initial formulation in seventeenth-century political thought, has continued progressively to expand its ambit of toleration to all religions—far beyond its initial mandate to institute peace across Christian denominations. Essays in this volume revisit and revise this narrative. Religious liberty even in its earliest formulation in European history was an unsteady and unstable concept, the result of what Ian Hunter has termed a "'circumstantial casuistry' of historically embedded political concepts" as opposed to a principled commitment to the separation of church and state. Indeed, importantly, as Hunter shows, the rival conceptions of religious freedom that emerged in early modern Europe "have proved inscrutable to both normative philosophical ordering, and to sociohistorical reconciliation."

We can see the stubborn multiplicity in the deep incompatibility even among early modern European conceptions of religious liberty. In theological argument, Martin Luther's sixteenth-century "freedom of all Christian believers" was and remains deeply incompatible with a Catholic theology that resolutely rejected both the 1555 Peace of Augsburg and a Protestant notion of freedom of conscience. In legal doctrine, the *cuius regio, eius religio* principle (which made a ruler's religion the religion of his entire realm) at the heart of the Augsburg Settlement was later repudiated by the Westphalian Treaties of 1648, proving Georg Jellinek's aphorism that history, not jurisprudence, teaches the true principle. And in seventeenth-century political thought, John Locke's conception of religious toleration developed in the context of the Anglican Settlement was deeply incompatible with that advanced by Samuel von Pufendorf and Christian Thomasius writing in the context of German imperial public law and the Brandenburg-Prussian regime. What was pivotal to these arrangements was not neutrality but a casuistical delineation of a sphere of *adiaphora* (those things not necessary for salvation) in order to make much prior religious doctrine and practice subject to the regulation of civil law. Given the necessarily regional and contingent character of these understandings, subsequent philosophical attempts to ground religious liberty in transcendent principles have been unable to supersede the incompatibilities at the heart of the conception since its early history. Indeed, conflicts over religious freedom continue to result in a crazy quilt of local solutions.

These early histories and antinomies continue to be relevant for understanding the formulation of the right to religious liberty in contemporary international law and human rights discourse. For example, the textual structure of article 9 of the European Court of Human Rights can be seen to reflect the characteristic early modern bifurcation of the right into a *forum internum* of "thought, conscience and religion" to be protected absolutely, in contradistinction to a *forum externum* where the "freedom to manifest religion or belief" is said to be subject to various grounds of limitation such as the protection of "public order" and "the rights of others." In this structure, we see how a purportedly universal right in fact represents, in Nehal Bhuta's words, "a bricolage of rights forms derived from heterogeneous traditions and specific political projects." The multiple genealogies coexisting within the form of the right to religious liberty is equally evident in the First Amendment tradition in the United States, where competing historical and political conceptions of "establishment" and "free exercise" are repeatedly deployed and juxtaposed without any possibility of rational reconciliation.

The various histories and genealogies of religious freedom also carry with them unstated and often opportunistic assumptions about what counts as religion. While it may once have been the case in certain times and places that the reference was obvious, today that is no longer so. Today the word *religion* brings together a vast and diverse, even shifting, set of social and cultural phenomena that no longer convincingly underwrite and justify legal action in its name. To continue to use the word in law is to invite discrimination. Locating religion today is complicated by the contesting discourses within the academic study of religion. Historians, sociologists, and anthropologists construe the objects of their study differently. Furthermore, legal and political enforcement of rights to religious freedom and other related regimes of management, including toleration and accommodation of religious diversity, necessarily involve a dividing of legal religion from illegal religion—good religion from bad religion. Those separations are effected along an ongoing set of unresolved and competing dichotomies dividing religion as individual or communal, private or public, spiritual or material, belief or practice, chosen or given, Protestant or Catholic, Western or Eastern, peaceful or violent, utopian or locative, universal or particular.

Much research has documented the ways in which law produces normative conceptions of religion, with kings and courts—since ancient times—inventing and reinventing religious orthodoxy for a given community. Individuals and groups then attach to new normative conceptions of religion (produced in part through the discourses of religious freedom), and new constituencies are framed. The history of Thai state-building illustrates this process. At least five different traditions of Buddhism existed in what is now Thailand. At the end of the nineteenth century, in a modernizing move responding in part to European and regional colonial pressures, the king decided to unify the *sangha* (the Buddhist monastic community). In deciding what counted as Buddhism, what counted as religion, *Sassana* (Buddhist teaching) was repurposed to mean "religion" to ensure that the Thai state would have religion as the foundation of its national identity. This new establishment resulted in, among other things, the repression of local Buddhisms. Examining legal definitions of Muslim identity in colonial India also illuminates the distortions that occur in and through the process of translating social realities into legal categories. Through an examination of Ahl-i-Hadith and Ahmadiyya controversies in colonial India, British courts produced and relied upon particular legal fictions concerning Islam: the fiction of a singular, clearly bounded, readily identifiable Muslim community and the fiction of mosques as public spaces open to all members of that community. The fact that the colonial legal apparatus came to define who was a Muslim according to a certain index of belief (the recitation of the Kalima, for instance) meant that it was, by definition, unable to recognize the ritual differences that provoked disputes in the first place. Rights to worship, in short, became rights claimable through one's status as "Muslim," a status that—while it acknowledged religious difference at one level (propositional belief)—occluded religious difference at other levels (ritual practice).

The essays in this volume provide many examples of such political and legal shapings of religion across the globe. Do these accounts mean that religious freedom is always a governance project, a flattening of "factual" complexity to suit particular regimes of domination? Are *religious* identities, practices, and communities unusually affected by these flattening processes—more so than other social realities—such that the legalization of religion remains distinctively problematic? How are religious self-understandings altered through processes associated with the liberal management of religious diversity? To what extent are the schematizing, routinizing tendencies intrinsic to law generated or amplified in modernity? Is there something distinctive about religion under modern legal technologies in this regard? If legality always requires translation or abstraction from complex social realities, what is actually being protected under the rubric of *religious freedom*? If law's role is to transform life—to misrecognize and transmute reality into rules and regularities legible to law—why do we pretend that law can recognize and protect religious lives and complexities?

Listening to the deployment of this phrase *religious freedom*, across many contexts and registers, we have come to see it as a deeply ambiguous, even at times intentionally duplicitous, legal standard in domestic and international law, one that is often dependent on parochial anthropological and philosophical understandings of the human and of human society. In the contemporary period, the deployments of religious freedom are multiple and contradictory: at times used to identify the virtuous and condemn the oppressor, at times used on behalf of women and minorities, and at others to serve narrow sectarian interests of missionaries, governments, and religious authorities. There are also significant and not yet fully explored connections among religious freedom advocacy, economic liberalization, and the "free market" model of religious growth.

US and UN reports often presume that religious freedom is universally valid and can be objectively assessed as a social fact. The present volume challenges this assumption by showing, through the work of various scholars working in a variety of geographical regions, that the meaning and practice of a right to religious liberty varies and shifts depending on the particular configuration of state-religion accommodation and the impact of other historical and transnational forces. Far from being able to be reduced to a question of compliance or noncompliance with a stable, uncontested norm that is being progressively disseminated globally (despite occasional setbacks), promoting a right to religious freedom shapes political and religious possibilities in particular ways, though always differently in different contexts.

These essays display a rich collection of histories and phenomenologies of religious freedom, but they are only a sampling. We, the editors, invite you to read further in the work of the many who have participated in this project and to join the conversation.

Selected Bibliography

Bhuta, Nehal. "Two Concepts of Religious Freedom in the European Court of Human Rights." *South Atlantic Quarterly* 113, no. 1 (2014): 9–35.

Hunter, Ian. "Religious Freedom in Early Modern Germany: Theology, Philosophy, and Legal Casuistry." *South Atlantic Quarterly* 113, no. 1 (2014): 37–62.

Jellinek, Georg. *The Declaration of the Rights of Man and of Citizen: A Contribution to Modern Constitutional History.* Westport: Hyperion, 1901.

PART I

Religion

Preface

Winnifred Fallers Sullivan

One of the most elusive and unstable aspects of the vociferous contemporary campaign for religious freedom is identifying precisely what counts as religion for both domestic and international legislation. On behalf of what exactly is this advocacy effort; what is included and what excluded by the word? In what ways do particular Christian histories and phenomenologies lurk within these deceptively universal formulations? How does a particular definition of *religion* imply a particular politics? Can we get beyond these entanglements? This section brings together seven essays that explore what might be meant by *religion* for religious freedom and the ways in which any such meaning is necessarily inflected by shifting connections among religion, law, politics, and freedom.

In their essays, Robert Yelle and Yvonne Sherwood trace the ways in which religion comes historically to be understood to float free of law and politics while remaining bound through those very separations to older and longer genealogies. Yelle insists that Judaism and Jewish ritual law as a negative image—as *the* negative image for the proposition that the state can never be the site for salvation—structures today's understanding that true religion is that which can never be in partnership with the state. Yelle emphasizes the urgent task of reading Christian theology in order to understand how unfree we are. For her part, unexpectedly bringing together the frontispiece to Denis Diderot and Jean le Rond d'Alembert's *Encyclopédie* with recent "religion or belief" legislation in the UK, Sherwood displays the always unstable tension between the modern would-be secular settlement, on the one hand, and an always shifting set of players representing the threat to that settlement, alternatively configured as theology, religion, or belief, on the other. Religion figures in this uneasy arrangement as radically free, emblematic of a free people and yet always also threatening to a contained, domesticated democratic freedom.

Focusing on the structural role of belief and morality in politics today, Elizabeth Shakman Hurd and Webb Keane highlight the work that is done when religion is conceived as belief. Keane contrasts religion as belief with religion as morality—drawing a necessary link with political theologies—dependent as they are on theological anthropologies in which morality is a matter of sensibilities divinely sanctioned rather than dependent on rational thought. Hurd emphasizes the seductive link to economic and political freedom when belief and choice are made primary, leading to the marketization and confessionalization of religion—and even to something very like mind control.

For these four contributors the dialectic between reason and faith lurks—sometimes on the surface, sometimes in the depths—as an unseen puppeteer, determining and redetermining the meaning of religion. The remaining three essays demonstrate how these abstractions act on actual bodies, rearranging persons and lives. The place of Theology in the Diderot frontispiece, placed ambiguously between Reason and Philosophy, serves as a type for the French Muslim schoolgirl who, in order to have her visible sign respected, must tread the fine line between non-negotiable choice and patriarchal imposition.

Courtney Bender illustrates the chameleon-like quality of separation as the bedrock of modernity even in the short span of the last fifty or sixty years of US history, showing how American religious sociologists have moved from a mid-twentieth-century understanding of religious pluralism as having a secularizing effect that tends to produce a common civic faith to an understanding of religious pluralism founded on a market model as the creator of vitalizing religion, allowing faiths, in her words, "to become truer versions of themselves." Both understandings affirm and underwrite an American exceptionalism that regards the United States as uniquely free in matters of religion—that religious pluralism, American style, leads inevitably to religious freedom—echoing Yelle's and Sherwood's depiction of a posited freedom that paradoxically underwrites an inflexible and intolerant politics.

Greg Johnson's and Rosalind I. J. Hackett's essays are, in a sense, protests from and for the margins to the devastating power of these realist revelations. Acknowledging the many critiques of the politics of religious freedom, they demand attention to the very specific ways in which that politics both disenfranchises and liberates those who have been excluded. The critique is shown to result in a second exclusion. Historically excluded by a religious politics that categorized the practices of African traditional religions and those of Native Hawaiians as not religion, now—just at a time when the possibility of inclusion in that politics begins to seem within reach—legal enforcement of international and national commitments to religious freedom are being delegitimated by the critique. Johnson shows how care for one's ancestors in Hawaii, particularly in the effort to enforce laws protecting burials, has taken center stage in a campaign for respect. Hackett describes active resistance to both Christian and Islamic efforts in sub-Saharan Africa to exclude the indigenous religious traditions of Africa from legal protection. As other essays in this volume show, the power of a claim to religious freedom is often most potent when it emerges from and negotiates within the context of a local politics and when, as Johnson notes, marginalized communities can call upon the powerful to honor their commitments—and shame them into putting their money where their mouth is.

There is little direct reference in any of these essays to academic definitions of religion, whether Durkheimian, Marxist, or Weberian, phenomenological, structural, or theological. Religious studies as a critical intellectual endeavor has had a mostly tangential relationship, at best, to interrogating the politics of religious freedom. Indeed, to the extent that the emergence of religious studies has contributed to an irenic celebration of religious universality and diversity, it has also contributed to the legitimating of religion as a space distinctively free of politics, as a space in which politics can be escaped. And most of its practitioners are advocates for religious freedom.

Enormous pressure is being placed on the word *religion* in the myriad of political and academic efforts to "understand" and "explain" a range of contemporary phenomena. The essays in this section direct our attention away from the utopian space of religious freedom to theology, philosophy, language, politics, economics, the media, and international aid work—not in a "religion and . . ." gesture but in order to illustrate the ways in which these other provisionally labeled and only fictionally independent domains are internal to and constitutive of religious life and it to them. Religion is returned in these essays to its embeddedness in and inseparability from the lives it shares, shapes, and inhabits.

CHAPTER ONE

Imagining the Hebrew Republic

Christian Genealogies of Religious Freedom

Robert Yelle

As a historian of religion, some of my recent work has focused on tracing the genealogy of what we call religious freedom in developments internal to European Christianity. My goal has not been to frame a normative theory of what limit ought to be placed on the freedom of religion in any contemporary jurisdiction, nor (apart from the effects of British colonialism on India) to trace the very different histories of the modernization of cultural traditions in other parts of the world, as these traditions have been shaped by the complex forces of nationalism and economic and technological development. My concern has been instead with tracing the entanglement of the origins of modern ideologies of freedom of religion, and of secularism more generally, with theological antecedents in keeping with Friedrich Nietzsche's understanding of genealogy as the uncovering of relations between categories that are ostensibly opposed—in this case, religion and secular law. This genealogical work does not depend upon a reification and reinscription of these categories, but instead takes its motivation from their effective separation in much contemporary discourse and the accompanying communication gap between lawyers and scholars of religion—two groups to which I happen to belong that rarely engage in productive conversation.

Several contributors to this discussion of religious freedom, including Elizabeth Hurd and Peter Danchin, have noted that intrinsic to the modern understanding of this concept is the idea that religion is a matter of private conviction rather than of public performance, a matter of belief rather than of ceremonial. This understanding of religion has commonly—and, I believe, correctly—been traced to tendencies that became dominant during the Reformation, as signaled by the Protestant critique of the Catholic ritual economy of salvation. It has less often been observed, however, that the separation of religion from such external matters was frequently expressed through more ancient Christian ideas, such as the distinction—of fundamental importance to the typological interpretation of the relation between the Old and New Testaments—among the natural, civil, and ceremonial portions of Mosaic Law. Natural or moral laws, such as "Thou shalt not kill," were supposedly universal and timeless; civil or judicial laws were the laws of a particular nation or people, and binding only on such people. The ceremonial laws of the Jews included ritual commandments such as those mandating the circumcision of male children and the offering of sacrifices. This last category of laws had supposedly been abrogated by the Gospel and by Christ's redemptive sacrifice that ended these rituals, which were regarded as no longer necessary for salvation. During the Reformation, many Protestants reinterpreted these ideas, posing again the question of the relationship between the civil and ecclesiastical powers, both within the Israelite kingdom when it existed and, subsequent to the promulgation of the Gospel, within a radically different economy in which, in Paul's terms, "grace" was opposed to "law."

Recently, Eric Nelson has argued that the notion of a Hebrew republic served as a model for thinking about the ideal relationship between church and state in early modern Europe, where this model influenced the development of religious toleration. Nelson also traces other important dimensions of our secular polity, including republicanism and ideas of land ownership and distribution, to theological discourses that took the ancient Israelite kingdom seriously as a model for present-day government. His approach combats the tendency of those—such as Mark Lilla—who represent the Enlightenment as having arisen sui generis, without connection to Reformation theology, and in so doing, adopt the secularist normative argument for the separation of religion from civil society as an objective description of historical reality. Nelson states, "[I]t may well be that we live, as Charles Taylor tells us, in a 'secular age,' but if so, we nonetheless owe several of our most central political commitments to an age that was anything but. And it seems reasonable that we will not be able to understand the peculiar fault lines and dissonances of our contemporary political discourse until we come to terms with that basic, paradoxical fact."

Nelson is not the first to make such claims. Henning Graf Reventlow, in his magisterial *The Authority of the Bible and the Rise of the Modern World*, carefully excavated the theological dimensions, and in particular the engagement with biblical typology, of such important contributors to secularism and religious freedom as Thomas Hobbes and John Locke. Joshua Mitchell also argued, "The central theoretical issue of the Reformation was this question of the meaning of Christ's fulfillment of the Old Truth. . . . This is no less true of Luther than of Hobbes and Locke. . . . Toleration, required because of the New Dispensation, entails that political power be wanting in matters of faith, that one be free of political power to be free to attain salvation. . . . [S]peculations on the meaning of biblical history are the threads that hold together the fabric of early modern political thought." As far back as 1895, Georg Jellinek noted that Reformation theology shaped the origins of religious freedom. Jellinek's work in turn informed that of Max Weber, although neither scholar was aware of the extent to which Christian anti-Judaism influenced secularism, and Weber's own biases against Rabbinic Judaism have been pointed out by such scholars as David Ellenson.

Recently, as a result of my own investigations into the role that Christian theological discourses played in the formation in early modern Europe of what we now call secular law, I have become increasingly convinced that part of what marks the Reformation discourse of secularism and religious freedom as Christian is precisely the use of Judaism as a foil or counterexample, in addition to the transformation of associated theological distinctions such as Paul's oppositions between "flesh" and "spirit," or "law" and "grace." This complements the work of scholars, such as David Nirenberg, who have shown how the idea of Jewishness has often served as a contrasting category or negative image for European civilization. Although it is clear that these transformations do not establish a simple continuity with what came before, they retain many traces of their origins, without a study of which our understanding of secularism and religious freedom remains incomplete.

There is a line that runs from Martin Luther's argument, in *The Freedom of a Christian* (1520), that "Man has a twofold nature, a spiritual and a bodily one," to John Locke's *Letter on Toleration* (1689), which concludes that "there is absolutely no such thing under the Gospel as a Christian Commonwealth." The idea that there exists a radical divide between internal faith and external performance, and that—predestination aside—only the former has to do with salvation, leads ineluctably, not to freedom, but to "freedom of religion." Luther, Hobbes, and Locke insist that Christians remain subject to the governing authorities, and as Perez Zagorin has pointed out, Luther himself was scarcely tolerant of religious dissent. Arguably in no other tradition has there occurred such a total bifurcation of spirit and matter. One thing that makes this doctrine distinctive is its claim that the state cannot in any sense be a site for salvation.

Thomas Morgan, in *A Brief Examination of the Rev. Mr. Warburton's Divine Legation of Moses* (1742), expressed the logical conclusion of this tendency when he insisted, paraphrasing Locke, that religion is a purely internal matter. Whatever is outside of us, and in the public domain, is not religious, but necessarily political and subject to the state:

> An established *Church* is certainly a Creature of State, and purely a political Thing; but an established *Religion,* or Religion established by Law, is an Absurdity and Contradiction. . . . Coercive Power can neither promote nor restrain Religion . . . can never enlighten the Mind, purify the Affections, or recommend Men to God . . . why then should you talk of *established Religion?* . . . Religion being purely a spiritual and internal Thing, consisting in the inward real Perswasion, Temper, and Disposition of the Mind, a Religion established by Law, can be nothing but an ecclesiastical Phantom, since the Law might as well make a God as a Religion.

Morgan held up the Jews as an example of the problems that come from confounding politics with religion: "The grand fundamental Error of that unhappy People from first to last, has not been Obedience to the Law in all its Parts, as a national civil Law supposed to have come from God; but mistaking and substituting it for Religion. . . ." According to this view, while there can be no such thing as a separation between church and state, there can also be no possibility of the state encroaching on true religion. This was the conclusion of a Protestant redefinition of religion as private or interior, and therefore as unconnected with ritual and the body, including the body politic.

The thesis of the impossibility of a "Christian Commonwealth" depended on the rejection of the Hebrew republic. Judaism was preserved in this secularizing dialectic as the negative image of Christian salvation or of a kingdom to come that was endlessly deferred as the *parousia.* I agree with Nelson on the importance of the Hebrew republic or Mosaic constitution to early modern political discourse. However, I take issue with his argument that toleration emerged not, as is commonly thought, out of the idea that church and state ought to remain separate but instead out of the Erastian notion that church and state ought to be collapsed and consolidated—as they supposedly were in the ancient Hebrew republic. It is true that the idea of the Hebrew republic permitted many laws that had been classified as "religious" and therefore as a source of contention among different sects to be reclassified as merely "civil" laws, which, even if legislated by God or Moses for the Israelites as a nation, had long ago ceased to be binding. It is also true that the Erastian consolidation of civil and ecclesiastical authority tended to reduce religious controversy. More important than either of these two developments, however, was the idea that, under the Gospel, religion is purely an internal, spiritual matter. Even in Hobbes, who was arguably the most thoroughgoing Erastian, such typological ideas are foregrounded. In *Leviathan*, Hobbes insists that Christ's kingdom is "not of this world" and that the inward condition (as opposed to external conduct) of a Christian, whether saved or damned, is not in any case accessible to the political authorities.

Condemnations of the Hebrew republic accelerated during the deist period, which exacerbated traditional Christian anti-Judaism. The deists, for whom true or "natural religion" (meaning the moral law) was universal and rational, abhorred the idea that salvation could depend on a particular historical dispensation given to a chosen people. The idea that religion requires revelation to be known is inconsistent with the deist idea that human reason is sufficient for salvation. Deists therefore rejected what Matthew Tindal referred to, in *Christianity as Old as Creation* (1730), as the "merely positive and arbitrary" ritual laws of Mosaic tradition. What deists most objected to was the manner in which these laws supposedly violated human autonomy, which depends on our ability to know and perform the moral law. Anathema to them was the idea of a God who could command us against reason and instinct, who demanded blood sacrifices and promulgated his statutes as arbitrary fiat, which required miraculous events to certify their authority. Morgan, in *The Moral Philosopher* (1738), rejected the idea that God would have commanded Abraham to sacrifice his only son, Isaac: "For, upon this Principle, . . . God may command the most unfit or unrighteous Things in the World by mere arbitrary Will and Pleasure. A Supposition which must unhinge the whole Frame of Nature, and leave no human Creature any Rule of Action at all." Carl Schmitt was right to point to radical Protestantism and Deism as moments of exclusion of both the miracle and the sovereign "exception."

A number of these ideas were taken up and systematized by Immanuel Kant, who defined Enlightenment in opposition to heteronomy, or the acceptance of external authority. Kant's thorough identification of religion with both reason and the internal sense of duty led him, in his *Religion within the Limits of Reason Alone* (1793), to label Judaism as "really not a religion at all but merely a union of a number of people . . . under purely political laws . . . [that] are directed to absolutely nothing but outer observance." Morgan, in *The Moral Philosopher II* (1739), had condemned Jews similarly for following arbitrary commands, noting that "their Obedience was only the Submission of Slaves, their Virtue nothing but a Restraint upon outward Actions, and their Repentance like that of a Thief or Murderer at the Gallows." Kant's and Morgan's versions of the Hebrew republic illustrate my objection to Nelson's argument: the Old Testament polity was retained under the Gospel dispensation not as a model to follow but as something superseded, preserved but also annulled (*aufgehoben*).

The redefinition of religion as freedom of conscience simultaneously "liberated" religion from control by the state and, to some extent, rendered this freedom nugatory. Indeed, the collapsing of religion into conscience or a purely internal condition is entirely compatible with any degree of enslavement of the body, now shorn of any spiritual value. That this is true is shown by Hobbes's argument in favor of an absolute sovereignty in which the ecclesiastical power has been collapsed into the civil. I therefore think Danchin is right to invoke Michel Foucault's description of Kant's kingdom of ends as a "contract of rational despotism with free reason."

In this we arguably see one of the distinguishing features of modernity that cannot be explained on grounds internal to the theological debates that form part of the genealogy of religious freedom. Instead there is the possibility of reading this trajectory as epiphenomenal to the rise of bureaucracy or the panopticon. While the line between inner and outer, private and public, is inherently unstable, it is in these extreme theological formulations of religion as utterly incorporeal that we witness the construction of religion as precisely that object which cannot come into conflict with the state. In other words, this redefinition of religion represented a strategy for conflict avoidance in the sense that it served the pragmatic objective of avoiding the possibility of intersection and friction between church and state, and that it was flexible (or slippery) enough to be deployed differently, according to convenience, in different contexts.

Although these theological debates ended long ago, we are arguably still witnessing their aftermath. The *Employment Division, Department of Human Resources of Oregon v. Smith* peyote case (1990) discussed by Winnifred Sullivan highlights an "endgame" very similar to that already outlined by Hobbes: the point at which religion vanishes from the perspective of civil society or ceases as an independent power. The push-back against *Smith* signals a rejection of this (dis)solution of the problem of religion. At the same time, the inadequacies of this solution, as applied to other cultures that do not share the same set of theological presuppositions nor the same trajectory of modernization, have become increasingly apparent. Where we go from here is a question that cannot be answered by genealogy.

The tentative sketch of the (Protestant) Christian genealogy of religious freedom outlined above is very much a work in progress. This is a project that will require an immense effort of excavation. Very few scholars at the moment, outside those in a few historical disciplines, have delved into the theological texts, an engagement with which would be necessary for the development of a more adequate genealogy of secularism and freedom of religion in its Christian form. This fact itself illustrates one of the legacies of secularism: the idea that, Max Weber's efforts notwithstanding, texts labeled as "theological" need not be taken seriously when considering the roots or contours of modernity. However, once we call into question the inevitability of the separation of religion from civil society—a separation that is not natural but depends on a particular tradition—then the rationale for disregarding such texts disappears, and what they lose in theological authority they gain in relevance as historical and anthropological data. Endorsing this project does not entail enforcing one particular account of the origins of religious toleration, but it does mean taking into account, in a manner that is more sustained and systematic than in previous efforts (and that must necessarily be cumulative and collaborative), the role of Christian theology.

Such a project may elicit, in response, a certain skepticism. Is theology being smuggled back into what ought to be a domain reserved for secular scholarship? Is a monolithic and essentialist—as well as possibly culturally chauvinist—claim for the importance of Christian or Western civilization to be allowed to displace true cultural diversity and, in this connection, to obscure a recognition of the multiple and varying ways in which religious freedom has historically been and is presently being negotiated in non-Christian and non-Western polities? Although some of the contributors to the present discussion—notably Yvonne Sherwood, Webb Keane, Ann Pellegrini, Cécile Laborde, and Courtney Bender— have taken note of the embeddedness, in varying ways, of modern notions of subjectivity and of the separation of church and state in Christian or specifically Protestant presuppositions, there are others who would direct us away from the project of excavating these presuppositions. Evan Haefeli, for example, points out that there is no single narrative of the rise of toleration that can cover all instances or provide "the" singular genealogy, and argues that "[t]he predominance of . . . Protestant thinkers in the scholarship on the history of toleration betrays its close alliance to the history of the rise of Protestantism. . . . Is it really our job to champion one narrative over the other?" Robert Hefner expresses a "general reservation with regard to current debates on religious freedom. . . . This simplification results in part from a tendency to conflate philosophical genealogies of religious freedom with a more comprehensive sociology of the real-and-existing varieties of religious governance." These are both legitimate criticisms of the project I have endorsed above, and in responding to them here, I mean to show that I take them seriously.

First, let me add my basic agreement with these scholars that a philosophical genealogy, which can only be at best a probable sketch of some major trends in the history of religious toleration, can never substitute for a sociological or anthropological account of different histories, models, and contemporary realities of governance of religion. I regard these projects as complementary rather than exclusive. This requires an admission that, frankly, we have something to learn from scholars who labor in other disciplines. I suspect that it is, in part, a difference in disciplinary perspectives and/or training that motivates Haefeli's and Hefner's skepticism.

That said, I do believe that a theological genealogy of religious freedom adds something to the discussion. I agree with Haefeli that it is our not our job to champion a monolithic narrative of secularization. I do think, however, that we are bound to provide some narrative or, to use a more hopeful word, some *account* of the rise of religious freedom; for what is the alternative to doing so? Moreover, I would argue that there is a pressing need for the sort of account I have sketched given that, recent efforts notwithstanding, a theological genealogy of secularism is by no means a dominant narrative. The dominant narrative, which is very close to what Keane calls the "moral narrative of modernity," remains that of a triumphant and fully nontheological secularism, as illustrated by Jonathan Israel's histories of the Enlightenment, or Mark Lilla's idea of a "Great Separation" between theology and politics in the early modern period. Therefore we already have competing or contesting—rather than monolithic—narratives. I would prefer to call my minority report a *counternarrative*. And we need more of these, not fewer.

As to whether or not, in the end, the genealogical process of excavation leads us to Protestantism: that, I think, is a question that can be answered if at all only through empirical study. It cannot be settled a priori. We must be prepared to let the chips fall where they may. Religious toleration is far too manifold and diverse a phenomenon to grasp with any single—much less such a simple—narrative as I have sketched above. No society, despite its best (or worst) efforts, can ever be religiously monolithic. This would go against both human nature and patterns of social interaction. Humans are seekers, as well as contrarians, while borders are porous. However, I don't see myself trying to construct a universal account of religious toleration. My efforts have been much more limited. I have been concerned with tracing some of the distinctive features of contemporary discourses of religious freedom in the modern West. These are not merely about religious pluralism, but are embedded in broader narratives of secularization. Whereas every nation has experienced some form of pluralism, arguably only Christian Europe incubated secularism.

The kinds of discourses that I have been attempting to outline, in necessarily cursory fashion, include features that are characteristic of certain Christian theological discourses. The modern opposition to ritual as heteronomy is reflected in Michael Lambek's observation that ritual conduct is both pragmatic and conforming: "one might say that what religion [as ritual] is not is freedom. Hence the very idea of freedom of religion is paradoxical." Both paradoxical and, I would add, distinctive. In no other tradition that I am aware of—not in Hindu Dharmashastra, not in Mosaic Law, and not, as far as I understand, in Islamic Shariah would this particular idea of religious freedom and antiritualism make sense.

Nor did there develop elsewhere the same division between "church" and "state" (or "religion" and "politics"), categories that are relatively meaningless when applied, for example, to ancient India. The fact that today we discuss the topic of "religious freedom" indicates that we are all, willy-nilly, still dependent on this distinction to some extent. It doesn't help us much in this regard to know that the Indian emperor Ashoka in the third century BCE gave state approval to the practice of different *dharmas* (a word that, in that context, could refer both to the specific teachings of the Buddha and to other rules of discipline—such as the Hindu Dharmashastra—that we now call religions); for what was meant by *dharma* did not incorporate the characteristic features that the category of religion now includes under a post-Christian dispensation, nor did the word *dharma* figure historically in the genealogy of the modern term "religion."

Although not focused on the idea of freedom of religion per se, Brent Nongbri's recent contribution to genealogies of the category of religion in early modern European sources, *Before Religion*, cites John Locke's effort to "isolate[e] beliefs about god in a private sphere. . . . [T]hese beliefs should ideally . . . be privately held, spiritual, and nonpolitical." Nongbri emphasizes the political factors, including the rise of the modern nation-state, that contributed to this definition of religion, and largely avoids a discussion of the theological background of, for example, Locke's thought. He nevertheless acknowledges that early scholars of comparative religion had "Christian presuppositions" that we have inherited to such an extent that "given the specifically Christian heritage of the category of religion . . . efforts to de-Christianize it are to some extent futile." In the context of the present discussion, what course of action does this conclusion counsel? Either we abandon entirely any discussion of "religion," or we work harder to reveal the Christian presuppositions of (freedom of) "religion." I suggest that the latter course would be more productive.

For that matter, the idea of a general secularization and disenchantment of the world, which is an evolutionary historical narrative of the highest order, and one that is closely linked to the narrative of religious freedom traced above, is unique to Christianity. This narrative emerged not, as Talal Asad has suggested, in romanticism, but instead in ancient Christian soteriological ideas that were taken up and reworked by Protestants: Eusebius's attribution of the decline of the pagan oracles to Christ's Passion; the idea that the Gospel ended the rituals of Mosaic Law and lifted the veil of Jewish mystery; and the notion that the charismata had ceased already in the time of the Apostles. Such ideas contributed to a radical realignment of subjectivity and cosmology; to the decline of belief in miracles, mystery, and magic; and even (as Carl Schmitt correctly noted) to the disenchantment of sovereignty in the political domain. It therefore matters a great deal that we expose such narratives, which continue to construct part of the architecture of this space we inhabit called modernity, not to reproduce such narratives uncritically but instead to reveal precisely how contingent they are, how indebted we remain to them despite (or rather because of) our lack of awareness of them, and therefore how unfree we are.

Selected Bibliography

Asad, Talal. *Formations of the Secular: Christianity, Islam, Modernity*. Stanford, CA: Stanford University Press, 2003.

Hobbes, Thomas. *Leviathan*. London, 1651.

Jellinek, Georg. *The Declaration of the Rights of Man and of Citizens*. Translated by Max Farrand. New York: Henry Holt, 1901.

Kant, Immanuel. *Religion within the Limits of Reason Alone*. New York: Harper and Row, (1793) 1960.

Lilla, Mark. *The Stillborn God: Religion, Politics, and the Modern West*. New York: Vintage, 2008.

Locke, John. *Letter on Toleration*. London, 1689.

Luther, Martin. *Freedom of a Christian*. Wittemberg, 1520.

Mitchell, Joshua. *"Not by Reason Alone": Religion, History, and Identity in Early Modern Political Thought*. Chicago: University of Chicago Press, 1996.

Morgan, Thomas. *The Moral Philosopher*. London, 1738.

——. *The Moral Philosopher II*. London, 1739.

——. *A Brief Examination of the Rev. Mr. Warburton's Divine Legation of Moses*. London, 1742.

Nelson, Eric. *The Hebrew Republic: Jewish Sources and the Transformation of European Political Thought*. Cambridge, MA: Harvard University Press, 2010.

Nongbri, Brent. *Before Religion: A History of a Modern Concept*. New Haven, CT: Yale University Press, 2013.

Reventlow, Henning Graf. *The Authority of the Bible and the Rise of the Modern World*. Philadelphia: Fortress, 1985.

Schmitt, Carl. *Political Theology: Four Chapters on the Concept of Sovereignty*. Translated by George Schwab. Chicago: University of Chicago Press, 2006.

Tindal, Matthew. *Christianity as Old as Creation*. London, 1730.

Yelle, Robert A. "The Trouble with Transcendence: Carl Schmitt's 'Exception' as a Challenge for Religious Studies." *Method and Theory in the Study of Religion* 22 (2010): 189–206.

——. "Moses' Veil: Secularization as Christian Myth." In *After Secular Law*, edited by Winnifred Fallers Sullivan, Robert A. Yelle, and Mateo Taussig-Rubbo, 23–42. Stanford, CA: Stanford University Press, 2011.

———. *The Language of Disenchantment: Protestant Literalism and Colonial Discourse in British India.* New York: Oxford University Press, 2013.

Zagorin, Perez. *How the Idea of Religious Toleration Came to the West.* Princeton, NJ: Princeton University Press, 2005.

CHAPTER TWO

On the Freedom of the Concepts of Religion and Belief

Yvonne Sherwood

In this essay I want to put a different spin on the question of religious freedom by exploring the terrifying freedom of the concepts of "religion" and "belief." In the first part, I examine how belief was first released as a potentially insurgent poltergeist, a shadow of politics and reason, at once more solid (less flexible, more intransigent) than its altogether safer counterparts but also more flimsy (less tangible) and further removed from "the real." In the second part of the essay I explore how the paradoxes and fears that accumulate around the strange space of believing escalate in recent legal definitions of "religion and philosophy" or "religion and belief."

The Invention of Belief

We have never needed the rise of al-Qaeda, so-called Islamism, or a hardline religious Right to terrify us with a resurgent specter of specifically *religious* (as opposed to purely *political*) terror. Rather than bearing down on us like some old specter of the Turk or Moor at Europe's gates, the terror of religion emerges—or "insurges" (if *insurge* can be made into a verb)—from within the standard definitions of religion squeezed out from Western epistemologies and politics. The inherited conceptual partitions that constitute and ground modernities leave religion and belief volatile, incendiary, and absolutely uncontained: in a real sense, entirely "free." This conceptual freedom collides (sometimes spectacularly) with the highly managed "freedom" of modern democracies and the conditions that we seek to impose on religion in law and public life. We define religion and belief as nonnegotiable, unconditioned. And then, crossing our fingers, we attempt to impose conditions on this home-grown flighty specter of "belief."

Consider, first, the positioning of religion or her once-young great-grandmother, Theology, in that primary architectonics of modern knowledge: the frontispiece to Denis Diderot and Jean le Rond d'Alembert's *Encyclopédie* (see fig. 2.1).

In a "temple" or "sanctuary" of truth, a host of clever girls clutch a range of instruments and accessories from compasses, set squares, cacti, and microscopes to harps, masks, and puppets. At the top, where all the action takes place, Truth is at the apex, attended by crowned Reason and, below her and to the right, Philosophy. Reason is lifting and Philosophy is arranging Truth's diaphanous veil. Awkwardly positioned between the two is Theology. In the words of Diderot's commentary, "A ses pies, la Théologie agenouillée reçoit sa lumière d'en-haut." (At her [Truth's] feet, Theology, kneeling, receives her light from above.) The phrase "*her* light" is pointed. Diplomatically (or tongue in cheek), the tableau fudges the issue of whether Mademoiselle Théologie has her own independent source of illumination or whether her light converges with—or is at least part of—the general radiance of Truth that, as Diderot says, "disperses the clouds." Miss Theology is at a tangent with and potentially independent from all that is going on around her. There's a strong possibility that she might dash out of the temple of truth at any moment should she be led to do so by *her* light.

This is a scene of obfuscation and diplomacy. It is a tableau of the awkward accommodation of religion and an emblem of modernity's wager, or "double-think," about religion. There is a founding nonsynchronicity between Reason and Theology, or belief. Theology's placement is deliberately obfuscated; she is close to the throne of Truth, but also strategically below it. Truth looks at her as if looking to her or, at the very least, taking her into consideration. Maybe Truth is a consummate politician, making Theology feel important and wanted, if not entirely believed.

At the same time Philosophy, her deputy, has an anxious eye and maybe a restraining hand on Theology, as if keeping her under surveillance, as if Philosophy were a prototype of the British MI5 Security Ser-

FRONTISPICE DE L'ENCYCLOPEDIE.

FIGURE 2.1. The frontispiece to *Encyclopédie, ou dictionnaire raisonné des sciences, des arts et des métiers*, edited by Denis Diderot and Jean le Rond d'Alembert. Drawn by Charles-Nicholas Cochin in 1764 and engraved by Bonaventure-Louis Prévost in 1772.

vice or the US National Security Agency. I am reminded of Immanuel Kant's image of philosophy as "the police in the realm of the sciences" (*die Polizei im Reiche der Wissenschaften*). As a tolerated heteronomy, an awkward surplus to the system, Theology seems to require more surveillance than her sisters. Theology plays no part in the unveiling of Truth, nor does she consult or even acknowledge her sisters. She seems to think it sufficient to "lend an ear to the oracle within oneself" (*nur das Orakel in sich selbst anhören*).

But there is no need to get too alarmist. Miss Theology looks peaceful and passive enough. She is not wearing a burka or carrying a knife. Though antique, she is not atavistic. She is no more "retro" than are her sisters. She is suitably *Abendländisch*: embodying the foundations of Europe as simultaneously Christian and classical—hence, relatively safe. In other words, she is still Theology—not religion, and not religions, plural, that more expansive category that includes darker apparitions. These will become more "natural" repositories of fanaticism, intolerance, and danger, thus saving Christianity by contrast. This tableau of nascent secularism precedes, or brackets out, Gil Anidjar's important story of how "Christianity invented the distinction between religious and secular" and "*made* religion," thereby "making religion the problem—rather than itself."

And yet, at the moment when Theology has not yet expanded into those religions that will become repositories for danger, we can see very clearly the structural volatility of homegrown theology's position. We have no idea what is being intimated to her through supernatural media, transmitting on an unknown frequency. She incarnates the unknown and the unknowable: *no longer "the gods" but her belief*. Modernity is the time when the mystery goes inside, to the inner sanctum, the "core" of the person. It is the time when the holy is privatized as "her belief."

If belief is the leftover space to describe that which is not of truth, reason, or philosophy, then it is potentially ubiquitous—and deliriously free. All thoughts that compel and draw us, but do not meet the rigorous entrance criteria to get into the enclosure of philosophy, are "beliefs." Sensing the danger, we contained belief by tagging it exclusively to theology or religion. This was a bold move, but, strangely, a believable one. The binary *religious versus secular* was invented to segregate the believers and keep the majority from wanting to join them out on the isthmus of belief. In the neat segregations of modernity, Theology and her granddaughters, the religions, became the special foci and repository for the maverick force of belief.

The Legal Operation of "Religion or Belief"

In the *Encyclopédie*, the maverick force of religion/theology/belief separates from philosophy, as a potential enemy of it and of the instruments of public reason. Henceforth we can do no more than keep insisting (somewhat anxiously) that true religion always believes in the rough equivalence of the voice of the gods and basic principles of civil obedience. We hope and pray for this and manipulate true religion in this direction, even as we betray our fears by anxiously reiterating to religion and all adherents what true religion ought to be, will be, must be (and in truth always has been). A recent reminder to religion can be found in a beautifully conflicted piece of recent British legislation , the Religion and Belief Regulations of 2003, taken up in the Equality Act in 2010. The document is on a continuum with the *Encyclopédie* and the division of labor between knowing and believing, or between philosophy and religion. But the key terms have undergone some curious twists.

In a giddy and bizarre demonstration of the freedom of the concept of belief, the legal odd couple "religion or belief" now means "religion or the secular equivalent of religion." *Belief* in this context means, effectively, "secular, not religious, but as intense as religious belief." In legal parlance, the secular equivalent of religion is also termed philosophy. Having been birthed as the awkward other of reason and philosophy, belief (in its legal sense) has become a synonym for philosophy (in its legal sense), and in law now means, effectively, "secular religion," or a "secular belief with the same kind of characteristics as religion." Following? One can reasonably expect a little confusion from the much-invoked alien from Mars, or an ambassador from one of the few still dissenting nonsecularized or nondemocratic modern states visiting on a fact-finding mission to learn how to better manage religion or belief.

The phrase "religion or belief" is an awkward response to the imperative of secularization. In being forced to come up with a secular cognate, religion is demoted, humiliated, pluralized, negated—and yet still sovereign. It still functions as the key coordinating concept, or at least the concept allowed to reign over the strange shadow state and outland of belief (the land that no other sovereign concept wants to rule). Religion remains the primary reference point for, and guardian of, the category of belief. The very phrase "religion or belief" suggests that a secular belief must meet the high entrance requirements set by religion, and this around that particularly religious assertion "I believe."

The ironies are legion. The committee that came up with the pairing "religion and belief" clearly did not consult religion scholars, who have spent most of their energy in the last thirty years decoupling religion from belief. In the field of religious studies, belief has undergone a strategic dethroning not unlike that of Queen Theology on the frontispiece to the *Encyclopédie*. Belief has been kicked into the sidelines as a Christian and colonial imposition. One would imagine that the question of "whether religion must be represented as something that derives from belief, as something with external manifestations that can ultimately be traced back to an inner assent to a cognitive proposition, as a state of mind that produces practice" would be deeply congenial and familiar to legal theorists and legislators. Which other discipline has so densely delineated all the distinctions between the *mens rea* (intention or state of mind) and the *actus reus* (guilty act)? Surely legal scholars would feel more comfortable with our preferred, if awkward, terms such as religious "affiliates" or "adherents," or the turn to privileging religious acts and performances. In law, only a potentially illegal or incendiary *act* or speech act triggers questions about belief. How ironic that even as the contemporary field of religious studies has striven for a law court model of religion based on witnessing and experience, law—oblivious to this— has reinstated and reinvigorated the old category of belief. This is even more mysterious since, in practice, law operates like the purest form of religious studies, ostensibly disavowing all prior knowledge and concentrating on deductions from observation. Symptomatically, implementation of the legislation has concentrated somewhat obsessively on visible symbols—most ostentatiously, various manifestations of a veil or a crucifix worn at work.

The phrase "religion or belief" reflects a turn from the singularity of a state religion and monotheism not to polytheism but to polyrepresentational societies. A polyrepresentational society is one that is able to demonstrate that it is able to act as if multiple gods and multiple religions exist (or exist for the believers). It is able to respect different personhoods and identities, understood as vials of inviolable belief. The recent renegotiation of the place of "religion and belief" is a response to the rise of representational politics organized around ascriptive identities: identities understood as rooted in inner nature or manifested in external bodily attributes. This relates to what I have termed elsewhere a new *iconography of democracy* based on new modes of representation, in all senses. Put briefly, even as the rubric of democratic equality leads to the principle of the substitutability of one individual for another (we are all equal, all the same under law), democracy compensates for the neglect of difference by identifying particular iconic individuals to become signs of democracy's concern or investment in care. In the mechanics of democracy, an elected member of Parliament represents or "stands for" his or her constituents. In the *symbolism* of democracy, an iconically protected person stands for the desire to protect or defend all people. There is an aesthetics or symbolism of democracy in which the good faith of a government, turned toward the individual, is shown through representative, selected personhoods or, in legal terms, "protected characteristics." Freedom is manifest in protection. "Religion or belief" stands as a sphere of protection alongside sexuality and gender, pregnancy and maternity, race, ethnicity, disability, and age. But "religion or belief" seems something of a misfit here. Though ethnicity and sexuality raise complex questions about choice and givenness, each identity category carries a sense of that which one uncontrovertibly and undeniably *is*: being pregnant, being gay, being bisexual, being sixty-five. By putting the phrase "religion or belief" on this list we create and legislate for a mode of believing that has a privileged relationship to essence. And this only intensifies a commonplace mode of thinking about religion. We talk about being or not being religious in a way that we would not talk about being or not being feminist or Marxist. Belief is a mode of thinking presumed to reach the parts of an individual that other thoughts (such as political ideologies) do not reach.

As a term of nonnegotiation (unlike an "opinion"), the obvious correlate for age, pregnancy, or sexuality in the realm of ideas is belief. Exceptionally and anomalously, religious belief is defined as a mode of thinking that is not, in a sense, chosen. It insists that it must be understood as defining or exceeding the individual, operating as an incontestable given such as sexuality or the color of his or her skin. Believing is understood as a form of agency that, paradoxically, takes us beyond decision to the point where it becomes that from which I cannot dissociate myself, that which cannot be wrenched apart from me except by violence—and hence a given, like sexuality or race. But because it is also understood as a particularly intense and nonnegotiable *thought*, and thoughts can change, belief teeters on the brink of collapsing back into something far less concrete and less worthy of legal protection than a category like race. There are clear indicators that religion is a far less robust category in law and public opinion than sex and race.

This awkwardness is beautifully articulated in the regulations for qualifying beliefs both religious and quasi-religious. They read as a strangely updated version of the question of the jailer at Phillipi to Paul and Silas in Acts 16:3. The question is no longer "What must I do to be saved?" or even "What must I do to 'believe'?" but "What must I do to be publicly recognized as 'believing'?" There are five criteria to be met in order to qualify as a public believer:

1. The belief must be genuinely held.
2. It must be a belief and not an opinion or view based on the present state of information available.
3. It must be a belief as to a weighty and substantial aspect of human life.
4. It must attain a certain level of cogency, seriousness, cohesion, and importance.
5. It must be worthy of respect in a democratic society, not incompatible with human dignity, and not in conflict with the fundamental rights of others.

Breaking with disciplinary decorums and refusing the limits of a purely legal commentary, we can attempt to elucidate the strangeness of "belief."

Looking at the first four criteria we learn that belief is weighty. Belief is substantial. Belief is serious. Belief is heavy. *But*—belief floats. It floats above knowledge or information or the verifiable. If it did not, it would not qualify as belief. Belief defies the laws of Newtonian physics. This is hardly surprising given that belief was a concept birthed as the other of science and its handmaids, reason and philosophy (in the other sense of "philosophy"—remember?). In contemporary legislation, belief, *by definition*, is that which has broken free from the safeguards of the empirical and material. It is heavy, weighty, inflexible—and absolutely free.

In its detachment from—or disdain for—knowledge or the verifiable, belief is like an opinion. But it is much heavier, weightier, and denser than an opinion; it has a mass index that is different from that of an opinion. *Opinion* implies diffidence, negotiation; the word itself implies that the thought knows that it could well be otherwise. Belief is distinguished from opinion by the depth to which it goes within the individual. Religion is the guardian of depth, as it is the guardian of belief.

These criteria are not based on the empirical observation of the lives of religious adherents. In practice and popular speech, people may lose and regain their religion; find religion; go through a religious phase; return to their religion; take on their partners' religion for reasons of love more human than divine, or they may espouse religion as a mask for realpolitik. Strangely, none of these commonplaces seem to rattle the faith in religion in law and public discourse, where religion continues to signify intensity, constancy, and depth. Without promoting the truths of demystification or declaring that religion does not exist, I wonder why we are so devoutly committed to the opposite position, where religion's purchase on depth and truth is regarded as unique. We habitually talk of belief as, by definition, "deeply held." This is even stranger given that religion is also seen as a privileged zone of fakery and dissimulation. (See, for example, Hussein Ali Agrama's discussion in chapter 25 of the present volume of constitutional legal theorist R. Kent Greenawalt's work on separating "the spiritual" from self-interest and secular advantage.) The fact that even the most ardent secularizers such as Richard Dawkins and Christopher Hitchens regularly use the phrase "deeply held convictions" or "deeply held belief(s)" suggests that the unique depth of belief has become something of a blithely rehearsed social creed.

This is what is so potentially upsetting and threatening about believers and their believing. In its *volatility* and *solidity*, belief does not simply defy the laws of Newtonian physics; it defies the laws of society, based on contract, negotiation, and compromise. Belief, the strange stuff that we have made, is by definition solid, immovable, and intransigent, but also unbounded, free. And this is why we fear, and feel the need to protect ourselves against, belief. Bad belief is that from which we must protect ourselves. But good belief becomes in contemporary terminology, a "protected characteristic." Because belief can be very bad and because everyone can be a believer, belief itself has to be protected from the inbuilt freedom and danger of belief.

Several commentators have already noted how an evenly hospitable gesture of "equality of religion or belief" is on something of a collision course with (for example) the Anglican Settlement in Britain or various concordats between the Catholic Church and democratic states. This is the obvious, but perhaps the more trivial, problem. The question does not stop with religion, for what is claimed is equality of "religion or belief." Law and society pledge to respect and protect the gods (lowercase) wherever they have gone. It legislates for myriad god effects, all over the place, even outside religion proper. Belief must be treated as holy, even as we have no way of knowing or policing the objects and investments of this chimerical force that we call belief and that we unleash as, by definition, "free." The protective mechanisms around belief can only ever be parsimoniously shared lest we all become believers and all start suing on grounds of discrimination against our belief.

Take, for example, the case of *Grainger v. Nicholson* (2009–10). In 2009, Tim Nicholson, former head of sustainability for the property company Grainger PLC, claimed that his redundancy (the elimination of his position) was an act of discrimination against his environmental beliefs. His legal team massaged his environmental "beliefs" into the forms set by the authoritative legal text. The legal team defending the property company argued that environmental commitments did not qualify because they were (merely?) *political* and a "lifestyle choice." The operative dichotomies were belief versus politics, belief versus opinion, belief versus knowledge, and sincerity or depth versus the mere: mere surface, mere choice, mere play. In November 2009 Justice Michael Burton ruled that "A belief in man-made climate change, and the alleged resulting moral imperatives, is capable if genuinely held, of being a philosophical belief for the purpose of the 2003 Religion and Belief Regulations" and added "In my judgement, his belief goes beyond a mere opinion." Nicholson was awarded a large out-of-court settlement that backed, with large sums of money, the legal reality and force of "secular belief." But this was something of a pyrrhic victory. Commitment to a belief in climate change was elevated to a protected status akin to religion but was placed in the outlands of the numinous and the dubious for all believers. In a beautiful demonstration of the ephemerality of belief, this led to an instant disavowal of the belief that had just been so ardently claimed. It turned out that belief had only existed qua belief within the confines of the courts, for the purposes of the case. Once the case was over it disappeared in a puff of smoke. Having been defined as indelible and irrevocable, belief was promptly disavowed. Climate change was emphatically *not* the equivalent of a "new religion" because it was not based on "faith or spirituality" but science, Nicholson told the press.

The ruling and its aftermath contained a strong element of deterrence; it became clear that it was not altogether a desirable thing to sue for protection on grounds of belief. To gain entrance, one must sever relations with good, solid, universally acknowledged things like science, fact, and knowledge. One must publicly confess to old ideas of a form of thought that cannot be substantiated and yet is so strong that it appears that it has chosen us rather than that we have chosen it.

Even as environmentalism was admitted (for the duration of the tribunal), as a belief, the ruling carefully controlled the parameters of qualifying belief. The judge offered humanism as an example of another kind of belief that would satisfy the criteria. Belief was being pluralized only in the most parsimonious way as, effectively, the "official unbelievers": those who don't believe in God (or gods) to such an extent that they get together in publicly recognizable groups in order to do so. This is the common way of paying lip service to the exorbitant demands of the secular. By giving a place at the table to humanist societies as, effectively, an "extra" world religion, and allowing them to function as an official "lack of religion," a state can appear to do justice to all the sites where the gods may have gone while in truth only protecting all the gods and the nongod (or rather their believers and adherents). As examples that failed to meet the criteria, the judge offered "belief in a political party or the supreme nature of Jedi knights."

Earlier we noted that Mademoiselle Philosophie looks like an undercover version of Kant's "police in the realm of the sciences," shadowing and watching Theology. In the legal formulations of 2003 and 2010, we find a far more explicitly Kantian performance of the scene of belief. The distinctions among opining, believing, and knowing looks as if it has been lifted straight out of Kant's *Critique of Pure Reason*. This is not just because legal scholars unwittingly repeat formulae that are over two hundred years old. What is attractive to modern democracies, loosely founded on Judeo-Christian virtue and committed to the protection and freedom of religion, is Kant's double-think around the notion of "belief." Kant is important because, just like Justice Burton, he both carefully delimits and valorizes belief.

In Kant's sphere of pure reason, as in the legislation of 2003 and 2010, judgment has three degrees: *opinion* (consciously insufficient, objectively and subjectively); *knowledge* (consciously sufficient, objectively and subjectively); and *belief* (only subjectively sufficient and objectively insufficient). As Kant notes, "The subjective sufficiency is termed conviction (for myself), and the objective conviction is called certainty (for everyone)." Clearly opining and knowing are parallel and less scary states, since the levels of objective and subjective sufficiency, or public certainty and personal conviction, agree. Belief is a mode of knowing that, "somewhat modestly," knows it is not knowing and knows it is not objective. But at the same time, "from the subjective point of view" it is an expression of "the firmness of our confidence." Belief is lopsided: heavy at one end and light at the other; firm at the level of "personal conviction" and entirely weightless at the level of public certainty.

Belief is unbalanced and unpoliceable. For this reason it does not get a special permit to enter the limited access domain of pure reason. But this is not Kant's last word on the place of belief. True enough, doctrinal belief is "somewhat lacking in stability" and must be excluded from the court of pure reason. But it is "quite otherwise" from what he calls moral belief: "For here it is absolutely necessary that something must happen, namely that I must in all points conform to the moral law. . . ."

For Kant, moral belief is the miraculous force that compels universal faith in human liberty, dignity, and equality (as well as God and immortality). Similarly, in the words of the fifth criterion of the Employment Equality Regulations, "[The belief] must be worthy of respect in a democratic society, not incompatible with human dignity and not in conflict with the fundamental rights of others." This is another version of that quintessentially modern hope and prayer that Mademoiselle Théologie/Religion will not turn against her industrious sisters, and not be as crude as to point to significant differences between her light and Reason's light.

Belief is a free radical that can attach itself to anything. By definition we cannot secure in advance the objects of belief. Having unleashed this flighty specter, the fifth criterion in the Employment Equality Regulations appears as a hopeful attempt to recapture—or, at the very least *manage*—the chimera of belief. The first four criteria create and unleash belief as a vague force that is not answerable to anything. They give belief free reign. Indeed, they define belief *by* this free reign. And then, in a distinctly late-modern twist on political theology, they try to manage the believing subject who has become sovereign, in a potentially exceptional relationship to law, by virtue of proven possession of "religion or belief." The fifth criterion attempts to squeeze the genie back into the bottle: it attempts to negotiate with the very quality that it has defined as nonnegotiable belief. Only if it submits to overriding principles of *Würde* (dignity) can belief qualify as belief. It seems that one can only hope—or pray—at this point. Clearly the attempt to impose conditions on that which is unconditioned will have limited success. Given the criteria just outlined, it is clear that not all beliefs will agree to submit.

Not surprisingly, the tension among the first four criteria (unleashing belief) and the fifth (imposing conditions on belief) is regularly played out in the courts. In the ongoing battles of our vague, amorphous "freedoms," the freedom enshrined in "rights" and "equal rights" regularly goes a few rounds with "freedom of belief." Qualifying believers—for example practicing Christians—are regularly admitted as conforming to the fifth criterion because to question, let alone sever, the links among Christianity, equality, and liberty would be more than the mythology and demography of modern Western democracies could bear. But at the same time, religious believers are allowed to be in conflict with the rights of others, even as conformity to the fifth criterion is declared. Courts have issued controversial opt-outs on religious grounds from legislation concerning gender and sexual orientation, but never ethnicity or disability. The protected characteristics (sexuality/gender, pregnancy/maternity, race/ethnicity, disability, and age) are not equally established, equally protected, though all are responses to social and political ferment of very recent date. The conflict between religion and sexuality (and particularly homosexuality) has become an incendiary cultural flashpoint and a stage for the trial of competing freedoms because *religious belief and (homo) sexuality are more insecure and vulnerable than age, maternity, disability, or race.*

Every time an institutionalized belief is granted an exception from the demands of equality on the issue of sexuality, the judgment turns our attention back on the tenuous alliance and disequilibrium between "religion and [secular] belief." Why does opposition to homosexuality only count when God-endorsed or issued from an exceptional sacred space? Belief is a limited-membership club. There is no place at the table for purely political beliefs (known as "opinions")—that is, beliefs that cannot aggregate in official and large collectives, or beliefs that lack the institutional edifices and props of antiquity to assert their status and make their case.

Every time adjustments are made to the fifth criterion by way of concession to the undeniable compulsion of belief, belief becomes, so to speak, stronger and we highlight the insurmountable force of the chimera we have created. We reify the notion of belief as "nonnegotiable," "intransigent" (problematic for community), "inflexible," and "not real,"—and yet so real that one has to act as if it were more than real. We reinforce the strange and frightening set of terms that assemble around *belief*, a term that itself becomes an assembly point for recognized collectives that need to join, en masse, in order to meet the legal requirements to believe. Some beliefs are admitted, whereas others are forcefully and polemically excluded, but all remain entirely inside the court's absolutely amorphous and unpredictable definition of "belief."

We cannot escape the paradox that we have instituted: a tolerated and respected heteronomy—submission to the law of the (divine) other—within a worldview that prioritizes autonomy just as long as that heteronomy does not impinge on the day-to-day running of democracy or provide an alternative law to the legal system. No wonder that there continues to be such hysteria about Islamic sharia. *The threat of sharia crystallizes the institutionalized "heteronomy" or other law that we have always admitted (without any external provocation) around "belief."* Massively funded government-led enquiries into "radicalization" neglect to explore how the threat of radicalization is built into our own conceptualizations of belief. This delineation of belief as an exceptional and essentially religious category originates in the Enlightenment, but has recently been intensified to a fever pitch. By protecting belief and restricting the cabal of potential believers, we have generated another round of texts that mystify and spook us with "belief."

Clearly the religion or belief regulations are not attempting to reflect on epistemology or enquire into the actual operation of "belief" in society. The task is legal management. This is accomplished by placing some core concepts on the chessboard ("belief," "opinion," "choice," and "knowledge") and then adding, for good measure, the contrast between sincerity and the "mere" (the mere as moderate, but also the mere as on the surface, fake). The concepts and contrasts are deliberately loose and flexible. They allow for different arrangements of the pieces and different checkmate scenarios that will only work for a particular game. Words like *belief* or *knowledge* operate rather like the rock, paper, and scissors in the game. As paper covers rock, so belief wins over knowledge (under certain conditions, if the belief is adjudicated as having the requisite "depth"). In each case the outcome depends on how the relative strength and virtue of words like *belief* and *choice* are calibrated and the order or hierarchy in which they are placed.

The British regulations are a stark case of similarly awkward/flexible accommodations of "religion" as concept and protected characteristic. Clearly other European legislative bodies are playing similar games. Hussein Agrama's contribution in chapter 25 of the present volume (and, in particular, his discussion of the work of Mayanthi Fernando) suggests that a very similar set of word pieces have been operative in France in prohibitions against the Muslim veil. To argue that the veil is a "choice" is to argue for its virtue because it is freely chosen and not coerced. But then, to argue that the veil is a personal choice is to leave oneself potentially stranded without sufficient backing from mainstream authorities. Without sufficient support (which can be inflected, oppositely, as coercion), the case for the veil would be indefensible, flimsy, and stranded like those beliefs that do not come into court with sufficient numbers to count. The conflicting rationales for prohibition demonstrate just how flexible the range of outcomes can be when words like *belief* and *choice* are put into play. They also help us to reflect further on how law uses this moving bar of "depth." Trials of depth or sincerity place the law in the simultaneously sinister and absurd position of playing omniscient deity and peering into the soul. Ironically, the interior of the individual is to be examined by those public (secular) bodies that have always declared their commitment to a fundamental separation between private belief and public behavior in a citizen of the state. But more can be said about this strange trial of sincerity. In the implementation of sincerity tests, the operative spatial metaphor is *breadth* as well as *depth* and the spotlight is not simply on individual depth. Beliefs and practices cannot stand alone. They cannot spring up *de novo*. They must pass (vague) synchronic and diachronic tests. To be admitted, they must be validated in sufficient numbers, and they must have sufficient historical depth. Usefully, this often means that the qualifying beliefs are those supported by religious authorities and mandated by mainstream (qualifying and ancient) religious texts. But arbitration by appeal to the schismatic and divided terrain of text and authority allows considerable room for maneuvering. It allows us to assign weight and lightness in different measures to different religions and different practices within those traditions. It allows us to adjudicate on what will be deemed the central, authoritative, and true interpretation—which is to say the one we judge to be "not incompatible with human dignity" and in line with the aims of the modern state.

The equal and opposite rationales for banning the veil show just how much leverage can be extracted around this moveable bar of "depth." French Muslim women who seek to defend the veil must find, somehow, just the right amount of context: just enough validation for the veil to make it an obligation, mandated by the authorities, but not so much that this validation becomes "coercion." They must get the force of compulsion just right. This is akin to getting the weight of a qualifying belief just right in UK legislation. True belief must prove a certain excess, or transcendence, to distinguish it from knowledge. But it cannot exhibit the kind of excess that is potentially fanatical and not supported in the religious mainstream. It must be sufficiently heavy, but light enough to be flexible and ally itself with fundamental notions of human rights. Similarly, French Muslim women must show that they have been moved by something outside or beyond themselves without allowing the force to get so strong that it potentially turns them into the kind of dumb puppet-believers who say yes to anything. They must find just enough context (depth/breadth) to qualify as genuinely called and obligated, lifting them above the bar of mere choice (and mere opinion) into faith. Only the state holds the secret of where exactly this ideal medium point lies. It is difficult to imagine Christianity being set such an impossible, fairytale test. The pieces on the chessboard make it possible to checkmate from equal and opposite directions. In their quest for the very best kinds of religion, states do more than hope and pray.

Selected Bibliography

Anidjar, Gil. "Secularism." *Critical Inquiry* 33, no. 1 (2006): 52–77.

Diderot, Denis and Jean le Rond d'Alembert. *L'Encyclopédie.* Paris: Bordas, 1967.

Employment Equality (Religion or Belief) Regulations 2003. Accessed April 8, 2014 at http://www.legislation.gov.uk/uksi/2003/1660/contents/made.

Equality Act 2010. Accessed April 8, 2014 at http://www.legislation.gov.uk/ukpga/2010/15/contents.

Grainger plc and others v Nicholson, Employment Appeal Tribunal 3 November 2009 [2010] I.C.R 360.

Kant, Immanuel. *Critique of Pure Reason.* Trans. Norman Kemp Smith. London: Palgrave Macmillan, 2007.

Lopez, Donald S. "Belief." In *Critical Terms for Religious Studies*, edited by Mark C. Taylor, 21–36. Chicago: University of Chicago Press, 1998.

Sherwood, Yvonne. *Biblical Blaspheming: Trials of the Sacred for a Secular Age.* Cambridge: Cambridge University Press, 2012.

CHAPTER THREE

Believing in Religious Freedom

Elizabeth Shakman Hurd

Anyone who identifies as a believer . . . (though religious freedom is for believers and nonbelievers) . . . can come to our roundtable.—US ambassador-at-large for international religious freedom, Suzan Johnson Cook, Council on Foreign Relations, 2013

The category of belief is not so easily transferred from one society to another, and . . . those who seek to do so are subject to the consequences of their deed.—Donald S. Lopez Jr.

Like a good movie, the story of international religious freedom offers something for everyone. It pits cowardly oppressors against heroic saviors. It tells of the triumph of international law over those who refuse to adhere to global norms and standards. It proposes secular tolerance over violent religion. It is a story of human progress and emancipation, of transforming conditions of religious oppression to liberate individuals— particularly women and minorities—from their primitive and discriminatory ways. It is a story of the triumph of the free market, of the "real" freedom and "real" religion that are said to emerge naturally when government influence is stripped away from the religious lives of citizens. And today, especially, it is a story of the need for the US government and its friends to convince others—particularly Muslims—that they should endorse a particular model of religious liberty as a template for organizing and democratizing politics and society.

This essay challenges that story by focusing on a key aspect of the promotion of religious freedom. Religious freedom advocacy is often described as supporting a right to choose one's "religion or belief." Although religious practice is also considered, belief is understood to be the central and defining feature of religiosity. The implication is that there can be no religion without belief. Religious freedom advocacy also seeks to protect the right to choose one's religious belief or nonbelief. Choice is taken to be a defining feature of freedom.

What kind of religion, and what kind of religious subject, are presupposed and promoted through these efforts? What are the consequences of promoting religious freedom as the right to believe or not, and the right to choose among beliefs in a free religious marketplace? What is the historical background of these assumptions? Is it possible that state programs, international initiatives, and human rights instruments designed to secure a universal right to religious freedom in fact disseminate and instantiate a particular notion of the "free" believing—or nonbelieving—religious subject? Would it be possible to continue promoting religious freedom as a universal norm if the modern construct of belief, and its tireless partner, nonbelief, were understood as the product of a specific political discourse situated in history rather than as the mark of the sacred?

International religious freedom advocacy contributes to the normalization of (religious) subjects for whom "believing" is taken as the universal defining characteristic of what it means to be religious, and the right to believe as the essence of what it means to be free. As individuals and groups around the world submit to legal regimes of religious freedom, they are also submitting to a particular model of a free religious economy populated by believing and nonbelieving subjects. This transformative process shapes religion in specific and identifiable ways.

The Subject of Freedom

International authorities have attempted to define "religion or belief" for the purposes of legally guaranteeing religious freedom. For the UN Human Rights Committee, charged with monitoring member states' implementation of the International Covenant on Civil and Political Rights, religion or belief includes "theistic, nontheistic and atheistic beliefs, as well as the right not to profess any religion or belief." For legal scholar Malcolm Evans, "it is the freedom to believe and to manifest beliefs, subject only to those limitations strictly necessary to protect the rights and interests of others, which is the subject of human rights protection, and not the beliefs themselves." For the UK Foreign and Commonwealth Office, whether a belief is protected depends on its "cogency, seriousness, cohesion and importance": "The word 'religion' is commonly, but not

always, associated with belief in a transcendent deity or deities, i.e. a su-
perhuman power or powers with an interest in human destiny. The term
'belief' does not necessarily involve a divine being; it denotes a certain
level of cogency, seriousness, cohesion and importance. So not all beliefs
are covered by this protection. For example, if someone believed that
the moon was made of cheese, this belief would not be likely to meet the
test above." There is an interesting tension between these anguished attempts to define religion or belief for the purposes of international legal
regulation and the fact that most scholars of religion departed some time
ago from the equation of religion with interiority and belief. This course
correction has led to what Constance Furey describes as a "fundamental change in the way many religionists now think about the religious
subject . . . this scholarly trend in religious studies strongly undermined
the assumption that the object of the religionist's inquiry is (and should
be) a freely volitional subject." As Yvonne Sherwood puts it in chapter 2
of the present volume, religion scholars "have spent most of their energy
in the last thirty years decoupling religion from belief," which has been
"kicked into the sidelines as a Christian/colonial imposition." With this
shift in orientation, scholars of religion appear to be catching up with the
lived realities of religious experience.

Religious affiliation has always involved more than a choice between
belief and disbelief. Citing a colonial American minister from the Carolina backwoods named Charles Woodmason, historian Jon Butler re-
counts that he "observed religious bewilderment, fascination, repulsion,
confusion, and a distanced evasion, including indifference, rather than
unbelief or a choice between belief and unbelief, or atheism." The difficulty with equating belief and religion, Butler explains, is that "the laity
have seldom phrased their own views about religion in such dichotomous
and essentially exclusive ways." T. M. Luhrmann made a similar point in
the *New York Times* about contemporary American evangelicals:

> Secular Americans often think that the most important thing to understand
> about religion is why people believe in God, because we think that belief pre-
> cedes action and explains choice. That's part of our folk model of the mind:
> that belief comes first. And that was not really what I saw after my years
> spending time in evangelical churches. I saw that people went to church to
> experience joy and to learn how to have more of it. These days I find that it is
> more helpful to think about faith as the questions people choose to focus on,
> rather than the propositions observers think they must hold.

Viewed skeptically today by those who study religion both past and present, the arguably nonexistent freely volitional subject who chooses to believe (or not) persists and, strangely, looms large in the world of international religious freedom advocacy. The protection of international religious freedom as a universal norm hinges upon, and even sanctifies, a religious psychology that relies on the notion of an autonomous subject who chooses beliefs and then enacts them freely. This understanding of religion normalizes (religious) subjects for whom "believing" is taken as the universal defining characteristic of what it means to be religious, and the right to choose one's belief as the essence of what it means to be free. Anchoring and steadying this approach to religion is a specific, historically located figure of faith, and a particular, historically contingent notion of belief.

Talal Asad's account of the shifting and lived experience of belief calls into question the universality of the liberal democratic requirement that it is belief or conscience that properly defines the individual, thereby representing, for many liberals, the essence of religiosity. Asad dates this concept of belief to a new religious psychology and concept of the state that began to emerge in seventeenth-century Europe. In that theory, which is also at the core of John Locke's theory of toleration, belief should not be coerced because it affronts the dignity of the individual, and cannot be coerced because it is located in the private space of the individual mind. Authenticity, according to many liberal philosophers, "consists in the subject's ability *to choose* his or her beliefs and act on them." Donald Lopez has described this seventeenth-century notion as "an ideology of belief, that is, an assumption deriving from the history of Christianity that religion is above all an interior state of assent to certain truths." This discourse of belief was accompanied by a particular understanding of the secular state; as Asad explains, "Although the insistence that beliefs cannot be changed from outside appeared to be saying something empirical about 'personal belief' (its singular, autonomous, and inaccessible-to-others location), it was really part of a political discourse about 'privacy,' a claim to civil immunity with regard to religious faith that reinforced the idea of a secular state and a particular conception of religion."

Like Butler, Asad draws our attention to the shifting, lived experience of "belief." Experiences now translated as "belief" (*croyance*) were always embedded in distinctive social and political relationships and sensibilities. This is illustrated, as Asad explains, in Dorothea Weltecke's description of a young peasant woman named Aude Fauré who was brought before the Inquisition:

> She was unable, she said, to *credere in Deum*. What she meant by this, Weltecke points out, emerges from the detailed context. Aude Fauré took the existence of a God for granted. It was because, in her desperation, she could not see in the Eucharist anything but bread and because she found herself struggling with disturbing thoughts about Incarnation that she had no hope of God's mercy. It is not clear that the *doctrine* of God's body appearing in the form of bread is being challenged here; what is certainly being expressed is the woman's *anguished relationship* to God as a consequence of her own incapacity to see anything but bread. In short, it is not that our present concept of belief (*that* something is true) was absent in pre-modern society, but that the words translated as such were usually embedded in distinctive social and political relationships, articulated distinctive sensibilities; they were first of all lived and only occasionally theorized.

Like Furey, Butler, Sherwood, Lopez, Luhrmann, and others, Asad's discussion of "belief" complicates the notion of a universal right to religious freedom understood as the freedom to believe (or not). Inasmuch as the protection of religious freedom hinges upon and sanctifies a religious psychology that relies on a particular notion of an autonomous subject who chooses and enacts beliefs, and a particular notion of the secular state that does not (and cannot) coerce such beliefs, these projects privilege and elevate—often in law—particular forms of religious subjectivity while disabling and depriviledging others. In normalizing subjects for whom believing is taken as the universal defining characteristic of what it means to be religious, and the right to believe as the essence of what it means to be free, they exclude other modes of living in the world, as bodies in communities and in relationship to which they are obliged, without (necessarily) any attention to or concern for individual belief.

But belief itself is also limited. It is not free. Religion or belief, as Sherwood shows in chapter 2, "is a limited-membership club. There is no place at the table for purely political beliefs (known as 'opinions')—that is, beliefs that cannot aggregate in official and large collectives, or beliefs that lack the institutional edifices and props of antiquity to assert their status and make their case." The promotion of international religious freedom, then, is part of a larger story involving the costs and consequences of mistaking, in William Cavanaugh's words, "a contingent power arrangement of the modern West for a universal and timeless feature of human existence."

The momentum behind the legal globalization of the rights of believers and nonbelievers is formidable. Calls for an international convention to protect the freedom of religious (non)believers are urgently made. Prominent scholars such as Malcolm Evans have joined a chorus of experts warning that legal protection for religious freedom should be seen no longer as "only an option," as "it is fast becoming a necessity in order to prevent the further erosion of the position of religious believers in many countries." The international community has been charged with "developing a more precise understanding of what the freedom of religion as a human right actually entails, and to do so in a coherent and transparent fashion to which all interested parties can contribute" so that "we might then be better placed to develop the means by which it can be realised." There is a drive to settle on the norm, agree on a definition, and fix it in a convention. Legal protection for religious freedom is proposed as the remedy for a host of societal ills, from poverty and oppression to violence and discrimination. An international convention, according to Evans, would breathe new life into an anemic global consensus that has "done little to combat the rising tide of restriction, hostility and violence experienced by many religious believers." It would tackle head-on "the overriding problem, which is how to hold States to account for their own failure to respect and protect the rights of all believers." The reference to religion or belief, at least outside the United States, includes nonreligious belief as well. Not only religionists but also nonreligionists are defined by belief. It is said to include everyone.

Yet the historical particularities of the rise of a certain economy of belief, and its close ties and constitutive relationship to modern, post-Protestant notions of religion, subvert the promise of freedom implicit in Evans's international legal ambitions. Contemporary international religious freedom advocacy not only protects particular kinds of religious selves and subjects but also helps to create individuals and "faith communities" for whom choosing and believing, in the sense historicized by Asad and lionized by Evans, are seen as the defining characteristics of what it is to be religious, and the right to choose to believe (or not) as the essence of what it means to be free. To achieve this unity in freedom of belief—belief in belief, as it were—across communities of belief (and nonbelief), is what it means to have achieved "religious freedom." As

Evans insists, "faith communities must reject the superficial attractions of claiming or accepting such freedoms for themselves alone, and unhesitatingly support the freedom of religion or belief for all. Unless or until religious communities are prepared to champion for everyone the freedoms that they wish their own followers to enjoy, there is likely to be little opportunity for seriously furthering the freedom of religion or belief at all."

The identification of religion and faith communities with a right to freedom of belief and believers leaves little room for alternatives in which religion is lived relationally as ethics, culture, and even politics but without, necessarily, belief and, as a matter of command, not freedom. The foreclosure on religion without belief shuts out dissenters, doubters, and those on the margins of or just outside those "faith communities" celebrated by religious freedom advocates, whose voices are subsumed or submerged by the institutions and authorities presumed to speak in their name. It endows those authorities with the power to pronounce on which beliefs deserve special protection or sanction. And it occludes the fundamental instability of the notion of religious belief. Who decides what counts as a religious belief deserving of special protection and legal exemption rather than as some other form of belief?

Religious freedom advocacy is built around a particular notion of the "free" believing or nonbelieving human that is disseminated through secular international institutions and instruments. This freely choosing, believing or nonbelieving subject is, as Lila Abu-Lughod has observed of the human of secular liberalism, "everywhere—translated, resisted, vernacularized, invoked in political struggles, and made the standard language enforced by power." The subject of religious freedom is an autonomous individual defined by his or her freedom to choose to believe or not. To reiterate Suzan Johnson Cook's quotation from the epigraph, "anyone who identifies as a believer (though religious freedom is for believers and nonbelievers) can come to our roundtable." Today this believing/nonbelieving subject is normalized not only through US foreign religious engagement but also through a proliferating series of public international legal regimes and administrative initiatives that have adopted this template and have as their objective to promote the right to religious freedom. These initiatives promote a particular notion of (free) religion understood as a set of propositions to which believers assent, making religion, as Webb Keane has observed, "a matter not of material disciplines or of ritual practices . . . but of subjective beliefs."

A Transition into "Freedom Itself"

As individuals and states around the world submit to legal regimes of religious freedom—as many are doing at lightning speed due to diplomatic pressures, trade incentives, and other advantages to be accrued—they also assume a particular model of a free religious economy. Contemporary international religious freedom advocacy both presupposes and produces the neoliberal religious subject of the religious economies model: a rational, voluntary religious actor who seeks out the religious options that suit her best. This model of religious growth, associated with Laurence R. Iannaccone, Roger Finke, and Rodney Stark, is described in chapter 5 of the present volume by Courtney Bender, who writes,

> Where state regulation is absent . . . , religious groups are free to organize as they wish and rise or fall based on their abilities to appeal to religious consumers.
>
> Religious economies models borrow explicitly from the Chicago school of economics. So, in this model a rational, voluntary, religious actor will consistently seek out the religious option with the compensatory system that best suits her. Individual religious freedom is maximized in a religious marketplace where multiple firms exist. Competition has the effect of increasing religious vitality and fervor, rather than marking its decline, and creating an ongoing religious equilibrium.

Shaping actions and possibilities, advocacy for religious freedom and religious liberalization promote and protect forms of (religious) subjectivity that are particularly well suited to operate in a free market where the believer or nonbeliever can shop for, among other things, religion. The state's job is to create the conditions for the emergence and flourishing of rational, tolerant, believing or nonbelieving consumers of free religion under law.

Mathijs Pelkmans has tracked the asymmetrical effects of religious liberalization on religious and nonreligious groups in post-Soviet Kyrgyzstan, where state-sponsored religious liberalization arrived in a package deal with the liberalization of the economy and the global "war on terror." Everyone was bringing freedom. As Pelkmans shows, the combination of economic and religious liberalization and the securitization of Islam in the "war on terror" opened spaces for the flourishing of Christian missions while closing them down for Muslim reformist movements. The market model created conditions that were favorable to Christian missions because "it is encased in an international discourse in which Islam (except for its 'secular' or 'folk' variants) is readily equated with radicalism and terrorism." As a result, "sectarian" Protestant movements were classified as legitimate denominations while Muslim reformist movements were perceived as a threat to the government and suspected of links to terrorist organizations. Working in tandem with free market ideology and the strategic imperatives of the "war on terror," religious liberalization in Kyrgyzstan sanctioned particular ways of being religious that were understood to be modern and free. In this model, individuals are free to choose their religious beliefs (or lack thereof) qua individuals, like shopping in the marketplace for goods. Particular inhabitations of what the authorities denominate as free, orthodox, and unthreatening religion are elevated and enabled while other ways of relating to community, place, and tradition are rendered unintelligible or even threatening. The failure or inability of certain religious groups to participate in this "free" religious market are cast as problems inherent to the groups themselves, as failures to "cast off religious peculiarities so that they can participate in the thriving religious commerce of modern democracies, and in real, 'free' religiosity," as Bender argues in chapter 5 of the present volume.

Yet the transformation wrought by religious liberalization goes deeper. The marketization of religion incentivizes communities to define themselves according to particular understandings of what it is to be a religion. "Religions" begin to perceive themselves as they are portrayed in the religious economies discourse—as hidebound communities, static bodies of convention, and groups comprising individual believers. Boundaries are settled. Orthodoxy is established. Spokesmen are appointed. Distinct confessional identities are required to play this game: you can be this or that, but not both. As identities solidify, the ability to change and adapt is increasingly understood to be the exclusive purview of secular subjects and not religious ones. Those who are provisionally affiliated, those wishing to question or qualify their affiliation, those living with multiple affiliations, given or chosen, are left out in the cold—falling into the abyss created by the modern divide between the secular and the religious. The experiences and uncertainties that shape religious identification are squeezed into the either/or logic of confessional identity.

Some religions adapt more readily than others. Submission to a religious economies model incurs losses in human and religious diversity. In the case of Kyrgyzstan, liberalization benefited religious groups such as evangelical Protestants that had not been active or were only minimally active in the country prior to the reforms. Yet these losses can be difficult to calculate because the transition into religious freedom is not understood as the imposition of an American, or even international norm, but rather as a transition into freedom itself, as Bender explains, "The free market allows—and in fact trains—religious groups to be free: to cast off the cultural and political baggage or problematic connections to political life. What we confront in both religious economies models and the narratives of their sociological critics is much less a theoretical frame of pluralism than a political doctrine of freedom." Part of the strength and appeal of contemporary international religious freedom advocacy is drawn from its imbrication with this political doctrine of freedom. Religiously liberated subjects are not brought into a particular American or capitalist normative system. They are brought into freedom itself.

Conclusion

For Janet Jakobsen modernity is characterized by a "market-based sense of freedom" that, she notes, "is not the repression of activity, but it is the regulated enactment of activity along particular lines." International religious freedom advocacy participates in a market-based religious economy by regulating the enactment of religious activity along particular lines. It shapes activities, actions, and desires. "Freedom" is achieved through the identification and selection of "religion or (non)belief" as an individualized object chosen in a religious marketplace. Inducing particular desires and practices, the promotion of religious freedom enables particular ways of being religious, and being human, while disabling others.

In its stronger forms, international religious freedom globalizes the secular state's power over the individual. Appearing as a guarantee of the worth of the individual's own desires, it tells individuals and groups how to be religious, modern, and free. In regulating religious activity along particular lines, it privileges particular ways of being religious as deserving protection by the state or other authorities. It singles out authorized representatives of "believers" (and less often, "nonbelievers") for legal protection, reinforcing divisions and hierarchies within and between communities. It structures societies around religious markets that, though purportedly self-regulating, are shot through with political and economic inequalities. In its more insistent moments, contemporary religious freedom advocacy is a story of the costs in human dignity and difference associated with the attempt to make conscience or belief the measure of what religion is understood to be, and the freedom to choose one's belief the measure of what it means to be free. Aude Fauré was brought before the Inquisition at the beginning of this modern attempt at mind control. Today, as well, it is a global enterprise.

Selected Bibliography

Abu-Lughod, Lila. "Against Universals: The Dialects of (Women's) Human Rights and Human Capabilities." In *Rethinking the Human*, edited by J. Michelle Molina and Donald K. Swearer. Cambridge, MA: Harvard University Press, 2010.

Asad, Talal. "Thinking about Religious Belief and Politics." In *The Cambridge Companion to Religious Studies*, edited by Robert Orsi, 36–57. Cambridge: Cambridge University Press, 2012.

Butler, Jon. "Disquieted History in a Secular Age." In *Varieties of Secularism in a Secular Age*, edited by Michael Warner, Jonathan VanAntwerpen, and Craig Calhoun, 193–216. Cambridge, MA: Harvard University Press, 2010.

Cavanaugh, William. *The Myth of Religious Violence: Secular Ideology and the Roots of Modern Conflict*. New York: Oxford University Press, 2009.

Cook, Suzan Johnson. "Religious Tolerance at Home and Abroad." Panel presentation at the Seventh Annual Religion and Foreign Policy Summer Workshop, New York, June 25, 2013.

Evans, Malcolm. "Advancing Freedom of Religion or Belief: Agendas for Change." Lambeth Inter Faith Lecture, Lambeth Palace, London, June 8, 2011.

Furey, Constance M. "Body, Society, and Subjectivity in Religious Studies." *Journal of the American Academy of Religion* 80, no. 1 (March 2012): 7–33.

Jakobsen, Janet R. "Sex + Freedom = Regulation. Why?" *Social Text* 23, nos. 3–4 (2005): 285–308.

Keane, Webb. *Christian Moderns: Freedom and Fetish in the Mission Encounter*. Berkeley and Los Angeles: University of California Press, 2007.

Lopez, Donald S. , Jr. "Belief." In *Critical Terms for Religious Studies*, edited by Mark C. Taylor, 21–35. Chicago: University of Chicago Press, 1998.

Luhrmann, T. M. "Belief is the Least Part of Faith." *New York Times*, May 29, 2013. Accessed September 3, 2013 at http://www.nytimes.com/2013/05/30/opinion/luhrmann-belief-is-the-least-part-of-faith.html?emc=eta1&_r=0.

Pelkmans, Mathijs. "Asymmetries on the 'Religious Market' in Kyrgyzstan." In *The Postsocialist Religious Question: Faith and Power in Central Asia and East-Central Europe*, edited by Chris Hann, 29–46. Berlin: LIT Verlag, 2006.

———. "The 'Transparency' of Christian Proselytizing in Kyrgyzstan." *Anthro-pological Quarterly* 82, no. 2 (2009): 423–45.

UK Foreign and Commonwealth Office (FCO). "Freedom of Religion or Belief—How the FCO Can Help Promote Respect for This Human Right." June 2010. Accessed September 3, 2013 at http://www.fco.gov.uk/resources/en/pdf/global-issues/human-rights/freedom-toolkit.

CHAPTER FOUR

What Is Religious Freedom Supposed to Free?

Webb Keane

What is religious freedom supposed to free? That is, what is the operant understanding of "religion" behind the claims of religious freedom such that religion requires its own forms, practices, and concepts of freedom under the law? Is there something about religion that gives freedom of religion either a privileged or a peculiarly worrisome character different in kind from artistic, political, academic, journalistic, or sexual freedom? And to this list why not add occupational, associational or, say, economic freedoms? Or freedom of marriage? (The latter, for one, is certainly deeply implicated in the governance of religion.) As Elizabeth Shakman Hurd and Winnifred Sullivan suggest in the present volume, one thing that institutions of religious freedom commonly presuppose is a deep connection between religion (or at least some kinds of religion) and violence (or at least some kinds of violence) such that religion requires specific forms of juridical intervention or state neutrality.

This connection is an idea commonly said to lie at the roots of the distinctive forms of European church-state relations whose early emergence is conventionally identified with the Peace of Westphalia. Of course, the actual Western history of religious freedom is far more complex and contingent than any single narrative line or conceptual synopsis can capture. Ian Hunter notes that the legal and political arrangements in Europe were as much the product of local institutional cultures and pragmatic solutions to specific problems as they were expressions of coherent principles. And, as Michael Lambek, Nadia Marzouki, and others point out in this volume, the complexity only grows once we extend our purview beyond the Euro-American world. Moreover, the distinctiveness of religion is certainly an assumption about which doubts may be raised. Yet one way or another, the question of religion's distinctive character still haunts juridical and legislative efforts to deal with it. However contingent the local political and juridical arrangements may be, their plausibility and legitimacy within any given social and historical context presumably depends on the ways they tap into some basic underlying assumptions about the distinctive character of religion. In particular, to posit an essential link between religion and violence is to assume that religion is defined by special emotions and deep, even primordial, commitments that separate it from the forms of instrumental rationality supposed to underlie other forms of violence such as electoral strife, class conflict, or simple criminality. Cécile Laborde makes a crucial point in this volume: cheerful views of religion that define it as a matter of people's central moral commitments—for example, as Charles Taylor does in *A Secular Age*—harbor the unintended implication that religion is most authentic when it is most dogmatic.

Beyond this supposed inclination of religion toward violence, Hurd and Sullivan bring out two different dimensions of the presuppositions informing current legal and political debates about religious freedom. Hurd, drawing on Talal Asad and others, stresses the central place given to the concept of belief in discussions around the legal status of religion. Sullivan, attending to ways in which the concept of religious freedom is being reformulated in the contemporary United States, points to the anxieties about the moral nihilism that will supposedly result from any triumph of irreligion under the guise of separation of church and state. Even if belief and morality are not clearly distinguishable in actual practice, it can make a difference which one is stressed in the terms of any given form of governance.

The first of these dimensions, a focus on belief, tends to portray religions in the plural (I believe in the Trinity, you believe in karma). The focus on morality, on the other hand, can sometimes end up placing the relevant divide at a higher level of abstraction, between the presence and absence of religion altogether. Or at least this is how the situation is presently understood by many of the American religious groups whose opposition to liberal understandings of the separation of church and state is discussed by Peter Danchin, Ann Pellegrini, and Winnifred Sullivan in their contributions to this volume. And one might suggest these different emphases involve different degrees of implied consequentiality. Without wishing to overstate the case, it may be that freedom of belief is most easily accepted if one takes it to refer primarily to theological claims of no particular immediate and practical consequence, a view famously expressed by Thomas Jefferson in the words, "[I]t does me no injury for my neighbour to say there are twenty gods, or no god. It neither picks my pocket nor breaks my leg." If complete indifference is rare, more common may be the qualifying assurance that as long as a person at least *has* a religion of some sort, matters of content may be set aside. Perhaps something like this pluralist view underlies US senator John Breaux's remark a few years ago, when asked whether being Jewish would affect the political fate of Joseph Lieberman: "I don't think American voters care where a man goes to church on Sunday."

If, on the other hand, religion is above all a matter of moralities, it is easier to imagine dire social and political consequences might be incurred through the mishandling of the relevant freedoms. As Laborde points out, to the extent that religion centers on deep moral commitments, differences of religion can also be taken as threats to public order and thereby require state intervention. They are no longer about differing truth claims or ontologies, matters about which people may, at least at times, agree to disagree. Rather, in this view, religion is a crucial factor in what motivates and directs the impact people have upon one another. For reasons like this, according to Nehal Bhuta, freedom to manifest religion in states influenced by European laws has always been limited on the grounds that neutrality toward religion is merely an exception to the state's prior responsibility for public order. But in either case, whether one emphasizes religion as belief or religion as morality, what makes religious freedom a special case, requiring special protections, institutions, and interventions, is predicated on what one takes religion ultimately to be.

In practice the inner realm of belief is hard to cordon off altogether from the external realm of material practices whose social consequences might trigger state intervention. Even the most austere religions must still take *some* material form. The links between belief and materiality can raise thorny semiotic problems. Thus Hussein Ali Agrama argues in this volume that Egyptian law instigates "a particular modality of suspicion" such that disbelief, supposedly a private and inner matter, may be taken as evidence of more worldly kinds of corruption. Moreover, according to Saba Mahmood and Peter Danchin, this is not just a distortion of an otherwise straightforward principle of state neutrality. They too say that the Egyptian state cannot help but become involved in interpreting material practices as evidence for inner states. Nor is this confounding of protected interior belief and the less protected domain of exterior manifestation restricted to Egypt. In European courts, limitations on the right to manifest one's religion, the *forum externum*, evoke questions about the meaning and practical efficacy of those signs that might be taken to connect outer and inner, material and immaterial, public order and private conscience. Two famous court cases that resulted in opposed verdicts both turned on this semiotic problem: whereas in the *Dahlab v. Switzerland* case, the Muslim headscarf was ruled to be a provocation that might lead to explicit doctrinal assertions and thus incite conflict, in the *Lautsi v. Italy* case, the schoolroom crucifix was held to be merely a "passive symbol" with no consequences for non-Christian pupils.

Bridging the belief-focused and morality-focused views of religion is the idea of conscience and the freedoms it demands. The tradition of defining religion in terms of belief, to which Hurd refers, tends to privilege individual interiority and its sincere expression—thus implying a local semiotics by which externals are or are not taken to reveal inner states. Seen this way, individual interiority takes precedence over community ties, rituals, or institutional structures. One common result (if not a necessary one, for Hunter observes that there was a strong presumption in European confessional states that "faith cannot be freely chosen") is to treat religious faith as something about which the believer has made a decision. Indeed, as Taylor has argued, even the distinction between religion and irreligion—in his view of secular modernity—has become merely a matter of choice among more or less equally weighted options. This is one reason why the focus on belief seems to lead to a view of the plurality of religions as so many members of a set, differing in their content but alike in their kind: all "go to church on Sunday." And it is precisely because one's religious beliefs are, at least in principle, a matter of choice that they manifest an ethics of freedom, and, in the liberal tradition at least, the freedom of an individual's conscience. That is, they are ethical precisely because they are deep manifestations of freedom in principle; as the Lockean argument goes, one may only imprison a person's body, but not his or her conscience. Thus one might argue religious freedom, framed as a matter of freedom of conscience and centered on belief, becomes inseparable from a long history of thought about freedom of the will tout court. What makes religious freedom special, in this view, might be the way in which it articulates a fundamental basis for there even being any human freedom at all.

I have argued that the sincere belief model of religion is at the heart of a moral narrative of modernity such that to maintain a religious practice that is not centered on belief—to pay too much heed to (mere) rituals, icons, clothing, or dietary laws, for instance—is to remain backward. The moral narrative of modernity is a story about human emancipation and self-mastery. According to this moral narrative, modernity is a story of human liberation from a host of false beliefs and fetishisms that undermined freedom in the past. It is a narrative in which freedom as such is pitted against certain forms of religion, such that their elimination (and, in some versions, replacement with the religion of sincere beliefs but, in others, with no religion at all) is a condition for the fuller realization of human agency. Those who persist in their fetishisms are not merely behind the times; by denying the agency that is properly theirs, they can even undermine the gains made by others, such as secular liberals, over the course of that long struggle. In this light it is not only proponents of a strong religious presence in public life who worry about the social impact of moral differences; so do their opponents.

As many critics have observed, the focus on belief is not only narrow; it also tends to favor a propositional understanding of religious belief. This understanding contributes to, or at least is consistent with, the idea that a rational capacity for deliberation is a fundamental precondition for moral actions. The demand that one be responsible for one's thoughts can translate into a demand that those thoughts be available for rendering in explicit form. Thus a legal insistence on responsibility may entail a degree of pragmatic pressure on religious practices on the ground, rendering juridically unrecognizable those that fail to assert themselves with creedal authority. Moreover, when juxtaposed to the morality-oriented view of religion, this demand may give greater impetus to the long-standing effort to organize morality under a knowable, objectified organizing principle that seems to be a distinctive project of a scripture-based monolithic religion. Given the demands for coherence imposed by a discursively explicit system of belief, religious morality may take the law as its model, and it would seem only natural as well to appeal to the law for support.

The high value often placed on the propositional stance toward one's thoughts has become a general expectation within the frame of secularism. In this view, what freedom of religion frees is, in its most exemplary form, a set of ideas discursively available to the consciousness of individuals. Freedom of religion might be about practices and ethical commitments, but viewed in this respect its basis would seem to lie in freedom of thought. In some important versions, the sincere belief model of religion also involves a particular semiotic ideology according to which the material forms of religion are merely conventional and arbitrary expressions of immaterial ideas. From this point of view, the state's concerns with the *forum externum* could seem to be relatively disengaged from its inner counterpart, the *forum internum*. The distinction helps underwrite the various local differences between the ways in which inner belief and outer manifestation respectively are supposed to be scrutinized and regulated.

In the moral narrative of modernity, proper human agency requires self-awareness and reason. This must be facilitated by that semiotic ideology such that people come to recognize the true significance of words and objects. From the perspective of this semiotic ideology, any excessively strong responses to the desecration of sacred objects and texts, or to the legal regulation of such things as headscarves and crucifixes, can seem to be irrational and archaic restrictions on the freedom that people should claim for themselves. In this view, since the religious sign is merely a conventional expression of something else, such as one's thoughts or social identity, then its regulation under the law should weigh lightly on the believer. After all, what is really supposed to matter—those thoughts or identities themselves—would remain untouched.

In this regard, consider again the idea of religion as opposed to irreligion as a basis for morality. Religion understood primarily in terms of morality differs from that understood as first and foremost a matter of belief in at least two respects. First, it does not necessarily depend upon any particular discursive formation. We can see an example in Charles Hirschkind's account of a piety movement in Egypt, in which ethical self-cultivation aims less at the learning of or adherence to doctrines or verbally explicit sets of rules than it does at the inculcation of sensibilities, somatic responsiveness, and emotional dispositions. Second, the focus on morality may often (if not always and everywhere, as dissidents of conscience make clear) require us to understand the faithful in the context of larger communities. This is perhaps one reason why religious regulations in many places concentrate on domestic law. As Mahmood has observed, Egyptian law treated marriage and the household as special concerns of religion, appropriately handled within particular religious communities, in sharp contrast to other spheres of the law, which were the prerogative of state institutions. In broad terms this is consistent with a more general history of Euro-American modernity in which the domestic sphere comes to be demarcated as that domain of social life most appropriately governed by affect and the moral sentiments, in contrast to the economic rationality that should prevail in the marketplace or the strategic calculations of politics. The restriction of religious law to the domestic sphere, and association of both with the moral regulation of communal life (focusing on the behavior of women), may reinforce the identification of religion with the irrational world of emotions.

The confinement of religious law—that is, law directed *by* religion—to the domestic sphere has, of course, been challenged by a variety of religious political movements. Much of the current discussion of these movements centers on the challenges they pose to familiar narratives about the inevitable secularization of public life. But in many places the secularization thesis has never predominated. Consider the Pacific, where, as Matt Tomlinson and Debra McDougall point out, many public figures assume that "nation-states are the means and not the ends of Christian action." Although this claim inverts conventional social scientific understandings of means and ends, it still preserves some version of instrumental rationality operating in a knowable world. It offers a theological anthropology to account for human interests and to delimit the capacities for and constraints on legitimate political action that other legal and political traditions may leave only tacitly presupposed. This anthropology offers models of human agency directed by moral sensibilities, divinely sanctioned. Those who see politics as requiring a certain kind of morality, as is common not only in much of the Christian Pacific but also elsewhere—not least of all, the United States, as noted above—often take morality to depend on religious faith. This widespread view typically derives from a nested set of assumptions: that faith offers an ultimate foundation for morality, that appeal to theology is the necessary and sufficient justification and authorization for ethical actions, that scriptural or pastoral teachings offer moral guidance, and that religious institutions and practices are the chief practical means by which moral guidance is inculcated and those ethical demands made inhabitable, all reinforced through the discipline of life within a religious community.

One objection to this view, of course, is that it seems to render those who claim no religion, or whose religion is unrecognizable to others, as incapable of possessing a reliable moral compass. But in practice political theologies also encounter other difficulties of their own. Like religious politics elsewhere, the goal in the Christian Pacific is often totalization, a quest for a holistic world in which faith, morality, and political order work in harmony. Yet the very terms through which that goal is sought derive from the characteristically modern and secular divisions among domains that set religion as a sphere apart from others and subject it to distinctive forms of legal permission and constraint (and, in some traditions, immune to corruption by virtue of that very separation). But the fact of being paradoxical hardly disqualifies a political theology from social success and indeed may serve as a goad to still more strenuous efforts.

Can religious freedom be understood not just as the subtraction of religion from the public sphere (as Taylor puts it) in order to emancipate some prior, authentic, self-fulfilling human essence? Can religious freedom be understood as itself helping constitute an ethical lifeworld without posing it either as liberation *from* the moralities produced in religions or as protecting religions from secular threats *to* the moralities considered peculiar to them? And can it also be understood in such a way as to recognize those people whose ethical sensibilities are *not* grounded in religion? To return to my opening question, the answer depends in part on what understanding of "religion" is presupposed by the laws that regulate and protect it.

A great deal turns on what is supposed to make religion distinct, in contrast to other institutions, practices, and domains of social existence. The struggles over religious freedom are many things, to be sure. But there is a possible point of convergence between the worries of those who are compelled by religious sensibilities and their opponents; for they may agree on the stakes—namely, the problem of understanding what motivates politics, what determines the outcomes of political actions, and what should constrain them. Although it may be misleading to base the legal protection or control of religion on the notion that religion taps into deep and potentially dangerous emotional sources, it may be right to recognize religion as one (if only one) organizing category for efforts to grapple with the limits of instrumental rationality as a full account of what people are up to.

Selected Bibliography

Bhuta, Nehal. "Two Concepts of Religious Freedom in the European Court of Human Rights." *South Atlantic Quarterly* 113, no. 1 (2014): 9–35.

Calhoun, Craig, Mark Juergensmeyer, and Jonathan VanAntwerpen, eds. *Rethinking Secularism*. Oxford: Oxford University Press, 2011.

De Vries, Hent, and Lawrence E. Sullivan, eds. *Political Theologies: Public Religions in a Post-Secular World*. New York: Fordham University Press, 2006.

Feldman, Noah. "Orthodox Paradox." *New York Times Magazine*, July 22, 2007.

Hirschkind, Charles. *The Ethical Soundscape: Cassette Sermons and Islamic Counterpublics.* New York: Columbia University Press, 2006.

Hunter, Ian. "Religious Freedom in Early Modern Germany: Theology, Philosophy, and Legal Casuistry." *South Atlantic Quarterly* 113, no. 1 (2014): 32–62.

Jefferson, Thomas. *Notes on the State of Virginia.* Edited by William Peden. Chapel Hill: University of North Carolina Press, 1955.

Keane, Webb. *Christian Moderns: Freedom and Fetish in the Mission Encounter.* Berkeley and Los Angeles: University of California Press, 2007.

——. "The Evidence of the Senses and the Materiality of Religion." *Journal of the Royal Anthropological Institute* 14 (2008): S110–S127.

——. "Freedom and Blasphemy: On Indonesian Press Bans and Danish Cartoons." *Public Culture* 21, no. 1 (2009): 47–76.

Mahmood, Saba. "Sectarian Conflict and Family Law in Contemporary Egypt." *American Ethnologist* 39, no. 1 (2012): 54–62.

Mahmood, Saba, and Peter Danchin. "Immunity or Regulation? Antinomies of Religious Freedom." *South Atlantic Quarterly* 113, no. 1 (2014): 129–59.

Taylor, Charles. *A Secular Age.* Cambridge, MA: Harvard University Press, 2007.

Tomlinson, Matt, and Debra McDougall, eds. *Christian Politics in Oceania.* Oxford: Berghahn, 2013.

Warner, Michael. "Is Liberalism a Religion?" In *Religion: Beyond a Concept,* edited by Hent de Vries, 610--17. New York: Fordham University Press, 2008.

CHAPTER FIVE

The Power of Pluralist Thinking

Courtney Bender

It is hard to remember, but religious pluralism meant something quite different fifty years ago. We have so shifted our collective understanding of it, and this transformation has been so naturalized, that we have little common conception that this shift even happened and much less sense of its consequences. To put it succinctly, in the 1950s and through the 1960s, sociologists argued that religious pluralism and secularization went hand in hand, contributing to the development of a modern, shared "secular" faith that could support and was indicative of religious freedom. But since the 1980s sociologists have argued that religious pluralism leads to the religious vitality of many lively religious groups. The new model, like the old one, argues that religious pluralism in the United States is brought about by, and likewise promotes, religious freedom. Both positions have thus contributed as much to our collective imagination of freedom as they have to theoretical understandings of the same.

In this short essay, I can do little more than note the divergent *and* shared theoretical logics underpinning sociological studies of religious pluralism over the last half century. They develop from two quite different understandings of religion, the former tied to classical sociological theories and the more recent to liberal theoretical concepts. The differences are important, and they have not yet been adequately discussed or considered by sociologists of religion. That said, both the new and the old models of religious pluralism share a view that religious pluralism, however it is defined, is good for American freedom and American democracy. Calling attention to the enduring power of positive, pluralist thinking as well as to the radically different narratives in which religious pluralism and religious freedom have been linked helps us to consider both models anew. And as such, it might help open up new approaches to empirical studies of religion and new theoretical approaches to religion that might provide fresh theoretical and political leverage in engaging religious diversity and political opportunity both in the American context and in the international settings where the American model is held up as a gold standard of actually existing religious freedom.

This essay's title resonates (intentionally) with that of Norman Vincent Peale's 1952 bestseller *The Power of Positive Thinking*. Peale, a minister and psychologist, offered a version of self-help positive thinking strongly inflected with his Christian commitments. "Believe in yourself!" he began, encouraging his readers to maintain an optimistic outlook, and promising that those who could do so would experience a happier, healthier, and, perhaps, wealthier life. Despite the book's explicit Christian frame, Peale intimated throughout that the "universal laws of attraction" were a "reality" for everyone. In other words, anyone—Protestant, Catholic, or Jewish— could learn from his book.

Peale's book was widely panned by reviewers, but the emphasis that it placed on individualized, spiritualized approaches to religion emerged as a prominent example in Will Herberg's 1955 sociology classic *Protestant— Catholic—Jew*. Herberg argued that increasing interactions among Protestants, Catholics, and Jews in suburban enclaves, in schools, and on the factory floor were shaping a new religious culture in the United States. Intermarriage rates were rising, and it appeared that the political and social salience of religious differences was on the wane. Religious identities still mattered, Herberg noted, but they were increasingly linked to private religious belief. Being privately (and nominally) religious was an important part of being a twentieth-century American: indeed, being a good citizen meant partaking in the religious pluralism of Protestant-Catholic-Jewish America where everyone had a religious identity but where religiosity itself was increasingly expressed in a cheery and psychologized private faith, and where the public faith was committed to the "American way of life."

Herberg's work was written within a "classical" secularization perspective, in which (as Émile Durkheim and Max Weber variably suggested) religious pluralism was both a sign and carrier of modern secularity. According to this frame, increasing social differentiation and the rationalization of authority within its various domains left religion and its institutions bereft of their earlier powers. And while the demotion of state churches and their concomitant shrinking authority created op-portunities for new religious sects to develop, all religions had increasingly limited social and political power. The existence of plural religions in na-tions once organized around state churches was thus both a sign of secu-larity (the absence of a state church or a single church's hegemony) and also a social fact that hastened societies along their secularizing path.

American sociologists in the 1950s and '60s used this narrative to explain changes they observed in American religious life. Both Peter Berger's *Sa-cred Canopy* (1967) and Robert Bellah's essay "On Civil Religion" (1968) articulate a vision of American public life in which the public acceptance of multiple, private religious pursuits weakened strong and spirited sec-tarianism. The midcentury sociological narrative can be summarized as follows: religious pluralism, itself made possible by the demands of a secular government, is a sign of healthy democracy. The "religion" in this pluralism is primarily private choice, which becomes social as those private citizens unite around a "civil religion" in which respect for private belief is held up as an important aspect of civic belonging.

This midcentury understanding of the relationship between religious pluralism and religious freedom sounds archaic today, and its articula-tion of the freedom of private individuals celebrating in a shared pub-lic civil religion something akin to an interesting footnote. In contrast, the sociologists who study religious pluralism today make quite different claims about the relationships among religious freedom, pluralism, and democracy. This work has shifted the locus of attention from individual believers as carriers of "religious freedom" to religious groups; their competitive interactions come to define a quantifiable metric of religious freedom. This shift is significant for several reasons, not least of which is its implications for how sociologists identify the very "religion" that is free to support (American) democracy.

Why did sociologists of religion turn away from the models that had been so powerful in the 1950s and '60s? There are many reasons, of course, including theories falling out of fashion in the academy and the desires of a new generation of scholars to make their mark. But all of that aside, the usual answer that sociologists give is that *religion* changed in America: what *had* been private became public; Evangelicals became mobilized out of their pietistic torpor; immigration brought "new religions" to the United States; identity politics and social movements found resources in religious organizations to make political claims. Given the benefit of hindsight, many scholars now find the story of radical religious and social

upheaval in the 1960s and '70s to be an incomplete or misleading explanation. But, that said, sociologists working in this era often claimed to
observe "religion" working in ways that they had not predicted, and in
ways that demanded theoretical rethinking.

Of the many alternatives proposed, the "religious economies" model
rose to the fore as one of the strongest alternatives. Such a model, promoted by Rodney Stark, Roger Finke, and others focused particularly
on the question of the plurality of religions and its effects on religious
participation. In a marked turn from the earlier generation, this model's
proponents argued that religious plurality and vibrancy is a natural consequence of limited or absent state regulation of religion. In the United
States, therefore, religious vibrancy can be explained as the outcome of
a free religious market, one made possible by (or perhaps better put, *revealed within*) the separation of church and state. Where state regulation is absent—and in explicit contrast to what they understand as the
"European" situation of national churches—religious groups are free to
organize as they wish and rise or fall based on their abilities to appeal
to religious consumers.

The religious economies model borrows explicitly from the Chicago
School of economics; in this model, a rational, voluntary, religious actor
will consistently seek out the religious option with the compensatory system that best suits her. Individual religious freedom is maximized in
a religious marketplace where multiple firms exist. Competition has the
effect of increasing religious vitality, religious options, and religious fervor
rather than marking their decline. Thus, as the argument goes, a plurality of Protestants—Methodists, Congregationalists, Baptists, and even
Mormons—vie for members. Over time, the losing firms are those who can't
attract or hold members, and the ultimate winners are all those people
who can maximize their religious potentials in a firm of their choosing.
Normatively speaking, the religious economies model presumes that the
best religious market—that is, the one that is best able to allow "freedom
of religion" to thrive—is one in which choices are maximized: state mo-
nopolies not only limit options but also contribute to declines in religious
participation. As we can see, this model not only argues that competition
increases participation; it also builds this understanding on an implied
vision of modern humans as having some form of religious interests that
exist freely.

There is a clear contrast between the religious economies model's basic concept of religious pluralism and that of the earlier generation of

sociologists. In some respects, the model takes a much narrower view of religious pluralism altogether. Initially, sociologists' arguments and models were based on competition among Protestants (a Protestant pluralism)—a much more exclusive and less "diverse" pluralism than the midcentury sociologists' invocations of Protestant, Catholic, and Jew. As many sociological critics have pointed out, the religious economies model has often found it challenging to include data (often membership data) from religious groups that do not conform to a specific Protestant model of voluntary adult membership. And as others in history and religious studies have noted—insofar as Jews, Catholics, Native Americans, antebellum slaves, and others are uneasy fits—the religious economies model has quite explicitly advanced a theological norm within itself. Specifically, free-church Protestantism is the norm against which all other religious groups are measured as capable of being free and capable of forming the kind of religious actors who can defend "religious freedom."

The implications of these stories and their rather explicit celebration of particular kinds of religious "winners" are likely clear to many. We can, for example, consider the effects of the "illusion of the free market," the subject of Bernard Harcourt's recent genealogical critique of free market economics. As Harcourt argues, the concept of the naturally regulating, universal free market recurs in multiple generations of free market economic thought. Where the market is conceptualized as naturally existing, regulation becomes an enemy: the state's meddling poses a threat to the naturally developing and self-regulating equilibrium. But this is not all, of course, for, as Harcourt notes, the self-regulating free market is also threatened by those economic actors who are not able to self-regulate—those who are not free and rational. Whether such actors refuse to act as proper self-regulating economic actors or whether they cannot do so, they become understood as unnatural actors that interrupt the natural freedom of the market. Even as regulation threatens market equilibrium, it nonetheless plays an important role in policing and regulating those actors who also threaten its freedom. Harcourt argues, in short, that one of the effects of the logic of the free market is to designate those economic actors who are free of the need for regulation and those who are not so free, thus providing impetus for their regulation and surveillance (and perhaps reform and rehabilitation) by the state.

We can take an analogical step to consider how Harcourt's observation may relate to the current sociological understanding of the free market religion. The religious economies model views the failures of various religious groups to participate in the market as problems inherent in the groups themselves—failures, for example, to cast off religious peculiarities so that they can participate in the thriving religious commerce of modern democracies and in real, "free" religiosity. The model rarely if ever points to problems that might be inherent in the market itself: that it might not be as free as imagined, or that it might in fact be regulated or regulating.

Numerous sociologists have pointed out the limitations of the religious economies model; they have roundly challenged the robustness of its principal methods, data, and interpretations, noting that these elements have been found wanting on numerous occasions (for a review, see Mark Chaves and Philip Gorski 2001). Yet despite decades of critique, the basic premise of the religious economies argument—in particular, its emphasis on the free market of religion—persists in public discourse. It finds its way into policy discussions about religious freedom in the United States and abroad. In that respect, we can say that none of the challenges to this model have stuck. One has to wonder, why not? One reason, I believe, is that even the staunchest sociological critics of the religious economies model share its basic premise—namely, that a plurality of religious groups is needed to indicate a thriving religious freedom, and that the American example presents a clear case of actually free religion. While this premise is explicitly articulated in the religious economies model, it is also embedded in almost every recent sociological analysis of religious pluralism.

To take one prominent example, sociologist Nancy Ammerman explains in *Pillars of Faith* that expanding religious pluralism in the United States, increasingly inclusive of non-Christian groups, has been supported by an American civil public sphere wherein religions exist "without state authorities to enforce orthodoxy" and "without state regulation or state support." Striking a tone similar to that of the religious economies model she critiques, she observes that in the history of the United States each religious group's "attempt to create a more nearly perfect spiritual community was free to find its own fertile soil or perish." Whether a religious group flourishes or perishes is, therefore, up to the actors themselves. If they accept the system "nurtured in the pragmatic and pluralist democracy of the United States" they will flourish. And to those "non-Protestant traditions that have complained that they have been 'Protestantized' as they have accommodated to American culture," she answers that "whatever else [Protestantization] has meant, they are right that they have been pushed to adopt a basic commitment to live peacefully alongside religious others."

Ammerman and other sociologists critical of the religious economies model draw on organizational and cultural approaches that have been used in other contexts to investigate how implicit and explicit norms, regulations, and interactions shape social domains and enforce conformity. Scholars of religious organizations using these approaches have thus focused on the effects that regulations, enduring cultural norms, and interests in professionalization have on "new" entrants to the United States. For example, they note that Hindu groups building temples in the United States incorporate as nonprofit corporations, thus developing governance structures for religious communities that are quite distinct from historical patterns in India. Or they note how Muslim groups are actively working to develop "chaplains" and other leaders in their communities that expand beyond the roles of teachers and imams—in part to conform to changing expectations among American Muslims of what religious leadership entails and in part to expand sites of professional "interfaith" interactions in local and national contexts. Others have argued that American religious organizational structure promotes a "de facto congregationalism" that encourages all religious groups to identify adherents and members as voluntary participants in shared religious collectivities.

These approaches call attention to the ways that norms and regulations shape and refigure religions that may be new to the United States (for example, Hinduism and Islam) so that they map more comfortably onto an American religious grid. They therefore also have the potential to call attention to the exclusionary effects, regulatory pressures, and bureaucratic and legal complications that explicit and implicit norms pose for many religious groups. But sociologists employing these models have rarely focused on these issues. As we see, they prefer to explain how the transformations that religious groups experience work to make each new religious entrant a more spiritual, perfect, and free practitioner of their own religions. As these new entrants confront American norms of freedom, they become more free and likewise more "tolerant" of others.

In other words, these arguments presume that "religion" comes into its own in America, in all of the nation's manifest plurality. Insofar as religious groups willingly submit to freedom, they certainly change. But in this view transformation is not to an "American" norm with its own limits and favorites but rather into the norm of religious freedom itself. The free market allows—and in fact trains—religious groups to be free: to cast off the cultural and political baggage or problematic connections to political life. What we confront in both the religious economies model and the narratives of its sociological critics is much less a theoretical frame of pluralism than a political doctrine of freedom. In this oddly contradictory explanatory narrative, sociologists can recognize both that the American public sphere is not neutral toward religion and that this nonneutrality has the effect of making all religions "more free."

Two issues are worth pondering at greater length than this short essay will allow. First, we can consider the political consequences of our current concept of religious freedom. American public discourse about religion has abandoned an earlier vision of religious pluralism that focused on the plurality of private individual faith that united under a shared rubric of commitments to religious tolerance and religious freedom. As even Herberg and Bellah worried, a shared if thin common faith might falter, or it might in the wrong hands be transformed into religious nationalism. Against these troubling possibilities Americans currently identify a religious pluralism that is "strong," "robust," and—to be more precise—distinctive. But the pluralities of religious groups must demonstrate that they are different from each other, even as they must demonstrate that they are free from demands that might restrict their flourishing in this plural public sphere.

Except—as Harcourt's examples remind us—this freedom is an illusion. Having the midcentury sociological assessments of religious pluralism in view helps us to see more clearly the current illusions that guide research—for example, how sociological studies of religion have continued to reinforce the cultural logics of "actually existing" religious freedom in American political culture and how such studies seek out new immigrant groups that succeed at being free. Our positive pluralist thinking continues, even if the terms of that pluralism have changed: much as the "positive thinking" espoused by Norman Vincent Peale hid the mechanics of social institutions that shape human lives and their many contingencies, contemporary pluralist thinking hides the mechanisms through which we recognize religions as free or many, or why we even find these tallies and their evaluations useful or necessary.

Second, with these two contrasting theories of pluralism in view we can see more clearly how they share a deeper theoretical understanding of religion. Indeed, even though the new sociologies of religion and market models claim to have successfully offered an alternative theory to classical secularization theories, they have redoubled their theoretical commitment to an understanding of religion as institutionally differentiated from other social domains. Current public and political rhetorics of religious pluralism depend upon evidence of religion's multiplicity and its differentiation from other parts of social life. Indeed, it is only *through* plural differentiation that religion is free—it is only a secular state that separates "church" from other political, economic, educational, and cultural concerns that allows real religion to flourish.

This vision, in turn, returns to a concept of religion and the religious person as awaiting freedom: oppressed by social situations where politics, religion, and economics are durably entwined, the only possible future is for a politics of differentiation—one that is, in the United States, perpetually reproduced in interfaith pageants and other public rituals. To my ears, the sociological logics of secularization and their emphasis on social differentiation have become revived and reread through the religious imaginaries of liberal political theory, including the works of John Locke, Adam Smith, and John Stuart Mill. If this is the political tradition that currently hovers over sociology of religion (as I have argued in a recent essay), then it is time to consider these arguments directly, and at length, in order to untangle once more how religious freedom, economic freedom, and political freedom are tacitly or explicitly linked in recent research.

In doing so we would begin to seriously reconsider what it means to identify and research American religion—modern "secular" religion—as not ever "free" of its connections to politics or the economy. What would a sociology of modern religious life look like if it did not begin with the expectation or the view that social differentiation frees religion, politics, and economics from each other in the way that we have so frequently claimed? What if we would begin, for example, with Karl Marx's wry observations in "On the Jewish Question" that the privatization of religious identity in the American context does not mean that religious identity ceases to matter politically? Just as the act of privatizing property does not transform property into something of no interest to the state, he notes, so the privatization of religion does not make it free to be left to its own devices. While "man emancipates himself politically from religion by banishing it from the sphere of public law to that of private law," Marx writes, then "religion is no longer the spirit of the state. . . .

Religion has become the spirit of civil society, of the sphere of egoism, of *bellum omnium contra omnes*." What would our sociology look like if we looked closely at the ways that the privatization of religion, much like the privatization of property, becomes a site of new capacities for social and political distinction and regulation?

To sum up, the power of the pluralist thinking that currently holds sway in sociology—and in other parts of the social sciences as well—is both old and new. In the 1950s and '60s, sociologists viewed religious pluralism as contributing to the declining role of religious interests within the secular state, which could support private individual consciences along with a public iteration of religious toleration. At present, sociologists identify religious pluralism as the continued vitality of competing religious groups within the secular state. The plurality of groups (rather than a plurality of individuals with their own consciences) stands as the current sociological marker of thriving religious freedom.

The underlying shift, as many have noted, has fashioned free religion along the logic of the free market economy. Religious actors, like economic actors, pursue natural or inherent interests that will regulate the market (or civil society) in a balanced way, so long as regulation is minimized. State regulation of religion is consistently understood to undermine these pursuits—except insofar as regulation keeps inappropriately unfree actors from participating. We can also see that regulation appears to have a positive, recuperative role at times insofar as regulation might train religious groups and individuals how to be free versions of themselves.

While this market model of religious freedom and religious pluralism is "new," it nonetheless shares with the older version a conception of modern society as secular and differentiated. These concepts of secularity are shared in different ways by liberal political theorists and classical sociological theorists—traditions often viewed as oppositional, yet from this vantage point clearly linked in their modern visions of orderly, secular societies. Insofar as sociologists of religion today may be said to share more with liberal theorists' conceptions of natural and free religion than they admit, we find an opportunity to rethink, in a new way, how powerful the logics of social differentiation have been for our modern polities.

Sometimes I wonder what might have happened if sociologists of religion who encountered the "resurgence" of religion in the 1970s had turned their attention to the limits of the logics of social differentiation. How would sociologists today understand religious freedom, and how would we talk about plurality, if their attacks on earlier models had gone to the heart of secularization theory? More to the point, what might a sociology of religion look like now were we to really take this challenge seriously? Recent work, including Prema Kurien's incisive readings of American politics and Hinduism, Henry Goldschmidt's efforts to rethink religious and racial conflict in urban contact zones, and interdisciplinary conversations among legal scholars, sociologists and historians, such as those in the edited collections *After Secular Law* and *After Pluralism*, offer alternatives that either reject the terms implied by the so-called self-evidence of religion's plurality and differentiation, and call attention to the value of such claims within specific political and legal systems. As captivating and strong as this growing body of work is, I nevertheless hazard to guess that it will take more than one generation to shed the power that positive pluralist thinking holds over us. But if we do so, we might be in a better position to speak about the consequences of the legacies of these magical and enduring concepts.

Selected Bibliography

Ammerman, Nancy. *Pillars of Faith: American Congregations and Their Partners*. Berkeley and Los Angeles: University of California Press, 2005.

Bellah, Robert N. "Civil Religion in America." *Daedalus* 96 (1967): 1–21.

Bender, Courtney. "Pluralism and Secularism." In *Religion on the Edge: Decentering and Recentering the Sociology of Religion*, edited by Courtney Bender, Wendy Cadge, Peggy Levitt, and David Smilde, 137–58. New York: Oxford University Press, 2012.

Bender, Courtney, and Pamela Klassen, editors. *After Pluralism: Reimagining Religious Engagement*. New York: Columbia University Press, 2010.

Berger, Peter. *The Sacred Canopy*. Garden City, NY: Doubleday, 1967.

Chaves, Mark, and Philip Gorski. "Religious Pluralism and Religious Participation." *Annual Review of Sociology* 27 (2001): 261–81.

Finke, Roger, and Rodney Stark. *The Churching of America, 1776–1990: Winners and Losers in Our Religious Economy*. New Brunswick, NJ: Rutgers University Press, 1992.

Goldschmidt, Henry. *Race and Religion among the Chosen Peoples of Crown Heights*. New Brunswick, NJ: Rutgers University Press, 2006.

Harcourt, Bernard. *The Illusion of Free Markets: Punishment and the Myth of Natural Order*. Cambridge, MA: Harvard University Press, 2011.

Herberg, Will. *Protestant—Catholic—Jew*. Chicago: University of Chicago Press, 1955.

Kurien, Prema. *A Place at the Multicultural Table: The Development of an American Hinduism.* New Brunswick, NJ: Rutgers University Press, 2007.

Marx, Karl. "On the Jewish Question." In *The Marx-Engels Reader*, edited by Robert C. Tucker, 26–52. New York: Norton, 1972.

Sullivan, Winnifred Fallers, Robert A. Yelle, and Matteo Taussig-Rubbo, eds. *After Secular Law.* Stanford, CA: Stanford University Press, 2011.

CHAPTER SIX

Reflections on the Politics of Religious Freedom, with Attention to Hawaii

Greg Johnson

Tough Therapy

The essays collected in this volume have provoked me in a number of ways, especially with their combined penchant for probing raw nerves. Indeed, I didn't fully understand how raw—let's say conflicted—I was about religious freedom discourses and practices until this intervention was staged. In the spirit of therapy, then, we can begin: "Hi, my name is Greg, and I've led a carefree lifestyle, all along assuming that religious freedom is a good thing. I've been drinking this cocktail for years; it has become part of my identity as a morally enlightened scholar of indigenous traditions. Thanks to these scholars, I've been sober for three days."

More seriously, these essays put a finger on a tension many of us face in our work, whether conceptual or practical—namely, a sense that religious freedom, in principle, must surely be good, but that in practice it has many possible outcomes, intended and otherwise. Furthermore, these essays argue that the routinely problematic social lives of religious freedom agendas should cause us to reconsider the conceptual genealogy of the ideal itself. Indeed, these essays cut so deep as to have us ask, is there a "principle" of religious freedom that stands above or beyond histories, political agendas, and their sundry entailments? In their own ways and in their conjoined force, these essays provide ample reason for extreme caution when proceeding down the path of announcing, promoting, and analyzing religious freedom agendas.

I am sensitive to this cautionary message, but I can also imagine some good reasons for saying, "Hold on, might there be more to the story!" My work in indigenous traditions has conditioned me to be very sympathetic to native religious freedom claims, especially in contexts of land disputes, resource access, and burial protections. I continue to think religious freedom claims have a place—at least in the short run—if their primary role is to secure rights already enjoyed by majority publics by making otherwise inaudible concerns heard, about which I will say more in my conclusion. But I am certainly persuaded by the common trajectory of these fantastic essays, which together amount to a multilayered critical assessment of religious freedom, its current lives, and its undergirding substrata.

Reading the chapters that make up this volume, I can't help but think of religious freedom projects as a form of social eugenics. The sought-after outcome is to produce and reproduce a healthy social body—as defined by those who have the power to manipulate society at the level of policy. Who are the subjects? What are the outcomes of these experiments, intended and not? And, as Elizabeth Shakman Hurd asks, might there be other discourses and registers for pursuing shared goals that steer clear of these troubled waters?

These sorts of questions were posed to me in sharp relief on a trip to Odessa, Ukraine, in 2012. I was there as visiting faculty for the Re-Set School, a multiyear seminar on the study of religion, whose students come from throughout the former Soviet Union and who range from PhD candidates to associate professors. The particular session I attended focused on law and religion. It was a rewarding experience on a number of levels, not the least of which was the opportunity to hear religious freedom discourses articulated in ways quite different from what I've become accustomed to in the US context (for a detailed discussion of the post-Soviet situation, see Mathijs Pelkmans in this volume). Over the course of our week together, three basics rubrics about religious freedom emerged from the group. One seemed to carry forward a Soviet-era suspicion of religion and announced the importance of secularism and freedom *from* religion; another was a comparatively new and almost boundless enthusiasm for religion of all stripes—though its champions faced the usual difficulty of distinguishing between religion and not religion, a bind for any religious freedom agenda no matter how capacious its imagination; and the third was an interesting mix of nostalgia for and desire to protect historically dominant traditions (the Russian Orthodox Church, especially) while simultaneously warding off the threat posed by assertive proselytizing movements, especially Jehovah's Witnesses and the Church of Jesus Christ of Latter Day Saints.

As I discerned the contours of these positions I began to think of them in the following ways: *no cake, the whole cake,* and *just our slice of the cake.* Of course, each of these positions wanted to eat its cake and have it too. And that, as Winnifred Fallers Sullivan has argued in *The Impossibility of Religious Freedom,* is just the problem with religious freedom discourse in practice—it sets out its own conditions of impossibility and is constantly at counterpurposes with that which it proclaims to advance. In any case, each camp worked to articulate a vision for how its particular ideal of religious freedom could be designed, animated, and otherwise brought to life. From my position on the edges of the conversation— and I admit to having but a basic sense of the current social struggles involving religious life in the former Soviet Union—all three sounded quite a lot like social engineering. Such an ethnographic realization has the potential, of course, to catalyze self-recognition. So I began to puzzle over the ramifications of the politics of religious freedom contexts closer to home. I offer two brief reflections along these lines herein.

Of course, religious actors and institutions routinely refashion themselves to meet the conditions of law or to inhabit spaces framed by law, as Saba Mahmood and Peter Danchin have described in the case of Egypt, for example. The contributors to the Politics of Religious Freedom Project illuminate how law provokes religion, often in the direction of ossification, or its discursive equivalent, legalism. Of this dynamic one might say that law prefers to take others, religions included, the way it usually takes itself, which is to say legalistically—categorically framed, drained of the potential to surprise, and otherwise stiffened. In this way religious freedom produces religious dogmatism. Some "religions" resist, of course. But the costs of remaining flexible, metaphorical, and open-ended can be high, like not being seen or being dismissed out of hand. As Hurd points out, one cost of recalcitrance is illegibility.

The contemporary global propensity to want to engineer religious life in relation to states and publics is also a mixed bag for scholars of religion. On the one hand, our jobs got easier; we need not be half as perceptive as we are trained to be. The characters on the world's religious stage are now outsized versions of themselves—puffed up on steroids, battle ready, putting on a hell of a show, and eligible for "freedom." On the other hand, some of us can't shake the sense that this is a bit too easy and, hauntingly, that somewhere along the way we got worked into the experiment in ways we haven't adequately understood, as Sullivan has suggested. Whether through support for or criticism of religious freedom agendas, some of us worry about the degree to which we are engineers or have been engineered.

The Politics of Religious Freedom in Hawaii

What might consideration of contemporary Hawaii add to our understanding of the politics of religious freedom? Hawaii is geopolitically isolated, has a comparatively small native population (about 400,000 out of 1.4 million), and its legal system is a fairly predictable iteration of US law (with some intriguing state-level nuances). Hawaii is instructive in several regards despite and because of these apparent limitations to its relevance on the global stage. The fact that Hawaii is not politically volatile affords the space to contemplate dynamics there without feeling paralyzed by the life-and-death quality of religious freedom issues one feels when thinking about Egypt and other similarly explosive contexts. This is not to belittle the significance of Native Hawaiian religious disputes, for they often concern such weighty issues as the integrity of burials, and therefore, for some Hawaiians, the state of ancestors' well-being in perpetuity (see Michael Lambek in this volume), but it is to observe that military or revolutionary forces won't suddenly appear, brandishing lethal force or the power of brute intimidation. Hawaii is also "good to think" because it is exotic but not foreign. Expressions of Hawaiian religion clang against US law in ways that may seem somewhat familiar to those schooled in federal Indian law, but often with surprising Polynesian inflections. It is a great test case for what happens when "known" law must navigate uncharted (from its perspective) religious waters.

My first brief example concerns articulations of genealogy in a contemporary legal context. The shape of the family and family law in Hawaii changed in the wake of colonialism: in other words, genealogy isn't what it used to be. As Sally Engle Merry has shown, missionary sensibilities and Victorian law completely reengineered these domains. Yet today Hawaiians are engaging vast realms of cultural life with deliberate emphasis upon restoring ancestral integrity to contemporary ways of being. This "renaissance" includes, among other things, subsistence practices, language immersion, hula, open ocean sailing, various forms of rejuvenated ritual practice, and the protection of ancestral burials. Some of these endeavors have gained legal and political traction. By way of various federal and state laws, policies, and entities like the Office of Hawaiian Affairs, native cultural and religious ideals and practices inform day-to-day matters like land use and fishing rules.

Unfortunately, the laws and policies that make room for Hawaiian voices have little capacity to comprehend the cultural content of the stories they have solicited. The stories connect to different times, sensibilities, and sexualities. Royal incest, alternative spouse arrangements, and an incredible range of genealogical possibilities configure Hawaiian religious imaginations. Contemporary law is rather deaf to all of this. For one example of this mismatch—of law's solicitations and refusals—consider the case of Mahi, a story about the costs of resisting law's positivism. To be Hawaiian religiously is to read signs, to think metaphorically, to interpret oneself into history; Mahi did this and became legally illegible as a result.

Mahi's story, which I have explored at greater length in my essay "Courting Culture," goes like this: A protracted repatriation dispute erupted in the early part of this century that involved the Bishop Museum and sixteen different Native Hawaiian organizations. The dispute centered on the so-called Forbes Collection, eighty-three extremely rare Hawaiian objects taken by nonnatives from a burial cave near Kawaihae on the island of Hawai'i in 1905. For most of the twentieth century, the objects were held by the Bishop Museum. In 2002 a group called Hui Mālama, headed by Halealoha Ayau, received the objects on "loan" from the museum. Members of Hui Mālama then replaced the objects in their original burial cave location and then sealed the cave. Soon other Native Hawaiian organizations complained that they had not been consulted about the disposition of the objects and pointed out that the "loan" circumvented federal repatriation guidelines. The dispute became the subject of several Native American Graves Protection and Repatriation Act (NAGPRA) Review Committee meetings and then a court battle. It is a fascinating story with many twists and turns, including the fact that a federal judge ordered the cave opened in 2006 and had the objects returned to the museum, where they remain today while the competing Hawaiian groups work toward an agreement about the artifacts' future.

My point in recounting this is to draw attention to Ayau's next move. The sixteen contending Native Hawaiian groups had asserted their claims by way of "cultural affiliation." A stronger claim under the law is by way of lineal descent. The law stipulates that lineal descent may be demonstrated by Western bureaucratic means—birth certificates, tax records, and the like—or by traditional genealogical means. In the dispute at hand, if anyone could articulate a persuasive lineal descent claim, that party would trump all cultural affiliation claims and control the disposition of the objects. As it happens, in the late 2000s Ayau became aware of the Mahi *'ohana*, a family from the region of the cave that asserted that the burial cave in question belonged to its ancestor, Mahi. In the course of researching the claim, Ayau was told by a prominent genealogist that he too was related to Mahi. Ever resourceful and dramatic, Ayau gathered as much evidence backing this claim as he could and then presented it to the NAGPRA Review Committee in a most traditional fashion: he spoke *as* Mahi. This first-person accounting of the ancestors is a classic Polynesian trope, something Marshall Sahlins has called "the heroic I." Oratory in this fashion speaks the concerns of the present in the voice of the ancestors. It is also, manifestly, a discursive impossibility so far as scientific entities and legal bodies are concerned, judging from the baffled response of the Bishop Museum and the NAGPRA Review Committee: they didn't so much reject Ayau-as-Mahi as ignore him. Flesh and blood genealogy was simply too much to take, or at least to take in. Law, it would seem, didn't recognize whom it had invited to the table.

My second brief Hawaiian example responds through redirection to Sullivan's emphasis in her essay in this volume on the *Employment Division v. Smith* decision and its fallout. My point is this: if *Smith*, then *Lyng*. I think Sullivan is completely right to direct us to *Smith* and its progeny. Undeniably we live in the world *Smith* made; more modestly but significantly, though, we also live in the world *Lyng* made. *Lyng v. Northwest Cemetery Association* (1988) was a Native American sacred lands dispute from the *Smith* era that made clear that the United States wasn't about to budge on control of "its" lands. While the decision was devastating for American Indians' claims upon public lands, what *Lyng* has yielded over time is increased attention to consultative processes between native groups and the government in the context of land use and access. This consultative spirit also configures repatriation and burial protections contexts, at least in the United States by way of the NAGPRA and state laws, including those in Hawaii.

Consultations among native groups, the government, and various other parties has rightly been celebrated as a step forward in taking indigenous claims seriously, especially with regard to religious evidence and oral tradition. In a substantial number of cases contesting groups have reached mutually agreeable settlements that take into account religious sensibilities in ways lost by the rougher handling of law proper. But meaningful consultation necessitates a case-by-case approach and is therefore administratively cumbersome, time intensive, expensive, and very taxing on the patience and goodwill of all parties. My worry is that post-*Lyng* laws and policies that stipulate consultation are insufficiently institutionalized. Changing administrations, financial crises, and fading institutional memory, among other perils, can emaciate consultative processes, reducing them to a shadow of their former selves or, indeed, as is happening in Hawaii, to nothing at all.

In Hawaii, state burial law enables considerable protection for Native Hawaiian graves and sets out a robust consultation model through monthly meetings of burial councils on the major islands. Historically these councils have had strong Native Hawaiian representation and leadership. From the time of the law's inception in 1990 until very recently, Hawaiian burials have arguably enjoyed more integrity than in any period since James Cook's arrival in 1778. However, in the last several years things have turned sour. The State Historic Preservation Division has dropped the ball on supporting the councils and has been weak in its implementation of the law in general. The state has failed to appoint council members in a timely fashion, regularly cancels meetings for lack of quorum or other administrative reasons, and otherwise has offered little oversight of key processes. Additionally and critically, the state has grown soft in its requirements for developers, particularly with regard to policing requirements concerning archaeological inventory surveys, which are intended to locate and record burial sites and features of religious significance. Absent these surveys developers can proceed as if the law doesn't exist. In this context, then, we have the politics of religious freedom in another key: a dirge about administrative failure.

Nowhere is this failure more apparent than in an unfolding burial dispute in downtown Honolulu, where more than six hundred *iwi kūpuna* (ancestral remains) have been dug up in the course of a construction project. As I have described in "Varieties of Native Hawaiian Establishment," the dispute concerns Kawaiahaʻo Church, a famous Congregationalist church with a significant Native Hawaiian membership. This is no simple story about Hawaiians versus Christians; it is a complex and unfinished epic about the ways diverse groups of Hawaiians are struggling over the meaning of the past in the present and the ways in which law supports or fails to support various agendas therein.

In 2004 the church announced plans to build a new multipurpose facility. Constricted as it is by the congested nature of its location, the church made plans to build over a portion of its cemetery. The congregation was consulted and an application was made to the State Department of Health for a mass disinterment permit so that burials could be moved as necessary within the boundaries of the cemetery to make room for the new footprint of the building. State burial law allows for this kind of activity within known, maintained cemeteries. However, the building plans included various infrastructure elements that entailed digging outside of the cemetery boundaries. This area, as documented by oral tradition and earlier archaeological surveys, is known to contain Hawaiian burials that predate the church. This component of the plan should have triggered state-level review and a thorough archaeological inventory survey. The state failed to enforce this legal requirement and the church began construction in early 2009. Shortly thereafter, in the course of initial trenching for a sewer line, sixty-nine *iwi kūpuna* were encountered and disinterred.

Hawaiian cultural and religious leaders immediately challenged the state to enforce its burial law and the church to stop the project. Neither was responsive and tensions began to mount. Protesters regularly picketed the church, media coverage ballooned, and still no relief was in sight. Two civil suits were filed, including one by longtime activist Dana Naone Hall. Consider the scope of the opening paragraph of her suit, which reads, "This complaint is based on the failure of Kawaiahaʻo Church and various public entities to fulfill their legal obligations pursuant to HRS Chapter 6E, the public trust doctrine, Native Hawaiian rights, and HRS Chapter 343. In this instance, government entities have failed to act with a level of openness, diligence and foresight commensurate with the high priority commanded under the laws of our state." Initially successful in stopping construction, Naone Hall was then denied standing in the case and construction resumed.

Naone Hall appealed the decision of the First Circuit Court, successfully winning a temporary halt to construction while the appeal was pending. Meanwhile, a Hawaii Supreme Court decision on the Honolulu rail project (*Kaleikini v. Yoshioka*) lent support to Naone Hall's charge that the state had failed to implement the burial law through bypassing the archaeological inventory survey requirement. In the spring of 2013 the Intermediate Court of Appeals ruled in favor of Naone Hall, shoring up the status of the burial law in the process. Both the state and the church petitioned the state's Supreme Court to consider the case, which it did, upholding the Intermediate Court of Appeals ruling in December of 2013. At present (April 2014), the matter is back before the First Circuit Court. Meanwhile, the State Historic Preservation Division has continued to fall further into crisis. Even if legal rulings restore a modicum of integrity to the burial law, the administrative arm of the state now appears too weak to lift the burden created by Kawaiahaʻo Church. Yet—surprisingly, perhaps—taking up the slack for state administrative failure, Native Hawaiian activists are filling the void, emphasizing the importance of due process and policing the state when it fails in this most basic of democratic tasks.

Not Quite Ready to Quit

Reflecting on the essays that make up this volume in the context of the "problem space" (see Hussein Ali Agrama in this volume) of contemporary Hawaii, and having participated in broader debates about religious freedom and secularism, I have come to the following basic tentative conclusions about indigenous religious freedom claims in the context of contemporary politics.

Though it is not a common position for a scholar of indigenous traditions, I agree with those, including Bruce Lincoln, who argue that all religions are undemocratic insofar as they rely upon differential access to putatively other-than-human sources of authority for their legitimacy. My point pertains to how authority is constituted and perpetuated in religious traditions, not the relative degree of apparent well-being various traditions achieve for those whose lives are configured by them. To be sure, some religions are less hierarchical than others, and it is clear enough that some religions exert far fewer and less severe claims upon human attention, comportment, and actions than do others. In practice some religious traditions appear quite egalitarian, if not democratic, especially in small-scale societies. It is also well established that religious motivations and actions have at times been instrumental in challenging abuses of power and authority, a fact that should hold in check any equation of religion with wholly domineering tendencies. Nonetheless, I still side with those who insist, in principle, that religious claims should not constitute grounds for special authority or rights within democratic settings. I am persuaded that rights and "freedoms" should be adjudicated according to "this-worldly" criteria subject to critical open scrutiny and debate. Beyond concerns about religious authority, I share the worry of other contributors to this volume who have pointed to the open-ended and opaque ways "religion" is invoked in all discursive arenas, including popular speech, legal discourse, and academic analyses. Thus, I agree with the editors when they assert that to speak of "religion" in law is to invite discrimination and, I would add, plain old-fashioned confusion.

All of that said, the still reverberating and wildly unequal historical context of nondominant religious freedom claims changes the practical equation from my perspective. Put simply, no democracy has been fully democratic and no secular society fully secular. Colonial and postcolonial histories, for instance, illustrate time and again how dominant religions prosper alongside and profit from within putatively secular states, often with profound and long-lasting consequences for minority traditions. And yet, for a variety of historical reasons, most modern settler society democracies embrace some ideal or another concerning religious freedom. This regard for religious liberty—however impossible to implement adequately, let alone coherently—has had the effect of occasionally enabling minority representatives to win a seat at the table of governance, as in the case of the NAGPRA Review Committee and island burial councils in Hawaii. Increasingly, if still rarely, those representatives have succeeded in making their concerns audible in other than religious registers, or in terms analogous to dominant religious tropes, and have influenced political and legal outcomes accordingly. Meanwhile, when they articulate religious claims in locally focused indigenous religious terms they tend to remain ignored. At the same time, when dominant religious institutions wish to flex political or legal muscle they need not speak in religious registers in order to make their case insofar as their interests are "naturally" recognized by secular regimes.

So long as this asymmetrical pattern obtains, my view is that nondominant groups should have legal recourse to religious freedom claims as a means to having their voices and concerns recognized, an admittedly undemocratic route to a potentially more democratic destination. Practical political theory should hold out a space for special recognition (religious or otherwise) for nondominant peoples until scenes like that at Kawaiaha'o Church disappear from the drama of cultural struggle.

Selected Bibliography

Johnson, Greg. "Courting Culture: Unexpected Relationships between Religion and Law in Contemporary Hawai'i." In *After Secular Law*, edited by Winnifred Fallers Sullivan, Robert A. Yelle, and Mateo Taussig-Rubio, 282–301. Stanford, CA: Stanford University Press, 2011.

——. "Varieties of Native Hawaiian Establishment: Recognized Voices, Routinized Charisma, and Church Desecration." In *Varieties of Religious Establishment*, edited by Winnifred Fallers Sullivan and Lori G. Beaman, 55–71. Burlington, VT: Ashgate, 2013.

Kauanui, Kēhaulani. *Hawaiian Blood: Colonialism and the Politics of Sovereignty and Indigeneity.* Durham, NC: Duke University Press, 2008.

Lincoln, Bruce. *Gods and Demons, Priests and Scholars: Critical Explorations in the History of Religions.* Chicago: University of Chicago Press, 2012.

Merry, Sally Engle. *Colonizing Hawai'i: The Cultural Power of Law.* Princeton, NJ: Princeton University Press, 2000.

Sahlins, Marshall. *Islands of History.* Chicago: University of Chicago Press, 1985.

Sullivan, Winnifred Fallers. *The Impossibility of Religious Freedom.* Princeton, NJ: Princeton University Press, 2005.

CHAPTER SEVEN

Traditional, African, Religious, Freedom?

Rosalind I. J. Hackett

G iven my associations with Uganda over the last few years, it might be expected that I would address the internationally infamous Anti-Homosexuality Act or the problematic KONY 2012 campaign that aimed to raise awareness and provoke action against Joseph Kony and the Lord's Resistance Army. Both initiatives flow from the demonization of a feared other; it is instead the various strategies to limit, if not eradicate, "traditional" forms of religious belief and practice in many parts of Africa that interests me in the present context. Human rights debates in Africa have largely excluded the question of religious freedom, and even the question of whether this category includes indigenous religions.

I have been observing and analyzing religious trends in various parts of sub-Saharan Africa for several decades, with a particular focus on new religious movements, variously termed "minority religious groups," "sects," or "unconventional religious groups." My years of living in southern Nigerian cities afforded me valuable insights into the workings of complex religious landscapes. As democratization, neoliberalism, media deregulation, and global religious activism increasingly change the stakes of coexistence among religious groups, and between such groups and the state, the management of Africa's increasingly competitive religious public spheres has become a more compelling area of investigation. How do state and nonstate agents act to facilitate or limit the public functioning and recognition of some or all religious organizations? How do the resources they draw on, such as globally circulating ideas about "international religious freedom," serve to frame what counts as (good or bad) religion, and which constitutional or statutory provisions are they informed or bound by in negotiating religious diversity? How much do local histories, politics, and demographics continue to influence the balancing of majoritarian and minoritarian religious interests?

In a recent article, "Regulating Religious Freedom in Africa," I explored the legal and extralegal strategies used to keep religious groups in check, noting that African states frequently defend limitations on religious practice and association as being in the public interest. Elsewhere I have also paid some attention to the growth of mass-mediated forms of religious expression in Africa and the capacity of these media forms to open up new possibilities for religious communication, often providing increased visibility and audibility for minority religious groups. Yet this recent liberalization of the media sector across Africa also replicates or generates patterns of exclusion and discrimination through the granting of licenses, transmission power, broadcasting access, and program content.

The angle I want to pursue here is the treatment of indigenous forms of African belief and practice in light of these postcolonial reconfigurations, or what Jean and John Comaroff term the Age of Millennial Capitalism. African traditional religions were particularly vulnerable during the earlier phases of Christian and Muslim missionary activity and colonization. The current dominance of Christianity and Islam is well evidenced by the 2010 Pew Forum project "Tolerance and Tension: Islam and Christianity in Sub-Saharan Africa." Still largely perceived as premodern, with ambiguous status as either religion or culture, indigenous religions struggle for public recognition and equal treatment under the law. Customary practices such as marriage and initiation rituals are vulnerable when states harmonize their legal systems and promote policies of detribalization. Moreover, African indigenous or traditional religions are hampered by being part of a generalized and heterogeneous category with no clear designation or centralized leadership. This situation recalls some of the legal battles faced by American Indians in trying to prove that their traditions were "religious" so that they could enjoy constitutional protection, as discussed by Tisa Wenger in her appositely titled book on the 1920s Pueblo Indian Dance Controversy, *We Have a Religion.*

While it is Muslim-Christian relations in Africa that command current geopolitical attention, we should not overlook the fact that sub-Saharan Africa provides some of the most instructive examples of how indigenous religions are still religious freedom misfits. The case that local forms of religious belief and practice have been subject to ongoing delegitimization by the state in collusion with missionary religions and postcolonial elites has been most forcefully made by Kenyan legal scholar Makau Mutua. He writes pointedly of the constitutional silence and refusal to acknowledge the existence of African religions or cultures in the country of his birth as well as in many other postcolonial African states. Moreover, Mutua contends that the "liberal generic protection of religious freedoms," with its guarantees of the right to manifest, propagate, and change one's religion, favors mission-related religions and is ultimately inimical to indigenous African religions and lifestyles.

Furthermore, Mutua argues, limitations on religious freedom for reasons of "public morality" and "public health" targeted the elements of traditional religious practice that many colonial states found problematic, even abominable. Such fears and statutory tests perdure in modern times. In a Pew Forum report on restrictions on religion worldwide from 2006 to 2009, Brian Grim notes that, after Christians and Muslims, members of "tribal or folk" religious groups are the second most commonly harassed group in Africa (in twenty-three countries). In sub-Saharan Africa the harassment is generally linked to accusations of witchcraft, ritual sacrifice, and charlatanistic healing practices. Nigeria's booming video and film market, known as Nollywood, has helped perpetuate negative stereotypes across Africa about traditional cultural practices; so, too, has the sensationalist media coverage of purported ritual abuse of African children suspected of witchcraft, whether in Africa or the diaspora. Evangelical and Pentecostal movements generally lead the fray in demonizing indigenous religious and cultural practices.

South Africa is one of the optimal places to explore current debates over the status of traditional African religion(s) in a modern postcolonial state. The radical transformation from apartheid to democracy generated a wealth of public debates, policy initiatives, and scholarship on matters pertaining to discrimination and self-determination (see Waheeda Amien's chapter in this volume on the recognition of Muslim marriages). On the face of it, according to the country's 2001 census, traditional forms of religious belief and practice appear to be almost nonexistent (at 0.3 percent). Nearly 80 percent of the population identifies as Christian. But as the contributors (mainly legal experts) to the most valuable book *Traditional Religions in South African Law* underscore, the defining and classifying of these religions is still a live issue. The authors discuss a number of recent legal cases that have tested the evenhanded treatment of traditional religions under the new constitutional protections for religious freedom. The conflation of traditional religion and culture, and an emphasis on communal identity, proved problematic in some human rights cases, as exemplified in the public outcry and lawsuit (the *Smit NO and Others v. King Goodwill Zwelithini Kabhekuzulu and Others* case, 2009) over a ritual bull slaughtering in a revived Zulu First Fruits festival. While the case brought by animal rights activists was eventually dismissed for want of factual evidence, Christa Rautenbach argues that demonstrating that the festival was "religious" and not "cultural" in nature (despite their interdependency in practice) would have afforded greater protection from the judiciary. Similarly, Jewel Amoah and Tom Bennett note the surprising lack of reference to religious beliefs in legislative efforts to reform the laws of African customary marriage; they see this as ongoing evidence of the way that indigenous African religions are being treated as "incidents of African culture," depriving them of the legal deference shown to other religious communities.

Another critical and contentious issue, ably discussed by Nelson Tebbe, is the outlawing of witchcraft by government and human rights organizations. While the practice of naming witches may be permitted under free speech and religious freedom, so too may limits on the practice because of its often violent consequences. These new laws have led to backlash from South Africa's pagan and Wiccan communities, such as the South African Pagan Rights Alliance. Furthermore, the problems of trying witches in state courts and allowing religious experts to give evidence would compromise constitutional prohibitions on government involvement in religious affairs.

Because of her background in politics, broadcasting, and higher education, Nokuzola Mndende, one of the leading advocates of African traditional religion in South Africa today, is highly critical of the ways her religious heritage continues to be mis- or underrepresented by media organizations. As conveyed by the title of her 2009 book *Tears of Distress: Voices of Denied Spirituality in a Democratic South Africa*, Mndende finds it problematic that traditional religion is often represented in the public sphere by "white reverend gentlemen," African Christian converts, and syncretistic diviners, and that it only gains legitimacy as an appendage to Abrahamic religions or as a secularized form of traditional healing. Mndende calls for "affirmative action" by the South African government to redress the fate of "disadvantaged religious communities." It remains to be seen if the South African Charter of Religious Rights and Freedoms (in whose drafting Mndende has participated) will provide any such benefits.

Marleen de Witte's insightful work on the neotraditionalist Afrikania Mission in Ghana also addresses the challenges facing such revivalist politicoreligious movements as they seek to be modern and African. These local struggles are bound up in decades of subjugating encounters with missionaries, colonialists, and scholars (whether of anthropology or comparative religion). De Witte provides a rich discussion of how Afrikania seeks to negotiate the new media opportunities and constraints, knowing that how it represents its "traditions" and "spiritual power" to the predominantly (Pentecostal) Christian Ghanaian public is critical to its survival as the principal face of African traditional religion in Ghana. She argues that this overly intellectualist focus on "representation" has been at the expense of the practices and concerns of shrine practitioners. Some feel that traditions of secrecy have been sacrificed in the quest to produce a modernized "world religion." Furthermore, De Witte describes Afrikania's position as "difficult and ambiguous" as it seeks to defend "superstitious" religious practices, such as libation, as part of its nationalist heritage project, even when these run afoul of "universal" human rights norms embedded in the Ghanaian constitution.

David Chidester has long claimed that the "inventory" of religious elements that have come to characterize African traditional religion (belief in God, veneration of ancestors, sacrifice, initiation, divination, and healing rituals) is a product of "colonial containment" and "Christian theological appropriations." Birgit Meyer observes too that Protestant missionaries in colonial Ghana attempted to "lock" people up in their own culture to prevent the development of syncretistic beliefs that might threaten the colonialist and nationalist project. In his book on the wild and surprising religious creativity of South Africa, Chidester discusses how, under the postapartheid national motto, Unity in Diversity, political leaders have drawn on indigenous religion as a national resource, whether as the spiritual dimension of heritage projects or through rituals at key national and international events such as the World Cup in 2010. He also considers how traditional religion finds its way into religious tourism, school syllabi, global Zulu spirituality, New Age neoshamanism, and traditional sovereignty. Facilitated by South Africa's new democratic dispensation, these "transactions," as he terms them, are often contested by those seeking to protect their sense of religious integrity, whether African traditionalists or devout Christians. It is worth noting that the popular African concept of Ubuntu (shared humanity, humanism) did not find its way into the revised 1996 constitution, leading many to view the omission as an act of de-Africanization.

While the government of South Sudan is taking encouraging steps to include traditional religions in its new political dispensation, as noted by Noah Salomon in this volume, the reality is that only one African state, the People's Republic of Benin, officially recognizes traditional religion in its constitution, granting it a national public holiday. In Nigeria the International Congress of Traditional Religion and Culture has advocated (unsuccessfully) for similar state recognition. This may account for why some groups such as Godianism, a traditional religious expression of Nigerian nationalism at the dawn of independence, now known as the Global Faith Ministries of Chiism, have reinvented themselves as modern, family-friendly, and heritage-oriented. Cultural tourism, especially if it receives the UNESCO World Heritage imprimatur, is a way to attract state support for traditional religious festivals, as evidenced by the internationally renowned Ọṣun festival in Nigeria's Ọṣun State. Another strategy is for traditional religious practitioners, especially healers, to create associations that promote their interests in the public sphere. The Zimbabwean National Traditional Healers Association and OrisaWorld, a global association to promote Yoruba religion, would be cases in point. The latter would be a vivid example of the strategic role that diasporic communities can play in the promotion and protection of traditional religious practices in their home countries. We should not neglect to mention the capacity of academic publications to legitimate the category of traditional religions for wider audiences, from the landmark work of John Mbiti in the 1970s through to recent texts such as *Orisa Devotion as World Religion.*

While foregrounding indigeneity has been arguably more strategically successful than ethnicity in protecting the rights of traditional African religions, the indigenous rights option as a tool for social and political mobilization turns out to be a less viable alternative, as the criteria in Africa for deciding who is indigenous are far "murkier" compared to the first peoples of the Americas; in the view of Dorothy Hodgson it tends to be used to refer to those with distinctive lifestyles, such as pastoralists and hunter-gatherers, and those who have special relationships to land and lineage. Some would claim that all Africans are indigenous.

An increasingly influential source for data on religious freedom around the world is the annual US State Department International Religious Freedom report, produced since 1999. Even a brief examination of the Africa reports can reveal the challenges faced by those trying to quantify and evaluate the rights pertaining to indigenous religious entities in national contexts. To begin with, the report writers face a problem of *sources* for demographic data. If the source is a census, it is not always clear whether there was an entry for traditionalists or was it rather a default category such as "other" or "remainder." In other words, some of the politics of recognition is embedded in the checkbox and is unquestioned in the reports. Then there is the possible bias of mainstream religious sources for data on nonmainstream religious groups. Clearly there is some reliance on data derived from the registration of religious organizations—a politically charged process if ever there was one, especially if there are tax preferences and legal benefits—but in the majority of instances governments do not register traditional religions. They may also be excluded from official or unofficial lists of religions. Only occasionally is the relative absence of traditional religious leaders from state or public events alluded to in the reports more generally or the fact that traditional religion is often represented at public events by traditional rulers (who are not religious functionaries and who may actually be Muslim or Christian, or some other religious affiliation).

The US State Department country reports are predicated on the status and activities of distinct religious organizations or groups. Several of the report writers make reference to the challenges of *categorizing* traditional religions, mainly because of their conflation with ethnicity and cultural practices. There are frequent references to the fact that many Africans (overtly or covertly) incorporate traditional beliefs and practices (such as visits to diviners and healers and ancestral veneration) into their Christian and Muslim lifestyles or practice them "in tandem" (see, for example, the Burkina Faso 2011 report). Another major challenge for the report writers, as for any researcher trying to analyze a religious landscape, is how to classify those eclectic, often urban, groups or movements that draw on elements from a variety of religious sources (e.g. indigenous, mystical, metaphysical, Indian, Christian, Muslim). These neotraditional (or some might say pseudotraditional) movements end up in the "syncretist" box, which seems guaranteed to lessen the chances of public recognition on most fronts. The report writers do not draw out the implications of this on the religious freedom credit or debit scale. In sum, this brief excursus into these globally circulated reports throws up the data deficit, as well as categorizing problems, in relation to indigenous African religions.

Anthropologist Ronald Niezen also sheds light on the ambiguity and paradoxes surrounding the concept of "indigenous religion," leaving us in no doubt about the effects of human rights activism and public and popular mediations of human difference in a globalizing era. Recent moves to grant institutional, protective space to indigenous expressions of "spirituality" not only essentialize and objectify traditional forms of belief and practice but also translate and recast them to appeal to cultural outsiders who formally or informally adjudge these rights' claims. Legal scholar Martin Chanock reminds us that cultural differences are not simply given but have their roots in the "intellectual history of empire." For that reason, the claim that rights are "cultural" (and, by extension, "religious") needs to be challenged in the same way that the claim that human rights are Western rather than universal has been challenged. Chanock emphasizes the strategic yet ambivalent role played by elites in postcolonial Africa in the creation and representation of cultures. He rightly notes that the processes of cultural formation and "branding" are increasingly linked to globalized advertising rather than social structure. A case in point would be the controversial Ghanaian traditional priest, Nana Kwaku Bonsam, who has built his fashionable image via modern media. This critical development seems to have been missed, Chanock argues, in human rights debates over "culture."

Just as Chanock advocates for rights and culture questions to be pursued "'beneath' that of constitutions and rights declarations" into the world of known oppressions and political interests such as family law and land law, both often linked to religion, Harri Englund demonstrates that abstract, elitist, and neoliberal ideas of individualized freedom in Malawi are counterproductive to struggles against poverty and injustice. As an anthropologist he proposes that more attention be given to the politics of translating human rights discourses into particular cultural contexts. Such ethnographic work can unmask the inequalities associated with rights talk in contemporary African contexts, as we have seen in relation to "religious freedom" and "traditional religion" in the course of the present essay.

Despite the undermining of African states by neoliberal policies and unreliable governance, the national level remains indispensable for thrashing out respect for what Lourens du Plessis terms a "jurisprudence of difference." As adumbrated above, the interpretation of the relationship between religion and culture proves more consequential for traditional or indigenous African religions than individualized notions of religious freedom in relation to a secular state. The rise of enterprising traditional religious leaders who are reconfiguring their identities in Africa's competitive religious public spheres, at times supported by diasporic (online) communities (as with the case of Yoruba religion), further problematizes attempts to define these "religious minorities" as discrete groups that are entitled to nondiscrimination on the grounds of religion. That notwithstanding, the local and global debates over what counts as "African," "traditional," "indigenous," "religious," and "freedom" are all vital grist for the religious freedom analytical mill, as well as for the development of constitutional governance in Africa.

Selected Bibliography

Amoah, Jewel, and Tom Bennett. "The Freedoms of Religion and Culture under the South African Constitution: Do Traditional African Religions Enjoy Equal Treatment?" *Journal of Law and Religion* 24 (2008–9): 1–20.

Bennett, T. W., ed. *Traditional African Religions in South African Law.* Cape Town: University of Cape Town Press, 2011.

Chanock, Martin. "'Culture' and Human Rights: Orientalising, Occidentalising and Authenticity." In *Beyond Rights Talk and Culture Talk: Comparative Essays on the Politics of Rights and Culture*, edited by Mahmood Mamdani, 15–36. New York: St. Martin's Press, 2000.

Chidester, David. *Wild Religion: Tracking the Sacred in South Africa.* Berkeley and Los Angeles: University of California Press, 2012.

Comaroff, Jean, and John Comaroff, eds. *Millennial Capitalism and the Culture of Neoliberalism.* Durham, NC: Duke University Press, 2001.

De Witte, Marleen. *Spirit Media: Charismatics, Traditionalists, and Mediation Practices in Ghana.* Amsterdam: Amsterdam School for Social Science Research, University of Amsterdam, 2008.

Englund, Harri. *Prisoners of Freedom: Human Rights and the African Poor.* Berkeley and Los Angeles: University of California Press, 2006.

Hackett, Rosalind I. J. "Religion, Media, and Conflict in Africa." In *The Wiley-Blackwell Companion to African Religions*, edited by Elias Kifon Bongmba, 483–88. New York: Blackwell, 2012.

———. "Regulating Religious Freedom in Africa." *Emory International Law Review* 25 (2011): 853–79.

Hodgson, Dorothy L. "Becoming Indigenous in Africa." *African Studies Review* 52, no. 3 (2009): 1–32.

Meyer, Birgit. "Christianity and the Ewe Nation: German Pietist Missionaries, Ewe Converts and the Politics of Culture." *Journal of Religion in Africa* 32, no. 2 (2002): 167–99.

Mutua, Makau. "Returning to My Roots: African 'Religions' and the State." In *Proselytization and Communal Self-Determination in Africa*, edited by A. A. An-Na'im, 169–90. Maryknoll, NY: Orbis, 1999.

Niezen, Ronald. "Indigenous Religion and Human Rights." In *Religion and Human Rights: An Introduction*, edited by John Witte Jr. and M. Christian Green, 120–34. New York: Oxford University Press, 2011.

Nwauche, Enyinna S. "Law Religion and Human Rights in Nigeria." *African Human Rights Law Journal* 2 (2008): 568–95.

Olupona, Jacob K., and Terry Rey, eds. *Orisa Devotion as World Religion: The Globalization of Yoruba Religious Culture*. Madison: University of Wisconsin Press, 2008.

Pew Forum on Religion & Public Life. *Rising Restrictions on Religion*. August 2011. http://www.pewforum.org/files/2011/08/RisingRestrictions-web.pdf.

Quashigah, E. K. "Legislating Religious Liberty: The Ghanaian Experience." *Brigham Young Law Review* 2 (1999): 589–601.

Rautenbach, Christa. "Umkhosi Ukweshwama: Revival of a Zulu Festival in Celebration of the Universe's Rites of Passage." In *Traditional African Religions in South African Law*, edited by T. W. Bennett, 63–89. Cape Town: University of Cape Town Press, 2011.

Tebbe, Nelson. "Witchcraft and Statecraft: Liberal Democracy in Africa." *Georgetown Law Journal* 96 (2007): 183–236.

US Department of State. "International Religious Freedom Report, 2011: Burkina Faso." http://www.state.gov/j/drl/rls/irf/religiousfreedom/index.htm?dlid=192685.

Wenger, Tisa. *We Have a Religion: The 1920s Pueblo Indian Dance Controversy and American Religious Freedom*. Chapel Hill, NC: University of North Carolina Press, 2009.

PART 2

History

Preface

Elizabeth Shakman Hurd

The seven essays collected in this section underscore the fragile, contingent, and interested origins of religious freedom and toleration and explore their imbrication with specific histories of governance, politics, and power. The authors insist on the embeddedness of religious freedom and minority rights in larger local, national, and global struggles. They question the existence of a single model of religious freedom or religious toleration to which all should aspire or assent. And they stress the partisan and power-inflected contexts in which trajectories of religious freedom and toleration are cobbled together in specific times and places, highlighting the unexpected alliances and unanticipated consequences that characterize these histories.

Several common themes thread through these essays. One is a shared emphasis on the shifting and variable coalitions that emerge to sustain various understandings of religious freedom across time and space. The authors in this section are committed to unveiling the unlikely alliances, exploring the unexpected tensions, and decentering the pretensions to universality that animate these histories. Writing on Ceylon/Sri Lanka at the cusp of independence from Britain, Benjamin Schonthal problematizes the presumption by international authorities (such as UN special rapporteurs) that religious freedom stands outside of struggles for power, serving as "a polestar that can guide political action without being contaminated by it" by presenting the specific historical conditions in which particular and partial conceptions of religious rights jostled for authority at a formative moment in modern Sri Lankan history. Taking stock of a series of controversies involving different conceptions of religious freedom in India, Nandini Chatterjee charts the clashes between religious freedom conceptualized as jurisdictional autonomy versus religious free-dom conceived as social justice, justifying state intervention following the promulgation of the Indian constitution in 1950. Examining the his-tory and politics of the Coptic question as it intersects with the transna-tional politics of religious freedom in Egypt, Saba Mahmood finds that, "far from being a universally valid, stable principle, the meaning and practice of religious liberty have shifted historically in the Middle East, often in response to geopolitical struggles, the expansion of modern state power, and local regimes of socioreligious inequality." As Evan Haefeli concludes, and others in this section concur, the problem with the his-tory of toleration—and the history of religious freedom—is that again and again it passes off an inevitably partisan narrative as a universal one.

A second thread running through this section is the detailed descrip-tion of the staggering diversity of political, social, and legal arrangements and settlements that have risen and fallen under the rubrics of "religious freedom," "religious toleration," and "religious liberty" across space and time. From the Edict of Nantes to Protestant congregations in southern India in the 1830s; from the Coptic community in postcolonial Egypt to shifting religiopolitical coalitions in the twentieth-century United States; from nationalist struggles in Ceylon/Sri Lanka; to the nonliberal pil-lared social structure of the Netherlands these authors demonstrate the quixotic—and ultimately intellectually and historically indefensible—nature of any attempt to define and delimit religious freedom, toleration, or liberty absent close attention to the specific local and transnational contexts in which the construct has been deployed and contested. Da-vid Sorkin, for instance, catalogs and contextualizes the very different meanings of what was known as "Jewish emancipation" across Europe over the course of the long nineteenth century, emphasizing the trade-offs made by various communities in exchange for legal and political recognition by the state. As Chatterjee concludes of her cases in a claim that also applies to the other contributions, "the precise body or subject whose freedom was advocated in each of these debates, and the variety of protagonists involved in these instances of advocacy, varied widely."

Samuel Moyn's essay substantiates this claim by charting the dra-matic shift in orientation among conservative Catholics in the United States for whom, prior to Vatican II, religious freedom had been rejected outright as a catalyst of secularism. In a mid-twentieth-century United States riven by Cold War geopolitics, conservative Catholic Americans recuperated and repurposed religious freedom (which went from "disease to cure") in an effort to stave off secularism and communism. This "Catholic pivot" also opened the door for contemporary alliances with evangelical Protestants, for whom religious freedom would stand not as part of a secular culture of individual choice and social tolerance but as a "keystone principle in the search for communities of belief, practice, and sentiment that subordinate individual choice to religious morality." Like the contributions by Schonthal, Chatterjee, and Mahmood, Moyn's essay stresses that local and national histories of religious freedom cannot be extracted from the broader global and transnational forces and histories that shape them.

From a form of state endorsement and establishment (Chatterjee, Moyn), to a technique of governance reflecting shifting interests and strange coalitions (Hefner, Mahmood, Moyn, and Sorkin), to a nationalist invective against colonialism (Schonthal), religious freedom appears in these essays as a shape-shifter, grasped occasionally and glimpsed peripherally if at all. One is left with a decentered, rehistoricized set of narratives wherein that which travels under the heading "religious freedom" is seen as partial and contingent, often discriminatory, always partisan, surprisingly variable, and—most of all—fleeting.

CHAPTER EIGHT

The Problem with the History of Toleration

Evan Haefeli

The problem with the history of toleration is not that no one is study-ing it. There is now a rapidly growing number of books and articles approaching the topic from a number of angles and in several different countries. These histories address what is alternately called toleration or tolerance, an anachronistic distinction that pervades the literature. When and why people began to think this was a meaningful distinction remains to be determined. It was not significant before the modern era, and thus is difficult to distinguish in earlier periods. Nonetheless, most contempo-rary scholars insist they mean two different things: the first being the for-mal laws and policies of states, the second being the ideas, attitudes, and personal practices of individuals. However, they are inconsistent in their usage of the terms. What is designated toleration in some studies appears as tolerance in others—or the terms are simply used interchangeably. Ei-ther way, the problem with the history of toleration is also the problem with the history of tolerance, for although they may point to different di-mensions, historically the two are difficult to keep apart.

The problem with the history of toleration (or tolerance) is the as-sumption that it exists as an autonomous topic of study, separate from any particular social or cultural context, and that all of those studying it (regardless of where or when) are investigating the same thing. Tolera-tion is imagined to be distinct from the historical context within which it operates, even though local studies indicate that, in fact, we are de-scribing a diversity of arrangements, dynamics, and possibilities taking place in different societies at different times, for different reasons. There is, of course, a history of toleration out there. Anyone can immediately conjure up certain associations and images when the phrase is invoked. However, exactly what comes to mind would, I am certain, vary significantly depending on the mind in question. Is it the struggle of Jews for recognition in Peter Stuyvesant's New Amsterdam? Catholics in Ireland? Mennonites in Switzerland? Remonstrants in the Dutch Republic? The Greek Orthodox in the Ottoman Empire? Episcopalians in Scotland? Muslims in contemporary Europe? Hindus in Mughal India? Christians in Japan? And so on. These are a series of distinct partisan struggles among a variety of different groups. Different writers can and do come down differently on each of these issues. As historians is it really our job to champion one narrative over the other? When scholars assume that all of these different conflicts revolve around a shared set of values or tend toward a common goal, they tend to favor the aspirations of certain groups over others: usually of Christians over non-Christians, and within that, of Protestants over Catholics (for this reason, toleration is more easily associated with the Protestant British Empire than the Catholic Spanish or French empires).

Toleration is one group's recognition and accommodation, or even acceptance—to varying degrees and for different lengths of time—of the existence of another or others—in the case of this essay, the groups entail different religions or nonreligions. Toleration takes on different hues depending on several factors: the immediate parties involved, who has the power to set its terms, and whose expectations one credits when deciding whether it is toleration or intolerance (an accusation of a failed toleration). For example, the toleration of the Edict of Nantes guaranteed separate spheres of worship for Reformed Protestants and Catholics within France but, like the toleration of the Ottoman Empire, it did not permit further religious growth of the tolerated minority. According to Louis XIV, it was not even supposed to last indefinitely—merely long enough to allow Protestants to be persuaded to return to the Roman Catholic Church, something he claimed had happened by the time he revoked it, claiming it was no longer necessary. This was quite different from the toleration in Cromwellian England, which allowed a plethora of Protestantisms to thrive within certain broad limits. Yet, even as Cromwell's armies did their best to suppress Catholic worship most everywhere they went (denying them the basic rights that Huguenots had under the Edict of Nantes), they did not force Catholics to convert, and Jews were even encouraged to return to the country (albeit without official, legislated sanction). Finally, there is the tolerance of missionaries such as the Jesuits, who learned local languages, adapted to local cultures, and even permitted many aspects of non-European culture to continue provided that the individuals became Roman Catholics. They are often held up as models of tolerance in contrast to Puritan English missionaries, who generally insisted that the indigenous people convert first to English culture (in dress, economic behavior, gender roles, housing, etc.) before they could become proper Christian converts. On the other hand, the Jesuit method allowed indigenous people to be Catholic without fully incorporating them into colonial society. While toleration was at work in all of these situations, it was in different ways and to different ends. They are not all equal. Simply to employ the term without outlining its consequences is to privilege one or another version of tolerance over others.

Wittingly or not, historians usually adopt one or another partisan perspective when they write and argue as if there were a single proper form of toleration to which all others should adhere or a single ideal, like "religious freedom," to which all should aspire. Perhaps the greatest symptom of this problem is scholars' persistent failure to find a fully satisfactory form of toleration. With regularity, various manifestations of toleration are described as somehow incomplete, lacking, or—worse—actually a form of intolerance rather than tolerance. In fact, this "less-than-ideal" quality is inherent in toleration itself, which is not, has not been, and never can be an ideal state of existence, for it always has different content depending on the context, and not everyone will be equally satisfied by the same arrangements. Another indication that there is a problem is the repeated efforts by a range of scholars to define the terms *tolerance*, *toleration*, *religious liberty*, and *religious freedom* more precisely. Upon closer inspection, their definitions often do not match up—a clear sign that we are not always talking about the same thing after all, even when we try to. This difficulty suggests that we need to privilege the particular contexts within which they are deployed over abstract definitions.

Employing toleration in a decontextualized manner leads some historians to see it as an issue full of hypocrisy and contradiction, in part because it is becoming increasingly clear that a degree of hostility toward— and disapproval of—religious difference existed in many if not all cases. For example, in her account of the ambivalent position religious tolerance occupied in early modern England, Alexandra Walsham claims "toleration is a form of intolerance," not "religious freedom. Nor did it proceed from indifference or neutrality." Rather, it was "a paradoxical policy, a casuistical stance involving a deliberate suspension of righteous hostility and, consequently, a considerable degree of moral discomfort." Likewise, "persecution" was in the eye of the beholder. Those accused of it often defined their actions as a necessary "correction" to nudge individuals toward the path of truth and salvation and thus save their souls. To tolerate their errors and heresies would be to let them damn themselves; one man's persecution was another man's loving care for their eternal well-being. Here, toleration, intolerance, religious freedom, persecution, and neutrality all slip in and out of each other, each being held up to some presumed universal standard, and all of them failing to match up—a perfect reflection of the problem with the history of toleration.

Some scholars are beginning to insist on clearer, contextually rooted definitions instead of deploying *tolerance* and *persecution* as self-evident terms. For example, Andrew Murphy, addressing whether a dispute between Quakers in 1690s Pennsylvania could be considered an example of Quakers "persecuting" others who disagreed with them, notes the "answer to such questions depends, of course, upon how one defines" the terms—in his case "persecution, liberty, and conscience." This is an important step to take. Persecution, after all, is not a policy anyone ever defends as such. Even those involved with organizations most indelibly associated with persecution, like the Inquisition, would not describe themselves as persecutors but instead as enforcers of truth, conformity, or even evangelicals compelling false believers into a chance at salvation. Nonetheless, it continually appears in situations that otherwise could be described as tolerant. The intrusion of the term is a sign of a clash of priorities between two or more groups, especially in a Christian context where *persecution* has long had negative connotations while being persecuted has been taken as a sign of righteousness.

Thus, evaluating the history of toleration in any sort of objective manner is perplexingly difficult, for this history—like toleration itself—is a deeply partisan phenomenon. Far from being a stable category or experience, toleration, like history, is constantly in flux, for it is fundamentally a relationship, not a static condition, and it thus cannot be abstracted out of its constituent elements. Toleration is inherently an ongoing, ever-evolving relationship, the content of which varies significantly depending on the parties involved. For example, one can say that there was toleration in the Ottoman Empire as well as the British Empire, but the first bolstered a form of rule dominated by Muslims and the latter did the same for Protestants. Each group lived in a situation of tolerance but would have found itself living in very altered circumstances in the other's system. Does that make one or the other less tolerant? It depends, as Murphy says, on how one defines the term. It also depends on whom you ask and where you draw the line. Is it at the point of refusing to kill, imprison, or otherwise physically punish an individual because he or she is of a different faith? Perhaps this kind of "unmurderous" coexistence is part of the essence of "toleration," an opinion bolstered by the histories of tolerance that Protestants began to write in the early modern period, which held up the Inquisition's notorious autos da fé as the opposite of toleration.

The tendency to see toleration as a singular universal quality—as "the idea of toleration," as Perez Zagorin sees it—obscures the partisan dimension of toleration, and most notably its close association over the past five hundred years with Protestant Christianity. Likewise the tendency to treat toleration as a distinguishing feature of, say, Dutch, British, or American history confuses content and context to the extent that toleration almost becomes that which the Dutch or the Americans do—a standard that those who are not Dutch or American will never be able to live up to. This problem is exacerbated by the habit of many scholars to take a single manifestation or interpretation of toleration (most popularly for theorists of liberalism, John Locke) as representative of the whole rather than as what it is: merely one manifestation among many. In the case of Locke and the Anglo-American world it is, of course, a highly influential version of toleration. However, to assume that it is then a universal model by which all others, past and present, can and should be evaluated (or, conversely, upon which "liberal" toleration can be indicted tout court) is to confuse the general with the particular. That is the main problem with the history of toleration: it passes off a partisan narrative as a universal standard.

Another symptom of the partisan dynamic unwittingly preserved in the history of toleration is the assumption that one can find a person or place that embodies the ideal of toleration better than others. Was it the Persian Empire? The era of *convivencia* in medieval Spain? The Dutch Republic? Sixteenth-century Poland-Lithuania? Roger Williams's Rhode Island? Mughal India? Was it Sebastien Castellio? Erasmus? Pierre Bayle? Baruch Spinoza? Here, too, one's answer depends on one's predilections. The predominance of early modern European history and Protestant thinkers in the scholarship on the history of toleration betrays its frequently close alliance with the history of the rise of Protestantism as well as the rise to global dominance of Britain and the United States. Indeed, some thinkers make little distinction between the two. For example, the English historian John Coffey, noting that most Christians today consider "persecution with a mixture of revulsion and incomprehension" and view it "as antithetical to Christian faith," argues that this "tolerationist version of Christianity" is rooted in radical Protestantism, a tradition in which he includes John Locke's famous *Letter on Toleration* and which arguably "reached its fulfillment in the Virginia Statute for Religious Freedom and the First Amendment to the American Constitution."

Traditionally, Roman Catholicism has played the role of the great antagonist in histories of toleration: many of the earliest histories of the rise of toleration were also histories of the decline in power of the Inquisition. Roman Catholics have tended to embrace the cause of religious toleration (or, nowadays, religious freedom) only when they have been a minority faith: Elizabethan England, for example, or colonial Maryland, or the mid-twentieth-century conservative American Catholics described by Samuel Moyn in this volume. One need not hold this as a reproach against Catholics, for most of the great advocates of religious toleration have been members of a minority faith agitating for greater rights and recognition: Jews and Quakers in Cromwellian England; Lutherans in the Dutch Republic; Baptists almost anywhere; British Protestants in India. Indeed, one could say the same (at least for the first few centuries) about Arab and Mughal Muslims in their newly conquered lands in the Middle East and India, when they preserved local religious diversity rather than compel conversion. In all of these cases, the nature, effect, and understanding of the toleration shifted over time, as the religious makeup of the particular population in question changed along with other factors, political and otherwise.

One of the great transitions between the early modern and the modern period is the role that toleration, or religious freedom, has come to play in various groups' battles for wider recognition, acceptance, or power. In the earlier period, it was rare for someone to argue in favor of toleration or religious liberty per se without attaching it to the cause of a particular group. At the same time, when an individual did do so, such as the Baptists or Separatists who regularly spoke in favor of toleration of Jews, Muslims, and a variety of Christians, it clearly fit their partisan needs as members of a group that either had given up pretensions toward universal appeal or (more often) were convinced of the persuasive power of their message in any situation in which they could operate free of constraint. Likewise, when members of a Protestant establishment, such as Hugo Grotius or William Chillingworth, spoke up in favor of tolerating a variety of opinions it was also with the assumption that eventually the variety of opinions would coalesce around the truth, which they never doubted resided more in their faith than any other.

Ever since the Age of Revolution in the late eighteenth century, figures have increasingly spoken out in favor of religious tolerance and freedom as an ostensibly universal quality. However, here too one can easily detect a partisan dimension. American Protestants did not fervently advocate religious freedom in the nineteenth century because they anticipated the flourishing of Buddhism in the United States but instead because it helped to justify the predominance of Protestants in a nation without an established church and a growing Roman Catholic minority. Likewise, Roman Catholics have not now embraced the cause of religious freedom because they believe it will diminish their position within the United States. On the contrary, it is proving (as it has since the days of US independence) a powerful tool for enhancing the prestige and influence of their church within the United States. Indeed, the US separation of church and state cannot be understood apart from the clashing ambitions of Protestants and Catholics in the nineteenth century. All of this is simply to point out that these diverse groups are not all advancing the same cause, their use of the same terminology notwithstanding. The struggle over religious freedom today has significantly different connotations than it did in 1780s Virginia, or 1650s Hamburg, or British India in the second decade of the 1800s, even though all of those can and have been described as cases for toleration.

By treating toleration as a distinct, clearly identifiable phenomenon rather than a problem that needs to be explained, we are in danger of depriving toleration of any analytical power while preserving it as the polemical tool that it has always been. My point is not to say that others have "it" wrong and I (or someone else) have "it" right. Rather, it is simply to emphasize how unstable a category toleration is on its own without any contextual referent. Given the relational nature of toleration, this dilemma should not be surprising. Can there ever be a situation in which what is really at stake is an abstract quality that stands above the constituent parties? States that claim to rise above the partisan dynamics of toleration can always be shown to be merely adding a different twist to the relationship between their religious constituencies, be it the

United States with its vaunted religious freedom or the self-proclaimed secular states of India, Turkey, or France. To deploy the term *tolerance* without specifying the context and makeup of the toleration in question is to adopt and champion a particular partisan stance, often one with deep roots in European history. It is not to employ a powerful, never mind objective, category of analysis. Indeed, an unexplored problem in the history of toleration is that modern scholars' expectations regarding religious freedom and pluralism, with a wide range of faiths coexisting peacefully in a pragmatic acceptance of the primacy of economic profit over religious purity, are in fact often little more than a positive spin on the vociferous criticisms of antitolerationists. The idea that toleration of one group would or should lead to the toleration of many more (or even all) did not originate with advocates for toleration like Locke or the Quakers; it came from their opponents, who presented it as a nightmare situation. What, then, are we advancing if this is our assumption of what toleration is or should be?

The partisan dimension of religious tolerance need not be read as a sign of hypocrisy, contradiction, or a fatal flaw in thinking. Rather, partisan implications should be accepted as inherent in the topic of toleration itself: they are the "core" of the phenomenon. As long as one expects toleration (or reifies it as a concept or phenomenon) to stand above all parties, it will always appear flawed and compromised, for it cannot do so. Toleration, however described, whether as an ideal state of being, or religious freedom, religious liberty, secularism, or pluralism, can never attain an objective status or transcendent condition. Toleration is a relationship—and a deeply, inescapably partisan one, for it involves a relationship between two or more different parties, none of whom will be equally satisfied with whatever their particular relationship happens to be at a given moment. Given the difficulty of writing a history of toleration that is not partisan, the least we can do is be open about this difficulty, and to emphasize context over abstractions when we chart its history.

There are many reasons to keep the context of toleration in sight whenever we trace out a particular history, not least of which is by not doing so we often inadvertently advocate for a position held by a particular group in the past, including the views of antitolerationists. If objectivity is well nigh impossible, the best we can do is to be as specific as possible, pointing out who is involved in any particular arrangement of toleration and how they are affected. All of these situations can and do change over time, and not always in the same direction. It is not a story of rise or fall; it is a story of changing relationships among different groups. As long as that difference persists, then there is toleration in play (whether the authorities will it or not). Toleration ceases to be in play only in situations dominated by efforts to deny, suppress, or erase those differences (regardless of the reasons for doing so). This separate history of intolerance and antitoleration faces similar problems of definition and scope as that of toleration, and there are certain histories (such as that of the Jesuit missionaries) that could arguably fit within both categories, making even this distinction difficult to draw.

Rather than evaluate the relations (some more fraught than others) among different religious groups along a presumed universal scale of tolerance, we should focus on the specifics of the situation at hand. Only once we can appreciate how the "rise" of tolerance in a particular place, such as Ireland, would affect the relationship between the various groups involved (in this case, a demographic majority of Roman Catholics versus smaller populations of various Protestants, including Presbyterians, Baptists, Quakers, and the Church of Ireland but not, before the nineteenth century, Jews, Muslims, or other non-Christians) can we then embark on a fuller discussion of what it is we are talking about when we talk about religious freedom (see, for example, Saba Mahmood's suggestions with regard to the Middle East in her essay in this volume).

Toleration is not something that can be improved to a higher or superior state. We would do well to abandon our habitual use of vertical terminology when describing toleration (as more or less, as rising or falling) in favor of lateral terms (wider, narrower), for the later form focuses on the number of parties involved, while the former one implicitly judges the situation via criteria that would apply better to some groups rather than others. There is not, and never has been, a situation of toleration in which all participants were equally satisfied with the results. It is time to step back from this impossible ideal and instead examine actual situations, how and why they have emerged and changed, and where they might be leading.

The challenge for today's world, in which global awareness and implications are unavoidable in a way they were not in the sixteenth century, is to come up with an approach to the history of toleration that can capture its perpetually evolving character. Although it has been intimately associated with the rise of Protestantism, it is no longer limited to that history. However widespread and powerful religious unity and conformity was in medieval

Europe, one could still find exceptions even then—bits of diversity that brought questions of toleration alive long before the appearance of Protestants. And if one goes back further, to the late Antique period, then one returns to a world of religious diversity in which the Roman Catholic Church was but one of many contenders. (Indeed, for the fervently Christian Roger Williams, everything went downhill after the conversion of the emperor Constantine and the fusion of his church with his empire.) Toleration in some form or another has been around for a long time; it will not go away, though it will change. We need to move away from models of rise and fall, progress and decline, and toward capturing the perpetual motion machine that toleration really is. Only then will the ideas of long-gone Protestants retain relevance in a world where now Catholics take the lead as advocates of religious freedom and Protestants are beginning to denounce it as a pernicious force undermining their spiritual welfare.

Acknowledgment

The author would like to thank Teresa M. Bejan and the editors for their thoughts and suggestions on earlier drafts of this essay.

Selected Bibliography

Coffey, John. *Persecution and Toleration in Protestant England, 1558–1689.* New York: Longman, 2000.

Forst, Rainer. *Toleration in Conflict: Past and Present.* Cambridge: Cambridge University Press, 2013.

Grell, Ole Peter, and Bob Scribner, eds. *Tolerance and Intolerance in the European Reformation.* Cambridge: Cambridge University Press, 1996.

Hamburger, Philip. *Separation of Church and State.* Cambridge, MA: Harvard University Press, 2002.

Murphy, Andrew. "Persecuting Quakers? Liberty and Toleration in Early Pennsylvania." In *The First Prejudice: Religious Tolerance and Intolerance in Early America*, edited by Chris Beneke and Christopher S. Grenda, 143–65. Philadelphia: University of Pennsylvania Press, 2011.

Walsham, Alexandra. *Charitable Hatred: Tolerance and Intolerance in England, 1500–1700.* Manchester, UK: Manchester University Press, 2006.

Zagorin, Perez. *How the Idea of Religious Toleration Came to the West.* Princeton, NJ: Princeton University Press, 2003.

CHAPTER NINE

Religious Minorities and Citizenship in the Long Nineteenth Century

Some Contexts of Jewish Emancipation

David Sorkin

In this essay I outline some of the issues involved in discussing religious minorities and citizenship in the long nineteenth century that are relevant to the study of Jewish emancipation or the acquisition of civil and political rights across Europe—a subject for which, surprisingly, there is no adequate monograph. As I engage the topic I am constantly reminded that I am unable to discuss Jews' status without understanding two intimately related issues: the status of other religious minorities across Europe and the ever-shifting and protean nature of citizenship. Yet in both these regards there is a similar impediment.

Social science scholars of "citizenship" have tended to follow T. H. Marshall's 1950s' tripartite model of civil, political, and socioeconomic citizenship. Marshall aimed to render inevitable, and thereby vindicate, the emerging welfare state, focusing on the issues his three categories generated. Although he dealt almost exclusively with the United Kingdom, he hardly mentioned religion. This was a striking absence given that religion had had an irrefragably prominent role in the emergence of both civil and political citizenship in the eighteenth century and the first half of the nineteenth: dissenting Protestants, Catholics, and Jews were the excluded groups who publicly struggled for inclusion. Nevertheless, Marshall did not accord religion the status of an independent, let alone a significant, factor. Sociologists and political scientists such as Andreas

Fahrmeir who have built on Marshall's categories have followed his precedent, thus depriving religion of a constitutive function in the empirical development of citizenship. At the same time, they eagerly pronounce religion's ever-decreasing importance by invoking the metahistorical narrative of secularization.

Historians' approaches to the question of citizenship are equally unhelpful. There is, for example, a large and excellent scholarship for early modern Europe's *ancien régime* devoted to toleration and the status of religious minorities. Scholarship by Ole Peter Grell, Christiane Berkvens-Stevelinck, and others focuses on persecution, discrimination, and expulsion; it does not, by and large, directly address the issue of citizenship, especially the local and municipal citizenship that were foundational in many parts of Europe. Even the more recent social historical scholarship on the practice of toleration such as Benjamin Kaplan and Stuart Schwartz does not extend to questions of citizenship. The scholarship for Europe from the French revolution onward does address citizenship, yet tends, with some significant exceptions (e.g., Rainer Liedtke and Stephan Wendehorst on the status of Protestants, Jews and Catholics in Europe), to subsume the subject of religion and religious minorities to the topic of nationalism and national minorities. As Inis Claude perceptively phrased it over a half century ago, "As the spirit of nationalism took hold, the guaranteed *rights* continued to be primarily religious ones, but the protected *groups* tended to assume the character of national minorities."

I will focus on the period from 1781 to 1925, the chronological arc of the long nineteenth century extending from Joseph II's Edicts for Protestants, the Greek Orthodox, and Jews in 1781–82 to the Minority Rights Treaties following the Paris Peace Conference in the 1920s. The conceptual arc extends from the question of toleration that had dominated the early modern or post-Reformation period at one end to the increasing dominance of the question of national minority rights in the late nineteenth and early twentieth centuries. My aim is to pose questions, formulate some analytical issues, and offer observations. I make no claim to providing answers.

The 1780s witnessed a shift from the question of toleration to that of equality. As is well known, this shift took place under the auspices of the French Revolution. Less well known is that it may have taken place virtually concomitantly under Joseph II's reforming enlightened absolutism and that Joseph's policies influenced the revolutionaries in France and many governments in the first half of the nineteenth century. Joseph's October 13, 1781, Edict of Tolerance granted Lutherans,

Calvinists, and the Greek Orthodox legal standing, albeit a lesser status, in the Habsburg lands for the first time since the Counter-Reformation. Their marriages were now legal. Moreover, he ended the policy of trying to destroy crypto-Protestant communities through forced emigration or "transmigration" (sending them to distant corners of the empire) that his mother, Maria Theresa, had practiced throughout her reign. In keeping with that lesser status, they were given the right of "private worship" that, following the Peace of Westphalia, meant "no chimes, bells, steeples, or public entrance from the street so as to simulate a church."

In keeping with his treatment of Christian minorities, Joseph issued his famous Edict of Tolerance for Jews of Vienna and Lower Austria on January 2, 1782. It aimed "to make the Jewish nation useful and serviceable to the State" by opening all occupations, admitting them to schools, and requiring that they use German in official documents. In the following years Joseph issued edicts for Jews in other parts of the empire—Silesia, Moravia, and Hungary (1781–83)—as well as individual laws (1783–89) until his final 1789 edict for the Jews of Galicia (the territory acquired during the first partition of Poland). In this edict Joseph released Jews from their separate semicorporate existence by abolishing their collective autonomy and integrating them into the existing corporate society. The edict "confer[red] on the Jews living in Galicia all benefits and rights that the rest of our subjects enjoy" so that henceforth "the Jews of Galicia will have the same rights and duties as other subjects." This incontrovertibly constituted parity and represented the absolute limit of what could be accomplished in corporate society. Does it deserve the term *equality*? Something similar could have occurred in czarist Russia. Catherine II's 1785 Charter to the Towns granted Jews, who were acquired through the first partition of Poland, equality with other urban dwellers. Had this legislation been fully implemented these Jews would have had the best legal status among Jews virtually anywhere in Europe.

The shift from toleration to equality took place in France in the transition from late absolutist reform to early revolutionary "regeneration" or transformation. Already in January 1784 Louis XVI had issued a new edict for the Jews of Alsace in which he abolished in perpetuity the "body" or "transit" tax (*péage corporel, Leibzoll*) otherwise applicable only to cattle. Significantly, for the first time this document referred to the Jews of the northeast as subjects of the French crown, "all our subjects," though this may have been inadvertent and the formulation was at best oblique. In a subsequent decree of July 10, 1784, the king revoked this rhetoric by speaking of "the Jews of Our province of Alsace." Louis

XVI's reform program of the late 1780s also included his November 1787 Edict of Tolerance, inspired by his brother-in-law Joseph II, which recognized the existence of Calvinists and granted civil rights "to register their births, their marriages and their deaths" (the right to marry solving the problem of legitimacy and inheritance), the right to practice their religion in private (public observance remained the privilege of the Catholic Church), and the right "to pursue their commerce, arts, crafts and other professions without being troubled or disturbed on the pretext of their religion." Calvinists were also explicitly instructed not to repeat the mistake they allegedly made under the Edict of Nantes by constituting themselves as "forming in our kingdom any particular body, community or association." (Because the edict used the term *non-Catholics*, the Jews of the northeast tested whether the edict applied to them as well. It did not.) Louis XVI then began the process of reforming the Jews' status; he is reported to have said to Guillaume-Chrétien de Lamoignon de Malesherbes, his minister, "you have made yourself a Protestant, now make yourself a Jew."

The early National Assembly (December 24, 1789) added to the 1787 edict's grant of civil rights the Declaration of the Rights of Man and Citizen's promise of political rights by admitting to eligibility for office and "civil and military employment" all "non-Catholics." That decree explicitly excluded Jews. A law of December 1790 restored to the descendants of exiled Protestants the right to reclaim French citizenship. One form of religious equality came in December 1791, when non-Catholics could apply to use public buildings for their worship.

Jews in France gained political rights in two stages. A decree of January 28, 1790, for the Sephardic Jews of the south confirmed their existing privileges and admitted them to the civic oath. A decree of September 28, 1791, granted the Ashkenazic Jews of the northeast political rights by abolishing their existing privileges. By this time, after two years of debate, the stakes were considerably reduced: the moderates who championed it were fearful that the king would repudiate the new constitution and that more radical republicans would seize power.

Napoleon Bonaparte revisited the entire revolutionary legacy, including the Protestants' and Jews' status. In the Organic Articles (April 6, 1802) he created a new administrative mechanism for Protestants in the state supervised *consistoire*; the state undertook to pay Protestant ministers' salaries. He imposed a similar administration on Jews in 1808 when he also issued the so-called Infamous Decrees that, for a period of ten years, reduced the Jews of Alsace to a status of partial equality by limiting their economic endeavors and mobility. Napoleon partially excluded Jews in a period (from 1803 on) when the nation was envisioned as a family writ large. In framing that bill Napoleon's ministers scrutinized Joseph II's Edict of Tolerance of 1782. Czar Nicholas I's ministers did the same in Russia; in trying to formulate the first comprehensive legislation for the Jews in Russia in 1804 (acquired through the partitions of Poland), the ministers adapted Joseph's Edict. It should also be noted that Napoleon's decrees had an afterlife: though allowed to lapse in France in 1818, they remained in force in parts of the Rhineland until 1848. Joseph II's edict similarly remained in force in most of the Habsburg lands until 1848.

This starting point yields a number of observations. First—and it goes almost without saying—citizenship has to be studied in context. It makes no sense to ask why a minority did not enjoy rights or equality in a society in which equality or rights did not exist, or why it enjoyed some rights but not others if no group enjoyed those same rights. An obvious example is that the meaning of "emancipation" or gaining rights meant different things for Jews and other religious minorities across Europe—indeed, even in the same country. As we have seen, for the Sephardic Jews of the south emancipation meant a confirmation of existing civic privileges plus a grant of political rights, whereas for the Jews of Alsace it entailed a release from all previous privileges as the prerequisite for admission to citizenship. This was part of a larger pattern. In parts of western Europe— for example, England, Holland, and the south of France—emancipation meant acquiring political rights because the Jews' civic rights (freedoms of residence, occupation, and religious observance) were largely in place. Jews slowly resettled in England (from 1656 on) without a charter or Jewry law. In this "statutory vacuum" they achieved civic and some political rights on an ad hoc basis either through the gradual removal of disabilities or the confirmation that they did not exist, often through court decisions that established unassailable precedents. "Emancipation" of Jews in England turned exclusively on political rights. The repeal of the Test Act for Dissenters (1828) and Catholics (1829) left Jews the only religious group without political rights.

Jews had gained permission to settle in Amsterdam in the 1590s. At that time individuals had begun to acquire "minor" municipal citizenship, which was not heritable, and which accorded rights of residence and freedom of occupation except for retail trade and most crafts, and excluded them from public office. Other religious minorities (Catholics, Mennonites, Lutherans, and Presbyterians) were similarly prohibited from public office, yet their citizenship was heritable. Jews suffered from more economic restrictions than Catholics, yet—like Lutherans, who were also considered to be an immigrant group—had the right of public worship. (Catholics worshiped in "clandestine" churches.) Emancipation for Jews, Mennonites, Lutherans, and Catholics came with the French-sponsored Batavian Republic.

In contrast, emancipation for Jews in Central Europe, and here I would include Alsace as well, meant a release from their former corporate or semicorporate existence. In other words, emancipation was "out of" corporations and "into" civic and/or political rights. To repeat, in France the admission of Ashkenazic Jews to citizenship (September 28, 1791) was predicated on "a renunciation of all privileges in their favor"—namely, the abrogation of their communal autonomy. The preamble to the Prussian Edict of 1812 correspondingly declared "all laws and regulations concerning Jews [issued] heretofore . . . as abolished." In Eastern Europe, and especially in czarist Russia, in contrast, emancipation meant integration "into" estates (as was also the case in Joseph II's edict for Galicia). When Alexander II allowed Jews to qualify as merchants of the first guild in 1859, for example, they acquired the privileges that adhered to that status, including the all-important right of residence in the Russian heartland—that is, outside the restricted Jewish Pale of Settlement that, since 1835, had kept Jews in the territories of the former Polish-Lithuanian Commonwealth.

We need also to be attentive to the actual requirements for citizenship, or the very definition of citizenship, since these shifted over time. Usually historians distinguish between two legal traditions of citizenship in Europe: *jus soli*, or citizenship based on residence, and *jus sanguinis*, or citizenship based on descent or ethnic/national membership. At times scholars such as Rogers Brubaker have argued that France represents the *jus soli* tradition and Germany the *jus sanguinis*, yet that generalization is imprecise. French law, for example, oscillated between the traditions. Jews were first admitted to political rights in 1790–91 when the law was based on residence (*jus soli*). When Napoleon demoted the Jews of Alsace to a form of conditional emancipation in 1808 modeled on Joseph II's edict, France's law was based on descent (*jus sanguinis*). Moreover, it was French law that introduced citizenship by descent (*jus sanguinis*) to most of Europe.

In the German case it is important to note that the one word *Bürger* incorporates two meanings: "citizen" and "bourgeois." Nineteenth-century developments required a further distinction between state

(*Staatsbürgerliche Gleichberechtigung*) and local citizenship (*Privat-bürgerliche Gleichberechtigung*) or between state members (*Staatsange-hörige*) and citizens with political rights (*Staatsbürger*). Throughout the nineteenth century, including the Wilhelmine Empire, local citizenship was primary, either state citizenship derived from local or municipal citizenship, or later German citizenship derived from state citizenship—for example, being a citizen of Bavaria made you a citizen of the empire. Moreover, the German states also employed both legal traditions of citizenship. Citizenship was tied to residence (*jus solis*) in most German states between 1815 and 1913; only with the 1913 Citizenship Act did *jus sanguinis* gain uncontested supremacy.

Citizenship has to be studied comparatively. We need to compare the status of a minority religious group with other minority religious groups as well as with the majority religion in the same society. Joseph II's edicts first for minority Christians and then for Jews are an example. We cannot logically scrutinize the legal status of Jews in England without comparison to the status of Anglicans on the one side and dissenting Protestants and Catholics on the other. This is important because there was often a hierarchy or precedence in the equalization of status. One could say that this began after the Peace of Westphalia, when the recognition of the "three religions" (Catholicism, Lutheranism, and Calvinism) began to spill over to others such as dissenting Protestants and Jews. In England the order was dissenting Protestants, who gained relief in the 1770s and '80s, then Catholics, who were emancipated in 1829, and finally Jews, who gained emancipation in 1858. (Fahrmeir has asserted that "in Britain, the systematization of the law of subjecthood occurred in the 1840s after the emancipation of the religious minorities.") In France, as we have seen, Jews followed Protestants. In Italy, or at least in Piedmont, Protestants and Jews gained rights together with the revolution of 1848.

This order or precedence reveals a significant development in the course of the nineteenth century. Many thinkers formulated, and many countries embraced, the idea of the "Christian" state or society with the intended result that "Jews" and "Judaism" became the excluded "other." In this binary Jews would always be last in line for rights and first in line for exclusion, vilification, or victimization. In post-Holocaust Europe, in contrast, that binary has been replaced by a triangulation. The postwar American coinage of a "Judeo-Christian" tradition now enjoys a peculiar renaissance in Europe, especially on the political Right. By allowing thinkers to claim the legitimacy of Jews and Judaism, it has made Muslims and Islam the "other" and thus also last in line for rights and first in line for vilification and victimization. Significantly, in pre-Holocaust Europe there was no equivalent concept to the "Judeo-Christian" tradition in circulation.

It is important to remember that the introduction of citizenship for religious minorities was not a one-time affair. Formal legislation was often at odds with—or at least in tension with—actual practice; there was a problem of continuing discrimination despite, or directly in response to, virtual or full equality. That discrimination could take various forms or have various origins. Some of it derived from the "small print" of legislation or the "tenacity of older legislation." Some of it came from what Wendehorst describes as "administrative practice."

France can serve as an example of the need to read the small print. Jews suffered various forms of discrimination until the Third Republic. Rabbis, unlike Catholic priests and Protestant pastors, did not gain state salaries until 1831. The Quai d'Orsay (or French Foreign Office) endorsed the "blood libel" during the 1840–41 Damascus Affair, when Jews were accused of the ritual murder of a monk—that is, using his blood to bake Passover matzos—thereby impugning French Jews' moral character and thus their claim to citizenship. Finally, the demeaning medieval Jewish oath (*more Judaico*) was not fully abolished until 1846 and not without a struggle. Similarly for Protestants, the Bourbon Restoration in its 1814 charter (article 5) declared Catholicism "the religion of the state" while also guaranteeing the equality of all religions (article 4), thus symbolically demoting Protestants and Jews to second-class status. Through administrative practice local authorities forced Protestants to build new churches on the outskirts or in the suburbs of towns, thus reviving practices reminiscent of the era of the Edict of Nantes (*Auslauf*). Protestants were not allowed to build churches freely anywhere in France until the 1840s. Napoleon III again discriminated against Protestants, according only the right of private worship; Protestants went so far as to turn to England as a protector. Protestants and Jews felt fully emancipated only with the Third Republic's secular turn after 1879 and the introduction of universal suffrage.

One obvious criterion of political integration is office holding and state appointments. Protestants and Jews were conspicuously integrated in the Third Republic. In the first republican government in 1879, according to Pierre Encrevé, fully half of the cabinet members were Protestants. The Third Republic saw the full flowering of what Pierre Birnbaum has termed "state Jews"—that is, Jews who served the state as high civil servants, university professors, and military officers; there were some twenty-five Jewish generals.

Germany offers an instance of the "tenacity of older legislation." After full emancipation in 1871, Jews and Catholics continued to find themselves discriminated against in appointments in the judiciary and education. The problem was the tension between federal law, which promised equality, and state law, which often did not. As Peter Pulzer has argued, the "Jewish question" and the "Catholic question" in Wilhelmine Germany were in fact together a constitutional question. Yet the two religious minorities suffering discrimination were at odds on the issue. As a tiny percentage of the population, Jews wanted appointments on the basis of individual merit. Many Catholics favored a proportional system that would raise their numbers to reflect their sizable share of the population.

In Britain Catholics gained civil equality in 1829 with the repeal of the Test and Corporation Acts. Yet here the "small print" and older legislation persisted: for example, Catholics were restricted to private observance. They were not allowed to serve as chaplains in the army and navy until 1866; the requirement that they make a declaration against transubstantiation to hold office was not abolished until 1867. New legislation exacerbated the situation; the 1851 Ecclesiastical Titles Act prohibited a Catholic hierarchy. One sign of resistance to equality and the resulting prospect of integration is violence. Violence against Catholics, including rioting, was a recurring phenomenon in Britain, especially around such public displays of Catholic identity as the Orange-Catholic parades in centers of Catholic population (Manchester, Liverpool, Glasgow, and London). Such violence tended to subside from the 1870s on.

The study of minority rights is also a study of the process by which a society in general created rights. Some nineteenth-century thinkers suggested that the legal status of a religious minority, often the Jews, was the index to the humanity of the larger society. Some neo-Marxist postwar historians have seen the status of the minority as the index to the development of civil or bourgeois society. In the cases of Italy, Austria-Hungary, and Germany, historians have understood the equality of religious minorities to be part of the process of national unification and the combined triumph of liberalism and nationalism. More recently historians such as Wendehorst have suggested treating the position of minorities as a means to understand national integration, which they take to be a complex and multifaceted process.

I am not sure whether these approaches are mutually exclusive. What is important about the way we conceive of the large process of minority rights is whether or to what extent it enables us to address the issues of how the state or larger society defined the minority religion and to what extent the minority religion's continuity remained legitimate and viable. In other words, are religious minorities gaining rights in a "homogeneous" nation or nation-state that can only accommodate them if it is presumed that they will ultimately disappear? Or is the situation one in which the minority needs to adjust itself and redefine its religion to fit a dominant tradition? And how hegemonic and imperious is that tradition? An obvious example in this regard would be France's republican tradition of *laïcité*. In the *consistoire* Jews and Protestants had to accept a state-imposed administrative mechanism that was entirely alien. To what extent did this touch on the essentials of faith? To what extent did it affect merely the *adiaphora*—extraneous matters—or the external administration of religion? Today, are Muslim women's head coverings essentials of their faith or merely *adiaphora* that can be subjected to state control? Or is state control a symbolic issue with little regard for its repercussions for the minority religion?

Imperial Germany presents an example of a presumed homogeneity. Many of the very German liberals who championed the Jews' emancipation as a virtual article of faith also presumed that the Jews would ultimately disappear as a distinct group. For these liberals, becoming German unquestionably also meant becoming Protestant (current German proponents of this position would say "Christian"). This was a tradition that ran from Wilhelm von Humboldt, who championed unconditional emancipation in the intragovernmental debates in Prussia in 1809, to Theodor Mommsen, who defended the Jews against Heinrich von Treitschke's attacks in the so-called Berlin Anti-Semitism Controversy in 1881. This was the same Germany in which Otto von Bismarck waged a war against independent Catholic institutions as subversive (*Kulturkampf*) because they were allegedly loyal to a foreign power (the papacy); he also deported tens of thousands of Catholic Poles and Jews (1885–87). To repeat, in the German states and the newly unified Germany there was a prominent tradition among liberals of desiring religious and cultural homogeneity as essential to national unity.

The long nineteenth century ended in the aftermath of World War I—for our purposes in the minority treaties that accompanied the creation of the successor states of east central Europe and were, in Carole Fink's words, "history's first experiment in international minority protection" that included religious equality and freedom. These treaties drew on an important development in the nineteenth century: the recognition of religious freedom in international law. This was an ambiguous enterprise in which victorious powers tended to impose on smaller states requirements by which they themselves refused to abide. At the Congress of Vienna, England, Austria, Russia, and Prussia imposed on Holland and Belgium, in an effort to unite the two, absolute religious equality (Treaty of Eight Articles, article 2). Holland accepted the provisions in its constitution; the Belgian assembly of notables initially rejected it, though an independent Belgium enshrined these provisions in its 1831 constitution. England, France, and Russia similarly imposed religious equality on the newly independent Greece (February 3, 1830), even though none of them could honestly make that claim for their own country. This pattern continued at the Congress of Berlin (1878; by then England and France could claim to have met the formal criteria, although Russian still could not), which required that full political equality be extended to citizens of all faiths in the new Rumania, Bulgaria, Serbia, and Montenegro. With the Minority Rights Treaties the victorious powers required the new states, especially Poland, to guarantee minority rights but refused to issue a universal statement that would have required the same of themselves. (US president Woodrow Wilson refused because of the implications for Jim Crow laws and his resegregation of the civil service.)

Did "minority rights" simply replace the question of religious equality or freedom because it was already established in international law? Or did nationalism simply subsume the issue of religion to its other concerns? Did the two converge? Whatever the answer, it does seem to me that a scholarship on citizenship that ignores or neglects the subject of religion and religious minorities cannot provide an adequate account of the development of citizenship in general.

Selected Bibliography

Berkvens-Stevelinck, C., J. Israel, and G. H. M. Meyjes, eds. *The Emergence of Tolerance in the Dutch Republic*. Leiden, Netherlands: Brill, 1997.

Brubaker, Rogers. *Citizenship and Nationhood in France and Germany*. Cambridge, MA: Harvard University Press, 1992.

Claude, Inis L. *National Minorities: An International Problem*. 2nd ed. New York: Greenwood, 1969.

Fahrmeir, Andreas. *Citizenship: The Rise and Fall of a Modern Concept.* New Haven, CT: Yale University Press, 2007.

———. "Nineteenth-Century German Citizenships: A Reconsideration." *The Historical Journal* 40, no. 3 (1997): 721–52.

Fink, Carole. "The Minorities Question at the Paris Peace Conference: The Polish Minority Treaty, June 28, 1919." In *The Treaty of Versailles: A Reassessment after 75 Years*, edited by Manfred F. Boemeke, Gerald D. Feldman, and Elisabeth Glaser, 249–74. Cambridge: Cambridge University Press, 1998.

Grell, Ole Peter, Jonathan Israel, and Nicholas Tyacke, eds. *From Persecution to Toleration: The Glorious Revolution and Religion in England.* Oxford: Oxford University Press, 1991.

Grell, Ole Peter, and Bob Scribner, eds. *Tolerance and Intolerance in the European Reformation.* Cambridge: Cambridge University Press, 1996.

Grell, Ole Peter, and Roy Porter. *Toleration in Enlightenment Europe.* Cambridge: Cambridge University Press, 2000.

Kaplan, Benjamin. *Divided by Faith: Religious Conflict and the Practice of Toleration in Early Modern Europe.* Cambridge, MA: Harvard University Press, 2007.

Kates, Gary. "Jews into Frenchmen: Nationality and Representation in Revolutionary France." *Social Research* 56 (1989): 231–32.

Liedtke, Rainer, and Stephan Wendehorst, eds. *The Emancipation of Catholics, Jews and Protestants: Minorities and the Nation State in Nineteenth-Century Europe.* Manchester, UK: Manchester University Press, 1999.

Maclear, J. F. *Church and State in the Modern Age.* New York: Oxford University Press, 1995.

Marshall, T. H. *Citizenship and Social Class, and Other Essays.* Cambridge: Cambridge University Press, 1950.

Pulzer, Peter. *Jews and the German State: The Political History of a Minority, 1848–1933.* Detroit: Wayne State University Press, 2003.

Weil, Patrick. *How to Be French: Nationality in the Making since 1789.* Durham, NC: Duke University Press, 2008.

Wendehorst, Stephan. "Emancipation as a Path to National Integration." In *The Emancipation of Catholics, Jews and Protestants: Minorities and the Nation State in Nineteenth-Century Europe*, edited by Ranier Liedtke and Stephan Wendehorst, 188–206. Manchester, UK: Manchester University Press, 1999.

CHAPTER TEN

Varieties of Religious Freedom and Governance

A Practical Perspective

Robert W. Hefner

A s Elizabeth Shakman Hurd's and Saba Mahmood's contributions to this volume remind us, the received wisdom in Western policy circles today emphasizes the necessary synergy between democracy and religious freedom. What I wish to suggest in this essay is not that this policy truism is wrong, but that it is sociologically too simple, and that the oversimplification can result in ill-conceived prescriptions for pluralist religious freedom. The relationship postulated in the received model overlooks the fact that, even in the West, the slow consolidation of electoral democracy in the nineteenth and twentieth centuries coevolved with not one but a variety of regimes for religious governance. Moreover, until the great secularizing surge of the mid- to late twentieth century, most of Western Europe's regimes of religious governance were not liberal in today's politicophilosophical sense of the term; indeed, some are not even today. Rather than religious freedom being a sine qua non of modern democratic politics, then, religious governance in Western Europe appears to have been structurally underdetermined and discursively plural in rationale and form.

Our appreciation of the more complex history of religious governance in the West does not necessarily deny the normative importance of religious freedom in contemporary debates about religion and democracy. Indeed, as I hope will be clear in the following pages, I personally endorse such efforts, at least where—as is the case in significant portions of the Global

South today—they resonate with the aspirations and circumstances of local actors and open—rather than narrow—popular understandings of and engagements with "religion." To understand such resonances, as well as the alterities and resistances that ideas of religious freedom may encounter, it behooves us to complicate our understanding of the genealogy of democracy and religious freedom in the West. I do so here by way of three points.

The first is that democratization in the modern West did not give rise to a stable and uniform practice of religious liberty but to a variety of governance regimes that, in most countries, secured religious freedom for some faith communities while restricting rights and privileges for those outside the imagined national community. Second, the form religious freedom and governance took in each Western country was not the result of faithful conformity to preconceived liberal principles, but of path-dependent struggles among different religious and class coalitions, all attempting to project their influence and public ethical ideals upward into the structures of religious governance. Third, the resulting varieties of religious governance seen in the modern West remind us that the *practice* of religious freedom was never the result of a unitary principle or hegemonic discourse, liberal or otherwise. Inasmuch as this is the case, those interested today in promoting—or critiquing—efforts to develop a more inclusive practice of religious citizenship in the world would do well to direct their attention to not just abstract principles of individual autonomy but the situated practices, coalitions, and balances of social power that ultimately determine what ethicoreligious traditions come to be authorized as "religions," and which among the several varieties of religious governance in social contention prevail.

Behind my comments is a general reservation with regard to current debates on religious freedom. There is a tendency among proponents and critics of liberal freedom alike to overintellectualize and homogenize the genealogy of religious freedom in the modern West. This simplification results in part from a tendency to conflate philosophical genealogies of religious freedom with a more comprehensive sociology of the real and existing varieties of ethicoreligious practice and governance. Although philosophies of religious freedom offer insights into the ways in which human rights and subjectivity were imagined and rationalized by intellectual elites, the struggles that gave rise to different systems of religious governance everywhere involved a more diverse assortment of actors, discourses, and powers, and a more varied array of ethicoreligious imaginaries than those premised on ideals of individual autonomy and freedom of belief alone.

More important, the individuals and groups involved in such contests came to subscribe to notions of religious freedom, where they did so at all, on grounds that had as much to do with group identities and interests, and the struggles and social pacts through which both were advanced, as they did any ontological commitment to individual autonomy or the sanctity of personal belief. As I have suggested with regard to Muslim democrats, all evidence suggests that there is today a similar diversity of motivations and political ontologies operative among those in the Global South who have concluded that some variety of religious freedom is congruent with their own needs and aspirations, even where liberal philosophical ideals of individual autonomy may not be.

This situation may strike some philosophically inclined analysts as odd. However, the circumstance of political actors subscribing to ostensibly liberal understandings of freedom, gender equality, or religious tolerance on ethical and epistemological grounds different from those of Western philosophical liberals is, in fact, widespread in the contemporary world. To take but one example, it is just such an approach that underlies the efforts of Muslim pluralists, like those of Khaled Abou El Fadl and Ziba Mir-Hosseini, to affirm the ideals of religious freedom and gender equality on specifically Islamic grounds. For researchers and analysts, the pervasiveness of examples like these underscores the need for us *not* to assume that the act of publicly subscribing to some liberal (or other political) value is the result of a single and shared ethicophilosophical discourse or rationale.

Inasmuch as the reasons for subscribing to an ostensibly liberal ideal like religious freedom can be epistemologically varied, when speaking of modern notions of religious freedom it may be more sociologically realistic to speak of a range of "civic pluralist" commitments within which liberal religious freedom is but one variety. In adopting the phrase we may be better able to recognize that rights of personal and confessional freedom are at times secured through social pacts and arrangements that recognize group identities and concerns, as well as practices of "religion," more varied than those highlighted under philosophical liberalism.

Varieties of European Religious Governance

As the sociologist David Martin pointed out more than a generation ago, and as historians of religion like Hugh McLeod or political scientists like Ahmet Kuru, Jonathan Fox, and Alfred Stepan have more recently reminded us, there was no single pattern of confessional freedom in modern Western Europe during the long century in which electoral democracy took hold. Not a single European democracy, including laicist France, adopted the American model of a constitutional wall of separation combined with a relatively competitive *and* religionized public sphere. The majority of Western European countries recognized a state religion or (less commonly) several state-approved religions; most still do today, as Stephen V. Moensma and J. Christopher Soper, as well as Alfred Stepan, note. Most regimes of religious governance countenanced religious education in public schools. With a few notable exceptions like France, the majority of European countries still do today, though the aims of the courses in some schools are shifting from indoctrination *into* a particular faith tradition to education *about* religions. Most European states also provided tax revenues for the maintenance of schools, houses of worship, hospitals, and religious associations.

Although some European countries extended state support to several religious communities, no European country provided equal treatment for the entire array of religious communities resident within its borders. In this sense, full religious freedom for most of the modern period was not universal, but selective and conditional. As Jonathan Laurence puts it, "Every religious community that has joined the national fabric accepted certain restrictions on its freedoms and autonomy at the moment of recognition: from the use of local clergy who preach in the local language, to abandoning distinctive dress in the public sphere." As with Jewish communities in the late nineteenth century and Muslim communities in Europe today, the precise terms for admission to the ranks of state-recognized religions were usually not explicitly specified in constitutions or legislation. The framework was instead the incompletely discursivized product of social struggles and political pacts among representatives of different religious and class coalitions.

Today some supporters of religious freedom might be tempted to dismiss these examples as illiberal and undemocratic and leave the matter there. But my point is simpler and more analytic: these and other examples demonstrate that the history of democratization is not the story of the progressive maximization of any single democratic value, whether the autonomy of the individual or some other, but an evolving balance among several, sometimes discordant, public ethical values along with the social groupings that served as their carriers. The negotiations taking place between select representatives of Muslims and state authorities in Western Europe provide a contemporary example of this phenomenon, as John Bowen and Jonathan Laurence have demonstrated. However, the history of religious governance in modern Europe's consociational democracies, the Netherlands and Belgium, shows that the pattern is anything but new.

Consociational Governance

Until the 1960s, the Netherlands—a laboratory for many Western ideas on republican freedom and economic liberalism—had a political and religious system organized around guaranteed group representation by way of what were known as religious "pillars" (*verzuilingen*). This arrangement was the pacted framework within which democratization in the modern Netherlands emerged, and it was premised on a more pluralized yet communitarian notion of citizenship than acknowledged in North Atlantic liberal models of democracy. Formally recognized in the constitution of 1917, the pillars were vertical social structures based on the Netherlands' four major ethicoreligious groupings: Roman Catholics, Orthodox Protestants, Reformed Protestants, and secular humanists. Since the 1990s efforts have been made—still not fully successfully—to secure state recognition for a fifth pillar, the growing community of Dutch Muslims.

In their heyday, the pillars were social and not ecclesiastical organizations, governed by a nonclerical administrative board. Established in the aftermath of the nineteenth century's struggles among Dutch religious communities and secular humanists, pillar administration provided state funds for religious education, hospitals, and other social services. Even labor unions were organized along pillar lines. Although regarded as prerequisites for the democratic peace, the pillars were controlled by leaders in a way that was, as the sociologist Anton Zijderveld has put it, "rather authoritarian and elitist," even if allowing a "remarkable social and political pacification." Civic peace and religious freedom were thereby secured by way of mechanisms that were as much vertical and corporatist as they were liberal.

Western Plurality and the Global South's Diversity

The point of this comparison is not to suggest that religious governance in Dutch society was somehow an exception to the Western liberal rule. On the contrary, the consociational example is interesting because it makes more salient processes and tensions endemic to democratization and religious governance across all of Europe from the mid-nineteenth century to today. Even as electoral democracy was being established, the emerging system of religious governance had as much or even more to do with group interests and strategic pacts as it did any foundational commitment to religious freedom or individual autonomy. The precise balance of religious rights and exclusions also showed the imprint of specific national cultures, struggles, and compromises, as John Madeley has shown. One could say that the history of religious freedom in the modern West looks very different when seen from the perspective of mundane struggles over religious education and state financial support for religious buildings rather than, say, liberal philosophers' political ontologies.

It is also useful to make practice-based comparisons like these because the politically contingent situations they evoke are far closer in organization and political dynamic to the religious landscapes in much of today's Global South. In matters of religion and governance, of course, there is no single Global South or "new majority." The religious and political heritage varies greatly in different countries and regions. What *is* similar between parts of the Global South and modern Europe, however, is the way in which urbanization, mass education, and the heightened mobility and plurality of people, goods, and ideas have given rise to new religious and ethical imaginaries and, with them, calls for regimes of religious governance capable of accommodating the new plurality. As was and is still the case in the West, the precise form of these appeals has varied. In countries where national identity has long been fused with a more or less established religious community whose borders are policed by well-entrenched elites, pluralism and religious freedom, even in a consociational form, may appear or be portrayed as intrusive and inauthentic. Elsewhere, as in parts of sub-Saharan Africa or East and Southeast Asia, the relative weakness of a hegemonic world religion may allow a more open and competitive religious market. Even here, however, the task of scaling up from religious diversity to a public ethical and legal framework that explicitly embraces pluralism is anything but guaranteed, dependent as it is on the passions, interests, and bottom-up struggles of different religious and class formations.

The implications of this analysis for proponents of religious freedom are by no means dire, but they are cautionary. They imply that progress toward a sustainable and inclusive religious freedom depends not only or even primarily on the constitutional affirmation of principles of individual freedom but on the creation of a public culture and alliances of interest across and within public ethical communities. No less important—and, again, contrary to some philosophical representations of religious freedom—the social motivations for popular support of religious freedom may have as much to do with the recognition of *group* identities and interests as it does any self-conscious commitment to the autonomy of the individual.

Rather than a counsel of pessimism, however, this prescription is as I understand it quietly encouraging. It suggests that religious or—as I prefer to call it, subsuming it within a more plural, less individualistic, and contingent ideal—*civic pluralist* freedom is a condition to which people in diverse societies can and will aspire because it allows them to resolve certain problems of coexistence in conditions of deep religious and ethical difference. Inasmuch as this challenge is pervasive in contemporary societies, we should not be surprised to see that many non-Western moderns rally to some variety of civic pluralist freedom. Equally important, and as has always been the case in Western democracies, even where people in different societies aspire to such pluralist freedoms their reasons for doing so may well be based on ethicoreligious ontologies more varied than those highlighted in liberal philosophy's imaginary of autonomous individuals.

Selected Bibliography

Abou El Fadl, Khaled. *Speaking in God's Name: Islamic Law, Authority and Women*. Oxford: One World, 2001.

Bowen, John R. *Can Islam Be French? Pluralism and Pragmatism in a Secularist State*. Princeton, NJ: Princeton University Press, 2010.

Fox, Jonathan. *A World Survey of Religion and the State*. Cambridge: Cambridge University Press, 2008.

Hefner, Robert W. "On the History and Cross-Cultural Possibility of a Democratic Ideal." In *Democratic Civility: The History and Cross-Cultural Possibility of a Modern Political Ideal*, edited by Robert W. Hefner, 3–49. New Brunswick, NJ: Transaction, 1998.

———. "Human Rights and Democracy in Islam: The Indonesian Case in Global Perspective." In *Religion and the Global Politics of Human Rights*, edited by Thomas Banchoff and Robert Wuthnow, 39–69. Oxford: Oxford University Press, 2011.

———. "The Study of Religious Freedom in Indonesia." *Review of Faith and International Affairs* 2, no. 2 (2013): 18–27.

Jackson, Robert. "European Institutions and the Contribution of Studies of Religious Diversity to Education for Democratic Citizenship." In *Religion and Education in Europe: Developments, Contexts and Debates*, edited by Robert Jackson, Siebren Miedema, Wolfram Weisse, and Jean-Paul Williame, 27–55. Münster, Germany: Waxmann, 2007.

Kuru, Ahmet. *Secularism and State Policies toward Religion: The United States, France, and Turkey.* Cambridge: Cambridge University Press, 2009.

Laurence, Jonathan. *The Emancipation of Europe's Muslims: The State's Role in Minority Integration.* Princeton, NJ: Princeton University Press, 2012.

Madeley, John. "A Framework for the Comparative Analysis of Church-State Relations in Europe." *West European Politics* 26, no. 1 (2003): 23–50.

Martin, David. *A General Theory of Secularization.* Oxford: Blackwell, 1978.

McLeod, Hugh. "Introduction." In *The Decline of Christendom in Western Europe, 1750–2000,* edited by Hugh McLeod and Werner Ustorf, 1–26. Cambridge: Cambridge University Press, 2003.

Mir-Hosseini, Ziba. "The Construction of Gender in Islamic Legal Thought and Strategies for Reform." *Hawwa* 1, no. 1 (2003): 1–28.

Moensma, Stephen V., and J. Christopher Soper. *The Challenge of Pluralism: Church and State in Five Democracies.* Lanham, MD: Rowman and Littlefield, 1997.

Stepan, Alfred. "The Multiple Secularisms of Modern Democratic and Non-Democratic Regimes." In *Rethinking Secularism*, edited by Craig Calhoun, Mark Juergensmeyer, and Jonathan VanAntwerpen, 114–44. Oxford: Oxford University Press, 2011.

Zijderveld, Anton C. "Civil Society, Pillarization, and the Welfare State." In *Democratic Civility: The History and Cross-Cultural Possibility of a Modern Political Ideal,* edited by Robert W. Hefner, 153–71. New Brunswick, NJ: Transaction, 1998.

CHAPTER ELEVEN

Religious Freedom between Truth and Tactic

Samuel Moyn

A self-described coalition of "Catholics and Evangelicals together" recently defended religious freedom in a manifesto printed in *First Things* in March 2012. The coalition—which originated in a 1994 pact—includes a number of notable Americans, like the late Charles Colson and George Weigel, with endorsements from the archbishops of Chicago, New York, and Philadelphia, along with many others. According to the statement, the situation is unexpectedly urgent. After the fall of the Soviet Union, "throughout the world, a new era of religious freedom seemed at hand." But now it is blatantly clear that the scourge of intolerance—especially secularist intolerance—persists. The current "peril" for religious freedom is global, given forces like communism and Islam that often trample it. On unclear evidence, the statement goes so far as to say that "the greatest period of persecution in the history of Christianity" is occurring right now. It calls for a response abroad in how "the foreign policy of the United States and Canada" are conducted. But religious freedom is also threatened within.

All this is very interesting. The statement is rooted in the vision of the founder of *First Things*, the late Father Richard John Neuhaus, and it is imbued with the spirit of his resounding complaint that "the public square is naked" in the United States—roughly, that our common discourse suffers from the alleged banishment of religious commitment and justification. The new statement portends a continuing period of strife over the meaning of religious freedom and the everyday management of

secular public space. It is significant that the group situates itself historically. Religious freedom is deeply rooted in the West, the statement explains. The group offers a "genealogy" (its term) of the principle, starting
with Jesus and running through Lactantius, Roger Williams, and Martin
Luther. And then, rather remarkably, the statement leaps to the last half
of the twentieth century, most especially Vatican II's *Dignitatis Huma-
nae* (1965).

I want to take up some of that history in this short piece—but first
let's consider the contemporary politics of the statement. It may have appeared too late to welcome the US Supreme Court's "ministerial exception" case that, in January 2012, limited the scope of antidiscrimination
law in the name of religious freedom. With perfect timing, however, the
statement coincided with the politics of the accommodation President
Barack Obama famously offered, constricting reproductive choice in
view of objections based on the same principle as the Supreme Court ruling. Some might see those developments as illustrating the considerable
force of religious sentiment, and the power of the norm of religious freedom, in American public affairs. Outside the United States, the *Lautsi
v. Italy* case decided in March 2011 by the European Court of Human
Rights suggests a similar conclusion. A prominent law professor based
in the United States, Joseph Weiler, actually invoked Neuhaus's slogan
in his appellate defense of the continuing presence of crucifixes in Italian schoolrooms, and the decision by the court's Grand Chamber to side
with him suggests that religious freedom and public Christianity maintain a healthy communion.

This coalition of American Christians, however, is still worried, as it
explains in a crucial paragraph. "Proponents of human rights, including governments," it writes, "have begun to define religious freedom
down, reducing it to a bare 'freedom of worship.' This reduction denies
the inherently public character of biblical religion and privatizes the very
idea of religious freedom, a view of freedom such as one finds in those
repressive states where Christians can pray only so long as they do so
behind closed doors. It is no exaggeration to see in these developments
a movement to drive religious belief, and especially orthodox Christian religious and moral convictions, out of public life." In view of such
fears, I write to ask how serious a "genealogy" of this coalition's preferred understanding of religious freedom is required to understand its
own current advocacy. It may seem strange, given recent academic trends
doubting the validity of secularism, to bracket worries about it in order

to investigate instead the lineage of the worry that privatization of "orthodoxy" is normatively misguided or practically discriminatory—an argument that unites the coalition of evangelicals and Catholics around the contemporary critique of secularism. In view of the coalition's statement, however, this agenda seems pressing. Where did the strategy of insisting on the "inherently public" character of religion come from, especially one grouping some Catholics in alliance with American evangelicals?

The defense of Christianity as an "inherently public" religion is nothing new; but until very recently Catholicism—and especially conservative Catholicism—considered the principle of religious freedom to be the disease rather than the cure. The failure of various mid-twentieth-century political attitudes led to an Americanization of Catholicism in which religious freedom made unprecedented inroads. It did so, however, as the new way that "inherently public" religion was pursued—one in which American Protestantism suddenly became model rather than stigma.

Most people know—though the statement doesn't mention—that Catholic authorities generally rejected religious freedom prior to Vatican II. In its scandalous indifference to truth, religious freedom, Pope Leo XIII explained in *Immortale Dei* (1885), is little more than slavery to falsehood. According to this encyclical on "the Christian constitution of states," Catholicism must stand against the theory that

> all questions that concern religion are to be referred to private judgment; that every one is to be free to follow whatever religion he prefers, or none at all if he disapprove of all. From this the following consequences logically flow: that the judgment of each one's conscience is independent of all law; that the most unrestrained opinions may be openly expressed as to the practice or omission of divine worship; and that every one has unbounded license to think whatever he chooses and to publish abroad whatever he thinks. Now, when the State rests on foundations like those just named . . . it readily appears into what and how unrightful a position the Church is driven.

In the mid-twentieth-century crisis, when liberal democracy was destroyed, it was therefore not out of nowhere that Catholics frequently voted with their feet in favor of explicitly Catholic states in crisis circumstances (in Austria, Portugal, and Spain before World War II, and then Croatia, Vichy France, and Slovakia during the war) and fascist states when this first best option was not available (in Germany and Italy before World War II and most of Europe during the war). Indeed, forsaking state capture still seemed radical in the late 1940s, when powerful Vatican forces remained stalwart in their defense of the older view that an endorsement of religious freedom made sense only as a "hypothesis" in those situations in which Catholics were in the minority—as in the United States—rather than a general principle or "thesis." (Leo XIII proceeded this way, for instance, in first taking note of American Catholicism in his encyclical *Longinqua Oceani*, 1895.)

The end of World War II famously gave birth to a new, widespread compatibility of Catholicism with liberalism, including liberal rights. Yet through the 1950s, and in fact through Vatican II, the Roman Catholic Church as a whole still opposed religious freedom, against a strong set of dissidents like Jacques Maritain and others. After the war, figures like Cardinal Alfredo Ottaviani (the last head of the millennial inquisition) continued to inveigh against religious freedom, offering Spain, where clericofascism in a majority Catholic country had survived, as the ideal model. Indeed, Ottaviani and his allies, in a dramatic series of events, nearly derailed Vatican II's declaration on religious freedom, which was the most high-profile and visible part of its work precisely because it was by no means uncontested.

In short, the idea of religious freedom as the key buttress of inherently public religion—the key pillar of the *First Things* statement—was painfully acquired. Among Catholics it had to be developed against those who insisted that "inherently public" religion needed to be immunized against the idea of religious freedom, with its Protestant, liberal, and privatizing implications. Long censured as a principle that brought ruin on Christianity, religious freedom now seemed a tool to buttress it.

It is not obvious why the switch happened. In my opinion, it was a process in which the geopolitics of the Cold War mattered most, as certain principles like freedom of conscience once denounced by a reactionary church got a second look. The stimulus for this was provided by a frighteningly secularist enemy against which the United States now stood as principal opponent, after an interwar period in which different choices—and serious mistakes—were too often made. Once tasked in Catholic political thought as a catalyst of secularism, religious freedom found itself recuperated as a crucial tool to stave secularism off. No wonder, then, that in privatizing faith, liberalism in the United States still seems analogous—for this coalition—most of all to communism. (As the statement explains, "the totalitarian temptation . . . seems to exist in all forms of political modernity.")

The adoption of religious freedom in the face of the totalitarian danger also allowed an unprecedented move in the direction of Protestantism, once denounced as the source of modern ills. It permitted American life to become a model—though many Catholics had commonly associated it with modern, individualist, and materialist error. Catholics like Maritain, for example, promoted America on the grounds that it showed how religious freedom promoted rather than undermined Christianity. In the nineteenth century, Catholic thinker Alexis de Tocqueville's attitude toward Protestant America was that it had figured out, by disestablishing the church, how to make Christianity more publicly powerful than ever. His message to Catholic reactionaries at home who denounced America as godless was that they needed to know how strong Christianity can become precisely among those who have given up the campaign to capture the state. "I shall wait until they come back from a visit to America," Tocqueville wrote of his reactionary opponents. Maritain, who had once attacked America, spent World War II there, forging alliances with theologians like John Courtney Murray, who followed him in marginalizing the thesis/hypothesis model. Murray, under Maritain's influence, became the most pivotal figure in Vatican II's work on religious freedom.

Murray faced a difficult uphill battle within the church—which made the declaration of religious freedom at Vatican II its single most controversial aspect and indeed one that nearly got derailed. Ottaviani and his faction succeeded in postponing consideration of the declaration in 1964, which caused a major international uproar. It was only the pope's decision to side against the reactionaries the next year that saved the proposal. The text of the papal declaration makes clear that it now seemed that endorsement of the principle of religious freedom undermined global secularism more than risked it. "Men of the present day want to profess their religion freely in private and in public," the declaration states, before turning this novel Catholic view against the Soviet Union. "[But] there are forms of government under which, despite constitutional recognition of the freedom of religious worship, the public authorities themselves strive to deter the citizens from professing their religion and make life particularly difficult and dangerous for religious bodies."

That conservative Catholics and evangelical Protestants rally around religious freedom together is nothing like a continuation of Tocqueville's America. Yet this is not simply because Tocqueville lost the argument in his time, with the unedifying politics of the twentieth century following and the Cold War finally prompting the Catholic pivot. It is also because, after World War II, mainline Protestants in the United States turned religious freedom into a more genuinely liberal and privatizing principle than ever before in this country's history. If the Catholic transformation with respect to religious freedom was fateful, this mainline Protestant move was equally so, for in making it, mainline Protestants may have sealed their doom—and provided a short-term boost to privatizing liberalism that did not secure itself in American life for long. After all, the evangelical ascendancy away from mainline coastal fortresses, which are today so depopulated, opened the door to the other side of the equation for today's conservative coalition—not to mention to the rise of American conservatism generally.

This side of the story, concerning the transformation of American Protestantism, is as replete with irony as the Catholic side, with many contingencies and surprises lying behind the current configuration. As a series of excellent historians have shown, in the mainline Protestant culture so dominant among cultural and governmental elites in the nineteenth century and beyond, the First Amendment's protections functioned in part to discriminate against Catholics. And if it was after World War II, in the era of *Everson v. Board of Education* (1947), that religious freedom became "liberal," as David Sehat has penetratingly demonstrated, it was only to set the stage for mainline Protestantism's demise. As David Hollinger and others have argued, the mainline move in the direction of pluralism and tolerance made its most fundamental bequest to the secular culture of diversity that increasingly defined America. At the same time, Protestant religiosity was left to expanding evangelical precincts moving from the south to the west and ultimately creating a strong electoral and cultural basis for a massive shift in America to the right. It is no wonder that it is evangelical Protestants joining together with conservative Catholics to interpret religious freedom not as part of a broader and secular culture of individual choice and social tolerance but instead as a keystone principle in the search for communities of belief, practice, and sentiment that subordinate individual choice to religious morality.

The strange fact today, in summary, is that the principal defenders of American religious freedom, defined as recognition of the "inherently public" role of faith, could not have been in coalition at any other time. Even in postwar America the coalition was not inevitable, and ending the story at Vatican II also leaves aside the very recent years when this coalition came together in what some have seen as a disturbing pact— one that certainly did not follow from a deeply rooted past alliance.

Attractively, the group pauses at the start of its text, mindful of the injunction about casting the first stone. It alludes vaguely to some prior period when "Christians have also employed the state as an instrument of religious coercion." But this passing allusion doesn't interfere with the spotty history the statement goes on to give. After its acknowledgment that mistakes have been made by politicized Christians, the statement concludes that "memory of Christian sinfulness . . . gives us all the more reason to defend the religious freedom of all men and women today." But everything then turns on what the "inherently public" forces deploying the principle of religious freedom really aim to achieve.

History won't settle America's debates about what religious freedom means. None of the above implies that religious freedom is itself new. Scholar of religion Elaine Pagels has hit on a passage in church father Tertullian, who claimed an amazingly long time ago, *"It is a fundamental human right, a power bestowed by nature, that each person should worship according to his own convictions*, free from compulsion." Yet seen from a different angle, this very right is one that some of its most current partisans, in a new coalition, only discovered recently. If so, the uncomfortable parts of the principle's trajectory matter fully as much as its inspirational parts in showing that the principle is far from straightforward, for it is as much a novel tactic as it is an eternal truth.

Selected Bibliography

Evangelicals and Catholics Together. "In Defense of Religious Freedom: A Statement of Evangelicals and Catholics Together." *First Things*, March 2012.

Hollinger, David. *After Cloven Tongues of Fire: Protestant Liberalism in American History*. Princeton, NJ: Princeton University Press, 2013.

Moyn, Samuel. "From Communist to Muslim: Religious Liberty in European Human Rights Law." *South Atlantic Quarterly* 113, no. 1 (2014): 63–86.

Pagels, Elaine. *Revelations: Visions, Prophecy, and Politics in the Book of Revelation*. New York: Penguin, 2012.

Sehat, David. *The Myth of American Religious Freedom*. New York: Oxford University Press, 2011.

Tocqueville, Alexis de. *Democracy in America*. Translated by George Lawrence. New York: Harper, 1966.

CHAPTER TWELVE

Religious Freedom, Minority Rights, and Geopolitics

Saba Mahmood

The right to religious liberty is widely regarded as a crowning achievement of secular-liberal democracies that guarantees the peaceful coexistence of religiously diverse populations. While all members of a polity are supposed to be protected by the right to religious liberty, religious minorities are understood to be its greatest beneficiaries in the protection it accords them to practice their beliefs freely without fear of state intervention or social discrimination. Conventional wisdom has it that religious liberty is a universally valid principle, enshrined in national constitutions and international charters and treaties, whose proper implementation continues to be thwarted by intransigent forces in society such as illiberal governments, religious fundamentalists, and traditional norms. Inasmuch as the Middle East and the Muslim world in general are supposed to be afflicted with the ills of fundamentalism and illiberal governments, then the salvific promise of religious liberty looms large. In this brief essay, developed more fully elsewhere in my work, I would like to question this way of thinking through a consideration of the career of religious liberty in the modern Middle East.

As I will show, far from being a universally valid, stable principle, the meaning and practice of religious liberty have shifted historically in the Middle East, often in response to geopolitical struggles, the expansion of modern state power, and local regimes of socioreligious inequality. Rather than treat the history of the Middle East as simply one of aberration from a Western norm of tolerance, in what follows I would like to consider how this history makes us rethink the normative claims enfolded in the current advocacy for the right to religious liberty and the universal good it is supposed to facilitate. In offering these reflections my intent is neither to promote nor to reject the right to religious liberty but to force us to consider the contradictions and paradoxes that lie at the foundation of this much-coveted right.

Let us consider briefly the historical trajectory of religious liberty in the late Ottoman Empire, which offers an interesting contrast to its historical unfolding in Western Europe. The modern conception of religious liberty—with its attendant notion of individual conscience and belief as the proper locus of religion—was unknown in the Ottoman Empire until well into the mid-eighteenth century. As is well known, under the Ottoman system "the people of the book" (Christians and Jews) were granted limited collective autonomy over certain juridical affairs (including issues of marriage, family, and worship) but were otherwise treated as socially and politically unequal to Muslims. This juridical autonomy was one of the primary ways in which the Ottomans managed to rule over an immense diversity of religious faiths for over six centuries. It is important to note that this "nonliberal model of pluralism" was different from the liberal model in that each religious community's autonomy was justified not in terms of group versus individual rights but in terms of a political order in which difference was paramount. The Ottomans did not aim to transform political difference into sameness as does the modern nation-state; instead various contiguous religious groups were integrated through a vertical system of hierarchy in which Muslims occupied the highest position. Notably, the liberal individualist notion of civil and political equality that makes the modern conception of freedom of belief possible was not the paradigm in this premodern period.

Things started to change slowly, of course, with the birth of the modern state, wherein the terms *majority* and *minority* came to serve as constitutional devices for managing differences that the ideology of nationalism sought to eradicate, eliminate, or assimilate. The Ottoman Empire formally adopted the right to religious liberty in 1856 (under the famous Hatt-i Hümayun decree) largely under European pressure. This was far from a benign attempt on the part of Europeans to promote religious tolerance in Ottoman lands: their own record toward "Christian dissidents," much less non-Christian minorities, was hardly tolerant at the time. Instead, the European pressure was a product of long-standing geopolitical struggles between Christian European states and the Ottomans.

Christian European rulers had made repeated attempts throughout the sixteenth century to assert their right to protect Christian minorities within Ottoman territories. As long as the Ottoman Empire was strong it was able to accommodate these pressures without compromising its sovereignty, but once Ottoman power started to decline it was unable to resist Western European incursions on behalf of Ottoman Christian groups. As early as the sixteenth century, Ottoman rulers had granted special privileges—known as "capitulations"—to Western European traders that ensured a considerable degree of self-government in matters of criminal and civil jurisdiction as well as freedom of religion and worship. Eventually, as Ottoman power declined, these privileges came to apply not only to Western traders but also to European missionaries and eventually indigenous Ottoman Christian communities (what were then called "Eastern Christians"). Notably, no parallel privileges existed for non-Christians residing in territories ruled by Christian empires at the time. Malcolm Evans, in his magisterial history of the right to religious liberty, notes, "Within this framework, the role of Western European States as protectors of the religious freedom of their subjects within the Ottoman domains easily elided into a claim entitling them to champion the liberties, religious and otherwise, of all Christians in the Empire."

When Ottoman rulers adopted the modern conception of the right to religious liberty in 1856, the fate of non-Muslim communities in the empire was only formally, not substantively, transformed. As historians of the late Ottoman Empire point out, for the Ottoman rulers the right to religious liberty served as a dual means to fend off increasingly powerful Christian missionary movements on the one hand and to shore up the Islamic character of the empire on the other. The empire had already lost large parts of its territory (one-third by 1878), and the Ottoman reformers were eager to bring Christians who had become protégés of foreign states (under the system of capitulations) back under the jurisdiction of the Ottoman state. For many Ottoman Christians, however, the right to religious liberty served as a means of claiming Western protection against systemic discrimination, in the process transforming their identity and self-understanding.

In contrast to the Ottoman rulers and Ottoman Christians, religious liberty meant something quite different to the European missionaries who had considerably expanded their activities in the Muslim world by the nineteenth century. For these missionaries, religious liberty was a crucial means for securing the right to proselytize freely among Muslims and Christians without constraint from existing laws and prohibitions against religious conversion. In Egypt, for example, Euro-American missionaries, who had failed to win converts among Muslims, concentrated their energies on Coptic Orthodox Christians whom they had long regarded with disdain and outright contempt as practitioners of a depraved form of Christianity. Notably, American and European missionaries enjoyed the protection of British colonial authorities in Egypt, and, as Heather Sharkey points out, the colonial period (1882–1918) was the apex of missionary activity in the region. The advantages accorded to Westerners under the Ottoman capitulations proved to be crucial for the missionaries in gaining access to Egyptian rural and urban populations. These missionaries made ubiquitous use of international diplomacy and colonial and foreign offices of Anglo-American governments in their cause, internationally advocating for the adoption of religious liberty in forums as diverse as the League of Nations, the Paris Peace Conference, the US government, and the British Foreign Office. The recent passage of the International Religious Freedom Act by the US Congress (1998) to promote the right of religious liberty (particularly of Christians) in the Middle East must be placed within this long geopolitical history in which Western powers have often violated the principle of state sovereignty under the guise of promoting religious tolerance; no non-Western nation-state in modern history has been able to exert the same pressure to advocate the rights of religious, racial, or ethnic minorities living in Western European and American societies.

Given the history I have tracked here, it is important to realize that the meaning of religious freedom has varied historically in the Middle East depending on the geopolitical position of the players. Furthermore, the career of the right of religious liberty has hardly been one of secular neutrality in the region. Through much of its modern history, the right to religious liberty has served as a means to either promote campaigns of religious proselytization to win Christian converts or to consolidate the majoritarian ethos of the emergent modern state. This history forces us to consider how religious liberty is not simply a juridical means of protecting the individual believer from state coercion. Rather, and crucially, it is a technique of national and international governance whose proper exercise has always entailed concerns of realpolitik.

One may ask at this point, how the religious minorities of the Middle East have been affected by these geopolitical struggles over religious liberty. The answer to this question varies, of course, depending on the history of each nation-state in the region. If we take the example of Coptic Orthodox Christians in Egypt, the largest Christian population in the Middle East, one would need to start with the history of the long-standing rivalry and struggle between Western and Eastern Orthodox Christianity (of which Coptic Christianity is a part). Alistair Hamilton points out that, starting with the Roman Catholic Church and throughout much of modern history, Western Christendom viewed Coptic Christianity as a primitive form of Christianity whose salvation could only come from the West. This view was further entrenched by the wave of Protestant missionaries, initially sent from Europe (Anglicans, Episcopalians, and Lutherans) and later the United States (Presbyterian Evangelicals), none of whom had success with Muslim converts and concentrated their energies on the Copts. In light of this rivalry, it is not surprising that Coptic Christians historically resisted European offers of patronage to "protect and represent" the Copts against Muslim rule. Thus—unlike, for example, the Maronite Christians of Lebanon, who made strong alliances with French colonial powers—the Copts were at the forefront of the anticolonial struggle against the British and were equal players in the shaping of the nationalist project between 1920 and 1950 (Egypt gained independence from colonial rule in 1952).

Despite this distinguished history of Coptic resistance to colonial rule and the enshrinement of the right to religious liberty in the Egyptian constitution, Coptic Christians have continued to suffer from various forms of formal and informal discrimination in postcolonial Egypt. In recent years, the discourse of religious liberty has become a dominant idiom in the Coptic struggle against social and state policies that marginalize Copts on the basis of their religious identity. In this struggle, however, religious liberty once again is not a stable signifier but means very different things to different groups.

At the heart of the contested meaning of religious liberty in Egypt is a political system that has enshrined the Coptic Orthodox Church as the sole representative of the Coptic community and created a church-state entente that makes it difficult for secular-lay Copts to change the terms of debate. As a result, the Coptic Church tends to deploy a communitarian understanding of religious liberty that serves to consolidate its authority over the religious and social life of its followers. This conception sits in tension with an individualist notion advocated by secular human rights activists grounded in the Universal Declaration of Human Rights and the International Covenant on Civil and Political Rights (ICCPR), both of which privilege notions of personal conscience, belief, and individual choice. The Euro-American Coptic diaspora, in alliance with an increasingly powerful Christian evangelical global network, champions a third concept grounded in article 27 of the ICCPR that foregrounds a collective conception of religious freedom as the right of a marginalized minority. Finally, the Egyptian government promotes its own narrow conception of religious liberty aimed at securing the Islamic character of the Egyptian nation and its sovereign power to determine the meaning and scope of religion in society.

It would be wrong to assume that religious liberty consists of simply protecting certain groups or individuals from the exercise of state power (that is, drawing the separation between church and state firmly and resolutely). The people who are supposed to benefit most from the modern principle of religious liberty—namely, religious minorities—are not merely protected from abuses of state power but are also transformed by virtue of their subjection to the calculus of state and geopolitical power in unique and unpredictable ways. The shift, for example, from a group-based understanding of religious liberty to an individualist one in international legal discourse is more than a conceptual one; it also affects the substantive meaning and practice of religious liberty as well as the kinds of subjects who can speak in its name.

In concluding this essay, let me point out that these contrastive deployments of religious liberty are often read as the cynical instrumentalization of an otherwise noble principle in the service of realpolitik or corrupt ends. Seen in this way, the principle itself—its logic, its aim, and its substantive meaning—remains unsullied by the impious intentions of the empires, actors, and states that have sought to promote or subvert it. Such an argument needs to be complicated for several reasons. As I have shown, far from being a measure of a culture's intolerance, religious freedom has been tied from its very inception to the exercise of sovereign power, regional and national security, and the inequality of geopolitical power relations in the Middle East. These differential meanings must be understood, I want to insist, not simply as opportunistic deployments of a single noble principle but as reflective of the contradictions and paradoxes internal to the conceptual architecture of the right to religious liberty itself and its global history. Inasmuch as the right to religious liberty is enabled by conditions of geopolitical inequality and differential sovereignty between the First and Third Worlds, it behooves us to rethink the global good its advocates often promise to all peoples of the world. Indeed, if the universal promotion of religious liberty has been ridden with colonial and neocolonial agendas, then how does one grapple with the legitimate and important question of providing protections to religious minorities across the Western and non-Western divide? What other procedural, legal, and social mechanisms do modern polities make possible that can be separated from the exercise of geopolitical domination, interests, and power? Is such a separation possible not just conceptually but practically given the intractability of politics in all human rights struggles of our times?

Selected Bibliography

Evans, Malcolm. *Religious Liberty and International Law in Europe.* Cambridge: Cambridge University Press, 2008.

Hamilton, Alistair. *The Copts and the West, 1439–1822: The European Discovery of the Egyptian Church.* New York: Oxford University Press, 2006.

Mahmood, Saba. "Religious Freedom, the Minority Question, and Geopolitics in the Middle East." *Comparative Studies in Society and History* 54, no. 2 (2012): 418–46.

Sharkey, Heather J. *American Evangelicals in Egypt: Missionary Encounters in an Age of Empire.* Princeton, NJ: Princeton University Press, 2008.

CHAPTER THIRTEEN

Ceylon/Sri Lanka

*The Politics of Religious Freedom
and the End of Empire*

Benjamin Schonthal

In May 2005 the United Nations deployed to Sri Lanka its special rapporteur on religious freedom, Asma Jahangir, with the mandate of examining the growing violence between Buddhists and Christians on the island. In a highly publicized visit, Jahangir stayed in Sri Lanka for nearly two weeks, interviewing politicians, religious leaders, human rights activists, and lawyers. Returning to Geneva, she produced a final report that linked the island's religious strife to the government's failure to adequately protect religious freedom. Her conclusion announced:

111. The right to freedom of religion or belief is a universal right enjoyed by all human beings and therefore by members of all religious communities, whether old or new and whether they have been established in a country for a long time or recently.

112. In this context, the Special Rapporteur condemns all acts of religious violence and intolerance that have been committed in Sri Lanka against any religious communities, but also within religious communities. These acts depending on the circumstances constitute violations, or unlawful limitations of the right to freedom of religion or belief.

113. The Sri Lankan Government has to fulfill its positive obligations under the right to freedom of religion or belief of all its citizens, irrespective of the religious community to which they belong. These positive obligations include,

first and foremost, the prompt investigation of any act of religious violence of intolerance, the prosecution of all perpetrators and the awarding of compensation to the victims of these violations.

In Jahangir's report, the term *religious freedom* names multiple referents. It refers to an ideal social condition, one in which persons live unburdened from unwanted encroachments on their "religious" lives. It also refers to a set of legal norms designed to bring about that social condition, norms that Jahangir takes to be embodied in UN charters, particularly in the International Covenant on Civil and Political Rights. In both uses, religious freedom is opposed to violence and intolerance, such that the "restoration" of religious freedom depends upon dealing with the causes and consequences of violence (i.e., prosecuting perpetrators and compensating victims).

Jahangir's multivalent use of religious freedom is by no means unusual. Increasingly, when one looks at the writings of policy makers, human rights activists, and even scholars, one sees that the term *religious freedom* names not one singular object *in* the world but an argument *about* the world. The standard argument goes something like this: governments should work to create an ideal social condition (religious freedom) through the elaborating and enforcing of discrete rules (rights to religious freedom) that if properly administered set the conditions for peaceful coexistence among members of a polity. Cast as an argument, the logic of religious freedom depends upon a quasi-Platonic separation of aspired-to ideals from degenerate realities. The appeal of religious freedom lies precisely in its assumed extraction from—or, rather, elevation over—the hurly-burly of politics and the one-sided interests of partisan groups. The pacific and pacifying powers of religious freedom seem to derive from the fact that religious freedom (in its social and legal manifestations) stands outside of struggles for power as a polestar that can guide political action without being contaminated by it.

The problem with this vision of religious freedom—and the religious rights understood to effect and protect it—is that it tends to obscure the specific, historical conditions that lead to the drafting of religious rights in the first place. Religious rights did not spring forth into history fully formed and self-interpreting; laws designed to protect religious freedom were in all cases born in drafting committees, honed through negotiation, and marked—dare I say it—by the pocks of political conflict. What Evan Haefeli says of toleration in this volume one might also say of religious rights: they are "polemical tools" used in political battles. Religious free-dom and religious rights are not the antitheses of fractious politics; they are the outcomes of politics.

The marks of political conflict can be seen clearly in the language of re-ligious rights, if one knows where to look. In most cases, the marks are not found in the dictionary definitions of those words used to make law, but in the strategies of legal borrowing and omission used to frame law. Drafts-persons use verbatim borrowing to signal distinct political affiliations and to silence political opponents. One's choice of terms bears the marks of political calculation and struggle as much as—if not more than—the marks of negotiated settlement. As such, one should not read religious rights as transcending politics but as recoding and transmogrifying it—transforming struggles for power into struggles over the language and laws used to moralize power.

Religious Rights at Empire's End

To see this process, one has to begin with the texts of religious freedom provisions and to work backward. To do so is to treat religious rights not as the solution to the problem of religious strife or persecution but as a problem itself, or at least as an object to be explained: Why this render-ing of rights and not another? Why religious rights at all? Why now?

Take, for example, the legal rendering of "religious freedom" from a draft constitution in Sri Lanka from the I940s. The text reads, "Freedom of conscience and free profession and practice of religion, subject to pub-lic order and morality, are hereby guaranteed to every citizen. The [Free Lanka] Republic shall not prohibit the free exercise of any religion or give preference or impose any disability on account of religion, belief or status." This statement appears unremarkable, even vaguely familiar—a bland collection of legal guarantees similar to those found in other trans-national religious freedom instruments, such as article I8 of the Univer-sal Declaration of Human Rights and the International Covenant on Civil and Political Rights (ICCPR). The statement guarantees citizens' rights to freedom of conscience, religious practice, and free exercise, and prohibits discrimination on the basis of religion. Much like the ICCPR, it prescribes certain limits on these freedoms (in the interests of "public order and morality"). Also like the ICCPR, it blends together positive and negative freedoms, freedoms *to* profess and practice, and freedoms *from* state impediments to religion and discrimination on the basis of religion.

Given the language of the Sri Lankan statement, one would expect that such an expression of religious freedom would not be controversial or alarming to political leaders. Indeed, if one looks at the meanings of the words themselves, there is nothing to suggest such polemics. However, if we look again, situating this iteration of religious freedom in its own historical context, it appears anything but anodyne. For politicians at the time, the statement was extremely provocative, both in its language and format. Far from a bland promise of religious freedom, it was a carefully crafted protest against empire. Coded within the language of religious rights was an only partially concealed strain of invective against British colonialism and a strong call for a more activist, more radical, more India-like nationalist movement.

This otherwise banal-seeming statement of religious freedom was, in fact, a key salvo in a contentious political battle taking place in late colonial Ceylon. The paragraph on religious freedom was one of thirteen paragraphs of rights compiled in a bill of rights, all of which were embedded in a draft constitution for "Free Lanka." The constitution was prepared in 1943 by a group of Ceylonese politicians who hoped it might serve as a legal charter under which the British Crown would transfer powers of self-government to a local Ceylonese parliament. A key feature of the draft was that, unlike other drafts prepared at the time it was not produced in consultation with British officials; it was the work of a cohort of young nationalists—affectionately and disparagingly dubbed the Young Turks—who rejected the idea that an outgoing British government should "give" to Ceylon the legal charter that announced its independence. Ceylonese would demand self-rule from the British, and the Young Turks would lead the charge.

In the broadest sense, the Young Turks included a section on fundamental rights in their constitution in order to mark their anticolonialist bona fides. They recognized that in the 1940s fundamental rights were taboo for Crown constitution makers. British legal advisers who participated in the drafting of independence constitutions throughout the colonies followed a Colonial Office policy regarding "bills of rights": they were not to be included. Legal historian S. A. de Smith quotes one influential British constitution maker of the period, Ivor Jennings, as saying "an English lawyer is apt to shy away from [fundamental rights] like a horse from a ghost." Officially, British legalists opposed justiciable bills of rights because they were not part of modern English law and because, they argued, such rights might undercut parliamentary sovereignty by requiring that the future legislators adhere to certain core political values as defined by current legislators—a requirement that would, therefore, inhibit legal institutions from adapting to new circumstances, values, and ways of life. Unofficially British legalists recognized an inconvenient friction between bills of rights and the colonial project as a whole: if the Crown were to acknowledge and entrench fundamental rights as absolute and binding on governments, it would risk exposing the illegitimacy of colonialism more generally, insofar as colonial governments acted without consideration of such basic rights.

The drafters of the Free Lanka constitution recognized this and framed religious freedom as a fundamental right (situated within a longer bill of rights) as way to amplify the anti-British tenor of the draft. In speeches, newspaper articles, and letters to overseas' organizations, especially the Indian National Congress, the drafters directly linked the push for fundamental constitutional rights with the campaign for independence from British rule. These advocates claimed that the British, as participants in the newly formed allied United Nations, were bound by the "human rights" expressed in the Declaration by the United Nations and therefore must acknowledge and grant to Ceylonese the same basic rights as they granted to others. In a manifesto drafted slightly later, the drafters of the Sri Lankan religious freedom provision even outlined a program of "five freedoms" for Ceylon—deliberately echoing Franklin Delano Roosevelt's famous fourfold formulation—of which the first was "The Freedom from Foreign Rule."

By articulating religious freedom through the idiom of fundamental rights, drafters gestured toward sources of legitimacy that were separate from (if not directly dominant over) the British Crown. They plotted religious rights, and their constitution as a whole, within a legal and philosophical terrain that treated rights *not* as benevolences extended by rulers but as guarantees that conditioned the legitimacy of rule itself: governments did not authenticate rights; rights authenticated governments. This alternative approach to the legitimacy and the origin of rights had radical implications. On the one hand, drafters were able to (and did) criticize the colonial government's legitimacy by accusing it of failing to grant adequate fundamental rights to those who lived in Ceylon. On the other hand, they simultaneously claimed *as* a fundamental right "the right to independence and a free constitution"—thereby analogizing the political independence of the island to the corporeal independence of its citizens.

The young nationalists' push for a chapter on fundamental rights was calibrated to not only echo human rights discourse among the Allies but also to signal affinity with the work of the Indian National Congress (INC) and its successive efforts across the Palk Strait to produce a Declaration of Fundamental Rights for the subcontinent in 1928, 1931, and 1944. Many of the Young Turks praised the INC for its more strident, assertive, powerful strain of anticolonial nationalism, one that they felt the Ceylonese politicians ought to emulate. Members of the Young Turks had very close relations with the INC, attending important meetings of the congress between 1920 and 1948 (such as those at Ramgarh in March 1940 and Bombay in July 1942) and emulating key features of its politics, including the emphasis on "national dress" and policies of rural uplift. By 1940 there was even talk of the Ceylon National Congress joining the INC as a branch organization. During this period of close engagement between the two congresses, Ceylonese nationalists indicated publically their approval of the declarations of fundamental rights produced by the INC in the Nehru Report of 1928, then in the Karachi Resolution of 1931, and in the recommendations of the Sapru Committee in 1944. The Young Turks' constitutional bill of rights—and its section on religious freedom—was influenced by the Indian model, and in 1945 members even drafted their own separate Declaration of Fundamental Rights which reproduced virtually verbatim the bills of rights contained in the Nehru and Sapru Reports. The Young Turks therefore hoped to use the INC's language of fundamental rights to signal their alignment with radical anticolonialism in South Asia more generally and to remake the Ceylonese independence movements in the image of the Indian ones.

Yet the drafting of the religious freedom paragraph in the Free Lanka constitution also targeted a more immediate local audience. The paragraph on religious freedom was designed in opposition to another paragraph on religious freedom that had been framed, only months earlier, by Jennings, one of Britain's leading constitutional scholars at the time and the author of the derisive assessment of fundamental rights quoted earlier. In a separate constitutional draft read by the Young Turks, Jennings proposed to ensure religious freedom by placing certain minimal limits on the lawmaking powers of parliament. In Jennings's version, religious freedom was to be secured by preventing lawmakers from enacting bills that would confer advantages or disadvantages on particular religious communities, impinge upon the "free exercise" of religion, or "alter the constitution of any religious body." When compared with Jennings's formula, it was not only the inclusion of religious rights within a bill of rights that distinguished the nationalists' draft but also the nature of the rights chosen. Whereas Jennings rendered religious freedom through a series of negative legislative prohibitions, the nationalists framed religious freedom in terms of positive as well as negative liberties, prescribing not only limits on government's powers but also guarantees of state protection for religious lives. Their limits and guarantees would apply not only to legislatures and lawmakers, but to all agents and actions of the republic.

More notably, the difference between the Young Turks' and Jennings's drafts reflected a distinct conflict in the politics of legal borrowing. Jennings modeled his religious freedom paragraph on provisions contained in the Ireland Act of 1920, a law ratified by the British Parliament, which, though it permitted limited Irish "home rule," maintained London's claims to the island. In an opposing move, the nationalists' paragraph on religious freedom took its language from the 1937 Constitution of Ireland, a document that aimed to establish total Irish independence from the British. As one of the Ceylonese drafters, Joseph A. L. Cooray, put it, the "Free Lanka" Constitution drew from a text that effected in Ireland "a definitive break with the past" and "conduct[ed] what, in law, was a revolution." For legal professionals and politicians at the time the implication was clear: the Young Turks demanded independence modeled on the more complete sovereignty of Ireland post-1937, not the partial sovereignty of Ireland in 1920.

Yet the anti-Jennings thrust of the Young Turks' work had also had a more academic, historical significance. In following the INC in its push for fundamental rights, the Young Turks were also taking sides against Ivor Jennings in an academic debate with one of his best-known scholarly interlocutors: Harold Laski, a constitutional scholar with whom Jennings had taught at the London School of Economics. Laski had been a significant inspiration for the drafters of fundamental rights in India, and it was Laski's legal theories that had provided much of the academic justification for demanding a bill of rights in what would become the new Indian constitution. During their time at the London School of Economics, the topic of bills of rights had divided Jennings and Laski, and in the years that followed Jennings argued consistently (until the late 1950s) against the inclusion of fundamental rights in constitutions, while Laski insisted that specially elaborated bills of rights were essential as mechanisms for preserving human freedoms. Many of those who were instrumental in

defending fundamental rights in India and Ceylon had been students of
Laski, and these former students presented the Ceylon Congress with not
only an alternative template of constitution making but also an alternative constitutional scholar on whose authority they might rely.

Rereading Religious Rights

We can now view the Young Turks' construction of religious rights in
a new light: as a polemic against British colonial policies, particularly
Crown opposition to bills of rights; as the affirmation of a vision of legal
sovereignty (drawn from the nascent human rights discourse of the allied
United Nations) that rendered colonialism illegitimate and treated constitutions not as something "given" by colonial powers but as something
claimed by citizens; as a demonstration of Ceylonese solidarity with the
Indian National Congress and its more aggressive anticolonial nationalism; as a rejection of the constitution-drafting work of Ivor Jennings and
an affirmation of alternative theories of constitutional law (those of Harold Laski); and as a claim to full and complete sovereignty in the manner
of Ireland after 1937, not after 1920.

Rehistoricized, the language of religious freedom and religious rights
represents not the transcendence of discord—a movement toward shared
affirmation of a single moral and legal good—but instead the transformation of discord into competing legal ideas and ideals. That is, the legal
syntax of religious rights, read against the grain and examined in context,
reveals the very thing that discourses of religious freedom and religious
rights tend to elide: the fragile, contingent, interested, political origins of
religious rights and the embeddedness of rights discourse in larger local,
regional, and global struggles for power and control.

The nationalists' paragraph on religious rights was not included in
Ceylon's independence constitution. And this is part of the story too.
What determined the shape of religious rights in 1940s Sri Lanka (and
elsewhere in South Asia) was not simply a concern with the importance
of resolving religious disputes or protecting religious communities but a
preoccupation with ensuring that the language chosen signaled the right
alliances and the appropriate politics. In Ceylon, where the handover of
power occurred exclusively by way of negotiation with the British Crown,
colonial politics prevailed over anticolonial politics, and Jennings's draft,
rather than the nationalists' draft, served as template for the 1948 Ceylon

Constitution. In India, where anticolonial movements had much greater influence on the process of decolonization, a new, more nationalistic constitution (completed by a sovereign Constituent Assembly just after independence) cast religious freedoms in the idiom of fundamental rights. In each case, the rhetoric of religious freedom bears the marks of struggle more than resolution. It imprints the politics of the 1940s: the politics of fundamental rights, the politics of colonial resistance, and the politics of constitution making in the twilight of empire.

Selected Bibliography

Ceylon National Congress. *25 Years—But Yet!* Colombo: n.p., 1946.

Cooray, Joseph A. L. "Human Rights and Their Protection in Ceylon." In *Constitutional Government and Human Rights in a Developing Society*. Colombo, Ceylon: Colombo Apothecaries, 1969.

De Silva, K. M. *A History of Sri Lanka*. Colombo, Sri Lanka: Vijitha Yapa, 2005.

De Silva, K. M., and Howard Wriggens. *J. R. Jayawardena of Sri Lanka*. 2 vols. London: Anthony Blond Quartet, 1988.

De Smith, S.A. *The New Commonwealth and Its Constitutions*. London: Stevens and Sons, 1964.

Ewing, K. D. "Law and the Constitution: Manifesto of the Progressive Party." *Modern Law Review* 67 (2004): 734–52.

Jahangir, Asma. *Report of the Special Rapporteur on Freedom of Religion or Belief, Asma Jahangir, on Her Mission to Sri Lanka. U.N. Doc. E/CN.4/2006/5/ Add.3 (Dec. 12, 2005)*. Accessed March 15, 2012 at http://daccess-dds-ny.un.org /doc/UNDOC/GEN/G05/166/64/PDF/G0516664.pdf?OpenElement.

Laski, Harold J. *Liberty in the Modern State*. New York: Harper, 1930.

———. *The Rise of European Liberalism*. Edited by John Stanley. New Brunswick, NJ: Transaction, 1997.

Parkinson, Charles O. H. *Bills of Rights and Decolonization: The Emergence of Domestic Human Rights Instruments in Britain's Overseas Territories*. Oxford: Oxford University Press, 2007.

Roberts, Michael, ed. *Documents of the Ceylon National Congress and Nationalist Politics in Ceylon 1929–1950*. 4 vols. Colombo: National Archives Department, 1965.

Welikala, Asanga. "The Failure of Jennings' Constitutional Experiment in Ceylon: How 'Procedural Entrenchment' Led to Constitutional Revolution." In *The Sri Lankan Republic at 40: Reflections on Constitutional History, Theory and Practice*, edited by Asanga Welikala. Colombo, Sri Lanka: Centre for Policy Alternatives, 2012.

CHAPTER FOURTEEN

Liberty as Recognition

Nandini Chatterjee

Adopted in 1950, article 17 of the Constitution of India legally abolished untouchability, the ancient Hindu system of social discrimination, forbidding its practice in any form and making the enforcement of any discrimination arising out of this disability a criminal offense. At the same time, the constitution guaranteed freedom of religious belief and practice under article 25, the autonomy of religious institutions under article 26, and the right of religious and linguistic minorities to establish and administer educational institutions under article 30. There was an obvious contradiction between these two sets of constitutional provisions, one aimed at social justice and the other at ensuring religious freedom, a contradiction that subsequently produced a very substantial volume of case law and legal scholarship. Recent scholarship on legal and political developments elsewhere, such as Winnifred Fallers Sullivan's essay in this volume, suggests that this contradiction is less locally specific than was earlier believed.

In decisions since the 1990s, the US Supreme Court has asserted the transcendence of law, prohibiting the use of certain intoxicating substances in worship or gender-based discrimination in state-subsidized schools run by churches and religious groups. In reaction an unprecedentedly broad spectrum of groups has begun demanding protection for the autonomy of religious institutions as a principle in its own right. As Sullivan's essay suggests, this inchoate but increasingly intractable demand is less about doctrine or religious ceremony and more about jurisdictional autonomy of something far less defined than church (hence "religion") and the state. Sullivan sees this genre of claims as a naïve effort to create something akin to the *ancien régime* establishment despite, or because of, the historical fact that Americans have never experienced such a legal and institutional connection between church and state.

In this essay I will reflect upon the possibility that the claim of jurisdictional autonomy in fact implies and entails a demand for state support—a form of establishment. As with early modern English republicans deploying the neoclassical idea of liberty of the body politic, any such claim of freedom seeks not mere nonintervention by the state but also demands state recognition of prior constitution—of the body that seeks to be free. The implications of such recognition and endorsement are naturally variable and depend on the social location of the specific claims. But I would argue that in all cases legal demands for religious freedom encapsulate and entail a formal recognition by the state of persons, institutions, material belongings, and social groups as constituting the religious body whose freedom is sought.

I will apply this idea to three sets of legal and political contests in India, stretching from the 1830s to the 1990s. The first set of debates concerned the internal regulation of a religious community—specifically, the arraignment of caste hierarchy in certain Protestant congregations in southern India in the 1830s. The second set, stretching from the 1930s to the 1960s, consisted once again of the regulation of caste—this time in relation to Hindu religious institutions. The last set deals with legislation, legal disputes, and administrative developments related to privately managed, state-supervised, and state-subsidized educational institutions, which have acquired the administrative nomenclature of Minority Educational Institutions. Religion and social hierarchy (in the culturally specific form of caste) thread in and out of all these disputes, as do debates over the content and purpose of religion and the appropriate authority for determining these. Above all, what connects all these disparate disputes is the persistent appeal to religious freedom, albeit articulated in various vocabularies. Unsurprisingly, the precise body or subject whose freedom was advocated in each of these debates, and the variety of protagonists involved in these instances of advocacy, varied widely. Nevertheless, in all of them the advocates of liberty explicitly sought state endorsement of their positions, in some cases more successfully than others. I will discuss the implications of actual or proposed state endorsement of such claims in my concluding comments.

I begin with the story of a diverse, fractured, and small religious community, statistically significant only in the southern part of the Indian subcontinent. There have been ancient Orthodox churches in India since the fourth century CE, possibly even from the first century, and Catholic congregations led by Counter-Reformation European missions have existed since the sixteenth century. But Christianity entered the demographic map of India only with large-scale group conversions of the most marginalized Indians—*dalits* (the erstwhile "untouchables") and members of various indigenous groups incompletely incorporated into any of the overarching religions and officially designated "tribals"—in the late nineteenth and early twentieth centuries. My first set of disputes relates to Anglican mission churches in the period immediately prior to such mass conversions. These disputes, which took place in the 1830s, were about the doctrinal acceptability of caste-based segregation in the mission churches, and, as a corollary, about the appropriate authority for making and applying the rules of religious life.

In 1826 the second Anglican bishop of Calcutta, the metropolitan of India, Reginald Heber, had observed the practice and concluded that caste was similar to its European eponym *casta*—being the result of natural social divisions and hence doctrinally neutral, or at the most akin to the "prejudices" of the ancient Jews and hence deserving Pauline tolerance. Historians of Protestant missions note that subsequent incumbents, especially Bishop Daniel Wilson in office 1832–58, came to the conclusion that caste was indeed part of the Hindu sacral complex, a hindrance to the spread of Christianity, and inhumane, and therefore to be discarded. What have remained unexamined in scholarship are the regulatory mechanisms through which this social discipline was imposed on the erring Indian congregations.

In 1829 even before the reforming Bishop Wilson had arrived, a new generation of Continental Pietist missionaries employed by the Anglican Society for the Propagation of Christian Knowledge Mission provoked a schism in the Indian—or, in missionary parlance, "native"—congregation of the Anglican Church in Mysore. They did so by insisting on, among other things, the desegregation of church services and the deployment of a lower-caste pastor to minister to the congregation. Following the expulsion of the poet Vedanayagam Pillai, one of the most eminent members of the congregation, the recalcitrant upper-caste segment of the congregation attempted to distance itself from what it saw as ritually polluted religious ceremonies by holding services in the churchyard. When prohibited from doing so by the missionaries, this segment petitioned the British governor of Madras, complaining of deprivation of the upper

caste members' collective property—the church that had been built with
their contributions. Using more exalted and shorter lines of communication with the political authorities, Bishop Wilson was able to convince
the government of India (and in turn the government of the presidency
of Madras) that the dispute merely concerned matters of ecclesiastical
discipline and hence was exclusively within the jurisdiction of church authorities. The Court of Directors of the East India Company—that is, the
ultimate political authority for British-ruled India at that time—wrote
from London approving of this outcome. Unsurprisingly the congregation split, and Anglican commentators reported with disgust that the Roman Catholic Church was not above welcoming the insubordinate Indian
Christians into its fold.

By the 1930s the dramatis personae had been significantly rear-
ranged, but the plot remained similar. The denunciation of caste as inhumane, socially regressive, and un-Hindu had become a widely (although
by no means universally) shared position among Indians—especially the
public-spirited, the reformists, and the nationalists. Indeed, under Mahatma Gandhi's leadership, the Indian National Congress required its
members literally to sign on to a renunciation of caste as the prerequisite
of membership. Among the many disparate social agendas embraced and
appropriated by the Congress in the twentieth century was the "temple
entry" movement—that is, the efforts of *dalit* leaders to breach the centuries of prejudice that had excluded them from Hindu religious buildings.
Thus during the 1933 debates in the semi-elected Imperial Legislative
Council (which made laws for all of British-ruled India), the nationalist-
reformists assumed a position similar to that of the Pietist missionaries,
with the difference that their procaste opponents consisted not of Hindu
templegoers in general, but the powerful and entrenched managers of
the very wealthy and lightly supervised Hindu religious institutions. The
Shankaracharya of Puri, one of the most important *mahants* (poorly
translatable as "abbot") in the country, sent a telegram of protest: "Do
you really claim that questions relating to medicine, engineering, etc.,
and to religious faith can be determined by referendum and especially by
legislators not returned on such tickets or that it is moral or even constitutional to force such decisions on sincere Sanatanists however misguided
you may deem them? Why this playing to the gallery and dancing to the
tune of renegades from Sanatanism and true constitutionalism? Surely
this is unworthy of you. Reflect and turn back. It is not too late now."
The Shankaracharya, quite like the Pietist missionaries of a century ago,

was making a claim for the state recognition of the autonomy of religious institutions and, even more specifically, for the recognition of the existing structure of authority within them. That the Shankaracharya was a trained medical doctor before entering his religious life perhaps explains his conceptualization of religious authority as deriving from professional specialization rather than ordination or spiritual achievement.

These conservative efforts to prevent the reformist reconceptualization of the content of religion, limits of religious community, and structure of religious authority were defeated to some extent, the reformist victory being enshrined in the Indian constitution, promulgated in 1950. Article 25, which guaranteed freedom of religion, was qualified by clause 2, which provided, "Nothing in this article shall affect the operation of any existing law or prevent the State from making any law . . . b) providing for social welfare and reform or the throwing open of Hindu religious institutions of a public character to all classes and sections of Hindus."

The law almost begged for the slew of cases that followed, all hinging on the inherent contradiction between religious freedom conceptualized as jurisdictional autonomy and religious freedom conceptualized as social justice and justifying state intervention. Quite like the upper-caste Indian Anglicans who, when defeated, chose to be Catholics, those opposed to such changes attempted to position themselves legally in terms of alternative non-Hindu religious identities.

In a famous case decided by the Supreme Court of India, Gouda Saraswath Brahman trustees of the temple of Sri Venkataramanah in Mulki, South Karnataka, attempted to keep their temple free of pollution by *dalits* by claiming that it was a denominational temple and hence entitled to limit its benefits to members of the denomination or those admitted at their discretion. In response the activist court stated that the constitutional clauses enabling the state to open Hindu temples to all Hindus (including *dalits*) overrode all other considerations. The Gujarati Swaminarayan Sampradaya or Satsangis took this pattern of oppositional argument one step further, claiming not to be Hindus at all. Chief Justice P. J. Gajendragarkar, an activist judge if there ever was one, refused the Satsangis their route of escape through religious redefinition, informing them that the constitutional obligations of modern Indian Hindus remained incumbent upon them. In another important case involving authority over Hindu religious institutions, the Madras High Court explained why the Indian judiciary could take an openly activist stance and restrict the interpretation of religious freedom in the cause of social justice. The case tested the constitutional validity of an act that was passed by the state of Madras in 1951 that reinforced the power of a government department called the Hindu Religious and Charitable Endowments Commission to inspect and supervise Hindu temples and *maths* (monasteries) and audit their accounts. The law was the product of campaigns spread over a century, all aiming to make Hinduism ethical and democratic and Hindu religious property subject to the wishes of a Hindu religious public. Opponents argued that the law conflicted with the other religious freedom provision in the Indian Constitution, article 26, which provided that:

> Freedom to manage religious affairs: Subject to public order, morality and health, every religious denomination or any section thereof shall have the right
>
> > to establish and maintain institutions for religious and charitable purposes;
> >
> > to manage its own affairs in matters of religion;
> >
> > to own and acquire movable and immovable property; and
> >
> > to administer such property in accordance with law.

Explaining why these and other freedom of religion clauses did not offer a secure escape route from the reformist agenda of the Indian state, judges noted that India was not America—in India there was no rigid wall of separation between church and state.

This reformist confidence quickly waned in the aftermath of the horrors of a secularist and unconstitutional government (the so-called Indian Emergency of 1975–77) and the subsequent rise of politically successful ethnonationalism, describing itself as "Hinduness" or *Hindutva*. Ironically this political development led not only to the spectacle of Hindu ascetics doubling as demagogues but also to the intensification of the policy and politics of minority recognition. Indian critics suggest that such politics entails treating minorities and other groups based on ascriptive identity as "vote banks"—that is, likely to vote collectively for a party or leader that endorses what is asserted and recognized as key demands of the group. In practice, "vote bank" politics consists of a vicious circle of constant negative stereotyping and victimization in politics, media, and social life, compensated by strategic concessions to self-styled but government-recognized "community leaders." As the most studied instances demonstrate, such concessions tend to be made to patriarchal individuals and entities, achieving two sets of recognition at once—the claim of such entities to represent the community, and the claim by the wider public that the community is backward, politically deviant, and exceptional.

Once again this process has produced a side stream of institutional developments that have attracted less attention but nevertheless represent a crucial stage in the history of defining and recognizing religion in the context of governance. This consists of the legal and bureaucratic rise of the category known as Minority Educational Institutions (MEIs). The concept of MEIs is based on article 26 (see above), and article 30 of the Indian Constitution, which states, "All minorities, whether based on religion or language, shall have the right to establish and administer educational institutions of their choice." The question that has occupied the Supreme Court of India several times since the 1950s, but with increasing frequency since the 1990s, is the degree of autonomy from state supervision this article entails for an educational institution established by a group defined as religious and specifically considered to be a minority. Examining recent cases in detail reveals how the social parameters of the contest over religious freedom have evolved in India since the 1950s. The most important distinction is that rather than ritual hierarchy, contests over the freedom of religious institutions are now explicitly over the allocation of scarce resources such as educational facilities and government employment.

In 1992 the Supreme Court decided that St. Stephen's College, one of the most prestigious colleges in northern India and originally established by the Anglican Cambridge Mission to Delhi, could reserve no more than 50 percent of its places for Christian students. Traditionally St. Stephen's had never achieved anything more than a smattering of Christian students and until that point had demonstrated no particular inclination for admitting them over others. The question of religious autonomy was precipitated by the college's effort to seek freedom from the cumbrous entrance procedures of Delhi University, with which it was affiliated. The college did so by arguing that it had the right to define and manage its own admission procedures per article 30 of the Indian Constitution. This victory was subsequently questioned several times in the Supreme Court, and in 2002 an eleven-member constitutional bench concluded that the right of St. Stephen's and other MEIs to institutional autonomy was necessarily compromised by taking state aid and accepting the consequent obligations, such as a transparent process of admissions and attention to merit in selecting candidates for higher university and professional degrees.

These and several other disputes led to the formation of the National Commission for Minority Educational Institutions in 2005, which offered bureaucratic umbrella protection to institutions deemed MEIs against potentially unconstitutional intervention by supervisory bodies, such as affiliating universities. Arguably, shorn of the constitutional framing of its case, such protection would have been unnecessary for St. Stephen's College, for the Supreme Court's plea for efficiency and merit was indeed its main concern. Legal developments have their own momentum, however, and despite predictions of doom from (non-Christian) Indian notables, many of whom had been educated at St. Stephen's, the college has undergone important changes in its social orientation, not only declaring itself a "Christian foundation" on its website but reserving 40 percent of its places for Christian applicants, including *dalit* Christians. It is possible that, in this case, an artificial legal definition (as a Christian institution and hence an MEI) may have moved this institution toward performing the socially transformative role that it never essayed thus far.

There is, however, a further aspect to the St. Stephen's case that complicates what might have been a story of progress toward equity and justice. The constitutionally provided and judicially confirmed autonomy of MEIs may have endorsed (or as with St. Stephen's, enabled) their reserving of places for members of the religious (or, in some cases, linguistic) community in question, but it has also afforded them a path of exit from affirmative action policies with relation to caste. Thus, of its 60 percent remaining places, St. Stephen's reserves 15 percent for non-Christian Scheduled Caste/*dalit* and Scheduled Tribe students ("scheduled" referring to the schedule or list of the Constitutional Order of 1950, which listed those groups so defined and hence entitled to benefit from affirmative action policies). The quotas maintained by St. Stephen's are far lower than the legal requirement for all other colleges affiliated with the University of Delhi. However, being an MEI, St. Stephen's is within legal bounds when not complying fully with affirmative action policies incumbent upon state-funded or state-supported educational institution. Recent legislation has restated such legal exceptions. For example, the 2006 Central Educational Institutions (Reservations in Admission) Act required all universities to reserve 27 percent of seats for "Other Backward

Castes" in addition to the 15 percent for Scheduled Castes and 7.5 percent for Scheduled Tribes already in place. Universities were also required to increase the number of places available so as not to reduce opportunities for admission available for other students. Minority Educational Institutions were explicitly exempt from this requirement. Being a "minority," then, offers autonomy from state intervention but also carries various other social implications.

*   *   *

In conclusion, then, we might ask, what do these claims and counterclaims over the nature, implications, and boundaries of religion do? It has been argued by some authors in this volume (Elizabeth Shakman Hurd, Webb Keane) that they produce a belief-centric understanding of religion such that ritual and practice come to be excised from what is—in a Protestant Christian perspective—considered to be true religion, and which (they argue) became the dominant paradigm because of the historical reality of colonialism with its hierarchies of knowledge and power. I do not entirely agree with this conclusion. It appears to me that, in spite of the demonstrably greater frequency of appeals to it, "belief" continues to be only one—and not necessarily the most important—way in which modern Indians, despite their colonial experience, define religion. When seeking liberty on a religious basis, whether they are seeking autonomy or social justice, disputants in the contexts I have described referred in variable combinations to authority, belonging, and ethics. In the debates within Indian churches, divided by race and caste, the dispute over church ceremonial and the control of sacred space was very much about establishing who was entitled to claim authority over both. Bishop Daniel Wilson's successful claim of institutional autonomy in that context translated into the state's recognition of his own authority within the church and that of European missionaries in charge of Indian congregations. This view of religious authority was challenged by Indian congregants positing a different principle—that of public property. Since they had paid for it, they said, the church was theirs in which to worship as they saw fit. The codefinition of property and the public is a neglected dimension in the history of religious modernization on the Indian subcontinent, one that can also be seen to be animating the efforts of Hindu, Muslim, and other reformists attempting—throughout the nineteenth and early twentieth centuries—to gain control over religious institutions and to dislodge those that they saw as corrupt, self-serving (as opposed to public-minded) priests. If this was the view of the improbably designated "father of modern India" Rammohan Roy (d. 1833), this was also the view of activist lawyers and judges such as Gajendragadkar. Between the 1930s and the 1960s, such reformers of Hinduism appear to have won a partial victory—hence the conservative efforts to reclaim their autonomy (and authority) through redefinition of themselves as not Hindu. That moment passed, and with the rise of a different model of populist Hinduism what we are now seeing is the legal and bureaucratic ethnicization of minority religions. Partly this is a defensive measure deemed necessary in the context of aggressive majoritarianism. On the other hand, it may also be, as I have discussed above, an unfortunate route of escape from social justice, which ironically replicates the Hindu conservative escapism of the 1950s and '60s. The implications have not been fully revealed.

Scholarship on religious change in the modern world has now reached the point at which we can reject the view that these developments are somehow exclusively or uniquely Indian. When in the 1960s eminent American scholars commented (largely negatively) on the Indian judiciary's predilection for unseemly meddling in religious matters, Marc Galanter struck a solo note by arguing that the Indian case was neither unique nor necessarily distinct from the American one. Anticipating Talal Asad, he observed, "No secular state is or can be merely neutral or impartial among religions, for the State defines the boundaries within which neutrality must operate."

But however universal these legal conundrums are revealed to be, it remains the case that they star in the spotlight only at specific moments and in certain contexts. In explaining the timing of such intellectual and political crises, one has of course to refer to geopolitical events and trends, but one might also argue for the importance of the social content. For example, it may appear that, as Sullivan points out, Americans have rather abruptly woken up to a problem that is neither new nor unique since, as with India, constitutional provisions for religious freedom and the quest for autonomy by religious denominations have been present since the moment of the birth of both nations. I wonder whether in understanding such disputes over religious freedom, the question to ask is not *why* but *why now?* If, as Evan Haefeli suggests in his contribution to this volume, toleration is inevitably a partisan phenomenon, then which element of the partisan equilibrium was shaken in the United States twenty years ago, around the time of *Employment Division v. Smith*? Not everything may be attributed to post-9/11 Islamophobia and its many results.

In India, as I have shown, there were very specific racial, social, and political contexts to the deployment of the arguments for religious freedom—alternatively imagined as institutional autonomy and social justice. Some of these contexts are better known than others, such as the legal transformation of Hindu ritual and social order, which saw the repeated deployment of article 26 in the 1950s and '60s, or the plaited politics of ethnic nationalism and ethnic recognition, which led to the clutching of articles 26 and 30 by those clubbed together under the bureaucratic appellation of Minority Educational Institutions. This shift entailed the reorientation of social activism on the part of marginal groups, from temples to the material means of social advancement—educational facilities, government jobs, political representation, and legal provisions for affirmative action. Seeking autonomy—in most cases from the supervisory authority of universities that they are affiliated with—or exemption from rules based on affirmative action policies, these institutions seem to be behaving in very similar ways to the post-*Smith* religious alliances in the United States, and doing so with some measure of success. India, it appears, has become more like America in the past half century.

Selected Bibliography

Bateman, Josiah. *The Life of Daniel Wilson*. London: John Murray, 1860.

Chatterjee, Nandini. *The Making of Indian Secularism: Empire, Law and Christianity, 1830–1960*. Basingstoke, UK: Palgrave, 2011.

Forrester, Duncan. *Caste and Christianity: Attitudes and Policies of Anglo-Saxon Protestant Missions in India*. Oxford: Oxford University Press, 1980.

Galanter, Marc. "Hinduism, Secularism and the Judiciary." *Philosophy East and West* 21, no. 4 (1971): 467–87.

Hasan, Zoya. "Gender Politics, Legal Reform, and the Muslim Community in India." In *Resisting the Sacred and the Secular: Women's Activism and Politicized Religion in South Asia*, edited by Patricia Jeffery and Amrita Basu, 71–86. New Delhi: Kali for Women, 1999.

Hudson, D. Denis. *Protestant Origins in India: Tamil Evangelical Christians, 1706–1835*. Grand Rapids, MI: Eerdmans, 2000.

Litt, Jurgen, Ancharlott Eschmann, Gayacharan Tripathi, and Herman Kulke, eds. *The Cult of Jagannath and the Regional Tradition of Orissa*. New Delhi: Manohar, 1978.

Mudaliar, Chandra. *State and Religious Endowments in Madras*. Madras, India: University of Madras, 1976.

Sastri Yagnapurushdasji v. Muldas Bhundardas. AIR 1966 S.C. 1127.

Skinner, Quentin. *Liberty before Liberalism.* Cambridge: Cambridge University Press, 1998.

Sri Venkataramana Devaru v. State of Mysore. AIR 1958 S.C. 255.

St. Stephen's College and others v. The University Of Delhi and others. AIR 1992 SC 1630.

T.M.A. Pai Foundation v. State of Karnataka. SCC 2002 481.

PART 3
Law and Politics

Preface

Peter G. Danchin

Contemporary legal and political discourse on religious liberty makes a number of distinctive normative claims. Simultaneously invoking notions of neutrality, secularity, freedom, and right, the claim is to have located a vantage point of universality somehow above or independent of the contingencies and disorder of politics, culture, religion and, indeed, of history itself. As the essays in this section show, however, it is a mistake to conceive of religious liberty as a single, stable principle existing outside of culture, spatial geographies, or power relations. Rather, religious liberty is better understood as a fractious, polyvalent concept unfolding through divergent histories in differing political orders. Each of these essays illuminates how different historical trajectories and genealogies coexist within the broad language of religious liberty, each submerging and reemerging in at times surprising ways to refract contemporary political conflicts and struggles.

The most striking aspect common to the essays is the kind of politics and political subjectivity that emerges when religious liberty is understood and contested as a matter of right. The idea of a *right* to religious freedom is in fact quite distinct from genealogies premised on the religious, political, and juridical casuistries spawned in the context of national religious settlements. The relation between "the state" and "religion" is usually cast as a political matter of negotiation and contestation among state actors and institutions and existing religious communities, groups, and traditions. But the notion of "a right" implies a legal/moral relation between the state and an individual legal subject as rights holder, as well as a background justification not only of the right itself but its distinctive function of holding others to correlative duties.

As Waheeda Amien observes in this volume, both of these trajectories of religious liberty are reflected in section 15 of the postapartheid Bill of Rights of South Africa, which on the one hand protects every individual's right to "freedom of conscience, religion, thought, belief and opinion" while on the other permitting legislation recognizing marriages "concluded under any tradition, or a system of religious, personal or family law" as well as any systems of personal and family law "under any tradition, or adhered to by persons professing a particular religion." It is fascinating to observe how current struggles and forms of engagement between the South African state and its Muslim communities are unfolding in legal reform efforts to recognize Muslim marriages and how this form of politics diverges markedly from the formal rights-based jurisprudence developed by the Constitutional Court under section 15.

Similarly, Nadia Marzouki describes how the right to religious freedom has not been the driving force in the Tunisian revolution nor prominent in the discourse of the ruling Islamist political party, Nahda. Rather, we see instead the efforts by Nahda and Tunisian intellectuals to redefine Islam today as "the source of an ethical and cultural project of collective introspection and reformation," a project that Marzouki tellingly sees as premised on a "moral narrative of modernity . . . in which the category of sincere [collective] belief plays the central role." Like the intractable and fractured debates unfolding in South Africa, we see the distinctive form of politics and legal contestation that arose following efforts by Nahda to include a new provision in the Tunisian constitution recognizing sharia as "the main source of legislation" and limiting freedom of expression on certain religious grounds.

The other essays further illuminate the surprising extent to which each of these issues—the subject of the right, its normative scope, and its theoretical justification—are essentially contested questions. It is often tacitly assumed that the subject of the right is the *individual*; the scope of the right is *conscience* or *belief*; and the justification of the right is either apodictic *reason* understood in broadly Kantian terms as an a priori subjective right that the individual gives to herself in accordance with universal moral law ("unconditional observance of a categorically commanding law of free choice") or some form of natural reason that yields an objective right to conscience in accordance with natural law.

These underlying ambivalences between subjective and objective conceptions of right, and autonomy and conscience as the proper object of the right, each coexist within the capacious abstraction of "the right to

freedom of religion or belief," and they help to explain both the extraordi-
nary power of the discourse as well as its characteristic antinomies. The
essays by Elizabeth Castelli and Winnifred Fallers Sullivan thus each vividly describe American Catholic conceptions of and activism around the
right to religious liberty. As Sullivan observes, the Catholic bishops paradoxically accept the priority of the religion clauses of the First Amendment ("our first liberty") just as they challenge the dreaded specter of
"secular humanism." And they do so explicitly in terms of a dominant
Enlightenment narrative that holds that this liberty is both exceptionally "ours" (America as the "particular guardian of freedom") as well as
"universal" (valid "for all nations and people who yearn to be free"). As
Castelli acutely observes, the Fortnight of Freedom announced by the
US bishops in 2012 begins on the feast day shared by St. John Fisher and
St. Thomas More, two martyrs who stood up to corrupt state authority,
and ends on US Independence Day, thus seamlessly weaving together
"the religious and national calendars around the broader struggle for religious liberty." Having accepted these foundations, the bishops then initiated a vigorous political and cultural campaign to contest the subject,
meaning, scope, and justification of the right, a struggle to be fought out
in the administrative, legislative, and ultimately judicial institutions of
the state.

Is the subject of the right the individual or does it include religious
groups and institutions, including "the church"? If it includes some account of "church autonomy," what is the state to do when the rights of
individuals conflict with the rights of the church? What must the state
do, for example, when the church acts to discipline or exclude one of its
own members in a way that limits or violates his or her freedom of conscience? How is the state to adjudicate this kind of normative conflict
arising *internal* to the right to religious liberty itself while remaining true
to its own foundational premises of neutrality towards religion and universality of the right?

As Lori Beaman's essay illustrates, these questions reveal the extent
to which long-venerated American doctrines of nonestablishment and
free exercise, far from being neutral or universal, in fact operate to encapsulate and entrench particular historical and cultural understandings
of both religion and right. These themes are further amplified in Ann
Pellegrini's essay, which, taking the landmark case of *Everson v. Board
of Education* as its launching point, shows how the "interstructuring"
of disestablishment and free exercise has generated a particular form of

Christian secularism in American public life that is both linked conceptually and historically to a "domesticated modern civic Protestantism"
while at the same time today confronting the "wild contemporary landscape of American religious pluralism."

A second theme running through the essays is the distinctive ways in
which the right to religious liberty functions as a modern technology of
secular governance and is integral to the power of the modern nation-
state. Both the structure of the right and its interpretation by courts
across a remarkably wide range of jurisdictions can be seen to rely on
a foundational distinction that significantly shapes the modern politics
of religious freedom. The first element, known as the *forum internum*,
defines the locus of religious belief and conscience as protected absolutely by law while the second element, known as the *forum externum*, is
where the outward expression or manifestation of this belief is subjected
to state regulation and sanction.

The *Employment Division v. Smith* case decided by the US Supreme
Court, which Sullivan argues has shaped the contemporary politics of
religious freedom in the United States, can be seen to be premised on
this distinction just as much as the Canadian cases of *Saguenay c. Mouvement laïque québécois* and *R v. Edwards Books and Art Ltd.* analyzed
by Beaman. My own contribution further shows how the more recent
decision by the US Supreme Court in *Hosanna-Tabor v. EEOC* draws a
remarkably similar distinction to that advanced by the European Court
of Human Rights to justify its contradictory rulings in the well-known
Lautsi v. Italy and *Dahlab v. Switzerland* cases. The US Supreme Court
asserts that its prior holding in *Smith*, that the right to religious liberty
does not require religious exemptions or accommodations from so-called
neutral laws of general application, was limited in that case to "outward
physical acts," whereas the *Hosanna-Tabor* case concerned "government
interference with an internal church decision that affects the faith and
mission of the church itself." In this set of moves, we see the essential
contestability of the subject and meaning of the right and at the same
time how this form of reasoning is both premised on and reinscribes the
underlying foundational distinction between inner belief and outward
manifestation that defines the exercise of modern secular power.

An important consequence of this normative structure is that it ends
up privileging the beliefs, values, and practices of the majority religious
tradition in any given polity and ensures that majoritarian values and
sensibilities become lodged in the very substance of a nation's laws. This

propensity across diverse bodies of jurisprudence illustrates the necessary intertwining between the religious and the secular that characterizes all modern polities despite different models of state-religion relations.

In conclusion, the conceptual architecture of the right to religious freedom can be seen to be premised on a paradox: on the one hand, religious freedom is said to be neutral toward religion and indeed neutrality is the leitmotif of modern religious liberty discourse whether in moral, legal, or political contexts. On the other hand, religious freedom as a technology of modern state and international legal governance is deeply implicated in the regulation of religion. This tension between inviolability and regulation, the essays suggest, is *internal* to the concept of religious liberty itself and serves to generate the distinctive antinomies and contradictions that we see arising in struggles over its meaning, justification, and realization.

CHAPTER FIFTEEN

Postapartheid Treatment of Religious Freedom in South Africa

Waheeda Amien

Introduction

Discussions in South Africa relating to religious freedom do not center on the extent to which religion can be excluded from the public sphere but the extent to which it can be accommodated. In the context of this article, I use the term *public sphere* to refer to that domain that is regulated by the state.

South Africa's willingness to respect religious freedom not only in the private sphere but also in the public sphere is as a direct result of its discriminatory-laden history under colonialism and apartheid. While race-based discrimination was the most obvious, religious discrimination was also invidious. Christianity was the dominant religion and was often used by the colonial and apartheid governments to justify their oppressive laws. For instance, marriages that did not conform to Christian values such as monogamy and heterosexuality were regarded as uncivilized relationships that were not worthy of legal recognition. Thus, potentially polygynous marriages such as Muslim, Hindu, Jewish, and African customary marriages, as well as same-sex marriages, did not enjoy the privileged position that Christian marriages enjoyed.

It was not until the introduction of democracy in 1994 and the adoption of South Africa's final constitution in 1996 that a commitment was made to foster a society that does not posit one religion above another and instead respects, appreciates, and celebrates religious diversity. This is evident in various sections of the constitution, including the following:

1) The Preamble of the Constitution makes reference to "God." It enjoins God to bless South Africa and protect its people. In Schedule 2, the Constitution enables an oath-taker to take the oath in the name of God or alternatively make an affirmation. The references to God in the Constitution acknowledge the existence and significance of religion in the lives of many South Africans.

2) Diversity of religion is respected through sections 9(1) and 9(3). Section 9(1) guarantees equal treatment of different religions. Section 9(3) identifies religion as a ground for unfair discrimination. Furthermore, section 16(2)(c) limits freedom of expression by prohibiting the promotion of hatred on religious grounds.

3) In particular, both individual and collective rights to freedom of religion are protected respectively in section 15(1), which protects every individual's right to freedom of religion and section 31(1), which protects the collective right of religious communities to practice their religion and to establish and maintain religious associations.

4) Religious freedom is further promoted through section 35(2)(f)(iii), which affords detained and imprisoned persons the right to interact with their religious counsellors, and section 235, which does not preclude religious communities from claiming a right of self-determination.

5) Section 181(1)(c) makes provision for the establishment of a Commission for the Promotion and Protection of the Rights of Cultural, Religious and Linguistic Communities to strengthen constitutional democracy.

6) Section 6(5)(b)(ii) enables the establishment of a Pan South African Language Board to promote respect for languages used for, among others, religious purposes.

7) Through section 15(2), religious observances can be conducted at state or state-aided institutions.

8) And finally, section 15(3)(a) permits the enactment of legislation to recognize, among others, religious marriages or religious personal or family law systems. In this way, the Constitution facilitates the creation of a semi-secular society that involves an intersection between religion and the state where the latter is encouraged to support religion.

In an attempt to ensure that religious communities do not use sections 15(3)(a) and 31(1) to legitimize religious practices that are constitutionally offensive, internal limitations were added. Therefore, section 15(3)(b) requires any legislation that purports to recognize religious marriages or religious personal or family law systems to be consistent with other constitutional provisions. Similarly, section 31(2) provides that a religious community may only exercise its right to establish, maintain, and join religious associations and practice its religion to the extent that it is not inconsistent with the Bill of Rights. Both internal limitations implicitly refer to, among others, the right to not be unfairly discriminated against on the basis of sex and/or gender. Thus, both limitations seek to ensure that, among others, gender-based discriminatory religious rules and practices do not permeate the legal framework of South African family laws.

In this essay attention is directed to the right to freedom of religion as encompassed in sections 15 and 31. I begin by summarizing the South African judiciary's approach to religious freedom. Thereafter, through the example of Muslim marriages and divorces, I consider the way in which South Africa has attempted to put section 15(3)(a) into practice.

Jurisprudence on Religious Freedom

South African jurisprudence on religious freedom has been shaped by four cases that have been decided in the Constitutional Court: *S v. Lawrence, Negal, Solberg* (1997); *Christian Education South Africa v. Minister of Education* (2000); *Prince v. President, Cape Law Society and Others* (2002); and *MEC for Education, KwaZulu-Natal, and Others v. Pillay* (2008).

In the above cases, the Constitutional Court interprets the constitutional provisions on religious freedom as permitting the South African state to subsidize religious institutions and allowing religious observances to be conducted at state or state-aided institutions provided they are not done in a coercive manner. For example, where a state or state-aided institution permits religious observances, members of that institution must not be made to feel that they are compelled to observe the religious ceremony that is conducted within that institution.

Where the state promotes and supports religion, the court further requires that it be done on an equitable basis. So if religious observances are permitted within a state or state-aided institution, then observances of different religions should be afforded the same opportunity and one religion should not be prioritized above another.

South Africa therefore incorporates a form of secularism that I call *inclusive secularism*, which accommodates religion in the public sphere. This is in contrast to what I call *exclusive secularism*, which involves a strict separation between religion and state in the public sphere.

The Constitutional Court also advocates the view that protecting religious freedom is intricately linked to appreciating religious diversity and that religious freedom should therefore be afforded maximum protection. As mentioned in the introductory section, appreciation of religious diversity is an important component of South Africa's democracy in light of its discriminatory past. Therefore, respect for religious diversity is also significant for the protection and promotion of human dignity.

At the same time, the Constitutional Court recognizes that religious freedom is not absolute. Where it conflicts with another right, the court requires a balancing test to be employed to ensure reasonable accommodation of religious freedom. This means that the court must consider the significant interest served by the law and the means used to achieve the purpose of the law. The balance also involves, on the one hand, not placing individuals and religious communities in the position of having to choose between their faith and the law and, on the other hand, not enabling individuals and religious communities to promote harmful practices in the name of religion.

Notwithstanding the constitutional protection of religious freedom and the jurisprudence described in the previous paragraphs that has been developed by the South African judiciary, courts still appear to be hesitant to engage with issues of religious doctrine. For instance, they prefer to leave the question of what constitutes the content of religion to the subjective interpretation of religious adherents. Yet if legislation were enacted to recognize and/or regulate religious marriages, the South African judiciary may very well have to explicitly apply their minds to issues of religious doctrine. It is to the issue of legislative recognition and regulation of Muslim family law, which encompasses Muslim marriage, divorce, and guardianship, custody of, and access to minor children, as an example of legislating religious marriages that I now turn.

Legislative Approach to Religious Freedom

In accordance with section 15(3)(a), the South African government initiated a process to ensure legal recognition of Muslim marriages. Given the spatial constraints of this paper, I consider only some of the implications for religious freedom that emanated from the process to recognize Muslim marriages.

In about 1999, the South African Law Reform Commission (SALRC) was tasked with drafting legislation to recognize Muslim marriages. The call for legal recognition of such marriages came from various quarters of the Muslim community and civil society. First, for the Muslim community, legal recognition of its marriages is important to the restoring of dignity after the colonial and apartheid governments failed to consider its marriages worthy of legal recognition and protection. Second, many members of the *ulamā* (Muslim clergy) advocate for legal recognition of Muslim marriages because they want their decisions relating to Muslim family law to be legally enforceable. Third, many Muslims and members of civil society require legal recognition of Muslim marriages so that Muslim spouses can access all the civil benefits that their civil law counterparts enjoy. Fourth, Muslim gender activists believe that recognition of Muslim marriages can enable Muslim wives to assert claims for Islamic law benefits that they are currently unable to enjoy. For instance, although Islamic law recognizes the value of unpaid labor in the home, the South African *ulamā* does not insist that this benefit should be afforded to women.

After extensive consultations with the South African Muslim community and broader civil society that spanned several years, the SALRC submitted a Muslim Marriages Bill in 2003 to the minister of justice and constitutional development. Seven years later, the Department of Justice and Constitutional Development (DoJ&CD) effected some amendments to the bill, which it thereafter submitted to the Cabinet of South Africa for approval. In 2010 the Cabinet approved the amended bill. The public was invited to make submissions on the 2010 bill by May 31, 2011. To date, the DoJ&CD has not informed the public about the outcome of the submissions and the draft legislation has not entered the parliamentary process for deliberation.

Several interesting observations have emerged from the process relating to the intended recognition of Muslim marriages. For the purpose of this essay, I shall focus on two: the different responses to the 2003 and 2010 bills, and the reasons for the delay in recognizing Muslim marriages.

Different opinions have been formulated in response to the two versions of the bill over the past several years. Indeed, there are those who support enactment of legislation to recognize Muslim marriages and those who oppose it. Yet, the matter is far more complex given that the support for and opposition to the draft legislation is multilayered and has exposed interesting bedfellows.

In the camp opposing the 2003 and 2010 versions of the bill, several players are identifiable. The most obvious are those Muslims who oppose any type of state regulation of Muslim family law by a non-Islamic state and prefer that the status quo be maintained. In other words, they would like the *ulamā* to continue regulating Muslim family law within the private sphere of the community. Some also advocate for the establishment of a shariah (Islamic law) court that they argue should be presided over by members of the *ulamā* who are authorized to deliver legally enforceable judgments. Others are pushing for Muslim arbitration tribunals to deliver legally enforceable arbitration orders relating to Muslim Personal Law (MPL), which encompasses Muslim family law and Islamic inheritance.

There are also those Muslims who feel that their Islamic schools of thought are not catered for in the draft legislation. The most prominent of the latter dissident voices follow the *Shi'a* tradition, which comprise a minority within the South African Muslim community.

Secular absolutists who favor a strict separation between religion and state are further located within the opposition camp. They ironically find themselves locking arms with those Muslims who reject state intervention in the affairs of the Muslim community.

The final component of the opposition camp is the gender advocates who expect the draft legislation to be absolutely gender-consistent before they will consider bestowing their blessings upon it. An example of a gender-inconsistent provision in the bill is the recognition of polygyny, which secular absolutists argue must be abolished. However, precedent for the legal recognition of polygyny already exists in the Recognition of Customary Marriages Act 120 of 1998 (RCMA). Both the RCMA and the 2003 and 2010 versions of the bill incorporate protections for polygynous wives. For example, a husband who intends to enter into a subsequent marriage is required to apply to court for approval of the written contract regulating the subsequent marriage and must show that he will maintain his spouses equally. Furthermore, the existing wives must be joined in the application, which will afford them the opportunity to voice their opinions on the subsequent marriage. Based on these protections, if the institution of polygyny is challenged, it is possible that the Constitutional Court may find that it has been "reasonably accommodated."

On the other hand, there are those gender activists within civil society and the Muslim community who support the enactment of legislation to afford legal recognition to Muslim marriages. They acknowledge that the 2003 and 2010 versions of the bill are open to challenge on grounds of gender equality. They argue, however, that if enacted, either version of the bill promises to provide more protection for women than they currently have. These gender activists adopt the view that there will be opportunities after the draft legislation is enacted to institute constitutional challenges against the gender-problematic provisions. Their main concerns with the 2010 bill relate to unequal divorce options for men and women and the limited sources that the bill recognizes for the interpretation of Islamic law.

While the 2010 bill recognizes different forms of divorce for men and women, women are not afforded the same right to repudiate their husbands and obtain a release from the marriage as men. The 2010 bill makes provision, among others, for the wife to be granted *khul'a* (no fault–based divorce available to the wife) provided her husband agrees to the amount of financial compensation that she must pay him in order for her to exit the marriage. In contrast, a husband may be granted divorce on the basis of *talāq* (no fault–based repudiation of the wife available to the husband) without requiring his wife's consent.

At the same time, there is a gender-friendly and religiously justifiable interpretation of *khul'a* that is not incorporated into the bill that enables a wife to release herself from the marriage by giving back her *mahr* (dower) without requiring her husband to agree to the amount that she gives him. So if the unequal divorce options in the bill are constitutionally challenged, it is possible that a court would adopt the gender-friendly interpretation of *khul'a* since it counterbalances the *talāq* and ensures an equal option of divorce for women. This is because enactment of legislation to recognize and regulate Muslim marriages will bring the interpretation of the legislation within the ambit of the judiciary. The judiciary would then have to interpret the legislation in a way that is consistent with constitutional imperatives. So if a religiously justifiable interpretation that is also consistent with gender equality were available, such as the gender-friendly interpretation of *khul'a* described above, the judiciary may be constitutionally justified and obliged to adopt it. This would also mean that the judiciary would have to depart from its current approach of cautious engagement with issues involving religious doctrine.

The second concern highlighted by gender activists is that the 2010 bill incorporates only the primary and secondary sources of Islamic law, namely, the Koran (Islamic holy book), the Sunnah (sayings and practices of Prophet Muhammad), Qiyās (analogical deduction), and Ijmā (consensus of Muslim jurists). It does not include subsidiary sources such as, among others, *maslahā* (public interest), *istihsān* (discretion to relax a rule where it would result in harm) and *'urf* and *adat* (customs and practices prevalent within the community). The rules derived from the aforementioned primary and secondary sources may not be able to address all the realities of the twenty-first century. Reliance on only those sources may result in the perpetuation of conservative rules that militate against women. Inclusion of an unlimited list of Islamic law sources therefore becomes necessary to ensure that Islamic law can be developed and applied in a socially responsive manner.

A third component—namely, moderate members of the *ulamā*—is further discernible within the camp supporting the enactment of legislation to recognize Muslim marriages. This group appears to make up the majority of Muslim jurists among the South African *ulamā*. They seem to understand that South African Muslims are a minority operating within a constitutional framework and that any recognition of Muslim family law will need to occur within that framework. They therefore seek to have the Islamic principles governing marriage incorporated into the draft legislation in a way that produces a balance between constitutional expectations and Islamic prerogatives. For these reasons, the moderate members of the *ulamā* supported the 2003 bill because for them it constituted a reasonable compromise.

However, moderate members of the *ulamā* have expressed dissatisfaction with the 2010 bill because it departs from the 2003 bill in two significant ways. First, the 2003 bill enabled adjudication of disputes arising from it to be presided over by Muslim judges from within the secular judiciary sitting with Islamic law experts as assessors. In contrast, the requirements that the judge must be Muslim and must adjudicate with Islamic law experts as assessors have been removed from the 2010 bill. In the opinion of the moderate members of the *ulamā*, the removal of the requirements relating to Muslim judges and Islamic law assessors as experts will render un-Islamic any decision arising from the 2010 Bill that is handed down by a secular judiciary. Thus, the 2010 bill appears to have been more secularized than the 2003 bill. At the same time, the inclusion of Islamic law sources that a court should rely on when interpreting Islamic law, which were not contained in the 2003 bill, means that in other respects the 2010 bill has also been more Islamized. It is unclear why the DoJ&CD made these changes when the 2003 bill had resulted from an extensive process of negotiations with various stakeholders. Perhaps there had been private conversations with the *ulamā*, which had resulted in the inclusion of specified Islamic law sources in the 2010 bill. Perhaps elements within the DoJ&CD are opposed to the establishment of what might have amounted to a Muslim bench adjudicating issues that arise from the Muslim Marriages Bill. One can only speculate at this point.

Second, the 2003 bill required binding mediation to precede the dispute going to court, whereas the 2010 bill proposes voluntary mediation to enable parties to settle their disputes prior to adjudication. The latter change is problematic for the *ulamā* because they most likely envisage the mediation process as the medium through which they would play a significant role in the management of disputes relating to Muslim marriages and divorces.

To date, no official reason has been given by the DoJ&CD to explain why, twenty years after the advent of democracy, Muslim marriages have not been afforded legal recognition, and especially since African customary marriages and same-sex marriages have been recognized. Legislative recognition of Muslim marriages appears to be going nowhere slowly, in part because the South African government treats the opinions of moderate members of the *ulamā* as representative of the general views of the Muslim community. Thus the current disagreement with the 2010 bill, especially by the moderate members of the *ulamā*, is most likely the main reason that the draft legislation has once again been placed on the political back burner.

The other likely reason for the delay in enacting either version of the bill is that the South African government lacks the political will to enact legislation to recognize Muslim marriages. In the first instance, the political imperative to recognize African customary marriages was overwhelming since the majority of the South African population is comprised of black Africans. Yet the same political imperative does not appear to exist for minority religious communities including the Muslim community, which makes up 1.5 percent of South Africa's total population. Second, several different politicians have occupied the office of minister of justice and constitutional development since 2003. The progress or stagnation of the process to recognize Muslim marriages seems to depend on their own political inclinations about whether or not the state ought to recognize and/or regulate minority religious marriages. Third, discussions about enacting legislation to afford legal recognition to Muslim marriages usually surface publicly at election times when the ruling party seeks to solicit Muslim votes. However, in the run-up to the 2014 national and provincial elections, the ruling party appeared to have adopted a different approach. Instead of highlighting the Muslim Marriages Bill, as it did during previous election periods, it sought to encourage members of the *ulamā* to register themselves as marriage officers in terms of section 3 of the Marriage Act 25 of 1961. Section 3 enables a person, who officiates a Christian, Jewish, Hindu, Muslim or other marriage to be designated as a marriage officer. When a designated marriage officer performs a religious marriage, he or she may simultaneously register the marriage as a civil marriage. The consequences of a civil marriage would then apply to the marriage and could be enforced in court. During April 2014 and in line with section 3, more than one hundred *ulamā* members from across the country received training as marriage officers and received their certificates from the Department of Home Affairs in a public ceremony held on April 29, 2014, in Cape Town.

Until recently, it appeared that many members of the *ulamā* were resistant to the idea of a civil marriage and only less than a handful were registered as marriage officers. Their resistance emanated from two issues: First, they were of the view that the default civil matrimonial property regime involving community of property is un-Islamic, since a traditional interpretation of Islamic law requires the parties' estates to be kept separate at all times. Secondly, polygynous marriages are not permitted under civil law. Given the sudden change in attitude by the *ulamā* to be registered as marriage officers, one wonders how the government managed to convince them to undergo training and become registered as marriage officers. In other words, why are civil marriages suddenly palatable to such a large number among the *ulamā*? Were they perhaps persuaded that the out of community of property regime is consistent with Islamic law, and that they could insist on parties entering into an ante-nuptial contract before agreeing to perform a civil marriage? That would explain why members of the *ulamā* are explicitly requiring parties to enter into ante-nuptial contracts to regulate out of community of property regimes in their civil marriages. As far as polygynous marriages are concerned, perhaps the *ulamā* have realized that registering a civil marriage will not preclude them from officiating polygynous Muslim marriages provided no more than one of those marriages is registered as a civil marriage.

To the extent that the *ulamā* members who are now designated as marriage officers proceed to register Muslim marriages as civil marriages, the initiative should be welcomed. Yet it will still not adequately address the challenge that Muslim women face to exercise a right to divorce without requiring their husbands' or a third party's consent. Muslim women may also not be able to access benefits that Islamic law avails to them since they may legally be perceived as having exercised a choice about which system of law applies to them when they agreed to have their marriage registered as a civil marriage. Thus, to enable Muslim women to exit their religious marriages and permit them to access Islamic law benefits, legislative intervention will still be required.

The delay in giving effect to section 15(3)(a) of the constitution by failing to enact legislation to recognize Muslim marriages indicates that the entrenchment of fundamental rights in a bill of rights does not guarantee their implementation. Instead, a strong and unapathetic civil society is required to hold the government accountable to its constitutional obligations. Therefore, those within the Muslim community and broader civil society who support the enactment of legislation to recognize Muslim marriages need to provide the political incentive for such enactment to take place. For instance, the Muslim community must take the lead in mobilizing and launching a strong and sustainable campaign for the recognition of Muslim marriages, which to date it has not done.

Furthermore, civil society should use the courts and launch a civil application against the government to encourage enactment. In 2009, the Women's Legal Centre (WLC), a nongovernmental organization that litigates gender-based precedent-setting cases, did just that and launched its application in the Constitutional Court in the case of *Women's Legal Trust v. President of the Republic of South Africa and Others* (2009). In that case, the Constitutional Court decided that there was no basis for the WLC to have had direct access to it and directed the organization to relaunch its application in the appropriate high court. The WLC's Constitutional Court application did, however, motivate the government to apply its mind to the 2003 bill; this resulted in the DoJ&CD's submission of the 2010 bill to the Cabinet and its subsequent approval by the latter.

More recently, the WLC brought an application on behalf of a female claimant in the Western Cape High Court in the case of *Faro v. Bingham NO and Others* (2013) and asked the court, among others, to recognize her Muslim marriage as valid under the secular Marriage Act 25 of 1961, or alternatively that the common-law definition of marriage be extended to include Muslim marriages. The court postponed the applicant's claim for hearing until August 2014, at which time it will consider her claim to have her Muslim marriage recognized as valid. Furthermore, the court ordered the government to report on its progress of the bill by July 2014. Presumably the court's decision to grant or not grant the claimant's application may depend on how much progress is made on the bill.

As indicated previously, a general consensus in favor of the 2003 bill had emerged from a widespread process of consultations within the Muslim community and broader civil society. Although not perfect, the 2003 bill had contained innovative mechanisms for the regulation of minority Muslim marriages within a secular legal framework. It is therefore unfortunate that the DOJ&CD had decided to effect changes to the 2010 bill without consulting the relevant role-players. The only way for the process to move forward now is for the DOJ&CD to revisit the problematic provisions of the 2010 bill with the concerned parties and to renegotiate and reformulate the challenged provisions.

As has been discussed here, the Constitutional Court requires reasonable accommodation of religion, which involves balancing competing state and community interests. In the context of Muslim marriages, this means that the religious concerns of the Muslim community must be reasonably balanced against the interests of the most marginalized and vulnerable members of the Muslim community—particularly women and children, whom the state is required to protect. If the state's responsibility to these citizens is realized, the current stalemate can be overcome by way of reasonable compromises. For instance, it is not practically feasible to require each dispute arising from the draft legislation to be adjudicated by a Muslim judge, if for no other reason than the fact that the South African judiciary has too few Muslim judges to ensure speedy resolution of bill-related cases. However, since South African judges are not experts in Islamic law, it could be reasonable to expect bill-related disputes— especially those involving religious interpretations that cannot be clearly gleaned from the legislation—to be presided over by a judge who sits with Islamic law experts acting as assessors. In fact, the latter could obviate the need for parties to produce their own experts, which in turn would reduce costs to the parties. Furthermore, adequate protection could be provided in the case of compulsory mediation as long as mediation orders can be appealed to the courts. Finally, it is reasonable to expect that the list of sources to interpret Islamic law should be kept as nonexhaustive as possible since this will enable interpretation and application of the bill to be responsive to the needs of the South African Muslim community.

Conclusion

This essay demonstrates that religious freedom in South Africa is treated as a right that is not simply relegated to the private sphere but can also be enjoyed, protected, and limited in the public sphere. The essay illustrates that incorporating personal law aspects of religion in the public sphere subject to limitations that protect gender equality may in fact be necessary to ensure protection for women's rights. South Africa is thus a good example of an inclusive form of secularism that acknowledges the reality of religious diversity and seeks to protect it in a nonabsolutist manner. South Africa has managed to bridge the public and private divide in the context of religion in a way that attempts to balance the interests of religious communities and the individual rights of women.

The most prominent manifestation in South Africa of the promotion of religious freedom, particularly in the public sphere, is through the implementation of section 15(3)(a) of the constitution by way of enacting legislation to recognize, among others, religious marriages or religious personal or family law systems.

If the DoJ&CD, South African civil society, and the South African Muslim community work cooperatively, enactment of legislation to recognize Muslim marriages can become a reality. Further consultations between the DoJ&CD and the relevant role-players are therefore necessary to ascertain the extent to which the 2010 bill can be changed to meet the needs and interests of those who will be affected by the draft legislation.

It is especially important for the DoJ&CD to not only pay attention to the voices of the *ulamā* but also to consult with Muslim women. The DoJ&CD needs to take seriously the call for legal recognition of Muslim marriages because every moment in which enactment of the bill is delayed is a moment more of oppression for the most marginalized within the Muslim community.

Selected Bibliography

Ackermann, L. W. H. "Some Reflections on the Constitutional Court's Freedom of Religion Jurisprudence." *Dutch Reformed Theological Journal* 43, nos. 1–2 (2002): 177–84.

Amien, Waheeda. "Overcoming the Conflict between the Right to Religious Freedom and Women's Rights to Equality—a South African Case Study of Muslim Marriages." *Human Rights Quarterly* 28 (2006): 729–54.

———. "A South African Case Study for the Recognition and Regulation of Muslim Family Law in a Minority Muslim Secular Context." *International Journal of Law, Policy and the Family* 24, no. 3 (2010): 361–96.

———. "Comparative Perspectives: South Africa." In *The Protections for Religious Rights: Law and Practice*, edited by James Dingemans, Can Yeginsu, Tom Cross, and Hafsah Masood, 4.370–4.415. Oxford: Oxford University Press, 2013.

———. "The Gendered Benefits and Costs of Legal Pluralism for Muslim Family Law in South Africa." In *Managing Family Justice in Diverse Societies*, edited by Mavis Maclean and John Eekelaar, 107–23. Oxford: Hart, 2013.

———. "Reflections on the Recognition of African Customary Marriages in South Africa: Seeking Insights for the Recognition of Muslim Marriages." *Acta Juridica* 13 (2013): 357–84.

Bekker, J. C., C. Rautenbach, and N. M. I. Goolam, eds. *Introduction to Legal Pluralism in South Africa.* n.p.: Lexis Nexis/Butterworths, 2006.

Christian Education South Africa v. Minister of Education 2000 (4) SA 757 (CC).

Du Plessis, L. "Religious Freedom and Equality as Celebration of Difference: A Significant Development in Recent South African Constitutional Case-Law." *Potchefstroom Electronic Law Journal* 12, no. 4 (2009): 10–34.

Faro v. Bingham NO and Others (4466/2013) [2013] ZAWCHC 159 (25 October 2013).

Fourie, Pieter. "The SA Constitution and Religious Freedom: Perverter or Preserver of Religion's Contribution to the Public Debate on Morality?" *Scriptura: International Journal of Bible, Religion and Theology in Southern Africa* 82 (2003): 94–107.

Heyns, Cristof, and Danie Brand. "The Constitutional Protection of Religious Human Rights in Southern Africa." *Emory International Law Review* 14, no. 2 (2000): 699–778.

MEC for Education, KwaZulu-Natal, and Others v. Pillay 2008 (1) SA 474 (CC).

Prince v. President, Cape Law Society and Others 2002 (2) SA 794 (CC).

S v. Lawrence, Negal, Solberg 1997 (10) BCLR 1348 (CC).

Ten Napel, Hans-Martien, and Florien H. K. Theissen. "The Judicial Protection of Religious Symbols in Europe's Public Educational Institutions: Thank God for Canada and South Africa." *Muslim World Journal of Human Rights* 8, no. 1 (2011): n.p.

Van der Vyver, Johan D. "Constitutional Perspective of Church-State Relations in South Africa." *Brigham Young University Law Review* 1999, no. 2 (1999): 635–73.

Women's Legal Trust v. President of the Republic of South Africa and Others 2009 (6) SA 94 (CC).

CHAPTER SIXTEEN

Religious Freedom in Postrevolutionary Tunisia

Nadia Marzouki

Since January 2010, numerous controversies have broken out in Tunisia around issues of religion and freedom of speech. They include the controversy about the broadcast of *Persepolis* on a private TV channel; the trials against several bloggers who had posted comments and images that were deemed blasphemous on the Internet; Nadia Al Fani's documentary *Neither Allah nor Master*; the trial against rappers who had written songs against the police; the attacks by Salafi groups against artistic exhibitions; and most recently, the saga around Amina Sboui and the Femen. Numerous Western observers and secularist activists in Tunisia have hastily juxtaposed all these controversies and created a coherent and alarmist narrative about how Tunisia is turning into an Islamist state where religious freedom and freedom of expression are crushed. Although this narrative has become increasingly influential in analyses of Tunisian postrevolutionary politics, it corresponds to a reality that is largely fantasized.

The Tunisian revolution was not about religion nor religious freedom. The rallying cry of demonstrators, *irhal* ("leave"), is the best expression of what made the revolt so specific. Tunisians did not take to the street for the recognition of an essentialized identity. (We are all "Islamist," or "proletarian," or "anti-French.") The ideal that emerged from the *irhal* movements is the "whatever" individual referred to by Giorgio Agamben. "Whatever" here does not mean indifferent or deprived of substantial value, but is rather "such that it always matters." An insistence on equality, irreverence toward any form of authority (*sultat*) and a suspicion of all types of privilege suggest that what Tunisians were calling for is a "solidarity that in no way concerns an essence." Claiming to speak in the name of Islam, *laïcité*, democracy, human rights, or the caliphate did not grant one a privilege any longer in Tunisian public debates. It simply gave one a right to argue "whatever." No politician, activist, or intellectual was immune from the risk of being silenced by a sneering, angry, or weary irhal. Religious freedom was by no means a driving force of the contestation. It is still a marginal issue of contention, in spite of what alarmist commentators try to suggest when they describe a country on the verge of civil war. The lively debates that have emerged in the aftermath of the uprisings express a plurality of competing—although not necessarily opposed—ways of living one's nascent citizenship. Notably, these debates are not essentially conceptualized as debates about "religious freedom." There is a blatant discrepancy between how Tunisians understand and experience the differences that exist among them and academic and media accounts of how these conflicts are supposedly understood.

In this essay I will first discuss the place of religion and religious freedom in the discourse of Nahda (the Islamist party that won 40 percent of the votes in the elections of October 2011) in order to show that these categories are not understood as discrete conceptual or lived realities. I will then turn to the discussion of some of the concrete debates that have erupted since the election. I will reflect upon how the increasing attempts to polarize the political field and public sphere are affecting the ways in which political parties and civil society understand notions of religion, freedom, state, and society.

Nahda's View of Religious Freedom

Tunisian and foreign secular organizations insistently call out Islamists on the issue of religious freedom with the hope of exposing their duplicity or unveiling their double-speak. But religious freedom has actually a very limited part in Islamists' current conversation, not because it is perceived as a divisive issue but because it is viewed as unproblematic and irrelevant.

When asked about religious freedom, most Nahda leaders give one of the following three explanations of why it needs to be protected. First, a theological rationale: compulsion has no place in Islam. Second, a historical-nationalist rationale: Tunisian culture is built on a very ancient history of cultural diversity that encompasses elements of Phoenician civilization, the Roman Empire, African traditions, Judaism, Christianity, and other elements. Finally, a political rationale: Islamists have experienced repression and torture under the regimes of Habib Bourguiba and Zine El Abidine Ben Ali; they know the importance of respecting freedom of expression and do not intend to submit any other group to the same type of arbitrary repression.

At the core of the movement's project is cultural authenticity, not religious conformity. Philosopher Ajmi Lourimi, a member of the Bureau Executif of Nahda and a scholar of Emmanuel Levinas, describes the current crisis in Tunisia as an "epistemological problem." The main challenge for Tunisians—and people from the Maghreb, more generally—is to deal with the "inferiority complex" caused by colonization. "We need to work so that all citizens gain a sufficient level of culture and collective awareness, to make sure that there will be no going back," Lourimi explained at a meeting organized in Tunis by the ReligioWest program of the European University Institute in March 2012.

Tunisian Islamists' insistence on the imperative of cultural authenticity represents a moral narrative of modernity that is analogous to the Western narrative of modernity, analyzed by Webb Keane in this volume, in which the category of sincere belief plays the central role. Just as Dutch missionaries defined interiority and sincerity as the core standard and site of modernity and true religiosity, Nahdawis insist on the reappropriation of cultural authenticity as the defining standard of modernization and development. A return to what is imagined as authentic Tunisian tradition is presented as the condition of modernization. Collective consciousness and cultural reformation are here the active agents of progress rather than individual conscience. But the idea of cultural authenticity serves also to mark a separation between what is deemed archaic (postcolonial *laïcité*, but also alien forms of religiosity expressed within the Muslim world such as the Saudi or even Egyptian ones), and what is modern (unity, reconciliation, and synthesis).

Tunisian Islamists have always had very little to say about religion. If they see religious freedom as a nonissue it is partly because they do not see religion as a problematic intellectual category but simply as an obvious part of reality (*waqa'*) and life (*hayat*). Islamist intellectuals' view on religion and politics is primarily informed by the writings of Rashid

Ghannouchi, who has long considered that the key line of confrontation in Tunisia is not between religion and politics but between society and the state. The crucial challenge is the protection of society from the state, not the protection of individuals from groups or of true belief from heterodox practice. Tunisian Islamists hold an optimistic view of society as a self-regulating and virtuous collective organization. Granted enough freedom, education, and economic opportunity, society will invent self-regulatory mechanisms that will lead to the development of piety and virtue and allow non-Muslims to live according to their own beliefs.

The project discussed and promoted by Tunisian Nahdawi leaders today can be described as a historicist, hermeneutical project of cultural reformation. It is based on a teleological view of the direction of Tunisian history and the place of Islam in this history. After the ruptures of the colonial moment, and of the authoritarian regimes of Bourguiba and Ben Ali, now is the time when Tunisians can regain consciousness of their history and reappropriate their past to better progress toward modernity. "The priority," Lourimi insists, "is not Islamization of society, but modernization." Key intellectual figures and leaders of Nahda such as Ajmi Lourimi, Abu Ya'areb Marzouki, and Rashid Ghannouchi describe the current context as a moment of dialectical synthesis that comes after a long period of estrangement and division. Their call for unity, reconciliation, and consensus—of national healing—is not strategic double-speak; it draws upon a deeply rooted Islamist sense of history in the postcolonial Maghreb. Mehdi Mabrouk, the current minister of culture, a sociologist, a former member of the secular Parti Démocrate Progressiste, and now close to Nahda (but not an official member), insists on Malekite heritage, Tunisian patrimony, and genealogy. During the Tunis ReligioWest meeting, Mabrouk stressed the need for unity and synthesis: "We need to find our Immanuel Kant, someone who will reconcile skeptics and dogmatics. We cannot stay in a state of division." Over the past months, Mabrouk repeatedly dismissed allegations that the Islamist-led government plans to engage in a plan of "Islamization of culture." He condemned those who resort to accusations of *takfīr* (disbelief) to silence artists and artistic production.

Mabrouk did trigger heated debates within the Tunisian and Arab artistic scene when he argued against the inclusion of a couple of sexy Lebanese female artists in the programming of the next Carthage Festival, a national cultural celebration that takes place every summer. But, notably, he did not justify this decision with reference to Islam but to good taste and high culture. This is not the "dictate of the proletariat anymore," he explained, partly in jest; there needs to be a "diktat of good taste." This combination of nationalism, social conservatism, and elitism resonates with most intellectuals and leaders of Nahda, who reject both miniskirts and Salafi outfits as expressions of alienation, romantically longing for the return of the traditional Tunisian *jebba* (robe). However adamant or undiplomatic the minister's statement may seem, it is much closer to, say, the position of the French Ministry of Culture on American movies and rap music than it is to a theocratic form of cultural repression. Ultimately, among the public, statements of this type are welcomed as subjects of satire and derision rather than as real sources of concern. When Mabrouk further explained what he meant by the "diktat of good taste," citing Hans Robert Jauss and Theodor Adorno, the young journalist who was interviewing him gently made fun of him and reminded him of the success of El General, the most famous Tunisian rapper. Here generational divides are as important—if not more so—as the so-called division between Islamism and secularism. For Tunisian Islamists, obstacles to a collective reappropriation of national identity do not come mainly from the west or the north but from Saudi Arabia, the Persian Gulf, or even Egypt and Turkey. While most Nahdawi leaders refrain from engaging in overt critique of Salafi groups or of the Islamist politics of neighboring countries, they strongly emphasize the originality and wealth of Tunisian cultural heritage, citing Tunisian Islamist reformers from the early twentieth century such as Tahar Haddad and Mohamed Fadel Ben Achour. In addition to this nationalist emphasis on Tunisia's own historical resources, Nahdawi intellectuals and leaders call for a comprehensive hermeneutical reformation. This, they argue, is more than a mere issue of random *ijtihad* (interpretation): Islamists, in collaboration with their supporters, need to develop a new methodology to reinterpret the past and see the present.

The way Nahda leaders and intellectuals define Islam today, as the source of an ethical and cultural project of collective introspection and reformation, echoes the way in which Italian philosopher Benedetto Croce talked about the Christian identity of Europe in 1942. In his essay "Why We Cannot Help Calling Ourselves 'Christian,'" Croce did not argue that "we" *are* Christians, or that "we" *must call ourselves* Christians. The phrasing of his title was an acknowledgment that Christianity as an unquestioned set of norms and institutions, as immune from critique, was dead. But the pamphlet was also an attempt to demonstrate why

Christianity could still have something to say to—and about—Europe. Christianity here was not opposed to secularism, atheism, or Islam but to the fascist and imperial politics of 1942 Europe and to the complicity of the Christian institutional church with this politics. Croce's essay is not a demand, but a proposition—almost a plea. It combined hope for a better future with nostalgia for a time when people were "all the more intensely Christian than they [were] free."

A similar combination of nostalgia and hope can be found in the discourse of contemporary Islamist thinkers and politicians. Longing for a golden age of Tunisian history and culture sustains a hope for emancipation from an era defined by postcolonial politics, authoritarian secularism, and state-sanctioned Islam. No matter how fierce Nahda's opponents are, there is wide support for the party's message and project, one that can be summarized in the same terms as Croce's statement: "We cannot not call ourselves 'Muslims.'" Such a performative statement stems from a realization of the inadequacy of the ideology of *shumuliyya* (integralism) to Tunisian society, but also from the conviction that Islam still has something to say about that society. The reference to Islam and the Muslim appellation are indeed polysemous, and may appear as empty signifiers to many. But this is precisely what defines Nahda's project; the reference to Islam is conceived as constraining, performative, and self-reflective rather than as imposed by some external force or institution. Only through this reference to Islam, Nahdawi argue, will Tunisians be able to reappropriate a sense of their own history. Ultimately, what matters is retrieving control of their history, more than adopting Islamically correct ways of being and governing. "Our existence depends on God," writes Gianni Vattimo, "because here and now we can't speak our language nor live our historicity without answering to the message that the Bible has transmitted to us." Ajmi Lourimi, an admirer of Vattimo, says something similar when he insists on the need for Tunisians to regain a consciousness of their history. The reference to God and Islam matters primarily as the enabler of "our" existence, "here and now."

*   *   *

While many Nahda intellectuals see the revolution as an opportunity for Tunisian history to reconcile with itself, leftist parties, by contrast, consider the victory of the Islamist party as a historical contradiction. Still heavily informed by the antireligious Marxist doxa, secularist-leftist parties cannot come to terms with the fact that they were not the major actors and beneficiaries of the revolution. The outrage they feel at this anomaly in the Marxist revolutionary teleology explains why some of them are now discussing the possibility of alliance with the main counterrevolutionary party, Nida Tounes.

The polarization of the public and political debate that developed in the wake of the victory of Nahda in the October 2011 elections has had a complex effect on the discussion of religious freedom. Although all parties opposed to Nahda and the troika government pose as the champions and guardians of religious freedom, what they actually advocate is a return to a form of state secularism of the same type as the one that was implemented under the authoritarian rule of Bourguiba and Ben Ali. Their definition of religious freedom implies that the state should monitor all religious activities and expressions (in schools, mosques, and charities) in order to prevent the empowering of Islamist parties and associations. These repeated attacks have in turn had an impact on Nahda's own approach to religion. The understanding of Islam in terms of national revival and cultural authenticity seems to be progressively giving way to attempts to defend religion as a discrete analytical category and as a distinct realm of life. A new discourse emphasizing the role of the state in protecting Islam is emerging, even though it is in sharp contrast with previous arguments about the need to protect society from the encroachment of the state.

Artists versus Salafis

Paintings of postrevolutionary Tunisia, caricatures mocking the successive governments, dance shows, songs, short movies, and plays have flourished since January 2011. While this new artistic *infitah* (opening) can only be encouraged, the form of engagement of Tunisian "revolutionary" artists raises several questions. Most of these artists have built their public identity based on a Manichean narrative of "us versus them." "Us" is the artists, defined as a homogeneous group that resists oppression and corruption; "them" primarily designates the Salafis and their Islamist allies, and, to a lesser extent, the "government" or "the police." An analysis of the content of these artistic expressions is beyond the scope of this essay. I simply want to suggest here that the public interventions of many Tunisian artists have largely reinforced the polarization of the public sphere. My point is by no means to minimize the importance of threats that some artists have faced from violent Salafi demonstrations and from the minister of culture's lagging response. That being said, it is also true that artists' public discourse has consolidated the narrative of an irreducible confrontation between the "good" (oppressed Tunisian artists fighting for freedom and gender equality) and the "evil" (the ugly, dirty, and bad Salafis, always represented as a faceless, soulless, shouting crowd). In many cases the cultural references and sources of inspiration of publically engaged artists come from Europe and the United States. The imaginary background of numerous artistic expressions combines elements from *V for Vendetta*, Wikileaks, the Occupy movement, and French feminism and laicism, with a dose of new orientalism thrown in. Tunisia often seems to act simply as a decor in which the figures of the mine worker and the stereotypical silhouette of the unemployed graduate or the "wounded of the revolution" have replaced the old orientalist tropes of veiled women and luxurious palaces. A 2012 YouTube video that went viral, showing dancers improvising on the streets of Tunis, illustrates well this tendency. The slogan through which the dancers present their initiative ("I will dance in spite of all") is entirely based on the "artists versus Salafis" narrative. The music, the outfits of dancers, the dance movements they chose give the impression that the performance could actually take place anywhere in the world. Tunisian markets, streets, and people appear simply as exotic decor.

There are more sporadic initiatives that do not situate themselves in this binary narrative. But the deeper inscription of the "artist versus Salafis" binary in the domestic political disputes and in international debates about religious freedom suggest that this divide will endure, at least in the short term. Unfortunately the sedimentation of this opposition contributes to the foreclosure of the broad scope of possibilities opened by the nonnormative references to *irhal* and "whatever."

Sharia and the Constitution

A heated debate broke out in February 2012, after the draft of a constitutional project attributed to Nahda was leaked to the social networks. According to article 10 of this draft, sharia should be established as the main source of legislation. Article 20 of this same draft stipulated that freedom of expression should be limited by respect for the sacred. On

February 3, Habib Kehder, a Nahda deputy and rapporteur in the commission in charge of the constitution, contended in a radio interview that
sharia would indeed be a major source of inspiration for the constitution.
The debate about sharia first took place outside the National Constituent
Assembly, in the public media, and within parties. The Tunisian public
expressed mainly three arguments. Supporters of Nahda and members of
what is loosely labeled as the "Salafi nebula" (Tunisian Salafism includes
various trends, from pacific pietism to groups who endorse violence) argued for the inclusion of sharia in the constitution as the main source of
legislation, noting that as Tunisia is defined primarily as a Muslim country, its Islamic identity should be reinforced after decades of authoritarian secularism. Groups and individuals closer to the secularist Left and
members of the educated, francophone elite (artists and academics), but
also a significant part of the pious, apolitical bourgeoisie (teachers, shop-
keepers, and businessmen) vehemently opposed this view. For them the
draft was yet more evidence of how threatening and untrustworthy
the Nahda-led government was. They stood for maintaining article 1 of
the 1959 constitution stating that "Tunisia is a free, independent and sovereign state: its religion is Islam, its language is Arabic and its regime the
Republic." For many, this article was arguably, in all its vagueness and
ambiguity, the best way to deal with possible conflicts and disagreements
concerning identity and religion. Finally, a small minority contended
that any references to sharia or Islam should be dropped and replaced by
a reference to freedom of religion, conscience, and expression.

The public debate about sharia was informed by the numerous controversies about freedom of religion and expression that took place at the
same time. The trial of the head of the private network Nessma TV, who
was accused of offending sacred values by authorizing the broadcasting
of *Persepolis*, amplified the fears of the anti-sharia side. The demonstrations of Salafi groups at Manouba University, who claimed the right of
female students to wear *niqabs* (traditional Muslim veils), also increased
the general fear of the hegemony of strict Islamic norms in the public
space.

The issue of sharia also triggered a major controversy within Nahda.
Initially the majority of Nahda members were in favor of the inclusion
of sharia in the constitution. The rationale of the pro-sharia advocates
ranged from an aggressive desire to assert Tunisia's Islamic identity to
a milder observation that sharia was already the material source of a
large part of Tunisian legislation. The Personal Status Code, aspects of

contract law, and rules regarding business transactions are indeed essentially informed by parts of Maliki law. A minority of members were worried about the consequences that the inclusion of sharia might have on Tunisia's international image and attempted to demonstrate that article 1 was sufficient to assert Tunisia's Islamic identity. A few intellectuals tried to propose a middle ground by suggesting that the objectives of sharia (*maqasid al-sharia*), rather than sharia, should be included in the preamble of the constitution; such is the view of philosopher Abu Yareb Marzouki, a supporter of Nahda who refuses to become an official member. Accounts of what exactly happened within Nahda differ, and no public record of the internal debate exists. On March 26, 2012, however, Rashed Ghannouchi publicly expressed during a press conference Nahda's renunciation of the reference to sharia. This term, he explained, is "a little blurred," and there is no need to add "ambiguous definitions" in the constitutional text that might "divide the people." The same day, Nahda issued an official statement declaring that the Bureau Executif had voted against the inclusion of sharia.

After the interruption of the summer of 2012, the discussions and negotiations within each commission resumed in September 2012, and the Tunisian National Constituent Assembly made a new draft public on December 14, 2012. From the point of view of secularists, this new draft represents a step forward for the defense of gender equality and religious freedom. However, Islamists managed to maintain a number of provisions that express their attachment to what they define as Islamic or Arabic tradition. In other words, the second draft manifests a stronger degree of compromise than the first one but remains unsatisfactory and worrisome for many.

One of the major sources of contention between secularists and Islamists was the inclusion of article 148, stating that "no amendment to the Constitution may cause prejudice to Islam" and defining Islam as "the religion of the state." For secularists, the explicit definition of Islam as the religion of the state ruins the positive ambiguity of article 1: "Tunisia is a free, independent and sovereign state. Its religion is Islam, its language is Arabic and its form of government is a republic." Due to its syntactic ambiguity, article 1 could imply that Islam is either the religion of the state or the religion of Tunisia. By unilaterally choosing between these two possible meanings, secularists argue, Islamists are trying to impose a vision of Tunisia whereby politics and religion are not separated.

Notably, Islamist deputies propose varying reasons to support pro-Islam articles. While some defend these statements on strictly religious grounds, most of them put forward a more complex type of reasoning that combines postcolonial and antiauthoritarian arguments with religious ones. The more robust acknowledgment of the Islamic and Arabic heritage is, in their view, a way to reconcile Tunisia with its precolonial history and to heal from what they see as a brutal rupture caused not only by colonization but also by Bourguiba's Western-oriented policy. They remind their secularist opponents that in its constitutional reform of 2002, Ben Ali used references to universal values and human rights as a pretext to implement other measures that reinforced dictatorship.

Conclusion: A Lesson from the Constitution of January 2014

On January 27, 2014, the Constituent National Assembly of Tunisia finally adopted its new constitution, with two hundred deputies voting for the text and twelve against it, with four abstentions. This positive outcome resulted from more than two years of crises, doubts, and fears, notably marked by the political assassination of deputy Chokri Belaid and party leader Mohamed Brahmi, the suspension of the assembly's work during several weeks, and two government reshufflings. But the constitution is also the result of an uninterrupted and passionate deliberative process that took place within and outside the assembly, in the media, within grassroots associations, in the streets, and in the universities, cultural organizations, and cafés during the countless strikes and demonstrations. Most important, the constitution belies the well-entrenched assumption according to which Islamist parties are by essence bound to establish theocracies. Ironically, the Tunisian constitution of January 2014 is one of the most protective of religious freedom in the Arab world even though it was passed by an assembly with a majority of Islamist deputies. The constitution defines the state as civil (*dawla madaniyya*), and its article 6 (§1) protects freedom of belief (*mu'taqid*) *and* freedom of conscience (*dhamir*). The constitutionalization of the protection of freedom of conscience, which implies the right to unbelief, and the ban on accusations of apostasy represent a groundbreaking change in the Arab world. Although these provisions have not been initiated by Nahda deputies, it is thanks to their assenting to the inclusion of these phrases that such a progressive constitution was passed. Nahda could have chosen to obstruct and oppose the vote, but instead the party chose to approve of the final draft in order to show its attachment to democratic rule. The constitution also acknowledges women's rights and gender equality: article 45 stipulates that the protections granted to women by the Personal Status Code of 1956 cannot be restricted and should instead be increased. Gender parity in future assembly is also defined as an objective of the constitution. True, there remain a few phrases that express some degree of ambiguity. For example, article 6 (§2) stipulates that the state forbids offense to the sacred. Orthodox secularists brandish this phrase as evidence that the constitution does not establish a truly liberal order whereby religion and sacredness are strictly bound to the spheres of the individual belief. They also contend that the maintaining of article 1 from the 1959 constitution, which defines Islam as the religion of Tunisia, introduces the theoretical possibility of a discrimination against non-Muslims. It is true that, if one abides by an orthodox definition of secularism and liberalism, the Tunisian constitution does not exactly conform to the secular-liberal cannon. But the same could be said of many constitutions, including the US Constitution; as is shown by Winnifred Fallers Sullivan, the two religion clauses of the First Amendment are so ambiguous that they often have been used as vehicles to establish the hegemony of culturally dominant understandings of what counts as religion. And a constitution cannot in and of itself resolve all the political, cultural, and social issues that may arise in the future. The likelihood of a constitution actually helping a people to solve their conflicts in the future is dependent on whether the constitution represents a real, long-fought-for compromise or an artificial freezing of political conflicts. Because the Tunisian constitution falls in the first category, there are reasons to be hopeful. By creating its own original path toward democracy, and through its unique, often tragic commitment to unity and compromise, postrevolutionary Tunisia has taught us an important lesson: a robust and authentic acknowledgment of fundamental rights can only emerge from the long, painful, and murky process of political dispute (in both senses of debate and conflict). If Tunisian deputies finally agreed on the inclusion of articles such as article 6 and article 45, it is not because of the abstract and artificial talk on international religious freedom that some Western organizations seek to promote as norms; it is only because, after debating and fighting for more than two years, they came to consider that such rights were coherent with Tunisia's own political trajectory.

Selected Bibliography

Agamben, Giorgio. *The Coming Community*. Minneapolis: University of Minnesota Press, 2003.

Je danserai malgré tout 2 (I will dance in spite of it all 2). December 8, 2012. Accessed April 26, 2014, at http://www.youtube.com/watch?v=kkFZSeFuGZM.

Kehder, Habib. "Habib Khedher Rapporteur Général de la Constitution: Parce Que Je Le Vaux Bien," Interview with Radio Mosaique FM, *Midi Show*. February 2, 2012. Accessed April 26, 2014, at http://archive.mosaiquefm.net /index/a/ActuDetail/Element/18129-Habib-Khedher-rapporteur-général-de -la-constitution-parce-que-je-le-vaux-bien.html.

Rorty, Richard, and Gianni Vattimo. *The Future of Religion*. New York: Columbia University Press, 2005.

Zeghal, Malika. "Competing Ways of Life: Islamism, Secularism and Public Order in the Tunisian Transition." *Constellations* 20, no. 2 (2013): 254–74.

CHAPTER SEVENTEEN

Beyond Establishment

Lori G. Beaman

Religious freedom and religious establishment have come to mean many things to many people. This is, in part, because of the shifting contours of the definition of religion itself (as has been pointed out by others in this volume, including Winnifred Fallers Sullivan and Elizabeth Shakman Hurd). But it is also because the nature of freedom is contested ground. The shifting nature of these two concepts makes normative assessment—religious freedom is good, religious freedom is bad—extremely difficult to carry out in any meaningful way. Further, when people advocate for or against religious freedom they are often talking about very different things. The measurement of establishment is equally nebulous.

It may come as a surprise to some that the discourse of establishment is not particularly resonant for many states, and as Hurd has so ably argued, religious freedom has taken on dangerously imperialistic overtones. These American standard bearers are generated by the First Amendment: "Congress shall make no law respecting an establishment of religion, or prohibiting the free exercise thereof. . . ." Establishment has become the base criterion by which the possibility of religious freedom has been measured. Discussing the relationship between these two concepts has become something of an intellectual cottage industry, which has been transformed into a national export. Nations that do not espouse the sort of constitutional disestablishment embraced (in theory) in the United States example are often suspect, as is their ability to support any sort of meaningful religious freedom. But disestablishment as a conceptual touchstone and ultimate goal does not translate especially well into other contexts nor, perhaps, even in the American context. A number of scholars, especially Sullivan, have seriously dented the establishment armor, pointing out that religious establishment has immobilized social institutions like law, preventing them from engaging in creative thinking about religious freedom. To be clear, when I talk about religious establishment, I am assuming that the constitutional prohibition of establishment has not been realized, nor is it ever likely to be, and that in fact what exists in the United States, following Sullivan, is establishment. I leave it to other scholars who are better equipped with knowledge of the US context than I am to articulate the contours of that establishment. It is perhaps the pretense of disestablishment's accomplishment that facilitates a certain dampening of religious freedom, such as that detailed in Sullivan's *The Impossibility of Religious Freedom*. Nonetheless, the myth of disestablishment continues to hold sway as the place from which to begin discussions about religious freedom. Further, there is some evidence to suggest that religious establishment, defined in US terms, has created space in some jurisdictions for religious minorities in public discourse. And, equally important, it has created space for the nonbelievers, atheists, agnostics, humanists, and the indifferent. The United Kingdom provides perhaps the best example of such an establishment, although the situation there is informed by historical and global confluences and tensions over who is entitled to a voice that are too complex to review here. National context is important in these discussions—including historical, economic, and cultural considerations. So then it becomes necessary to ask questions about why one country's "establishment" can impede religious freedom while another's might encourage it. I do not pretend to answer that in this chapter, but rather to reflect on these terms as they circulate in other contexts, especially in Canada.

My argument is not simply for a critical assessment of whether or not establishment exists but for a shift in analytical focus from the constitutional discourse on establishment and its attendant discussion of church-state relations to one that begins with different assumptions and questions. If the state is always assumed to have a relationship with religion in one form or another, the binary of establishment/disestablishment becomes possible, which would in turn shift the focus to mapping the contours of the myriad and dynamic ways in which that relationship works. It might then also be possible to step away from the freedom-disestablishment association that stifles critical and creative analysis. This in turn could prompt a more sophisticated treatment of power that would embrace a relational understanding of power rather than a narrowly hierarchical one.

Although it might be objected that an assumption of a relationship goes too far, evidence from a number of liberal Western democracies suggests that this sort of acknowledgment is realistic and accurate.

An example of the type of analytical shift in direction being suggested is illustrated by the work of James Beckford. In "The Return of Public Religion? A Critical Assessment of a Popular Claim" Beckford reviews the relationship between the British state and organized religion. He reflects on the often-heard yet contradictory statements that religion is enjoying resurgence in the public sphere and that religion is systematically excluded from public life. Beckford addresses this contradiction by pointing out that the state, political society, and civil society have never been neatly divided in Britain. He then outlines the British government's strategy for engaging with religion—a strategy that both blurs the line between state and civil society and manages religious and ethnic diversity. Beckford does not use the words *establishment* or *religious freedom* in his article and only specifically mentions "church-state" relations a few times. Yet the analysis is rich and insightful as Beckford layers religion, spirituality, state, and public together, highlighting the relational rather than hierarchical nature of these engagements.

It might be useful to complicate the discussion about religious freedom, then, by embracing two assumptions: first, that religious freedom means different things in different contexts, and thus an interesting analytical launching place might be an exploration of how (or whether) religious freedom is being used and by whom, rather than whether a state has an established religion; and second, that all states have a relationship with religion(s) and that it is not in fact always possible to make clear distinctions between the state and civil society in the first place. What emerges as being important, then, is the exploration of the nature of that relationship, the framing of interests, and the ways in which interests collude or clash. Does this mean that an analysis of (dis)establishment is never relevant or should be completely displaced from discussions of religious freedom? Not necessarily, but decentering establishment can yield some fruitful results. To illustrate, I will draw on a Canadian example.

Is there a religious establishment in Canada? Yes and no. The Constitution of Canada does not explicitly address establishment, but instead guarantees religious freedom in the Canadian Charter of Rights and Freedoms. However, the preamble to the Charter states, "Whereas Canada is founded upon principles that recognize the supremacy of God and the rule of law," and in section 29, recognition is given to the historic compromise that supports state funding for Protestant schools in Quebec and Roman Catholic schools in Ontario. Public discussions of religion sometimes casually mention that "we have separation of church and state" in Canada, even though this is not constitutionally true and, in fact, evidence from the constitution itself as just noted would support the opposite conclusion. Of course, it is arguable that mere mention of God in a constitution does not create establishment, as it were, but it should raise questions about how a state that juxtaposes God and the rule of law imagines God will or should act within that state. The state funding of public schools is important: only Christian schools were offered funding originally, and in some provinces this is still the case. Establishment is not an all-or-nothing endeavor; rather, its varieties are numerous, as Winnifred Fallers Sullivan and I have argued elsewhere; David Martin has also argued that there is a shadow establishment, and others have suggested similar conclusions. I have argued that a Christian hegemony exists that is embedded in social institutions and shapes not only the ways that religion is imagined but also shapes the construction of nation, values, citizenship, conceptual drivers like multiculturalism, and "othering" discourse. The point is that the secular is always entangled with the religious, and thus the question that is most interesting is *how* rather than *whether* they are entangled.

As Beckford argues is the case in Britain, in Canada the divisions have never been clear between state and civil society. The services of religious organizations were called upon by the state, for example, to deliver schooling to aboriginal children. This collaboration met the needs of both religion and state, the former to save the souls and missionize those they viewed as being uncivilized and in need of salvation, the latter to civilize and build a nation. Does disestablishment make sense in the Canadian context? Not really. The ongoing relationship between the state and religion, and their close intertwining to the point of being indistinguishable, mean that religion is so embedded in the social structure and institutions of this nation that it is impossible to untangle them from each other. Therefore any claim to disestablishment ignores the historically embedded power relations that shape contemporary developments. One of those developments has been the decision by the Canadian government to establish the Office of Religious Freedom.

In its election platform released in April 2011, the Conservative Party of Canada announced that it would pursue the establishment of the Office of Religious Freedom. In the June 2011 Throne Speech, the by-then

Conservative government announced that it was indeed establishing such an office. On October 3, 2011, the government held its first consultation meeting about the office. Subsequently the government came under criticism, primarily for its limited, conservative-Christian-heavy consultation process and for suspicion that the office would be principally concerned with securing and protecting Christian missionizing. Several things are of interest for the purposes of this discussion: first, one of the six people consulted was Thomas Farr, who was the first director of the US Office of International Religious Freedom; second, through the political speeches of its ministers, the government has consistently linked democracy and religious freedom, stating, "The long history of humanity has proven that religious freedom and democratic freedom are inseparable." Finally, both establishment and disestablishment regimes (in Canada and the United States, respectively) have been able to support the idea of such an office. In the Canadian context, the accusation that the inclusion of the Office of Religious Freedom violated the principle of separation of church and state was countered with the fact that Canada does not, in fact, have separation of church and state and that this idea is imported from the United States. In the United States, with its official disestablishment the Office of International Religious Freedom has been justified as an expression of the commitment to this ideal. It is clear that the meaning of the terms *establishment, quasi-establishment,* and *disestablishment* is highly fluid.

The more telling discussion relates to how religious freedom is being defined, by whom, and for what purposes. Preliminary descriptions by the Canadian office, for example, state that it will "monitor religious freedom around the world, to promote religious freedom as a key objective of Canadian foreign policy, and to advance policies and programs that support religious freedom." But it remains unclear what this means exactly. Will the Office of Religious Freedom concern itself with members of the Church of Latter-Day Saints who proselytize globally? Will it worry about Jehovah's Witnesses forced into military service in South Korea? Will the Office of Religious Freedom worry about Muslims in Switzerland who cannot build minarets, or Muslim women in France who cannot wear the *niqab* (traditional veil)? Or will it concern itself with matters closer to home, like *niqab*-wearing women in Canada who must strip off their face coverings to take the oath of citizenship? Whose religious freedom will be defended, and where? When on February 19, 2013, the Office of Religious Freedom was formally established and the

Canadian government finally appointed its ambassador of religious freedom, Andrew Bennett, an acting subdeacon and cantor with Ottawa's
Holy Cross Eastern Catholic Chaplaincy and St. John the Baptist Ukrai-
nian Catholic Shrine, the answers to these questions did not become any
clearer. According to Bennett, "Here's Canada's belief in what freedom
of religion is. Not only is it a Canadian principle, it's a universal principle." Although it is still too early to tell where the office will intervene,
given the process thus far there is little reason to believe that it will not,
as Hurd describes in this volume, sanctify a particular kind of religious
psychology that "relies on the notion of an autonomous subject who
chooses beliefs and then enacts them freely." Such an approach creates
a hierarchy of privilege for specific kinds of religion, all the while allowing the religious freedom crusade to continue under a guise of neutrality
and its sponsoring states to imagine themselves to be religiously "free"
and disestablished. The problem is, of course, that those states imagine
themselves to be religiously "free" and disestablished.

If establishment is not the question, what is? The preoccupation with
establishment and the adoption of it as a conceptual framework, repro-
ducing what Noah Salomon in this volume calls "the modern state's
voracious appetite for categorization," have distracted from critical engagement with a more sustained analysis of religious hegemonies. Constitutional freedom and disestablishment (in some cases), together with
declining participation in traditionally hegemonic religion (sometimes
simplified as "secularization"), have produced an intellectual compla-
cency regarding religion that has, despite volumes of critical scholarship,
often been imagined as static and conceptually solid. Assuming that
establishment—or religious hegemony—permeates state, civil society,
and political society (and that these are themselves fluid and interpenetrating categories) positions us for a different type of analytical gaze.
We may then see an ongoing metamorphosis that repositions religion in
certain circumstances as culture. One fascinating thing about this re-
positioning is its multisited dimension: in the United States, Canada,
and Italy, for example, religion has somehow become culture. But only
some religion can be cultural for some purposes. And the consequences
of one designation or another changes depending again on the context
and the power relations involved. To be more precise, a crucifix in a classroom or a municipal chamber can be imagined as cultural and as being
part of "our" heritage and, indeed, as a symbol of the foundation of
universal values and thus does not violate anyone's religious freedom.

Notably, though, a *hijab* can also be imagined as culturally specific (but not "ours") and therefore not *really* religion and, consequently, not eligible for protection under religious freedom provisions. Allow me to elaborate.

On May 27, 2013, the Quebec Court of Appeal decided in *Saguenay c. Mouvement laïque québécois* that neither the recitation of a prayer at the beginning of municipal council meetings in Saguenay, Quebec, nor the presence of either a crucifix or a sacred heart statue in council chambers (which is where the business of the city takes place) violates the human rights of nonbelievers—in this case the atheist complainant Alain Simoneau. At some point during his fight to have the prayer recitation stopped and the crucifix and statue removed, the Mouvement laïque québecois joined Mr. Simoneau in support. The Quebec Human Rights Tribunal found that Mr. Simoneau's rights were violated; the Court of Appeal disagreed. The following is the prayer that was (and still is) being recited before the council meetings:

> Dieu tout puissant, nous Te remercions des nombreuses grâces que Tu as accordées à Saguenay et à ses citoyens, dont la liberté, les possibilités d'épanouissement et la paix. Guide-nous dans nos délibérations à titre de membre du conseil municipal et aide-nous à bien prendre conscience de nos devoirs et responsabilités. Accorde-nous la sagesse, les connaissances et la compréhension qui nous permettront de préserver les avantages dont jouit notre ville afin que tous puissent en profiter et que nous puissions prendre de sages décisions. Amen.

> Almighty God, we thank you for the many blessings you have granted to Saguenay and to our citizens, such as freedom, growth opportunities, and peace. Guide us in our deliberations as members of the municipal council, and help us to take seriously our obligations and responsibilities. Give us the wisdom, the knowledge and the understanding to allow us to maintain the advantages enjoyed by our city in order that all can benefit from them and that we may make wise decisions. Amen. (Translation by Lori Beaman and Tess Campeau)

For those familiar with the 2011 *Lautsi and Others v. Italy* case from the Grand Chamber of the European Court of Human Rights, the following logic offered by the Quebec Court of Appeal will be strikingly familiar:

[88] Je retiens de l'opinion de ces experts que les valeurs exprimées par la prière litigieuse sont universelles et qu'elles ne s'identifient à aucune religion en particulier. Toujours selon ces experts, cette prière est conforme à une doctrine théiste moderne, ouverte à certains particularismes religieux non envahissants et raisonnables.

[88] What I've learned from the expert opinion is that the values expressed through the contentious prayer are universal and do not identify with a specific religion. Still according to these experts, this prayer complies with a modern theist doctrine open to non-obtrusive and reasonable religious denominations. (Translation by Tess Campeau)

The court notes that it is the duty of the state to protect the cultural heritage of society and frames the prayer, crucifix, and statue in that context under the broader rubric of the "common good" and universal values, a theme with a long history, as Robert Yelle points out in this volume. In the court's assessment, religion has two faces—one is not religion at all, but culture, or a broader imagining of religion that folds it into culture and renders it part of who "we" are. But in this same paragraph of reasoning, the court also preserves the space of religion, demarcating the prayer—if it *is* in fact religion—as complying with a "modern theist doctrine." The court, however, also distinguishes between reasonable religious denominations—and, presumably, unreasonable religious denominations. Objecting to such a prayer on religious grounds or atheist grounds thus becomes impossible—since the prayer is reasonable, opposition to it from either religious or nonreligious grounds is de facto unreasonable.

As mentioned above, the themes of universality, culture, and history are also at the heart of the *Lautsi* decision, which originated with a complaint by an atheist mother about the crucifix hanging in her children's classroom. In *Lautsi* a crucifix and Roman Catholicism were transformed in arguments by the Italian state from religious symbol and religion to cultural symbol and universal values. Thus, the crucifix on an Italian classroom wall was not just "religious" but "cultural" and part of Italian heritage. Although the court acknowledges the religious nature of the symbol, it also considers—and indeed there was extensive argument presented on this point—that the crucifix is an important part of Italian heritage and culture. This very point is picked up in *Saguenay c. Mouvement laïque québécois* to justify the court's conclusion that the prayer is universal and the symbols "heritage." The possibility that other religious traditions might enter into the classroom (through, for example, a *hijab*-wearing student) was taken as evidence in *Lautsi* of the openness of the classroom to religious diversity. The crucifix was presented as innocuous, noncoercive, passive, and universal, representing common values: "It is hardly necessary to add that the sign of the cross in a classroom, when correctly understood, is not concerned with the freely held convictions of anyone, excludes no one and of course does not impose or prescribe anything, but merely implies, in the heart of the aims set for education and teaching in a publicly run school, a reflection—necessarily guided by the teaching staff—on Italian history and the common values of our society legally retranscribed in the constitution, among which the secular nature of the State has pride of place." As in the *Saguenay* case, the transformation of the crucifix as a universal, inclusive symbol was qualified by the notion that this is a "correctly understood" interpretation, thus displacing the possibility of disagreement that will, ipso facto, be an incorrect interpretation. The Supreme Court of Canada heard an appeal of the *Saguenay* decision in October 2014; the decision has yet to be released, and so it remains to be seen how the Court will frame these issues.

The Quebec Court of Appeal decision, which explicitly relies on *Lautsi* for justification, is not an isolated case. A similar sleight of hand occurred when the Bouchard-Taylor Commission Report recommended the removal of the crucifix from the Salon bleu, the main chamber of the provincial legislature and the place where all of the legislative business of the state is presided over by a blatantly Christian symbol. The Bouchard-Taylor Commission, which was cochaired by sociologist Gerard Bouchard and prominent philosopher Charles Taylor, was formed to respond to what was worked up by the media as a crisis in accommodation. Public anxiety had been generated over *Multani v. Commission scolaire Marguerite-Bourgeoys*, in which the Supreme Court of Canada "accommodated" the religious practices of a Sikh schoolboy who wished to wear his *kirpan* (ceremonial dagger) to school. The court held that the schoolboy could in fact wear the *kirpan*, a decision that caused a media frenzy that increased public anxiety about publically visible religious minority practices (like the wearing of *kirpan*, *hijab*, *niqab*, and so on). The commission held public hearings, received some nine hundred submissions, and prepared a report about the so-called crisis in which it made recommendations. As mentioned above, one of those was to remove the

crucifix from the Salon bleu. The day the report was issued, the National
Assembly voted unanimously to keep the crucifix, stating that it was an
important symbol of Quebec's heritage and part of its history; Quebec
historically has had a Roman Catholic majority, and in fact the majority of Quebeckers still identify as Roman Catholic on surveys, despite
extremely low church attendance and a relationship with the church that
is probably best characterized as one of "love-hate."

Although some might like to imagine the story of majoritarian religion-
turned-culture as being unique to Quebec, there are similar traces of
a turn to culture as a safe space for majoritarian religion, specifically
Christianity, in the rest of Canada (as well as in the United States—see,
for example, *Lynch v. Donnelly* as well as Sullivan's discussion of *Salazar
v. Buono*). Soon after the enactment of the Canadian Charter of Rights
and Freedoms, Sunday closing cases in Canada engaged in similar
transformative exercises—most notably in *R v. Edwards Books and Art
Ltd.*, when the Supreme Court of Canada, in upholding the Sunday closing law, declared that Sunday as a day of rest had nothing to do with
Christianity or, at the very least, religious origins do not render a day of
rest religious. Using a logic similar to that in *Lautsi* and in *Saguenay*, the
court noted, "Our society is collectively powerless to repudiate its history, including the Christian heritage of the majority" and "[t]o say that
the States cannot prescribe Sunday as a day of rest for these purposes
solely because centuries ago such laws had their genesis in religion would
give a constitutional interpretation of hostility to the public welfare
rather than one of mere separation of church and State." Note the entry
of public welfare here, a theme that is later replayed in the *Saguenay* case
as the public good, and the reminder that Christianity, even if historical,
is the religion of the majority. The court combed through evidence of
Sunday closing in other countries—including Soviet Russia and Japan—
and concluded that because they do not have a history of Christianity
and still have Sunday closing that Sunday closing is not a religious or
specifically Christian practice. This conclusion ignores, of course, the
impact of globalization and the long reach of Christian empires such
as the United Kingdom, France, and the United States. The court concluded that the law was 'secular' while maintaining what Samuel Moyn
describes as the "healthy communion" between religious freedom and
Christianity.

R. v. Edwards Books and Art Ltd. followed hard on the heels of the
initially expansive understanding of religious freedom elaborated by

Supreme Court justice Brian Dickson in the first post-Charter religious freedom case, *R. v. Big M Drug Mart Ltd.*, in which the court struck down the Sunday closing law. In that case Justice Dickson explicitly recognized the possibility of the tyranny of the majority, stating,

> To the extent that it binds all to a sectarian Christian ideal, the *Lord's Day Act* works a form of coercion inimical to the spirit of the *Charter* and the dignity of all non-Christians. In proclaiming the standards of the Christian faith, the Act creates a climate hostile to, and gives the appearance of discrimination against, non-Christian Canadians. It takes religious values rooted in Christian morality and, using the force of the state, translates them into a positive law binding on believers and non-believers alike. The theological content of the legislation remains as a subtle and constant reminder to religious minorities within the country of their differences with, and alienation from, the dominant religious culture.

The strange turnaround in *Edwards Books* can be justified by legal scholars, but is odd by any other measure. What is interesting for the present discussion is the way in which the themes of history, values, religious majorities, universality, and culture play out in these cases. *R. v. Big M Drug Mart Ltd.* serves as a reminder of an alternative to the current move in law and in public discourse toward categorizing religion as culture, which effectively removes majoritarian religion from scrutiny and in fact positions those who object to it as unreasonable, militaristic, against the common good, or as "demanding" that all religion (or majority culture) be removed from the public sphere.

Within a week of the release of the Court of Appeal decision in *Saguenay*, yet another controversy erupted in Quebec, this time over the wearing of turbans on the soccer field. Despite the Fédération Internationale de Football Association's (FIFA) position on this (which allows the wearing of turbans), the Quebec Soccer Federation issued a statement that turbans were not to be worn on the soccer field. Then Quebec Premier Pauline Marois issued a statement defending that decision, relying on the idea of Quebec and common values: "Quebec is a welcoming society that wants to integrate all those who want to participate in its values, participate in this reality we represent collectively, which accepts differences but also wants to share common values." Her government also proposed a Charter of Quebec Values, which was originally proposed as a Charter of Secularism. That proposed charter became the focus of a divisive public debate in Quebec whose impact transcends the fact that a Liberal Party government has recently been elected. Given the all-party support for the retention of the crucifix in the Salon bleu, it is almost certain that those values will include the "cultural heritage" of majoritarian religion. As an interesting aside, when the new ambassador to the Office of Religious Freedom was asked whether the soccer controversy was something he might get involved in, he answered that the mandate of his office is about foreign policy and about defending freedom of religion in other countries: "In Canada we're very blessed to have institutions like the Charter of Rights and Freedoms and parliamentarians and legislators who actually act to defend these freedoms."

One objection to the observation that religion has been transformed into culture is that religion *is* part of culture. In part this is true, and it is important to bear in mind Courtney Bender's caution in this volume about our current infatuation with "differentiation," or evidence of religion's differentiation from other parts of social life (upon which, she argues, current uses of pluralism depend). But it is also the case that religion is separated out as an analytical and lived category both in law and in public discourse at certain times and for certain purposes. The point of this discussion is to highlight the power dynamics in that process, as well as to underscore the fluid nature of these categories and the possibilities for their transition. By constructing the practices of religious majorities as culture rather than as religion, they become a benign presence in the face of the (dangerous, offensive, alien) religious practices of the other or of the (also dangerous) godless atheist.

By pushing past establishment as a framework for analysis and exploring the ways that particular religious traditions, practices, and beliefs are woven through social institutions and practices, and in fact *assuming* that they do, we make possible a richer exploration of religious diversity and religious freedom. Using a conceptual model that captures the dynamic ways that religion changes and is socially constructed can open space to ask different sorts of questions than those under an establishment framework.

Acknowledgments

I would like to acknowledge the support of the Religion and Diversity Project in the preparation of this chapter as well as the ongoing financial support of my research through my Canada Research Chair in the Contextualization of Religion in a Diverse Canada. I am also grateful to Marianne Abou-Hamad and Tess Campeau for their editorial assistance.

Selected Bibliography

Baird, John. "Address by the Honourable John Baird, Minister of Foreign Affairs, to the United Nations General Assembly." 66th Session of the United Nations General Assembly, New York City, September 26, 2011. Accessed April 3, 2012, at http://www.international.gc.ca/media/aff/speeches-discours /2011/2011-030.aspx?lang=eng&view=d.

Beaman, Lori G. *Defining Harm: Religious Freedom and the Limits of the Law.* Vancouver: University of British Columbia Press, 2008.

Beckford, James A. "The Return of Public Religion? A Critical Assessment of a Popular Claim." *Nordic Journal of Religion and Society* 23, no. 2 (2010): 121–36. Accessed August 22, 2013, at http://tapir.pdc.no/pdf/NJRS/2010/2010-02-2.pdf.

Canadian Charter of Rights and Freedoms, Part I of the Constitution Act, 1982, being Schedule B to the Canada Act 1982 (UK), 1982, c 11.

Conservative Party of Canada. *Here for Canada.* Ottawa: Conservative Party of Canada, 2011. Accessed August 22, 2013, at http://www.conservative.ca/media /2012/06/ConservativePlatform2011_ENs.pdf.

Martin, David. "Canada in Comparative Perspective." In *Rethinking Church, State, and Modernity: Canada Between Europe and America*, edited by David Lyon and Marguerite Van Die, 23–33. Toronto: University of Toronto Press, 2010.

Seljak, David, Joanne Benham Rennick, Andrea Schmidt, Kathryn Da Silva, and Paul Bramadat, Department of Canadian Heritage. *Religion and Multiculturalism in Canada: The Challenge of Religious Intolerance and Discrimination, Final Report*. Ottawa, Ontario, Canada: Multiculturalism and Human Rights Program. Accessed August 22, 2013, at http://amicus.collections canada.ca/aaweb-bin/aamain/itemdisp?sessionKey=999999999_142&l=0&v =0&lvl=1&rt=1&itm=37402328&rsn=S_WWWbbaTMo33s&all=1&dt=%22 Seljak,+David%22 . . . &spi=-.

Sullivan, Winnifred Fallers. *The Impossibility of Religious Freedom.* Princeton, NJ: Princeton University Press, 2007.

———. "The Cross: More Than Religion?" The Immanent Frame, May 5, 2010. Accessed August 22, 2013, at http://blogs.ssrc.org/tif/2010/05/05/more-than -religion/.

Sullivan, Winnifred Fallers, and Lori G. Beaman, eds. *Varieties of Religious Establishment.* Burlington, VT: Ashgate, 2013.

CHAPTER EIGHTEEN

The Bishops, the Sisters, and Religious Freedom

Elizabeth A. Castelli

A t its March 2012 meeting, the Administrative Committee of the United States Conference of Catholic Bishops (USCCB) approved *Our First, Most Cherished Liberty: A Statement on Religious Liberty*, a document drafted by the conference's Ad Hoc Committee for Religious Liberty. The statement offers a brief sketch of purported threats to religious freedom in the United States, a highly compressed and partial history of religious freedom in America, a sober call to disobey "an unjust law" (never explicitly named, but almost certainly the 2009 Affordable Care Act [ACA] and its attendant administrative regulations concerning contraceptive coverage), and an exhortation to US Catholics to participate in A Fortnight of Freedom from June 21 through July 4 of that year—a period of prayer and activism during a time when "both our civil year and liturgical year point us . . . to our heritage of freedom."

The rhetoric of the bishops' statement is familiar to anyone who has followed conservative Christian activism around the cause of religious freedom in the United States over the last two decades or so, though the recourse of Catholic officials to such language is a relatively recent innovation. The bishops' definition of "religious freedom" or "religious liberty" is both opaque and expansive—in imitation of conservative Christian activism on the issue more generally. The bishops note the priority of the first amendment to the US Constitution and the priority of religious freedom ("our first . . . liberty") among the freedoms guaranteed by that amendment. Acknowledging that Americans are not alone in their claims concerning freedom ("Freedom is not only for Americans"), they nevertheless see the United States as exceptional in its relationship to it ("we think of it as something of our special inheritance"), viewing Americans as the particular guardians of freedom ("We are stewards of this gift, not only for ourselves but for all nations and peoples who yearn to be free").

The bishops go on to enumerate specific examples of "religious liberty under attack." By the logic of priority, the ACA-related mandate issued earlier in the year by the US Department of Health and Human Services requiring health insurance coverage for contraception (which the document calls the "HHS mandate for contraception, sterilization, and abortion-inducing drugs") holds pride of place in the list of instances of religious freedom under siege. The ACA requires that health insurance plans cover contraception without requiring cost sharing on the part of insured individuals. Although religious organizations and religiously affiliated nonprofit organizations enjoy exemptions from this general requirement, the USCCB has taken the position that *any* requirement of contraceptive coverage, including that for secular, for-profit employers' health care plans, constitutes a violation of religious freedom. Indeed, they argue that *any* legal requirement to provide contraceptive coverage constitutes a violation of religious freedom.

But the bishops also cite a number of other domains of purported constraint: the refusal by state and local authorities to use the foster care or adoption placement services of Catholic Charities because of the organization's unwillingness to place children with cohabiting or same-sex couples; Alabama's punitive anti-immigrant legislation, which made it a crime to harbor or transport undocumented immigrants, as some Christian churches do; the denial of official recognition of a Christian student group at the University of California Hastings College of Law because of the group's requirement that its leaders be Christian and abstain from extramarital sexual activity; and New York City's discontinuation of the practice of renting public school buildings to churches for weekend services, among others. Religion (a category represented in the statement exclusively by Christian examples) is under siege, the argument runs, on the federal, state, and local levels and on many different fronts.

But if the document seeks to catalog the wide range of threats to religious liberty, it is nevertheless primarily concerned with undergirding the bishops' campaign against the inclusion of contraceptive coverage under the ACA. The document sets the terms of the debate agonistically and dramatically; the ACA itself is nowhere named explicitly. Yet, given the rest of the content of the conference's religious liberty website (with "HHS Mandate" and "Conscience Protection" as featured subjects for activism), it certainly resides behind the characterization of "an unjust law [that] cannot be obeyed," a law that imposes the will of the state upon religious institutions and individuals. Arguing by analogy, the bishops juxtapose the need to disobey such an unjust law—a duty Catholics "must discharge . . . as a duty of citizenship and an obligation of faith"—to the religiously inflected arguments and actions of the US civil rights movement of the 1950s and '60s, using Martin Luther King Jr.'s "Letter from a Birmingham Jail" as their proof text. Strikingly, the bishops also take care to distinguish between "conscientious objection" to a societal requirement (unspecified, but one might think of conscientious objection to military service) from the requirement to resist an unjust law. One can imagine that the bishops are seeking to sidestep the question of all of the other ways in which tax dollars are used to support militarism, capital punishment, or other forms of state-sponsored violence to which religious individuals or institutions may object. Following the bishops' logic, opposition to these institutionalized forms of state violence does not rise to the status of opposition to "unjust law," which "cannot be obeyed," presumably because the bishops distinguish between contraception as a moral evil under all circumstances and state-sponsored violence (such as war-making) as sometimes justified (under the logics of "just war" theory), open to individual conscientious objection but not requiring full-scale collective opposition by all Catholics. Framing their opposition to the health care mandate in terms of religious freedom, it needs to be emphasized, is a strategic move that narrows the terrain significantly: to challenge the bishops' opposition to the health care mandate requires one to take a position against religious freedom.

When *Our First, Most Cherished Liberty* was publicly announced in April 2012, the USCCB also announced its initiative called A Fortnight of Freedom, a two-week period beginning on June 21, the feast day shared by Saint John Fisher and Saint Thomas More, and ending on July 4, US Independence Day. Fisher and More are commemorated in the Catholic calendar of saints' days as martyrs who stood up to the monarchy when it sought to wrest power from the church in sixteenth-century England. The USCCB document that announced the 2012 Fortnight of Freedom explicitly noted the significance and appropriateness of these two martyrs, whose deaths are remembered as lives sacrificed in a struggle against the overreaching of corrupt political authorities, establishing them as suitable role models for the contemporary moment. Framing the Fortnight event with Fisher's and More's feast day on one end and Independence Day on the other, the initiative wove together the religious and national calendars around the broader struggle for religious liberty. The bishops continued in the USCCB document to elaborate the theme of martyrdom by emphasizing other important feast days that fall within the Fortnight: the Feast of Saint John the Baptist on June 24, the Feast of Saints Peter and Paul on June 29, and the Feast of the First Martyrs of Rome on June 30. Collectively these feasts connect the contemporary Fortnight with the earliest martyrs, the foundation of the church, and figures whose deaths the church remembers as instances of the faithful executed by a powerful political entity—the Roman empire or its local political puppet (in the case of John the Baptist). By situating the Fortnight temporally in this fashion, the bishops linked the church's liturgical time with national time as well as the discourse of religious freedom with the discourse of persecution and martyrdom.

The citation of these particular saints is intentional and selective. Numerous other saints are also celebrated during this fourteen-day period in the liturgical calendar, including saints whose stories do not align so seamlessly with the religious liberty narrative. For example, June 26 is the feast day of Josemaría Escrivá de Balaguer, the Spanish priest who in 1928 founded the controversial, some might say notorious, movement Opus Dei. The organization enjoys Vatican favor but has come under considerable criticism from former members and other Catholics, especially around issues of secrecy and coercion. As the Jesuit scholar James Martin notes in *America*, the primary magazine for US Catholics, Escrivá himself emphasized the need for "holy coercion": "*compelle intrare* [make them come in] the Lord tells us." Escrivá's beatification in 1992 and subsequent canonization as a saint in 2002 were controversial, not only because of the nature of Opus Dei itself but because many within the church thought the promotion of Escrivá toward sainthood was premature: his case jumped the queue so that he was beatified before numerous others, not least of whom Pope John XXIII, the architect of the Second Vatican Council.

Among the many other saints whose feast days occur during the Fortnight of Freedom, two from the history of the early church particularly stand out: Irenaeus of Lyons on June 28 and Cyril of Alexandria on June 27. Irenaeus was the bishop of Lugdunum (now Lyons) in the Roman province of Gaul in the second century and is best known for his five-volume work *Contra Haereses* (Against Heresies). This work established the genre of heresiology and became a model for boundary-policing Christian writers in subsequent centuries. Like other ancient Christian writers in this genre, Irenaeus was concerned with documenting and refuting beliefs, teachings, and practices that he viewed as outside of the bounds of acceptability. In the process of describing and critiquing what he considered nonnormative, Irenaeus contributed to the formation and consolidation of what would become "orthodoxy." The people and communities he critiqued may have called themselves Christian, but it was Irenaeus's view that they were in need of pastoral discipline and correction—or, failing that, expulsion.

Cyril of Alexandria, meanwhile, lived two centuries later and served as the bishop of that multicultural and cosmopolitan Egyptian city, following his uncle Theophilus into office. Ancient historians and modern scholars alike offer captivating portraits of Cyril as a vitriolic partisan for orthodoxy, whose partisanship morphed easily into religiously inflected violence. Upon taking office Cyril confiscated the property and churches of sectarian Christians who opposed him. During his episcopacy he ordered the seizure of synagogues and their conversion into churches as well as the expulsion of Jews from their homes. He enthusiastically suppressed paganism in the city, including playing at least an indirect role in the murder of the influential neo-Pythagorean philosopher and scholar, Hypatia. He mobilized Egyptian monks in violent opposition to Christian sectarians, whom he and his allies deemed heretics.

In short, the Fortnight for Freedom calendar elevates a roster of martyr-saints whose feasts fall within its temporal parameters while ignoring other saints who represent a critical strand of church history commemorated during the same two-week period of time in the church's calendar—notably, the strand that includes the coercion-defending Escrivá, the heretic-hunting Irenaeus, and the violently intolerant Cyril whose zeal on behalf of doctrinal orthodoxy and religious purity produced anti-Jewish and antisectarian violence and what Ed Watts has called "the lynching of Hypatia." The bishops, in other words, seek to capitalize on the ideological charge and moral authority implied by martyrdom and persecution by placing themselves in a lineage of Christian martyrs when their political activism more closely mirrors that of an Escrivá, an Irenaeus, or a Cyril. This is not to suggest, of course, that their activism descends to the level of Cyril's religiously inspired violence, but that their continued insistence upon their own authority as the sole arbiters of correct teaching and practice—and their efforts to impose these teachings and practices upon others, Catholic or otherwise, by insisting that the ACA should never require contraceptive coverage for anyone—put them more naturally in the shadow of Escrivá, Irenaeus, and Cyril than in that of the first martyrs of Rome.

Turning to more contemporary US contexts, one can reasonably situate the bishops' activism within a lineage that allies them with the evangelical Christians whose activism led to the passage of the International Religious Freedom Act of 1998—activism that also successfully mobilized tropes of persecution and martyrdom in the service of the campaign, as I have shown elsewhere. Within the Catholic Church itself, one observes an increase in activism around international religious freedom and an increase in the discourse of persecution, accompanied by the view that this activism will help the church gain traction and coalition partners in other arenas. When the Italian government established the Observatory of Religious Liberty in 2012, for example, its inaugural conference in June of that year featured Baltimore's Archbishop William Lori as the keynote speaker. Lori is the chair of the USCCB Ad Hoc Committee for Religious Liberty and an outspoken critic of the ACA as a law that violates religious freedom. Meanwhile, an April 2012 conference at Catholic University of America titled "International Religious Freedom: An Imperative for Peace and the Common Good" sought to situate religious freedom as a key component in the achievement of global security. Archbishop Timothy Dolan of New York, the public face of the Fortnight for Freedom, gave the keynote address at this conference. Catholic University of America professor of international relations Maryann Cusimano Love also spoke there, arguing that the movement would do well to emphasize the intersecting categories of "women" and "security" and expressing the hope that such linkages would expand the church's ability to make common cause with groups working for women's rights internationally.

Acting under the aegis of religious freedom, the Catholic bishops have also lent moral and financial support to Catholic groups and individuals who have brought several dozen lawsuits across the country challenging the ACA. In April 2012, Justice Carol E. Jackson of the US District Court, Eastern District of Missouri, found for the defendants in one such suit—*O'Brien et al. v. US Department of Health and Human Services et al.*—against plaintiff assertions that the ACA violated the first amendment of the US Constitution, the Religious Freedom Restoration Act, and the

Administrative Procedure Act. This decision has not, however, fore-closed other suits, as the online clearinghouse for information on such suits makes clear (see the Becket Fund for Religious Liberty HHS Information Central website for updated information on these suits). The status of legal challenges to the ACA is a moving target. In May 2012, the Becket Fund for Religious Liberty HHS Information Central site carried the tagline, "55 plaintiffs, 23 cases, one constitutional mandate, and the go-to page for it all," whereas by October 2013 the same website listed "74 cases, over 200 plaintiffs" in a similar tagline. In October 2013, the site listed thirty-nine cases brought by for-profit organizations challenging the ACA. Of these cases, thirty had received injunctive relief, five had been denied injunctive relief, two had been dismissed, and two had been filed without further action.

It is within such a rhetorical and activist context that the bishops speak of religious freedom and seek to portray a consensus that aligns them with evangelical Protestants and Orthodox Jews, while excluding from the conversation other coreligionists who do not share either their ethical assessments of the particular issues under debate (e.g., access to medical services, reproductive freedom, etc.) or their political agenda. Consider, as just one example, the Religious Coalition for Reproductive Choice, which includes the Episcopal Church, most of the mainline Protestant denominations, the Unitarian Universalist Association, virtually all of the Reform, Reconstructionist, and Conservative Jewish governing bodies, and numerous Christian and Jewish national organizations. Moreover, while advocating for a public square in which religious arguments and actors move freely, the bishops frame the issue as one that sets a "naked public square" ("stripped of religious arguments and religious believers") in opposition to a "civil public square" ("where all citizens can make their contribution to the common good"), carefully disavowing any claim that they desire a "sacred public square" ("which gives special privileges and benefits to religious citizens"). "At our best," they write, "we might call this an American public square." Framed in this way, the very presence of religious arguments and believers is precisely what makes the public square "American." Their absence is, on its face, un-American. And yet, if the public square is a space of deliberation and debate, a space where arguments are evaluated and contested, it seems as though "religion" itself remains immune to contestation and critique—*in* the public square but not *of* it.

One could engage in an extended exploration of the way in which the bishops' framing of these issues—clearly beholden to nearly two decades of evangelical Protestant activism around religious freedom—depends upon a range of theoretical incommensurabilities, as the work of Winnifred Fallers Sullivan has so ably shown. One could further revisit the debates over the uneasy truce between religion and politics, church and state, that has been forged by recourse to the "Protestant secular," as Janet Jakobsen and Ann Pellegrini, among others, have diagnosed it. But what I prefer to do here is to engage in an imaginative exercise: what would it mean for the bishops to put their money where their collective mouth is and to defend religious freedom in their own polity—that is, within the Catholic Church itself? In other words, is there the possibility for religious freedom *within* the Catholic Church?

It should be noted that, on another Catholic horizon, the Vatican has decided that the exercise of what one might well call religious freedom on the part of American women religious—the exercise of conscience—is a problem requiring the intervention of episcopal oversight. In other words, the sisters are in need of some church-sponsored discipline and a reining-in of their faithful enactment of their commitments, governed by conscience. This action has been undertaken by the Congregatio pro doctrina fidei (Congregation for the Doctrine of the Faith), the modern incarnation of the Inquisition, which in the spring of 2012 issued its *Doctrinal Assessment of the Leadership Conference of Women Religious*. The report was the culmination of a process of critical investigation initiated by the Vatican beginning in early 2009, focused on the Leadership Conference of Women Religious (LCWR), an organization that represents 80 percent of Catholic nuns in the United States. Accused of "a rejection of faith [that] is also a serious source of scandal and . . . incompatible with religious life," objectionable "policies of corporate dissent" (on issues of women's ordination and homosexuality), and "radical feminist themes," the LCWR has become the target of disciplinary action by the Vatican.

This context is not the place to parse all of the details of the *Doctrinal Assessment*, which seeks "to implement a process of review and conformity to the teachings and discipline of the Church, the Holy See, through the Congregation for the Doctrine of the Faith." But in the context of the US bishops' expression of a deep commitment to the notion of religious freedom, it might be a worthwhile imaginative exercise to ponder the following question: What would a defense of religious freedom look like if the LCWR were considered "religion" in this case and the Vatican were considered "the state"?

Of course, the authors of the *Doctrinal Assessment*—all American cardinals, I have been told—would reject the question as I have framed it since they insist that faithful religious life can only be lived in "allegiance of mind and heart to the Magisterium of the Bishops," as they put it in the opening paragraph of the Assessment, quoting from John Paul II's 1996 Post-Synodal Apostolic Exhortation, *Vita consecrata*. In doing so, however, they rather show their hand. Religious freedom emerges as nothing more than a mode of shoring up the authority of the Magisterium of the Bishops, not a set of values that shelters and protects the acts of conscience undertaken by Catholic women religious in the United States. That is, there is a foundational paradox in the religious freedom enterprise insofar as it privileges the authority of the leadership of religious communities, thereby reinscribing often contested hierarchies and empowering *some* religious points of view over others. Yet ironically, in this case, recourse to a robust notion of personal conscience is an unambiguously orthodox position in Catholic moral theology and a fully justifiable exercise of religious freedom on the part of the nuns.

The LCWR itself has done a particularly eloquent job of defending the commitments and actions of its individual and collective members, asserting all the while their deep fidelity to the ethical demands of the Gospel, particularly in relationship to the poor. Their labor is grounded in a Gospel-based solidarity and a conscience-steeped discernment of priorities on the ground, which effectively sidestep the issue of episcopal authority in a fashion that the authors of the *Doctrinal Assessment* clearly find maddening. But the issue throughout the *Doctrinal Assessment* circles back over and over again to submission to the authority of the Magisterium, which, according to the Magisterium's representatives (bishops and cardinals, all) is the only position from which one can legitimately act. Such a closed loop of rhetoric and reasoning constructs and reinscribes authority through repetitious assertions of its own legitimacy. According to this logic, "religious freedom" is not a capacious category but one reducible to submission to institutional authority, authority that is defined solely by those who hold it. Indeed, some would argue that the very name Roman Catholic presupposes wholesale acquiescence to this logic—in other words, if one does not accept this logic, then one should simply relinquish the name and self-deport from the church.

The widespread outrage among Catholics in the United States in response to the *Doctrinal Assessment*'s attack on the LCWR—outrage that produced numerous thoughtful essays about the profound value and integrity of the actual work of Catholic nuns, vigils of support in cities across the country, and even the satirical Twitter hashtag #radicalfeministthemes—

has made it clear that, for many US Catholics, the actions of the Congregation for the Doctrine of the Faith do not, in fact, carry the authority they seek to reinscribe and shore up. These Catholics have also challenged the overarching logic of the hierarchy's "because we said so" defense of its pronouncements. Against the (obviously correct and even self-evident) observation that the church is not a democratic institution, the Catholics who defend the sisters of the LCWR nevertheless operate with a more expansive notion of "religious freedom," one that shifts the terrain of authority from the institution to the individual conscience. (Contrary to the commonplace framing of conscience as a specifically Protestant formulation, Catholic moral theology offers a robust theology of individual conscience, one that many Catholic moral theologians promote precisely as a counterweight to a theology too dependent upon the sole authority of the hierarchical Magisterium, which is to say the bishops.) On this shifted terrain, the Vatican emerges as the state (and it actually *is* a state, recognized by other nation-states and even the United Nations) that constrains the conscience-driven religious freedom of its citizens.

This reframing of the circumstances of the bishops and the sisters is, of course, only a thought experiment and one unlikely to hold sway with those, both inside the church and beyond its walls, who take the authority of the Magisterium for granted. But I would submit that it is a useful experiment because it opens up a broader discussion of the rhetorical use to which the category of "religious freedom" is increasingly committed by political actors in high-stakes debates in the postsecular age. When the bishops deploy the category of "religious freedom" and invoke the specter of persecution and martyrdom in the process, they seek simultaneously to affect policy in the broader society and to impose discipline within the church itself. In this they are more like the heresy-hunting and imperial bishops of the early church than like its faith-washed martyrs.

In its statement on religious liberty, the Conference of Bishops wrote, "The Christian church does not ask for special treatment, simply the rights of religious freedom for all citizens." Just for a moment, consider a restatement of that sentence: "The Catholic women religious and their allies in the church do not ask for special treatment, simply the rights of religious freedom for all members of the church." The radical impossibility of the restated sentence reveals the true character of the category of "religious freedom" in episcopal discourse—a category that underwrites the authority of the hierarchy, not the freedom of conscience of faithful Catholics.

Selected Bibliography

Becket Fund for Religious Liberty. HHS Mandate Information Central. Accessed May 1, 2012, at http://www.becketfund.org/hhsinformationcentral/.

Castelli, Elizabeth A. "Praying for the Persecuted Church: US Christian Activism in the Global Arena." *Journal of Human Rights* 4 (2005): 321–51.

Congregatio Pro Doctrina Fidei. *Doctrinal Assessment of the Leadership Conference of Women Religious.* 2012. Accessed 1 May 2012, at http://www.usccb .org/loader.cfm?csModule=security/getfile&pageid=55544.

Jakobsen, Janet R., and Ann Pellegrini, eds. *Secularisms.* Durham, NC: Duke University Press, 2008.

Martin, James, SJ. "Opus Dei in the United States." *America: The National Catholic Review.* February 25, 1995. Accessed May 1, 2012, at http://america magazine.org/opus-dei.

O'Brien et al. v. US Department of Health and Human Services et al. 2012. Accessed July 5, 2013, at http://law.justia.com/cases/federal/district-courts/mis souri/moedce/4:2012cv00476/119215/50.

Sullivan, Winnifred Fallers. *The Impossibility of Religious Freedom.* Princeton, NJ: Princeton University Press, 2005.

United States Conference of Catholic Bishops Ad Hoc Committee for Religious Liberty. *Our First, Most Cherished Liberty: A Statement on Religious Liberty.* 2012. Accessed May 1, 2012, at http://www.usccb.org/issues-and-action /religious-liberty/our-first-most-cherished-liberty.cfm.

Watts, Edward J. *Riot in Alexandria: Tradition and Group Dynamics in Late Antique Pagan and Christian Communities.* Berkeley and Los Angeles: University of California Press, 2010.

CHAPTER NINETEEN

The World That *Smith* Made

Winnifred Fallers Sullivan

In November 2011 the United States Conference of Catholic Bishops announced the creation of the new Ad Hoc Committee on Religious Liberty to be led by William Lori, the bishop of Baltimore. Addressing his "brothers" in the conference, and citing a wide range of authorities including John F. Kennedy, George Washington, Alexis de Tocqueville, Pope Benedict XVI, and Learned Hand, Lori explained the need for the new committee:

> For some time now, we have viewed with growing alarm the ongoing erosion of religious liberty in our country. . . . In failing to accommodate people of faith and religious institutions, both law and culture are indeed establishing un-religion as the religion of the land and granting it the rights and protections that our Founding Fathers envisioned for citizens who are believers and for their churches and church institutions. . . . Together, we will do our best to awaken in ourselves, in our fellow Catholics, and in the culture at large a new appreciation for religious liberty and a renewed determination to defend it.

The Ad Hoc Committee, along with other episcopal efforts, established an annual summer Fortnight for Freedom and a year-long Call to Prayer for Life, Marriage, and Religious Liberty to begin in Advent 2012.

Given the evidence of this and other calls to arms by the American Catholic bishops, as well as the ringing endorsement they have received from a remarkably wide range of public figures, it seems that many Americans truly believe that a zombie-like phenomenon called "unreligion" stalks the land, promoted alike by "law" and "culture," peddling aggressive secularism and displacing the rights that they say the "Founding Fathers envisioned for citizens who are believers and for their churches." Indeed, according to the Pew Research Center, "About half of Americans say the growing number of 'people who are not religious' is bad for American society." What is needed, the bishops say, is public recognition that "the freedom of religious entities to provide services according to their own lights, to defend publicly their teachings, and even to choose and manage their own personnel, is coming under increased attack."

There is much that could be said about the history of the Catholic Church and its dedication to the defense of religious freedom over the *longue durée*, and some of that story is told in other essays in this volume. The church as an institution is not easily characterized as being a part of the problem or part of the solution. This essay will focus rather on the company that the bishops are keeping today—and why the bishops' bellicose language accusing the administration of president Barack Obama of mounting a war on religious liberty seems to make sense to such a disparate and varied group across the religious and political spectrum. Beyond an evident self-interested concern with maintaining their authority inside and outside the church, there is a genuine urgency to the bishops' appeal, one that is legible to a surprising number of Americans. In the last couple of decades, numerous projects have been launched to advocate for religious freedom, in the United States and elsewhere, many warning of the dire consequences of failure. Suddenly, it seems, the protection of religious freedom is all that stands between us and nihilistic oblivion. For some a lack of religious freedom explains a rising tide of poverty, inequality, and even violence. How did it come to be that so many current concerns are being traced to a lack of religious liberty?

This view is not exclusive to the United States. Advocacy for religious freedom is a global phenomenon today, as many have detailed. And we have been here before. Religion and freedom, broadly conceived, are intertwined in the stories told about government in complex ways throughout history. A full accounting has yet to be done. But new alliances are being made today, alliances whose commitments are not wholly founded in a concern for freedom. The salience and urgency of a call for religious liberty today is deeply and problematically connected to a politics of fear and containment, for the churches and for other campaigners. It is at the same time, paradoxically perhaps, a call underwritten by the successful popularization of the romance of a kind of religious universalism. In this essay I confine myself to the recent US domestic context—and to the convergence of two linked threads in the multiple genealogies that have led us to this perplexing moment—that is, recent developments in First Amendment jurisprudence and the unintended consequences of the formation of religious studies as an academic field.

It is a commonplace in the academic study of religion today to observe that the word *religion* is manifestly conditioned by the history of its use and that it is deeply problematic, epistemologically and politically, to generalize across the very wide range of human goings-on that are now included in this capacious term. To speak of religion is always to elide and conceal much that is critical to understanding the deeply embedded ways of being often denoted by the shorthand term *religion*. It is also common now to note the very specific difficulty of definition that faces interpreters and enforcers of legal instruments purporting to protect and regulate the freedom of "religion." And yet, among scholars of religion, the temptation to hold at once a highly skeptical attitude toward the semantic reference of the word and a zealous commitment to religious freedom is almost irresistible.

American Catholic bishops have had their own fraught history with religion and with religious freedom, one that has periodically involved the shunning—or worse—of members of their own church who invoke claims to religious freedom and religious equality, American style, to justify their own dissent. The bishops now seem to wish both to claim it for their own, as Catholic and American, and at the same time to distance themselves from its implications when it comes to monitoring behavior within the church. By associating themselves with others with whom they share only this outward political commitment they are always also in danger of losing control of the narrative and falling into what the antimodernists in the church have identified as the sin of indifferentism. Why do the scholars of religion and the bishops both want to have their cake and eat it too?

One could begin the US story of religion and freedom at various points, beginning with events in virtually any of the last five or six centuries. Yet there is a sense in which the conversation began anew two and a half decades ago when the US Supreme Court decided *Employment Division v. Smith*. *Smith*, known as the peyote case, concerned a claimed constitutional exemption from narcotic laws for members of the Native American Church who ingest peyote in the context of a religious ritual. Justice Antonin Scalia's opinion for the majority in *Smith* held that the free exercise clause of the First Amendment to the US Constitution does not mandate a religious exemption, or accommodation, from neutral laws of general application when they impinge on the activities of religiously motivated folks, even if such laws effectively outlaw acts that are understood by those folks to be nonnegotiable religious obligations—even, as in the *Smith* case, acts that they termed sacraments.

The *Smith* decision was broadly received by religious conservatives in the United States as effectively and finally revealing the implacable (and widely suspected since the Bible reading and school prayer decisions of the 1960s) hostility of the federal government toward religion. But, much more important, the coalition of more than sixty religious groups that came together—and quickly and successfully lobbied Congress to overrule *Smith* with passage of the Religious Freedom Restoration Act (RFRA) in 1993—included both liberals and conservatives. Indeed, it included groups from across a very broad American spectrum politically and theologically. By thus defining itself in opposition to the government's perceived secularism, the coalition consolidated its common identity as religious. Baptists, Evangelicals, Jews, Seventh-Day Adventists, Presbyterians, Unitarian Universalists, Pentecostals, Quakers, and more: all agreed that religion itself—religion in general—was under threat as a result of the *Smith* decision. All recognized that what bound them together was the threat of secularism made evident by *Smith*. What united them and enabled them to speak across the historical, theological, and cultural gaps that had previously divided them was that they were all "religion." They needed to bury the hatchet and confront the enemy, an enemy they often denominate as secular humanism. *Smith* was seen as a wake-up call; it suggested that religion in the United States had become complacent about its irenicism, its inevitability, and its cultural entrenchment.

The subsequent institutionalization of a post-*Smith* politics has changed the legal and political language of religious freedom in the United States and abroad. RFRA was specifically intended to reinstate a balancing test for religious exemptions, forcing government to defend regulations that "substantially burdened" a person's exercise of her religion with an explanation of the compelling governmental interest that outweighed the burden on religious practitioners. While subsequently declared unconstitutional with respect to its effect on the actions of state governments, a raft of other more carefully drafted legislation, including the Native American Graves Protection and Repatriation Act, the International Religious Freedom Act, and the Religious Land Use and Institutionalized Persons Act at the federal level, as well as dozens of state laws—or, as they are sometimes known, mini-RFRAs—were passed, all designed to provide robust protection for religion. The aftermath of *Smith* also saw the development of a vigorous and well-funded specialized bar promoting the rights of religion in the United States and elsewhere.

While the decision in *Smith* led above all to an immediate tactical shift from constitutional appeals to the drafting of legislation intended to protect religion at every level (even local school boards), it has also arguably provoked a now further shift away from reliance solely on selective accommodations from secular law to robust jurisdictional demands for church autonomy or even church sovereignty, both domestically and internationally. In a series of cases considering the constitutionality of school voucher programs and of various social service projects grouped under the faith-based initiative, for example, the Court has held that the establishment clause of the First Amendment does not prohibit the recognition and direct funding of religious institutions by government. There is a new post-*Smith* accommodation between the two clauses, giving institutional religion new legal definition and relevance even while the rights of individuals are being eroded. This new accommodation looks a lot like what might once have been considered "established" or "sectarian" religion in an earlier American parlance.

American religious politics is not, of course, entirely produced by Supreme Court jurisprudence. But it is plausible, I think, to see *Smith* as a turning point in the consolidation of a broad religious alliance that is at work today, one that collectively opposes unreligion while each member aggressively seeks to shore up its own ecclesiological position. There is a sense in which *Smith*'s comprehensive rejection of religious reasons as constitutionally relevant invented religion anew—giving, at the same time, new life to the specter of unreligion. *Smith*, in part because of the high-handed rhetorical violence of the majority opinion and its refusal even to discuss Native American peyote use beyond a brief half-sentence reference, seemed to dismiss a carefully nurtured US religious multiculturalism with the back of a hand. The response of US religious groups has been impressive in scope and effect.

Whether religious freedom is a right belonging to the individual or to the group has lurked in the jurisprudence of this area for some time now as the broader implications of the alternate formulations of rights more generally haunt liberalism in a variety of ways. With respect to religion in particular, the question arises as to what extent a legal and political commitment to religious freedom implies a need for formal legal recognition of a self-governing capacity for churches and other religious institutions. The 2012 decision by the Supreme Court, *Hosanna-Tabor v. EEOC* (constitutionalizing a ministerial exception to the Americans with Disabilities Act, or ADA), is interesting in part because it brings to the fore a troublesome leftover issue for Americans and for others who would promote religious freedom—an issue with a long US pedigree but one made newly relevant by the challenge of *Smith*. A radical version of US disestablishment—never realized—might suggest that churches in the United States are and have been from the beginning (whether in Puritan New England or at the time of the making of the Constitution) understood ideally to be entirely voluntary and private, even ephemeral, organizations that survive or not due to the enthusiasm and pocketbooks of their congregants (and God's will), not transhistorical entities or public institutions legally defined, incorporated, and supported by the state. While lip service has long been paid to such a position in law and politics, the fragile voluntarism of the free church apparently now seems a slender reed on which to build a bulwark against unreligion. Older, tougher, *ecclesia* are being looked to.

Hosanna-Tabor originated in a claim for retaliatory dismissal brought by the Equal Employment Opportunity Commission on behalf of a fourth grade schoolteacher under the ADA. The employer, a Missouri Lutheran elementary school, defended, claiming that a judicially created ministerial exception to the ADA, mandated by the Constitution, exempted the school from compliance with civil rights laws protecting disabled Americans (and, most probably, with a collection of other protections for employees.) A version of the post-*Smith* alliance was mobilized once again in response. A remarkable number and range of religious institutions filed amicus briefs on *Hosanna-Tabor*'s behalf. Briefs were filed by some regular filers in religion clause cases and others less regular, some represented by well-known First Amendment lawyers and advocacy organizations; others were newer to the scene—many of them very strange bedfellows indeed. These organizations, like the RFRA coalition, represent a wide range of religious positions, including evangelical Christians, Hindus, Muslims, Catholics, Mandaeans, Methodists, Presbyterians, Afro-Carribean religions, Jews, Mormons, and Lutherans. What seems to have brought them together this time is not so much a common commitment to the right of religiously motivated individuals to a conscientious exemption from laws that burden their religious practice, as in *Smith*, but a common commitment to the robust assertion of a corporate jurisdictional autonomy from the state for religion, an assertion confirmed by a unanimous Court.

The muscular hierarchical demand of the rights of churches and other religious authorities, of which the *Hosanna-Tabor* decision is but one example, is a product of the world that *Smith* made. While some national constitutional orders outside the United States and most international human rights regimes are moving toward a more individualistic model of protecting religious freedom, one that focuses on the sincerely formed consciences of particular persons, whether religious or not, religiously motivated groups in the United States may be moving the other way, back toward what used to be called establishment—that is, government support of "pervasively sectarian" institutions—in a curious embrace of those churches and of the folks who run them, those who once seemed the very antithesis of American religion.

There is a tragic quality to this situation. A broad-based critique of secularism combined with the anxieties of contemporary international politics feeds a romantic yearning for the presumed holism of intact and homogenous religious cultures. Churches and other religious authority structures can no longer rely on the dissent of their followers from majority cultures. They are demanding secular backup in their efforts to impose discipline. Many religious individuals meanwhile worry about whether the interests of organized religions can continue to serve as a proxy for their own religious longings and their political interests.

*   *   *

On August 7, 2013, Secretary of State John Kerry, in a speech celebrating the creation of the new State Department Office of Faith-Based Community Initiatives, commented that if he were to return to college today he would major in religious studies. It was tempting to cheer. But I think that for those of us in religious studies the context of this announcement should prompt concern. Indeed, the context should suggest that in some important ways religious studies has failed in its oft-repeated objective to serve as a nontheological and apolitical discourse about religion. Speaking of humans as properly "safe guarders of God's creation," Kerry spoke of his belief that, in spite of religious diversity, "there is much more that unites us, and should unite us, than divides us. . . . All of these faiths are virtuous and they are in fact, most of them, tied together by the golden rule, as well as fundamental concerns about the human condition, about poverty, about relationships between people, our responsibilities each to each other. And they all come from the same human heart." Kerry affirmed the commitment of the US State Department to work in partnership with religious "leaders" and with religious "communities" to defeat extremists, neatly separating bad religion from good religion. Describing religion as a collective endeavor led by inspired religious leaders such as Mahatma Gandhi, Kerry finished with a quote from scripture: "For even the Son of Man did not come to be served, but to serve, and to give his life as a ransom for the many." Seeing religious studies as authorizing a constitutionally sanctioned partnership between church and state—one framed as religious liberty by the Catholic bishops, who, like Kerry, use the language of "religion" to include all believers—may seem a betrayal to those with a late-twentieth-century confidence in both the academic study of religion as a critical secular project and in a separationist reading of the First Amendment. For those with a longer historical view, however, it should be seen as business as usual, continuous with a longer US government partnership with those in the academic world eager to offer their work as a how-to manual for government: academically produced "knowledge" about Indian religions for the better government of Native Americans, expert witnessing about Mormons and others in service of moral reform, as well as various contemporary collaborations between American academics and the US government to combat religious "extremism" through the promotion of moderate religion.

Justice Samuel Alito's concurrence in *Hosanna-Tabor* nicely illustrates the complicity of religious studies in the governing of Americans. Affirming the Supreme Court's majority opinion's endorsement of a ministerial exception to the civil rights laws, Alito, like Kerry, parades a schoolboy competence in the sociology of comparative religions when he asserts that, while "minister" is historically a protestant religious office, all religions have analogous positions. As with much other cheap comparative work, universalizing the position of minister in this way does the double work of protestantizing American law by taking a protestant church office as the model for religious leadership while simultaneously effacing religious difference—difference internal to religious communities as well as among them.

This version of religious studies has its own authorizing court decision: *Abingdon v Schempp*. The *Schempp* decision is understood by many in religious studies to license the objective "nontheological" teaching of religion at public universities. Formally it does no such thing; *Schempp* concerned Bible reading in public schools. But the adoption of a few sentences as what historian Sarah Imhoff calls the creation myth of religious studies underlines the curious complicity between religion and government. A distinction between teaching religion and teaching "about" religion in the United States has come to enable not government neutrality but government reform of religion. The religion that has been taught in public universities under the auspices of *Schempp* is no less "theological" in many ways than the Bible and theology courses it displaced. It, too, mostly serves the church and the state, via what Will Herberg called the religion of the American way of life, often in the guise of an irenic religious perennialism. Establishment, not free exercise, is the natural way of government, in the United States and elsewhere.

The world that *Smith* made is the product of a complex convergence of shifts in First Amendment jurisprudence, a newly available language in which to express the universalism of human religiousness, a mid-twentieth-century innovation in the teaching of religion in the United States, and an assertive politics by would-be religious leaders. The shifting tectonic plates of alliance between religious and political power have dispossessed religion of its power to divide—and liberate. Those who speak in its name now do so in unison.

Selected Bibliography

Abingdon v Schempp, 374 US 203 (1963).

Employment Division v. Smith, 494 US 872 (1990).

Herberg, Will. *Protestant—Catholic—Jew*. Chicago: University of Chicago Press, 1983.

Hosanna-Tabor v. EEOC, 565 US (2012).

Imhoff, Sarah. "The Creation Story, or How We Learned to Stop Worrying and Love *Schempp*." *Journal of the American Academy of Religion* (forthcoming, 2015).

CHAPTER TWENTY

Religious Freedom in the Panopticon of Enlightenment Rationality

Peter G. Danchin

The contract may have been regarded as the ideal foundation of law and political power; panopticism constituted the technique, universally widespread, of coercion. It continued to work in depth on the juridical structures of society, in order to make the effective mechanisms of power function in opposition to the formal framework that it had acquired. The "Enlightenment," which discovered the liberties, also invented the disciplines.—Michel Foucault, *Discipline and Punish: The Birth of the Prison*

Michel Foucault famously described Jeremy Bentham's panopticon as a "cruel, ingenious cage" to be understood not as a "dream building . . . [but as] the diagram of a mechanism of power reduced to its ideal form . . . a figure of political technology." For Foucault, panopticism was "the general principle of a new 'political anatomy' whose object and end are not the relations of sovereignty but the relations of discipline: The celebrated, transparent circular cage, with its high towers powerful and knowing."

At the same historical juncture in the mid-1780s when Bentham was conceiving of his panopticon, the German philosopher Immanuel Kant was expounding what today is recognized as a revolution in moral and ethical thought. As Christine Korsgaard has noted, Kant compared his philosophical system to that of Copernicus, which explained the ordering of the heavens by "turning them inside out"—that is, by removing the earth from the center and making it revolve around the sun—in arguing that "the rational order which the metaphysician looks for in the world is neither something that we discover through experience, nor something that our reason assures us must be there." Rather, it is something that we "*impose upon the world*, in part through the construction of our knowledge, but also, in a different way, through our actions."

In his 1785 *Groundwork of the Metaphysics of Morals*, Kant advanced the idea of a third type of judgment that is known neither a posteriori by experience nor a priori independent of experience but is instead "synthetic a priori," known in such a way that it tells us something new about its subject yet independent of experience—on the basis of "reasoning alone." This conception of moral knowledge was premised on the skepticism of the Humean fact-value distinction and effectively severed the deep connection between moral claims and the broader vision of reality traditionally affirmed by many metaphysical systems and religious traditions.

Kant's philosophy had two revolutionary features; first, contrary to older traditions of Catholic natural law theory, it was *nonnaturalist*: the ground of moral obligation was to be sought not in nature, human nature, external (clerical or traditional) authority, or any contingent circumstances of the moral agent; and second, contrary to Protestant theologies of God as the moral lawgiver, it posited a new authoritative *source* of moral obligation now to be found a priori in metaphysical concepts internal to pure reason alone.

Moral judgment was thus to be given autonomously by the agent to herself—imposed upon the world—under the rational discipline of the categorical imperative. The first move defined *enlightenment* in terms of a particular conception of rationality—the right to "think for oneself" and be free of heteronomous (especially religious) sources of moral obligation, while the second move defined *freedom* as acceptance of what reason dictates as duty (one should always act in accordance with what one can simultaneously will as universal law).

Each of these moves involves fraught and contested claims. Recall again that these are not claims about the phenomenal world but instead an imagined *noumenal* or transcendental realm internal to a particular (Protestant) conception of human rationality. As Foucault himself observed in relation to Kant's 1784 essay *An Answer to the Question: What is Enlightenment?*, the "enlightenment" as posited by Kant is the discovery of an exit, a "way out," a "process that releases us from the status of 'immaturity'" (a state where religious authority takes the place of our conscience) by a "modification of the preexisting relation linking will, authority, and the use of reason."

This modification is premised on rationalist and pietistic conceptions of the two things Kant suggested fill the mind with awe as we contemplate how things *really are:* the starry heavens above, which reduce us to nothing, and the moral law within, which elevates us infinitely. This new moral economy marks the great reversal in ethical thought in modernity: what was previously *external* and *objective* (the authority of God) now became *internal* and *subjective* (the unstable coimbrication of autonomy and conscience in the double bind of "freely chosen conscience"), and what was previously *internal* and *subject* to God's natural order now itself became *external* and *objective* (universal reason in the disciplinary form of the categorical imperative).

As Ian Hunter has argued, these reversals had the remarkable effect of simultaneously rationalizing religion and sacralizing reason. In this sequence of moves, the concept of religion and its authority in political order were fundamentally altered. We see this along three main dimensions. First, it was now irrational (as defined by rationality itself) for religion to be a "source" of political or legal authority, as the only true or universal source of such authority is secular rationality, which holds that no value other than *freedom* understood as autonomy (the right of each person to decide for themselves questions of moral value) is true.

Second, religion as a category now became understood not as an external social fact but as an internal "value" located in the "inner mind" or consciousness of the individual as subject. Religion was thus an idea or a belief, true if at all in only a nonnaturalist or transcendental conception of moral value. Such belief was not a genuine insight into the character of reality but only the subjective attitude of the thinker who proposed and adhered to it. And third, the understanding of religion as "belief" or "conscience" became secondary to the master value of autonomy such that any genuine religious beliefs must be autonomously chosen and affirmatively assented to by the individual as a set of creedal propositions (subject to the overarching discipline of rationality itself).

In each of these propositions, Hunter points out, Kant's principles of morality and right were grounded in a comprehensive "Christian-Platonic anthropology deeply embedded in the history of north-German Protestant university metaphysics" according to which man was imagined as "the empirical harbinger of a pure rational being" (*homo noumenon*) who, by intelligizing "the pure forms of experience, and [governing] the will by thinking the 'idea' or form of its law [was] supposed to free himself from the 'sensuous inclinations' that otherwise tie the will of empirical man (*homo phenomenon*) to extrinsic ends or goods."

In this essay I wish to suggest that the modern politics of religious freedom are substantially shaped by and traceable to these intertwined genealogies of panoptic disciplinary power and Enlightenment rationality. The central features of this politics are first the use of the right to religious liberty as a technology of modern state governance (rights as *techne*) and second what Hussein Ali Agrama has termed the problem space of modern secular power that incessantly raises the question of where to draw the line between the religious and the secular. Each of these features empowers the state to determine the proper place of religion in social and political order and result in the continual entanglement of the state and religion in legal forms.

It is crucial to recognize, however, that such entanglements are not deviations from secularism but an expression of the underlying power that makes secularism possible, a power that generates religion itself as a category and views it through a particular modality of suspicion (see Agrama's contribution to this volume). Contrary to the repeated refrain of state neutrality, the success of this modality of power lies less in the restraint of the state from interfering in religion and more in the way that it serves as a means for the modern state to regulate substantive features of religious life and to declare certain religious practices indifferent to theology in order to make them consequential to state law. As a matter of coercive legal power and authority, the intertwined doctrines of secular neutrality and individual right thus operate quite distinctly from those imagined by Kant in the spheres of self-critical reason and voluntary ethics (although Kant did recognize the antinomies of reason and thus retained the notion of a public-private divide whereby reason would be "submissive" in its private use).

These two features and their implications for modern law and politics can be observed in the rights-based jurisprudence of otherwise quite different nation-states such as France, Turkey, the United States, and Egypt as well as in supranational rights regimes such as that of the European Convention on Human Rights. In cases raising claims of the right to religious liberty, these features generate two corresponding and recurring dilemmas for judges.

The first dilemma concerns the subject and object of what is often referred to as the *forum internum*, a sphere demarcated as "essentially religious" that is to be protected absolutely from interference. Is it the individual as subject who has the right autonomously to choose as object her own beliefs and convictions, religious or not? Or is the object instead the right to have and maintain a certain category of inner belief, such as "conscience" or "faith" understood in some sense as unchosen? Or is it not just individual persons but also religious groups and institutions as subjects who have the right to profess and maintain a religious tradition free of sovereign or other interference?

The second dilemma is to specify what constitutes a recognized manifestation of religion or belief in the so-called *forum externum* or, conversely, what constitutes an exceptional ground of limitation needed to secure important state interests such as public order or the rights of others. This is most clearly seen in cases such as *Kokkinanis v. Greece* (1993), in which the European Court of Human Rights was confronted with a conflict, between the right to proselytize on the one hand and the right of the target of proselytization to have and maintain a religion free of this activity on the other, and thus with the need to delimit the scope of competing rights claims while maintaining fidelity to the doctrine of neutrality. Inevitably, resolution of such conflicts involves not solely the limitation of the right in the *forum externum* but goes to the very nature and scope of the right in the *forum internum*. Once the *forum internum* is then broadened beyond individual belief alone, an entirely different conception of the right and of the criteria for inclusion and exclusion are created, as Saba Mahmood and I have pointed out.

Alternatively, as soon as the concept of public order is deployed to justify a limitation on the right to manifest religion in cases such as *Sahin v. Turkey* and *Dogru v. France*, it is axiomatically construed to encompass those fundamental rules, values, or principles that together define and are incorporated into the collective identity of the state. This inevitably results in a privileging of those majoritarian sensibilities, traditions, and customs that have become intimately linked with the legal and political order.

In order to address these questions, judges must paradoxically *go beyond* the calculus of secular neutrality and liberal rights and make determinations that are entangled with and premised on religious criteria in order to define a sphere "free" from the authority of the state and its norm of secular freedom (a private space of exception) or to recognize or limit a manifestation of religion in the name of public order or the rights of others (a second, public space of exception). This often tacit resort to heteronomy and religious sources of morality contradicts the opening premises of an autonomous rationality and of the right as neutral, objective, and universal. It further suggests that the secular character of the statist public order can never be neutral toward religion in any a priori manner and is constantly open to challenge for being either excessively religious *or* secular.

All religious freedom cases can thus be read as attempts by judicial reasoning to resist what Foucault termed Kant's "contract of rational despotism with free reason: the public and free use of autonomous reason will be the best guarantee of obedience, on condition, however, that the political principle that must be obeyed itself be in conformity with universal reason." In adjudicating any claim to religious liberty, judges are trapped simultaneously in the tower and circle of the modern panopticon of Enlightenment rationality. On the one hand they speak with authority in an objective register of right and reason as they gaze upon the category of "religion," while on the other they speak defensively in subjective registers of history and culture as they seek in vain to resist the disciplinary implications of the category of "freedom." This leaves their reasoning exquisitely caught in a fraught but familiar dialectic of power and illusion, ultimately unable to justify its own normative categories.

A substantial part of the confusion in modern jurisprudence lies in the fact that religious freedom and the *right* to religious freedom are not in fact coterminous ideas, either historically or conceptually. Their clashing vocabularies and bricolaged rights forms are nevertheless continually elided and entangled in complex ways such that today they are mutually constitutive in religious liberty discourse.

The notion of "religious freedom" implies a sphere of immunity or absence of legal regulation and concerns the issue of political authority. It is thus most closely associated with political secularism in the form of the putative public-private divide and varying relations between the state and religion(s). This kind of spatialization of power is imagined toward a private domain of social space where, although subject to state sovereignty, the authority of religion as a collective tradition and way of life is accorded legal recognition.

This inner or private space encompasses both religious beliefs and practices and historically has taken the form of politically negotiated religious settlements and varying religion-state arrangements that today continue to exist in states with widely divergent religious traditions. In this classical conception of religious liberty there is no necessary connection to the idea of individual rights. What is demarcated as "private" or "internal" is an open question that takes different institutional and normative form in different political orders.

On the metaphysical Kantian view discussed above, however, an entirely different spatialization of power is imagined. The notion of a *right* implies a rights holder and a background justification for the right and its distinctive function of holding others to correlative duties. In modern rights jurisprudence, all three of these issues—the subject of the right, its normative scope, and its theoretical justification—are essentially contested questions. In modern religious liberty discourse, however, it is often tacitly assumed that the subject of the right is the *individual*; the nature and scope of the right is to *conscience* or *belief*; and the justification of the right is either *apodictic reason* understood in broadly Kantian terms as an a priori subjective right the individual gives to herself in accordance with universal moral law or as *natural reason* understood in broadly Thomist terms as yielding an objective right to conscience in accordance with natural law.

Religious freedom on this account of right is fundamentally different. Freedoms contemplate activities so diverse that the precise acts cannot be defined a priori whereas rights stipulate defined conduct. The freedom to pursue a religiously defined legal regime, for example, of the kind Waheeda Amien discusses in her essay in this volume, comprehends a potentially infinite variety of activities comprising social life whereas the *right* to religious freedom requires the state—usually through a court, but also through legislation—to adjudicate and define the proper subject, scope, and justification of the right.

It is here that a dramatic shift in spatialization occurs. Once religion is understood in terms of the three features discussed above where (1) Enlightenment rationality posits (2) a conception of individual belief that is (3) autonomously chosen in the *forum internum*, then most of what was formerly internal and private is transformed into an external *manifestation of religion* now subject either to recognition or limitation by the state in the new, vastly expanded *forum externum*.

It is important to note that in this hierarchy of norms, freedoms are subordinate to rights since a right authorizes the holder to demand that the duty bearer does or does not do something that the duty bearer was formerly at liberty to treat as a matter of noninterference. The right to religious freedom in this way becomes the means to protect the individual not only from the harm of state interference but also from harms that flow from the exercise of freedoms. This is a shift of great consequence in disputes involving competing claims to religious freedom.

The recent decision in *Lautsi v. Italy* powerfully illustrates this structural logic. The Grand Chamber of the European Court of Human Rights here held that the compulsory display of the crucifix in public school classrooms in Italy was compatible with article 9 of the European

Convention on Human Rights. The case presented the court with the two dilemmas discussed above: first, given the Court's earlier reasoning in *Dahlab v. Switzerland* that an Islamic headscarf worn by a secondary school teacher in Switzerland posed a threat of pressure or proselytizing to students, whether the effect of the crucifix on the right to religious liberty of Mrs. Lautsi and her sons could be distinguished; and second, given the Court's earlier reasoning in *Sahin v. Turkey* that the proper place of a religious symbol such as the Islamic headscarf worn by a university student in Istanbul is the private sphere, whether the mandatory presence of the crucifix in Italian educational institutions could be justified.

The reasoning of the Grand Chamber on each issue is instructive. The Court held that the crucifix is a "passive" symbol, unlike the "active" nature of the Islamic headscarf at issue in *Dahlab* and *Sahin*, and thus posed no threat to the right of Mrs. Lautsi or her children "to believe or not to believe." Second, as a "symbol" the crucifix represented a state of belief that preceded it and was being recognized by Italy in the *forum externum* as a manifestation of culture, or tradition, or as broadly representative of shared secular values such as tolerance and even religious freedom itself.

The first line of reasoning rests on a particular understanding of what constitutes religion and a proper religious subjectivity while the second decides and spatially demarcates the proper place of religion in the Italian social and political order. Notably, the right to religious freedom was deployed here to *limit* the claims to freedom of Mrs. Lautsi and her children, while the secular power of the state was accorded a wide margin of appreciation to allow a conception not of the right but of the freedom to maintain the existing entanglement of the majority religious tradition with and within the public sphere and institutions of the Italian state.

Let us now turn to the prominent recent case of *Hosanna-Tabor v. EEOC*, in which a "ministerial exception" to antidiscrimination law was recognized for the first time by the United States Supreme Court. While the judgment was immediately hailed as a victory for religious freedom, it is the specter of the panopticon that haunts every page of the Court's reasoning.

Once again, the case presented the Court with the two dilemmas discussed above. First, could religious liberty be justified as a collective right, here attaching to religious groups and institutions as opposed to individual persons? Religious institutions don't have consciences per se—only their individual members do—though religious entities do have texts, traditions, rituals, and practices. If such groups or institutions are bearers of rights, what is the scope of that right, what forms of conduct and activity does it include, and with what legal consequences? Does the right generate, for example, a duty on the state not to interfere in some "autonomous" sphere (as yet undetermined) or to recognize certain group manifestations of religious practice? If so, why does this not pose the threat to the administrative state identified by Supreme Court Justice Antonin Scalia in *Employment Division v. Smith*, in which he stated that "permitting [a person] by virtue of his beliefs 'to become a law unto himself,' contradicts both constitutional tradition and common sense?"

Second, if a "ministerial exception" was to be recognized under the First Amendment, who is a "minister," and how could this be determined in a neutral way as between different religious traditions? If so recognized, how could the exception be justified to nonreligious groups performing the same activities to whom neutral laws of general application applied and to ministers themselves whose personal rights under these laws were now to be limited? How could this be neutral between religion and nonreligion? Some argument was needed to explain why religion was accorded special treatment either because distinctly burdened or under a special legal disability, an argument that itself could not be "religious."

For Chief Justice John Roberts, writing for a rare unanimous Court, the answers to these two sets of questions were to be found simply in "the text of the First Amendment itself, which gives special solicitude to the rights of religious organizations." In addition to textualism, the Court invoked two forms of historical argument, one looking at the original understanding of the First Amendment's religion clauses on the basis of which the Court (re)tells a founding story of the principled rejection after 1776 of the established Church of England and entrenchment of "disestablishment" and "free exercise"; and another interpreting the Court's own labyrinthine religion clause jurisprudence from which distinctly Protestant terms such as *church, minister, ecclesiastical, belief, faith,* and *mission* are neatly distilled and woven together in the Court's final *ratio* that "the authority to select and control who will minister to the faithful—a matter 'strictly ecclesiastical'—is the church's alone."

The jurisprudential reasoning in *Hosanna-Tabor* closely tracks the two dilemmas of how to demarcate the scope and content of the private sphere and how to justify either recognition or limitation of claims to religious liberty in the public sphere. The case further illustrates the recurrent and oscillating ambiguity of religious liberty when conceived as *both* a freedom and a right.

First, the privatization of churches (and religion more broadly) and their Erastian control by the state are the premises of freedom in the private sphere—a sphere *unilaterally* defined, protected, delimited, and increasingly regulated by the state itself. Regardless of how the sphere of conscience is delimited, the underlying assumption of this assertion of line-drawing power is the *denial* of the coercive authority of religious institutions in enforcing the demands of conscience. This is the critical point.

Any interest of the state in appointing officials to the church would arise only if either the church had a corresponding official role in the public realm of the state (as in England, where of the Church of England's forty-four bishops and archbishops twenty-six are permitted to sit in the House of Lords) or an agreement was negotiated between sovereigns (as is possible in Italy in its relations with the Holy See and Vatican City). It is difficult to see why the state would wish to appoint officials to a "free church" assigned the legal status of a voluntary association in the private sphere of civil society. If this is what is claimed to be a victory for religious freedom, it is a Pyrrhic victory. The churches have long ago ceded or been denied their former ecclesiastical jurisdiction and are now unilaterally "free" to select their ministers in private under the disciplinary gaze of the panopticon.

This legal understanding is expressly confirmed in the Court's opinion, which states that the ministerial exception is not a "jurisdictional bar" but a "defense" on the merits because "the courts have power to consider ADA claims in cases of this sort and to decide whether the claim can proceed or is instead barred by the ministerial exception." This, in Foucault's terms, is not a relation of sovereignty, but of discipline. The church has already been absorbed into the state, the former ecclesiastical jurisdiction has been collapsed into the secular and, in the words of Bradin Cormack, the temporal law has become "the rule against which the claim of conscience [is] to be measured."

Second, what is most interesting in *Hosanna-Tabor* is how the Court expands the notion of autonomy to include the church as a legal subject with a right to a certain sphere of freedom. But unlike in *Smith*, as soon the category of "religion" is broadened to include not only the *forum internum* of conscience but also the *forum externum* of manifestations of religion, conflicts arise with the legal jurisdiction of the state that potentially extends to any action implicating sovereign interests. In order to deal with the legal consequences of this move, the Court now seamlessly shifts in its reasoning from the language of autonomy to "conscience" and in effect analogizes the "inner conscience of the church" to individual conscience conceived as extralegal and prepolitical. The Court, in other words, seeks to identify a realm not merely of autonomy but of *sovereignty*—a jurisdiction in some sense independent of the state. As a sovereign realm, this must include not only decisions made for a religious reason but more broadly must ensure that "the *authority* to select and control who will minister to the faithful—a matter strictly 'ecclesiastical'—is the church's alone."

This turns the autonomy argument on its head. Indeed, this is the kind of classical argument for religious liberty that communitarian theorists have long adduced against Rawlsian liberals claiming the self to be prior to its ends and the right to be prior to the good. The communitarian argument hinges on both the moral importance of religion and the idea that religious liberty should protect those "who regard themselves as claimed by religious commitments they have not chosen." As Winnifred Fallers Sullivan has observed, the idea appears to be that churches are "prior to conscience," for it is in churches that the individual conscience is *formed*. This is a deeply theological argument that seeks to identify the proper attributes of religion and religious subjectivity. But it does so unilaterally—by an act of imagination rather than mutual recognition of sovereign relations—and it does so in an almost nostalgic gesture toward a now extinct legal relation that has vanished from the modern secular state.

How exactly does the Court know which matters are "strictly ecclesiastical" and which affect "the faith and mission of the church?" From a religious point of view, the scope of the "inner conscience of the church" is likely to be conceived more broadly than that permitted under the ministerial exception as delimited in *Hosanna-Tabor.* Conversely, from a secular point of view there are likely to be a host of activities and actions pertaining to the "inner conscience of the church" that raise interests and concerns pertaining to the proper exercise of legal jurisdiction.

Given the depth and scope of these complexities, the puzzle remains why the Court in *Hosanna-Tabor* so effortlessly assumes the compatibility between autonomy and conscience in the formulation of the ministerial exception. What appears pivotal for the Court is that the church "freely decide" ecclesiastical matters as a matter of right and that it have autonomy to control matters, even on nonreligious grounds, provided these pertain to the "inner conscience of the church." The first argument defines conscience in terms of autonomy while the second defines autonomy in terms of conscience. In this set of historically and culturally contingent moves, a Protestant understanding of "the church" and an Enlightenment conception of freedom are simultaneously asserted and naturalized.

This necessarily results in what Sullivan has termed a "protestant de facto establishment" privileging one religious subjectivity over others. This is evident as soon as the ministerial exception is considered in relation to different religious traditions, especially those historically seen to threaten either the security of the state (public order) or the rights of others (freedom of conscience and belief). Consider, for example, the vast governmental surveillance and monitoring of mosques in America since September 11, 2001. This has extended well beyond the application of the criminal law to suspected acts or support of terrorism. The government has directly targeted theological matters and established intrusive mechanisms to monitor the content of any religious speech believed to foster "fundamentalism" or "radicalism."

As Saba Mahmood has observed, the "effectiveness of such a totalizing project necessarily depends upon transforming the religious domain through a variety of reforms and state injunctions. . . . This has often meant that nation-states have had to act as de facto theologians, rendering certain practices and beliefs indifferent to religious doctrine precisely so that these practices can be brought under the domain of civil law." Muslim practice of and adherence to phenomenal forms of Islam—laws, scriptures, rituals, liturgies, and observances—potentially disturb such naturalized understandings of religion as conscience and conscience as autonomy.

The most glaring antinomy in *Hosanna-Tabor*, then, is the simultaneous exceptionalism and universalism of the Court's reasoning. This is important to understand more broadly as we witness the ongoing global war against "Islamic fundamentalism" and the global monitoring, promotion, and protection of the right to religious liberty (in countries apart from the United States) under the auspices of the International Religious Freedom Act of 1998 implemented through machinery such as the US Commission on International Religious Freedom. A better understanding of the underlying genealogies of the politics of religious freedom helps to make visible both the use of the right to religious liberty as a technology of modern state governance and the constitutive effects of the disciplinary power of the panopticon so as to see more clearly what is at stake for religious traditions and conditions within and beyond North-Atlantic modernity.

Selected Bibliography

Agrama, Hussein Ali. *Questioning Secularism: Islam, Sovereignty, and the Rule of Law in Egypt.* Chicago: University of Chicago Press, 2012.

Cormack, Bradin. *A Power to Do Justice: Jurisdiction, English Literature, and the Rise of the Common Law, 1509–1625.* Chicago: University of Chicago Press, 2007.

Foucault, Michel. *Discipline and Punish: The Birth of the Prison.* Translated by Alan Sheridan. New York: Vintage Books, 1995.

———. "What Is Enlightenment?" In *The Foucault Reader*, edited by Paul Rabinow, 32–50. New York: Pantheon, 1984.

Hunter, Ian. *Rival Enlightenments: Civil and Metaphysical Philosophy in Early Modern Germany.* Cambridge: Cambridge University Press, 2001.

———. "Kant's Regional Cosmopolitanism." *Journal of the History of International Law* 12 (2010): 165.

Kant, Immanuel. "An Answer to the Question: What Is Enlightenment?" In *What is Enlightenment? Eighteenth-Century Answers and Twentieth-Century Questions*, edited by James Schmidt, 58–64. Berkeley and Los Angeles: University of California Press, 1996.

Korsgaard, Christine. "Introduction." In Immanuel Kant, *Groundwork of the Metaphysics of Morals*, edited and translated by Mary Gregor, ix–xxxvi. Cambridge: Cambridge University Press, 1998.

Mahmood, Saba. "Secularism, Hermeneutics, Empire: The Politics of Islamic Reformation." *Public Culture* 18, no. 2 (2006): 323–47.

Mahmood, Saba, and Peter Danchin. "Immunity or Regulation: Antinomies of Religious Freedom." *South Atlantic Quarterly* 113, no. 1 (2014): 129–159.

CHAPTER TWENTY-ONE

Everson's Children

Ann Pellegrini

Everson v. Board of Education is considered a landmark of First Amendment jurisprudence. The 1947 case marks the first time the US Supreme Court held that the disestablishment provision of the First Amendment is binding on the states and not just on the federal government. The "incorporation" of the principle of disestablishment thus completed the task begun seven years earlier in *Cantwell v. Connecticut*, when a unanimous court held that free exercise applied to the states. In *Cantwell* the court overturned the convictions of three Jehovah's Witnesses who had been arrested for unlicensed soliciting and a breach of peace.

As conservative legal scholar Terry Eastland notes in his commentary on these two cases, "most of the religion-clause cases decided by the Supreme Court" in the wake of *Cantwell* have involved "federal litigation over religion-clause claims against states." This is in contrast, he observes, to the first 150 years of Supreme Court religion-clause jurisprudence when all of the very few cases heard by the court "involved claims against the federal government."

On the one hand this geographic shift has meant that formalized practices of religious establishment in individual states became subject to scrutiny and challenge. On the other, the application of the disestablishment principle to the states has also arguably contributed to the complaints of many Christians that a monolithically secular state is driving something called "religion" from public life, creating a state of siege for religious liberty and religious people. What this religious "something" is remains a contested question, as do assertions of "persecuted" Christians.

What is clear, however, is that in the last half century there has been an increasing regionalization of public conflicts over the place of religion and religious people in public life and in the state. This "and" is necessary: the public is not the state, a conceptual confusion that regularly trips up public debates about the meaning and practice of religious freedom in the United States. The state may not even be *the* state, if such a conception either turns the state into some sort of totalized superagent that acts without any internal incoherences or sets the state wholly apart from the institutions of civil society. Lori G. Beaman's provocative account in this volume of the way the Canadian state has historically called upon religious organizations to deliver essential social services, such as education for aboriginal children, shows how blurry the line is between the state and civil society, a blurring that can have the effect of installing Christian dominance—Beaman calls it "Christian hegemony"—into the state.

Christian dominance in US public life, while a truism, is itself not monolithic in practice. Instead we might better speak of religious cultures, plural, and of secular negotiations, also plural. Particular Christianities are dominant in some states and regions in the United States in ways that strain against a larger overlay of mainline Protestantism as the baseline for what both national religious culture and national secular identity have meant historically in the United States. I'll come back to this point.

Although he may seem like too easy a target, former senator and now former Republican Party presidential candidate Rick Santorum's conflation of the state and the public square is illuminating precisely because it is not exceptional. In a notorious February 26, 2012, appearance on ABC's *This Week with George Stephanopolous* Santorum proclaimed his expansive vision of First Amendment free exercise: "I don't believe in an America where the separation of Church and State is absolute. The idea that the church can have no influence or no involvement in the operation of the state is absolutely antithetical to the objectives and vision of our country. This is the First Amendment. The First Amendment says the free exercise of religion." Santorum went on to express his visceral disgust at those who would bar religious people from the public square, seamlessly shifting his focus. Making presidential candidate John F. Kennedy's famous 1960 speech to the Greater Houston Ministerial Association stand in as the ur-moment of this enforced bracketing of religion from all of public life, Santorum glossed Kennedy's speech: "To say that people of faith have no role in the public square? You bet that makes you throw up. What kind of country do we live in that says only people of non-faith can come into the public square and make their case?"

This is, pardon the pun, a rather gross misreading of what Kennedy actually said. But what interests me here is twofold: first, the way Santorum effortlessly elides the public square with the state and, second, Santorum's elevation of free exercise over disestablishment as the living pulse of religious freedom. Minimizing—if not outright denying—disestablishment licenses the hyperbole of Santorum's claim that the state can set no limits on the reach of "the church" into its operations. To be sure, Santorum's language was very colorful, but his analysis and the ressentiment it bespeaks are broadly shared among evangelical Christians and a growing number of conservative Catholics as well.

Claims that religious liberty is under siege in the United States are almost exclusively made by Christians conservatives—Evangelicals and, in recent years, American Catholic bishops. As Elizabeth A. Castelli notes in this volume, these conservative Christian actors seek a place for religious arguments in public debates (on its face, neither objectionable nor unconstitutional), but would restrict the scope of what counts as properly religious to those moral views that cohere with their own even as they would insulate their particular religious arguments from criticism and debate. This reduction of religion to the most conservative versions of Christianity and of religious liberty to the religious freedom of some Christians (a historically surprising evangelical-Catholic alliance, as Samuel Moyn points out in this volume) makes no room for a diversity of perspectives among Christians, let alone for the commitments of those many religious Americans who are not Christian and those many Americans who are not religious at all. Don't they have religious freedom, too?

As Janet R. Jakobsen and I together argue in *Love the Sin: Sexual Regulation and the Limits of Religious Tolerance*, it matters a great deal to possibilities for agonistic democracy and meaningful religious freedom whether one sees the two components of First Amendment religious freedom, disestablishment and free exercise, as separable or interstructuring. In our view—and we are hardly legal outliers on this question—disestablishment is the structuring condition for free exercise. Otherwise those who are religiously different or not religious at all may well find their lives not simply less admired and valued than those who belong to the dominant religion; they may find they have diminished legal status.

Nevertheless, in public political debates over the meaning of religious freedom, too often we see the very balkanization replayed by Santorum: proponents of more religion in US public life and in government (and let's be clear, not just of any religion, but of particular Christianities) lean heavily on the free exercise component and underplay disestablishment. Conversely, many secularists (though not all, to be sure) stress the absolute separation of church and state and minimize free exercise.

At least in principle, the appearance of religion in public spaces or the use of religious language and arguments in public debates need not equate to the state's endorsement of any religion at all; nor need it lead to religious dominance. To quote one of my favorite lines from Gilbert and Sullivan's *Utopia Limited; or, the Flowers of Progress*, "That's the theory, but in practice, how does it act?" Not so well, as it happens. This is because US public life operates under conditions of Christian dominance. Particular Christian practices and claims can "float," sometimes being overtly marked as religious, at other times passing as secular, resulting in a situation Jakobsen and I have elsewhere termed "Christian secularism."

The public itself (as an ideal) and public spaces, plural, in all their practices, are prepared in advance to credit Christian assumptions and value claims as integral to public life and national character. In such a context it can be hard for those who are religiously different and those who are not religious at all to get a word in edgewise. In addition, these same Christian assumptions can pass into the state as the secular logic of universal morality and civic order, as we have seen in numerous state laws banning same-sex marriage and restricting access to abortion. The rising fortunes of marriage equality for same-sex couples in the United States in no way undermine the above claim. On the contrary, the relatively rapid success of the marriage equality movement cannot be separated from a concurrent phenomenon: the continued and even hardened opposition to legalized abortion. Both these trends, which initially appear to be going in opposite directions (the one toward liberalism over sexual morality, the other toward conservatism), in fact promote a Christian secular *responsibilization* of sexuality with profoundly raced, classed, and gendered consequences. Wanna get married? You pass. Want or need an abortion? Not so fast. Abortion conjures raced and classed images of an out-of-control female sexuality. An unwanted or unplanned pregnancy, which can happen for so many reasons—including failed contraception or a failure to educate young people about contraception at all—is instead recast as a woman's failure in self-discipline and sexual morality. Michel Foucault could not have better anticipated this meeting of Christian and secular disciplines.

Although many liberal and progressive secularists had hoped, even expected, that the election of Barack Obama in 2008 heralded the end of religion's role in public debates and policy decisions, this hope has not been realized. On one level the hope was for an end to the influence of conservative religion—really, conservative Christianities—on policy making, particularly in issues concerning sexual life. But it was also, for many secularists, a desire for the elimination of any trace of religion in the US public sphere, as if religion were a toxin from which they needed or even had a fundamental right to be protected. This also shows too measly an understanding of the scope of religious freedom and the parameters of agonistic democratic engagement. Democracy does not always feel good. In everyday life we bump up against each other and may well be discomforted by differences we cannot assimilate or will not understand. This is among the reasons we need courts to protect the rights and freedoms of unpopular minorities: so that these bumps will not turn into overt violence or formalized exclusions. Encounters with difference, including moral difference, are not a hostile takeover nor taking away, nor an instance of "indoctrination"—whether of religious values or secular ones. (Given the entwinement of Christian values with the values of the secular in the United States, the "or" in that previous sentence needs critical pressure as well.)

In using the loaded word *indoctrination* I am invoking numerous heated debates about higher education and, in particular, the claim that universities are dominated by liberals and indoctrinate their students into secular values—thereby severing them from their families of origins. (Indeed, just such a claim was advanced by Rick Santorum in the very same interview in which he declared his nauseated response to church and state separation.)

The word *indoctrination* also makes a curious appearance in the *Everson* case. At issue were reimbursements approved by the township of Ewing, New Jersey, and paid out to parents for money they spent busing their children to schools, whether public or Catholic. A local taxpayer challenged the payments to the parents of parochial school students as an unconstitutional establishment of religion. A split court (5–4) held that the use of such public monies did not unconstitutionally establish religion in the state. Fascinatingly, even the four dissenters agreed with the

logic of justice Hugo Black's majority decision, which argued strongly
for Thomas Jefferson's famed "wall of separation" between church and
state. Indeed, the expansive terms of Justice Black's conception of disestablishment could easily have been penned by any one of the four dissenters. As Justice Black wrote for the five-member majority,

> The "establishment of religion" clause of the First Amendment means at least
> this: Neither a state nor the Federal Government can set up a church. Neither
> can pass laws which aid one religion, aid all religions, or prefer one religion
> over another. Neither can force nor influence a person to go to or to remain
> away from church against his will or force him to profess a belief or disbelief
> in any religion. No person can be punished for entertaining or professing re-
> ligious beliefs or disbeliefs, for church attendance or non-attendance. No tax
> in any amount, large or small, can be levied to support any religious activities
> or institutions, whatever they may be called, or whatever form they may adopt
> to teach or practice religion. Neither a state nor the Federal Government can,
> openly or secretly, participate in the affairs of any religious organizations or
> groups and vice versa. In the words of Jefferson, the clause against establish-
> ment of religion by law was intended to erect "a wall of separation between
> Church and State."

I always discuss the *Everson* case in my undergraduate lecture course
"Religion, Sexuality, and American Public Life." I sketch the basic issues
in dispute for this case, tell my students it was a split decision, and then
show them the above passage from the majority decision. In light of this
purple passage, I ask them what they think the holding was. Inevitably,
they think the court ruled *against* public funding for buses to Catholic
schools.

Like my students, I share the dissenting justices' puzzlement that the
majority could have put a bus-size hole in the fabled "wall of separation"
without recognizing the contradiction. The larger lesson, however, goes
beyond providing my students a quick course in First Amendment Jurisprudence 101; it is a reminder that the sharing of general principles—in
this instance the "wall of separation"—does not yet tell us anything about
how they will be set down in practice, especially on so messy a terrain as
religion. Moreover, the wall described in justice Robert H. Jackson's dissent seems to call for refortifying dominant Protestant notions of what
secularism should look and feel like in practice. He does so via a stun-
ning comparison and contrast between a Catholic emphasis on education

as indoctrination into faith and a—well, *what* exactly?—Protestant, secular, or hybridized Protestant-secular emphasis on neutrality and the value of mature adult "choice." Justice Jackson writes,

> It is no exaggeration to say that the whole historic conflict in temporal policy between the Catholic Church and non-Catholics comes to a focus in their respective school policies. The Roman Catholic Church . . . does not leave the individual to pick up religion by chance. It relies on early and indelible indoctrination in the faith and order of the Church by the word and example of persons consecrated to the task.
>
> Our public school, if not a product of Protestantism, at least is more consistent with it than with the Catholic culture and scheme of values. It is a relatively recent development . . . organized on . . . the premise that secular education can be isolated from all religious teaching so that the school can inculcate all needed temporal knowledge and also maintain a strict and lofty neutrality as to religion. The assumption is that after the individual has been instructed in worldly wisdom he will be better fitted to choose his religion. Whether such a disjunction is possible, and if possible whether it is wise, are questions I need not try to answer.

The spirit of education conjured in this passage may well reveal its own "romantic yearnings"—to draw on Winnifred Sullivan's language—for a unified secular culture. As the justice's toggle between not-quite-Protestant and not-*not*-Protestant suggests ("Our public school, if not a product of Protestantism, at least is more consistent with it"), this unified secular culture—the fantasy of it, at least—is linked historically and imaginatively to what religious studies scholar Robert Orsi describes as a "domesticated modern civic Protestantism" tolerable within the secular learning cultures of the academy that emerged in the late nineteenth and early twentieth centuries.

If this domesticated Protestantism did not need to plead its case in the classroom, this is because its style of personhood and structures of feeling were the very building blocks of secular public education—Protestant building blocks mistaken for walls of separation. Increasing religious diversity in the United States, including diversity among Protestants, has called many of Justice Jackson's operative assumptions into question. I suspect that the justices in the majority in *Everson* did not quite anticipate the wild contemporary landscape of American religious pluralism either.

But there are other important connections to Sullivan's discussion of "The World That *Smith* Made" and Peter Danchin's "Religious Freedom in the Panopticon of Enlightenment Rationality." Religious authorities now find themselves in the ironic position of appealing to the secular state to enforce sectarian orthodoxies. In 2011's *Hosanna-Tabor v. EEOC*, a unanimous Supreme Court held that a "ministerial exception" to Federal antidiscrimination law protected a Lutheran school from a teacher's claims that she was fired because of a disability. The decision elevated the ecclesiastical body of "the church" to the status of a legal subject possessing both a "collective conscience," in the words of Justice Roberts's opinion for the court, and the religious freedom protections previously accorded to individual adherents in their exercise of conscience.

The logic behind this decision has obvious, if as yet underexamined, echoes with a much more controversial decision a year earlier in *Citizens United v. Federal Election Commission*, when a split court found that First Amendment protections for political speech extended to the financial expenditures of corporations. Together, the decisions in *Citizens United* and *Hosanna-Tabor* chillingly forecast the legal arguments being made by Hobby Lobby and other private Christian companies for a religious exemption from the Affordable Care Act's contraception mandate. More than sixty lawsuits have thus far been filed against the Affordable Care Act by private "religious" corporations that assert that being required to provide contraception coverage for their employees would violate the company's conscience. The most prominent such lawsuit, *Hobby Lobby v. Sebelius*, reached the Supreme Court in 2014. As this essay goes to press, the court's ruling is pending.

The appeal to conscience and its formation moves easily between religious and secular contexts. *Hosanna-Tabor* concerned a private, sectarian school. But one of the ongoing and crucial laboratories for the contest between collective discipline and individual dissensus will be public school classrooms. The *mission*—a term I choose with great deliberation—that Justice Jackson attributed to the secular public classroom in *Everson* is not and never was innocent of religious domination. Those of us concerned about attacks on public education, from budget cuts to the conservative politicization of curricula, would do well to remember and mark the specific histories of domination on which we stand our ground in the name of First Amendment freedoms of religion and of speech.

Selected Bibliography

Eastland, Terry, ed. *Religious Liberty in the Supreme Court: The Cases That Define the Debate over Church and State.* Washington, DC: Ethics and Public Policy Center/ Grand Rapids, MI: Eerdmans, 1995.

Jakobsen, Janet R., and Ann Pellegrini. *Love the Sin: Sexual Regulation and the Limits of Religious Tolerance.* 2nd ed. Boston: Beacon Press, 2004.

Jakobsen, Janet R., and Ann Pellegrini, eds. *Secularisms.* Durham, NC: Duke University Press, 2008.

Orsi, Robert. *Between Heaven and Earth: The Religious Worlds People Make and the Scholars Who Study Them.* Princeton, NJ: Princeton University Press, 2004.

Pellegrini, Ann. "Feeling Secular." *Women and Performance* 19, no. 2 (July 2009): 205–18.

PART 4

Freedom

Preface

Saba Mahmood

The essays in this section expose the difficulties involved in defining the conceptions of freedom and religion ensconced in the right to religious liberty. Key to this rumination is the opening essay by political theorist Cécile Laborde, who asks if it is possible to do away with the special status assigned to religion in the right to religious liberty. Can one expand the kinds of beliefs that are extended state protection and whose practical demands the state might accommodate within reasonable limit? How would one normatively and abstractly define the substance and scope of such beliefs in order to extend them legal protection? Laborde argues against Charles Taylor and Jocelyn Maclure's recent proposal that, inasmuch as conscience is the proper locus of modern religion, it makes sense to extend state protection to other strongly held beliefs that exert a similar moral pull on individuals. Laborde argues that such a solution is problematic because it privileges the conscience and/or belief over practices and communal forms of life that may well exert a force on the individual similar to strongly held convictions. She remains sympathetic, however, to making the right to religious liberty normatively more capacious so as to accommodate a range of beliefs and practices that are not only religious.

A number of essays in this section spell out the challenges, conceptual and practical, that such a project runs into. The first question these essays raise is, who decides what kinds of beliefs deserve state protection? It is clear that the state and its juridical apparatus would ultimately select and deem certain beliefs worthy of protection while discarding others, but would the beliefs of majority and minority groups be judged and measured equitably under such an arrangement? The idea that the right protects individuals and their beliefs rather than groups or traditions may seem to get us out of this bind. But a number of essays in this volume cast doubt on this possibility by pointing to the structural prejudice built into the modern state's laws and policies for the customs and traditions of the majority that are at the heart of national identity and culture. This is not simply a bias characteristic of some nations and not others since the very concept of the nation-state, in its claim to represent "the people," necessarily privileges majoritarian beliefs, practices, and cultural values. Noah Salomon's essay discusses this in the context of the recently created state of South Sudan (2011) where Christianity stands in for national culture and overshadows other minority religions, including animistic African traditions and Islam. Similarly, the government's attempt to categorize the populace according to its faith affiliations forecloses and solidifies religious boundaries in a country where individuals and groups belong to a multiplicity of faiths and their religious practices cut across traditions. For a place like South Sudan, which has emerged out of a long civil war that was religiously defined, this state-driven project poses a challenge for future peace, as recent events have shown.

Michael Lambek's essay calls our attention to another kind of problem. Drawing on his decades-long research in Madagascar, Lambek argues that certain religious beliefs are more amenable to the state's political rationality and calculus than are others. As he describes it, there are a variety of ways of being religious in Madagascar that not only cross boundaries of faith traditions but also escape the logic of belief and conscience that takes the individual as its proper locus. What forms of epistemic violence are entailed in privileging the concept of individuality when one's sense of self is located not within the conscience (which can claim state protection) but is embedded within the personhood of ancestors, both dead and alive? Could one extend state protection to practices that escape the notion of "belief" and a clearly articulated sense of moral commitment? How would extending state protection to such practices normalize and transform them on a singular model of religion? Would such an inscription not violate the freedom that the right to religious liberty strives to expand and secure?

One may respond that—in the context of the extensive homogeneity that exists in Western liberal democracies, where the metalanguage of belief, individuality, and conscience is extant—it is important to expand the ambit of the state to protect a range of beliefs and practices that are analogous to religious ones. This response rests on the assumption that the modern liberal state can be a neutral arbiter between competing systems of beliefs, and the task is to implement this neutrality judiciously and rationally. Viewed from this perspective, the problem is that most Western liberal democracies are not neutral enough—but they have the potential of becoming so by expanding the scope of beliefs to which they extend protection. The essay by Hussein Ali Agrama in this volume challenges this diagnosis and prescription. For Agrama, the process by which the state judges a belief (religious or otherwise) to be worthy of protection entails a range of criteria, key among them its ability to distinguish whether the belief in question is sincere or deployed instrumentally to gain a material advantage. This distinction rests on a separation between the realm of material power and the realm of belief, a separation that the state is obligated to parse out and investigate, intervening and probing into the very realm of privacy that it is supposed to protect. Agrama also argues that—inasmuch as any nation-state is obliged to define a basic set of values around which a national consensus is constructed—minority sensibilities, beliefs, and practices always sit at odds with the majoritarian culture that defines these values. The values of the minority in any polity are therefore always more subject to the hermeneutics of suspicion, the question always open as to whether their beliefs are sincere or merely instrumental. This is not the result of the failure of the state to be adequately neutral in regard to the beliefs of its citizens, but, as Agrama concludes, is "built into the historical grammar of secularism and the consequences that follow from it."

Mathijs Pelkmans's essay provides a different vantage point on the issue. The former Soviet republics of central Asia inherited a different kind of secular state from the model prevalent in liberal capitalist societies. In the aftermath of the fall of the Soviet Union and the adoption of a liberal form of governance, the older model of religion-state relationship has been reformed. The right to religious liberty, as a central principle of the liberal model of governance, now characterizes the regulation of religion in central Asian republics. Pelkmans's essay is useful in that it shows how this is not merely a matter of adopting a principle but involves a range of realpolitik and geopolitical concerns that determine which religions are protected, which are deemed suspicious, and which are extended special protections in order to create a new liberal polity. Once again we are asked to direct our gaze at the practical political conditions, institutions, and arrangements in the context of which the right is exercised and which determine the substantive meaning and scope of the right.

The last contribution in this section, by political theorist Wendy Brown, asks provocatively whether religious freedom is oxymoronic. Brown answers this question in part by pointing to competing conceptions of "freedom" within liberal secular thought, none of which can be quite squared when brought under the rubric of religious freedom. Brown also points out that the right to religious liberty is built upon the foundational assumption that religion is (or should be) a private affair, ensconced in the conscience of the individual who prays to her god in the solitude of her beliefs. Received wisdom has it that when religion becomes privatized, the political and public realm can be shielded from its interventions and demands. Yet, as Brown asks, inasmuch as religious belief also entails the demand that one *submit* to divine authority, what happens when divine dictates contravene the reigning political order? What happens when one's conscience *requires* that one resist the (unjust) demands of the state, or when one's religious beliefs stipulate that one violate the secular mandate that religion be kept out of politics? What happens when submission to divine authority "becomes constitutive of individual sovereignty (freedom's fundament in liberalism)"? By drawing upon the lifework of two iconic figures in the history of liberal political thought—Socrates and Martin Luther King Jr.—Brown calls into question the neat separation that the liberal conception of religious freedom draws between the privacy of conscience and the publicity of political action. Brown forces us to consider that freedom—in its various formulations—is not necessarily opposed to submission (as John Stuart Mill for instance would have it) but subject to various forms of authority, whether it be the authority of God, state, reason, self, rights, or justice.

In sum, the contributors to this section on freedom insist that we unpack what "freedom" entails—conceptually, practically, politically, and religiously—when we invoke the right to religious liberty.

CHAPTER TWENTY-TWO

Protecting Freedom of Religion in the Secular Age

Cécile Laborde

I want to start with a paradox. In the secular age, as Charles Taylor has amply illustrated, religious belief no longer structures our social imaginary. Instead it has become one option, one possibility, among others: one of the ways in which we give meaning to our lives. The secular age, then, is characterized by the fact of pluralism—an irreducible pluralism of beliefs, values, and commitments. Yet we secular moderns also give special primacy to freedom of religion, which is standardly presented as the archetypal liberal right. So the paradox is this: how (and why) do we protect freedom of religion in an age where religion is not special?

Here's a plausible solution to this paradox. We could say, roughly, that freedom of religion is in fact a subset of a broader class of freedoms. So instead of seeing religion itself as a special good, we say that religion is one of the ways in which individuals seek the good for themselves. Exercising freedom of religion is one of the ways in which we exercise a more generic freedom—moral freedom. Let us call this an egalitarian solution to the paradox I started with. An egalitarian theory of religious freedom does not deny that religious belief is special and should be respected and protected. What it denies is that religious belief is uniquely special: it can and should be analogized with other beliefs and commitments. Many contemporary liberal philosophers are egalitarians in this sense. John Rawls argues that what the liberal state protects is our ability to form and pursue comprehensive conceptions of the good. Ronald Dworkin sees "ethical independence" as the core value protected by freedom of religion—his last book is entitled *Religion without God*. Martha Nussbaum connects freedom of religion to a conscientious search for "ultimate meaning."

In chapter 2 of this volume, Yvonne Sherwood analyzes the perilous and fraught analogy of the category of religion with similarly "intense" and "weighty" secular "belief"; in chapter 25, Hussein Ali Agrama critically assesses Taylor's theory of state neutrality toward religious and nonreligious beliefs. In what follows, I too focus on Taylor's version of the egalitarian approach: one he puts forward (with Jocelyn Maclure) in their book *Secularism and Freedom of Conscience* (originally in French as *Laïcité et liberté de conscience*). In it Taylor and Maclure put forward their own egalitarian theory of religious freedom, and a radically inclusive one at that: they argue that all "meaning-giving commitments" should be protected on the same basis as religious commitment. The volume is also fascinating when read as a statement of Taylor's political theory—a normative companion to the more historical, epistemological, and philosophical diagnoses of our contemporary condition found in his *Sources of the Self* and *The Secular Age*.

To put my cards on the table: I agree with Taylor and Maclure that normative egalitarianism is the right response, ethically speaking, to the deep moral pluralism of the secular age. What I shall suggest, however, is that they—like other egalitarian philosophers—have underestimated the profound tensions that beset egalitarian theories of religious freedom. What does it mean, exactly, to treat religious and nonreligious conceptions of the good alike? In virtue of what should nonreligious commitments and lifestyles be analogized with religious beliefs and practices? Equality is attractive, but what is the currency of equality? Equality of *what*?

In seeking to answer these questions, egalitarian philosophers are unavoidably drawn to making the kind of judgments that they would rather avoid: value judgments about the ethical significance of particular beliefs, lifestyles, and preferences. In other words, they cannot merely appeal to a principle of neutrality between conceptions of the good. They must identify, among nonreligious conceptions, those that deserve to be treated on the same plane as religious conceptions. They must, therefore, identify a criterion with which to determine what, within a particular system of beliefs and commitments, deserves to be respected and protected. In the end, these tensions can be traced back to the difficulties of identifying (even a thin) liberal theory of the good in the secular age—in a world where conceptions of the good are irreducibly pluralized, individualized, and subjectivized. In brief, the story I want to tell is also a very Taylorian story, for it is one that—like Taylor's early work—raises questions about liberal neutrality about the good.

*   *   *

Writing in the context of the Canadian debate about reasonable accommodations, Taylor and Maclure begin by defending the idea that members of religious minorities have a right, on nondiscrimination grounds, to enjoy similar opportunities to practice their religion as members of the majority. I have no quarrel with this idea, and have argued along similar lines in my book on critical republicanism and the *hijab* controversy in France. But I'd like to focus on their second main point—namely, that the question of reasonable accommodations raises a more fundamental problem: in virtue of what are religious believers entitled to special consideration in the first place? The debate about reasonable accommodations assumes that religious practice is respectable qua religious, and that existing accommodations of religious beliefs and practices are legitimate—that they protect a basic, fundamental good or value. But what is this fundamental good or value that freedom of religion protects? It is important to formulate an answer to that question. The law inevitably creates burdens for those who have to obey it, and if we are to provide a justification for exempting some citizens from these burdens, it had better be a strong one. A purely formal egalitarian answer (which analogizes burdens on majority and minority religious practice, to justify compensating members of minorities for purely external burdens) will not be sufficient. Why is religious conduct worthy of protection in the first place?

Taylor and Maclure answer that religious belief, for purposes of legal exemptions, should only be seen as a subset of a broader category of beliefs that deserve protection: "moral beliefs which structure moral identity"—what they call "meaning-giving beliefs and commitments." And this also covers a broad spectrum of nonreligious beliefs and practices—from secular pacifism to ecocentric vegetarianism through duties of care to terminally ill loved ones. The notion of meaning-giving commitments is broader than that used by other egalitarian philosophers. In contrast to Rawls, they do not insist that individual beliefs be "comprehensive" in scope, and they reject Nussbaum's emphasis on "ultimate existential questions." It is a feature of the secular age, they point out, that people's ethical commitments take the form of "fluid, eclectic set(s) of values" that are not integrated into a comprehensive whole and are not perceived as "unconditional rules for action." At certain times, however—such as during the illness of a loved one—the pursuit of certain core values become paramount and gives meaning and shape to one's life. In sum, we can say that Taylor and Maclure take the ethical pluralism of the secular age far more seriously than other egalitarian philosophers. Rawls and Nussbaum, it seems, still hold a traditionally religious understanding of the scope (comprehensive) and content ("ultimate questions") of what counts as a morally weighty secular belief.

Drawing on Taylor's rehabilitation of "ordinary life" in *Sources of the Self*, Taylor and Maclure detect pockets of moral depth in ordinary life—in the sudden encounter with finitude in the event of the death of a loved one, or in ecocentric vegetarians' profound convictions about the wrongness of meat consumption, to take their two favorite examples. What makes those commitments particularly weighty is that they allow individuals to act with integrity—where integrity is defined as congruence between one's perceptions of one's duties and one's actual actions. What the end-of-life caregiver and the ecocentric vegetarian have in common is that they both seek to act in accordance with their conscience. "Here I stand, I can do no other," as Martin Luther is thought to have said. Taylor and Maclure note that forcing someone to act against her deep conscientious convictions constitutes a "moral harm" equivalent to the kind of "physical harm" that justifies the special accommodation of citizens with disabilities. Thus, they conclude, citizens with intense, categorical, meaning-giving secular beliefs have a prima facie claim to be considered for exemptions from burdensome laws. The claim is only prima facie because there are limits to accommodation: the rights of others, the interests pursued by the law, the undue hardship caused by accommodations. But even if the claim is not favorably received, what is interesting is that Taylor and Maclure have considerably expanded the range of beliefs and commitments that have a claim to be considered for special protection. They have provided a novel philosophical justification for accommodation itself. To sum up, they reject both the content and the scope criteria for a secular belief to be as morally weighty as a traditional religious belief, but they retain a third criterion, which we could call the categoricity criterion. Secular beliefs are morally weighty when they prescribe duties of conscience.

*   *   *

So, have Taylor and Maclure solved the paradox I started with? Have they developed a plausibly egalitarian definition of morally weighty beliefs that is not biased in favor of religious beliefs yet adequately protects the underlying values expressed by the ideal of freedom of religion? My assessment comes in two parts. In the first, I draw attention to one significant virtue of their account, which is that it implicitly relies on a very Taylorian idea of "strong evaluation." In the second, I cast some doubts about the viability of the individualistic, Protestantized, subjectivist conception of strong evaluation that underpins their account.

Taylor and Maclure get to the heart of a key feature of freedom of religion—one that is strangely neglected by contemporary liberals. It is this: what Taylor said (in an earlier, seminal article) about negative freedoms in general—that they are empty without "strong evaluations" of what they allow the pursuit of—applies with particular acuity to freedom of religion. Freedom of religion, in contrast to more generic freedoms of thought, belief, and association, relies on a moralized distinction between valuable and nonvaluable activities and serves to protect a subset of the former. It is a freedom to pursue a specific end and activity: it refers to the pursuit of a conception of the good with a specific shape, content, and form rather than the means through which any conception of the good can be pursued. Furthermore, in the case of exemptions and accommodations, which is our focus here, freedom of religion generates demands of positive assistance in pursuing those activities. This means that, when adjudicating such claims, it must be decided which claim correctly expresses the values underpinning the general principle.

Even though they do not explicitly draw on Taylor's earlier writings, Taylor and Maclure are open about the need to make "strong evaluations" about the values that freedom of religion is supposed to protect. This confirms the long-standing Taylorian view that rights protect substantive values: we care about rights because of the good that they protect, which cannot be reduced to individual freedom of choice. So our authors do not shy away from openly perfectionist evaluations, setting "trivial" against "central" commitments and "mere preferences" against "core convictions." Such perfectionist discriminations, it seems to me, are inherent in any serious reflection about the value of freedom of religion. Perhaps this is an obvious point, but it is one that contemporary liberals—punctiliously attached to an ideal of neutrality toward the good—have not fully come to terms with.

Who, then, is to make the strong evaluations required to distinguish between meaning-giving and trivial commitments? Taylor and Maclure's emphatic response to this is: the individual claimant herself. Here they anticipate the charge—often leveled at Taylor's conception of positive liberty—that the idea of "strong evaluation" could give the state the authority arbitrarily to discriminate between better and worse ways to exercise one's freedoms. Instead Taylor and Maclure assert that "the special status of religious beliefs is derived from the role they play in people's moral lives, rather than from an assessment of their intrinsic validity." They defend what they call a subjective conception of freedom of religion, according to which only individuals—not the state, nor religious authorities—are in a position to explain which particular beliefs and commitments are key to their sense of moral integrity. Judges only have to assess whether such claims are made with sincerity (so as to rule out, when possible, fraudulent or pretextual claims). Yet ultimately the subjective conception of freedom points to the sovereignty of private, strong evaluations.

There is much to recommend in this account, to which I am very sympathetic. But it is also plagued by tensions and difficulties.

First, Taylor and Maclure effectively collapse religion into conscience and implicitly assume that the latter category is more inclusive than the former. But we may wonder whether this is the case, or whether anything is lost in the redescription of freedom of religion as freedom of conscience. Assume I am a devout Muslim; I observe Ramadan, say my prayers every day, wear the *hijab*, give *zakat* (alms giving or charitable giving), and send my children to Koranic school. Or assume I am a practicing Catholic. I observe Lent, try not to eat meat on Fridays, celebrate Easter, go to church every Sunday, have my children baptized and confirmed. For many Catholics and Muslims (but also other Christians, Jews, Hindus, and Buddhists) the religious experience is fundamentally about exhibiting the virtues of the good believer, living in community with others, and shaping one's daily life in accordance with the rituals of the faith. Those rituals are meaning-giving and are connected to believers' sense of their moral integrity.

Yet they are not duties of conscience, though they are often redescribed as such. The good religious life is a life of constant, difficult, ritual affirmation of the faith against the corrupting influences of the secular world. It is not often one in which one single obligation (say, wearing a particular dress, attending Mass) is so stringent as to promise eternal damnation if it is not fulfilled. Taylor and Maclure tend to reinterpret acts of habitual, collective, "embodied practices" of religious devotion as Protestantized duties of conscience. While such a description tallies with the individualization and subjectification of religious experience in contemporary societies, it also has two unanticipated consequences. First, it perversely encourages the most fundamentalist and rigid interpretations of religious dogma. It rewards those Christians who present their objection to homosexuality as a matter of conscience ("here I stand, I can do no other") over and above those habitual believers who seek to accommodate their religious life to a secularizing world, often with considerable unease and forbearance. So here's another paradox: in insisting that only beliefs that are intensely held—and experienced as categorical duties—should be candidates for "reasonable" accommodation, Taylor and Maclure accommodate those with the least "reasonable" beliefs. Of course it can be retorted that only claimants with intense and categorical beliefs are likely to be candidates for accommodation in the first place. But as the dilemma about accommodations is used to identify the values underpinning freedom of religion itself, legitimate questions can be raised about the broader implications of the reduction of religion to conscience.

At this point one may legitimately ask, why did Taylor and Maclure not opt for the weak interpretation of freedom of conscience—which protects all meaning-giving and integrity-constituting commitments—rather than the strong interpretation, which focuses on the more problematic category of conscience? The main concern seems to be about the proliferation of claims. Thus Taylor and Maclure plausibly note that values such as political ideals, professional fulfillment, and artistic creativity are meaning-giving and integrity-constituting. Yet they generally do not generate claims of special accommodation because they are linked to flexible and fluid, not overriding and stringent, obligations. It is only in exceptional cases—the ecocentric vegetarian and the caregiver of a terminally ill parent—that such secular beliefs generate something like an absolute categorical obligation. The strong interpretation of freedom of conscience, then, allows Taylor and Maclure to sketch a manageable theory of accommodations in which only beliefs with a certain degree of categoricity—conscientious beliefs—are accommodated. The administratibility of exemptions is, of course, a legitimate concern. But the singling out of categoricity as the necessary trigger for protection raises its own problems. It draws a normative wedge between two kinds of meaning-giving commitments, those that are inflexible and conscientious and those that are habitual and embodied. This has the effect of singling out individual conscience—as opposed to cultural or community membership—as especially worthy of protection.

In a Canadian context, where cultural identities often feature as the paradigmatic meaning-giving, integrity-constituting commitments, Taylor and Maclure's lack of reference to culture is surprising. In light of Taylor's seminal contribution to the normative theory of multiculturalism, one might have expected that *Secularism and Freedom of Conscience* would take seriously the cultural dimensions of religion instead of proposing a "Protestant" interpretation of what, within religion, is worth protecting. The upshot of their theory is that a sense of communal membership, of cultural identification, of ritualized practice, are not among the values that freedom of religion can be said to protect. Consider the following practices, which currently generate rights to exemption from general laws on grounds of religious freedom in various countries: accommodation of religious dress in the workplace, the ritual killing of animals for halal or kosher meat, tax exemptions for religious charities, church autonomy in the appointment of its leaders. None of these activities is properly described as a conscientious activity, and therefore it is unclear whether they would be entitled to accommodations under Taylor and Maclure's theory. Note that I am not saying that they should; I am simply pointing out this interesting paradox, that a self-proclaimed inclusive theory of freedom of religion actually excludes what most religious believers would take to be freedom of religion to be about. In the present volume Robert Yelle (chapter 1), Elizabeth Shakman Hurd (chapter 3), Webb Keane (chapter 4), and Peter G. Danchin (chapter 20) point out that religion has been construed as a matter of private conviction rather than of public performance. We could add that, even when freedom of religion relates to actual performances and practices (as it does in accommodation claims), it still draws its moral force from its presumed connection with individual conscience.

Second, let me now raise a connected difficulty with Taylor and Maclure's subjective notion of freedom of religion. While they only consider examples of morally admirable commitments (pacifism, caring for the sick, protecting animal rights) it is not difficult to think of a range of conscientious actions that may be morally trivial, morally wrong, or morally bad. In those cases, should individual strong evaluations be supreme or are different standards called for?

One issue is how to distinguish trivial from morally significant beliefs. Taylor and Maclure assume there is a consensual understanding of the difference between a morally trivial and a morally significant act. Yet, under conditions of deep moral pluralism, it is precisely those kinds of strong evaluations that are likely to be contested. Consider the standard defense by US courts (following the decision in *Employment Division v. Smith*) of the ingestion of peyote, an otherwise illegal drug. The use of peyote within some Native American rituals is considered by the Supreme Court as a spiritual act falling under the free exercise provision of the First Amendment (even if it does not generate a right to accommodation—as the court famously declared in the *Smith* case, as discussed in chapter 19 by Winnifred Fallers Sullivan). But what is interesting is this: while ingesting drugs merely to "get high" would count as a trivial, frivolous purpose, injecting drugs for spiritual purposes rightly falls under the category of a morally significant act deserving of protection. But let's also consider this: what if individuals not belonging to what the courts recognize as a "religion" sincerely claim that they are also using drugs for spiritual purposes? Does "spiritual purpose" extend to dealing with depression, seeking higher truths through controlled intoxication, or dealing with existential pain? In the secular age, how do we draw the line between the spiritual and the trivial, and who is to be the judge of someone else's spiritual integrity?

The other issue is whether freedom of conscience should permit individuals to do bad or unjust things. Taylor and Maclure avoid the difficult question of whether freedom of conscience positively protects a right to do wrong. One very preliminary hypothesis: in the philosophical tradition of thinking about conscience—whether Greek, Buddhist, Muslim, Jewish, Catholic, or Kantian tradition, to name just a few—conscience is respectable and admirable not only as a subjective individual faculty to live in conformity with one's own good; it is, more deeply, respected as the faculty to live in conformity with what one sincerely perceives to be the demands of the good. This is why Antigone's dilemma is so poignant: it vividly pictures a tragic choice between two objectively recognizable moral obligations. In the natural law tradition, conscience is the faculty with which individuals exercise practical judgment about how to apply a general objective moral law to concrete cases. Individuals are fallible, and consciences may err. But conscience is admirable because it is a sincere, though fallible, attempt to find the good. Conscience, therefore, cannot demand us to do evil, inhuman, or outrageous things, even though it can mislead us about the good. But if there is a deep (if complicated) connection between respect for conscience and a nonsubjectivist assessment of its content, then individual strong evaluations will likely be an unreliable guide about what conscience really requires of us.

*   *   *

Where does this leave us? To conclude, I see Taylor and Maclure's succinct but densely argued chapter as the most promising attempt to articulate the morally admirable human faculties traditionally protected by freedom of religion in ways that respect the deep pluralism of the secular age. I have pointed to some problems, which are not so much fatal flaws as unavoidable tensions within the politicolegal philosophy of religious exemptions.

My suspicion is that liberal neutrality about religion ultimately "piggybacks" on a baggage of ideas, conceptions, and values that originally made sense in a world comprehensively structured by a broadly Christian ethics. In that world, where early liberal ideas of toleration and freedom of religion were articulated, Christian ethics provided the moral framework within which "strong evaluations"—between good and evil, significant and trivial, and do on—were taken for granted. Then it could be coherently assumed that "religion" was a good thing, that any activity pursued under the aegis of religion was therefore also good, and that churches were alternative, self-standing sources of normativity to that of the state. Religion on that view operated as a normative "black box," the content of which the state could try to ignore. It is when this box is thrown open by the egalitarian impulse of the secular age that the need for new "strong evaluations" reappears. Yet those strong evaluations are inherently problematic in a world where there is no publicly validated religious or moral faith, and where the state is expected not to take sides between different ways of conceiving and living the good life.

Egalitarian liberals have struggled to define, in a way that is suitably nonsectarian and evaluatively neutral, the morally admirable faculties that traditional freedom of religion can be said to protect. Taylor and Maclure promisingly seek to locate those human faculties in the moral predicaments thrown up by ordinary lives and in the strong evaluations that individuals make in the process. Yet the emphasis on conscience tends to favor a Protestant understanding of what a religion is, and it also relies on an implicit, unarticulated theory of the good. All of this only illustrates one of Taylor's most profound contributions to political philosophy, pointing to the complex ambiguities that beset the liberal ideal of neutrality toward the good life. What I have sought to provide is the sketch of a Taylorian critique of Taylor—a modest testimony of the astonishing fecundity of his thought. In sum, Taylor's recent work points to the formidable challenges that await the still underdeveloped philosophical project of making sense of the ideal of freedom of religion in the secular age. That such a philosophical project is difficult and complex does not imply, of course, that it is not worth pursuing.

Note

A version of this essay was presented at "Charles Taylor at 80: An International Conference" held in Montreal on March 31, 2012.

Selected Bibliography

Dworkin, Ronald. *Religion without God*. Cambridge, MA: Harvard University Press, 2013.

Laborde, Cécile. *Critical Republicanism: The Hijab Controversy and Political Philosophy*. Oxford: Oxford University Press, 2008.

Maclure, Jocelyn, and Charles Taylor. *Secularism and Freedom of Conscience*. Translated by Jane Marie Todd. Cambridge, MA: Harvard University Press, 2011.

Nussbaum, Martha. *Liberty of Conscience: In Defense of America's Tradition of Religious Equality*. New York: Basic Books, 2008.

Rawls, John. *A Theory of Justice*. Cambridge, MA: Harvard University Press, 1971.

Taylor, Charles. "What's Wrong with Negative Liberty?" In *Philosophy and the Human Sciences: Philosophical Papers*, 211–29. Cambridge: Cambridge University Press, 1985.

———. *Sources of the Self: The Making of the Modern Identity*. Cambridge, MA: Harvard University Press, 1989.

CHAPTER TWENTY-THREE

Freeing Religion at the Birth of South Sudan

Noah Salomon

If you had the opportunity to start from scratch, without the burden of a permanent constitution or an entrenched legal system—if you were, in other words, a founding father/mother of a newborn nation—what relationship would you forge between religion and state? What creative ways might you devise to appease voices in the public sphere that call for separation of church and state as well as those that demand freedom of religion, both in the sense of freedom of conscience and communal autonomy? How might you solve the challenge of offering ample space for the religious diversity extant in your populace while crafting a model of citizenship upon which all can agree? While such a scenario might seem like a far-fetched fantasy, these were the very questions many South Sudanese were asking themselves in the summer of 2011, elated at the possibility of starting anew after a history of brutal civil war and colonial (African and European) occupation.

Yet while the excitement was palpable in those heady days following the declaration of independence on July 9, 2011, we must be wary of those who imagine that South Sudan, despite its limited infrastructure, was being created *ex nihilo*. Suffering still from unhealed wounds of civil war (and debts yet unpaid to those who fought in it), as well as a series of unreconstructed models of governance adopted in consultation with international aid and development organizations, South Sudan was, of course, in reality not starting from scratch. The neighborhoods of its capital, Juba, with names like *atla' bara* ("get outside") and *al-rujal ma fi* ("the men are not here"), were constant reminders, inscribed on the very geography of the place, that Juba was not long ago a garrison town of the Sudanese Army, which had gone through these neighborhoods violently clearing them of rebels. And yet the possibility of mixing these heirloom ingredients into a new stew was certainly present, and, around tables in newly constructed (or more often trailer-housed) government offices, hotel verandas, tea circles, and private salons, everyone from South Sudanese intellectuals, to the northern opposition exiled now in Juba, to returnees from rural Minnesota (or urban Uganda or Khartoum) were imagining the possibilities for forging a new future.

The possibilities, at least in those first days, were seemingly endless. Some stressed continuity with the past, riffing off the comments of the then Secretary-General of the Sudan People's Liberation Movement (SPLM), Pagan Amum, when he lowered the old Sudanese flag for the last time in preparation for the raising of the South Sudanese flag at the independence ceremony. (The SPLM was the former southern Sudanese rebel movement, then a national political party, and is now the party of the current government of South Sudan.) There he told the crowd that he would not be handing the Sudanese flag over to Khartoum in a gesture of good riddance but instead would hold on to it in the soon-to-be-formed national archive, in memory of the shared history, the shared struggle, and indeed the shared future that northerners and southerners have and would continue to experience together. Others imagined a cleaner break. One bilingual sign held high at the independence ceremonies read (and I translate from the Arabic), "From today our identity is southern and African and not Arab and Islamic. We are not the worst of Arabs, but rather the best of Africans (*min al-yawm huwiyatna janubiyya ifriqiyya, wa laysa* [sic] *'arabiyya islamiyya. lisna aswa' al-'arab bal afdal al-afariqa*)." The sign expressed itself well in Arabic—and was held up at a ceremony largely conducted in Arabic, still the de facto lingua franca of South Sudan despite official efforts to switch to English—but the English text on the sign that attempted to proclaim the same aspirations was difficult to parse: "We are not worst Arabs but better African". The clean break at which the crafters of the sign aimed could not be achieved overnight. The discursive historical reality of independence, of sharp, bold lines on the map, was matched in intensity by the sociological reality of entanglement (by choice and by force), of blurry lines. North and south could not be so easily disaggregated.

The tension between a national model that stressed continuity with the past and one that proposed a break with what was certainly a painful history plagued Muslims perhaps most of all. Muslim South Sudanese, who make up a significant portion of the population of South Sudan, are individuals whose very identity challenges the clean break between north and south. Islam came primarily from the north (from which the south was now separating), tying together families, trade routes, and pilgrimage networks, despite aggressive British colonial efforts to stop its spread to southern Sudan. These links between north and south—genealogical, economic, and confraternal—were not so easily sundered. While many non-Muslim South Sudanese had assumed that Islam was a political identity, somehow tied to the north, and imagined mass-conversion away from Islam coinciding with southern independence, South Sudanese Muslims insisted that to be southern and Muslim was not a contradiction in terms. Continuity with a past in which southern Muslims suffered discrimination in the north for being southerners and in the south for being Muslims did not seem like a good option to them. (I should note, though, that this discrimination was by no means universal: for example, in the case of the south Muslims were well integrated into the SPLM during the civil war and the south's deeper history certainly includes important Muslim leaders.) Indeed, the vast majority of Muslims with whom I spoke in 2011 favored southern independence and a clean break from the north, and were actively debating how Muslim identity had changed under the new political arrangements they had entered: South Sudanese Muslims had gone from being part of a national majority, to being a "minority group" literally overnight, and without traveling anywhere. The nature of "South Sudanese Islam" was being renegotiated, but most seemed to agree that the particular cultural stamp of the north would have to be transcended if the name of Islam was to wash out the stain of its bad reputation, acquired during the war, and flourish in the new state.

On the other hand, the notion of a clean break that sought to define South Sudan as explicitly non-Muslim (whether or not it was thereby "Christian" was a topic of debate, to which I will return below) and non-Arab made South Sudanese Muslims worry that the "New Sudan" imagined by deceased SPLM founder John Garang, which was to embrace Sudanese of all religions and ethnicities, was quickly taking on an ethnically and religiously exclusive color. Muslim communities feared persecution in the new state after decades of civil war in which Islamization, if not Islam, was portrayed as a prime adversary to southern flourishing. For example, the uneven (but active) banning of headscarves in southern public schools after the signing of the 2005 peace agreement, which reverted control of the south to southerners, led to protests in at least one major Muslim center I visited (the city of Malakal) and the founding of a private Muslim girls' school there. The banning of religious political organizations was taken by many Muslims to be directed at Islam, as Christian majority parties (under secular names) were certainly plentiful. Such incidents further raised suspicion that the equality and secularism that the new government was promising was a coded way of promoting "tyranny of the majority" and a state from which Muslim communities would be marginalized. The southern state's resistance to a quota system (in which a certain amount of ministries or parliamentary seats would be given to Muslims qua Muslims), under the logic of blindness to religious identity, led to a short-lived but significant armed rebellion in Northern Bahr el Ghazal—active during the days of independence, but now quelled—demanding 30 percent representation for Muslims in the new government.

The desire to "transform political difference into sameness," as Saba Mahmood has put it in her chapter in this volume, has certainly been at the top of the state's agenda in its quest to establish something called a South Sudanese citizen out of the dizzyingly diverse cultures, languages, and religions that make up the demographic landscape. What that "sameness" was to consist of, and what degree of diversity was still possible in spite of it, was a primary object of debate.

In a nation where neither tribes, nor regions, *nor even* individual families are traditionally divided on the basis of religion, how would South Sudan's adoption of the internationalist languages of religious freedom, and the concomitant division of peoples into rights bearing "religious actors," affect the existing social fabric? While there certainly have been Muslim communities across what is now South Sudan for some time, who have been, by all accounts, well-integrated into life there, I was surprised to find that the vast majority of Muslim leaders at the focal point of new tensions did not emerge from those communities but were recent converts. Why have these "new Muslims" taken on such a prominent role in the organizational structures of the emergent "Muslim minority"? What makes them, rather than individuals from the entrenched Muslim communities, so much more suitable for the formation of a Muslim civil society that the state seems to both fear and demand? Such individuals live in households that are extremely diverse (a father who follows the prophet Ngundeng, a Christian Mother, and Muslim son is not at all uncommon), and one wonders how (or perhaps if) this status quo will be interrupted by the emergent notion of confessional community that is being forwarded by Muslim organizations and state demographers alike.

At the same time, however, South Sudanese Muslims seemed to experience religion as a mode of being that did not necessitate the discarding of other modes of belonging (tribe, family, social class, etc.). Indeed, even the associational spaces themselves (Muslim councils and organizations, mosques, etc.) were not as restricted as one might assume. For example, at the Islamic Council for South Sudan office in Malakal, a good portion of the young men hanging out in the inner courtyard were in fact Christians: this space was by no means restricted as a Muslim gathering place. Families, as I indicated above, were equally diverse in terms of the religious identities of their members. Even individuals themselves were not always easy to categorize into one box or another. The modern state's voracious appetite for categorization may have trouble coming to terms with the absence of the kind of neat lines that the international regimes of religious freedom that it has adopted demand in order to dole out their goods (protection from "religious persecution," participation in networks with global "communities of faith," etc.). It is precisely the lack of a proper fit between religion as it is lived and religion as it is conceived in such projects that makes religious freedom endeavors potentially so parochial in their application, the bluntness of their instrument having significant capacity for exacerbating division rather than ameliorating it.

It was not only in regard to Muslim communities that the state's intervention into religion seemed ripe with tension. As I walked the streets of Juba, listening to the new national anthem played over and over ("Oh God, we praise and glorify you, / for your grace on South Sudan"), I wondered not only where Muslims would figure into the imaginings of this new nation but also where all the "African traditional religions" (or ATRs, as government officials called the variety of ancestor veneration, spirit, and divination practices extant in South Sudan) would figure into the national image. (See Rosalind I. J. Hackett's essay in this volume, for a discussion of how ATRs are managed and marginalized by states in a variety of African contexts.) While there was an explicit attempt to give time to Muslim and Christian prayer in official forums, such as at the independence ceremony when a Christian benediction as well as verses from the Koran were recited, symbols of these traditional practices were not present at the podium. The official party line seems to be that ATRs should be represented within the state, constituted as distinct faith communities (*dins*, as expressed in my interviews with government officials). However, scholars of South Sudan point out that to think of such "traditional" practices as distinct confessions does not represent the reality of South Sudanese who may identify as Christians, for example, and at the same time see no contradiction in maintaining their rites and rituals. One wonders, then, what effect the state's attempt to constitute such practices as discrete "religions" (and distinctly not part of what it means to be Christian) will have on those engaged in such practices, and whether it will make this kind of lived hybridity between Christianity and other modes of approaching the divine less sustainable, thus rendering Christianity and ATRs as much more polar forms of identity than they are currently.

Indeed, with South Sudan's government still in flux, one wonders what particular iteration of "religious freedom" will take root in the new state. The Transitional Constitution of South Sudan nowhere mentions "freedom of religion" but instead offers a very specific retinue of "religious rights" (article 23), perhaps fearing the power of religious groups were their freedoms stated absolutely. On the ground, the new government has not been shy about managing and taxonomizing religions, policing the line that divides religion and state and even the borders of religious orthodoxy itself. Government offices registered "faith-based organizations" and often rejected applications, for example, of Christian organizations "if the constitution of a particular group is not lining up with the biblical chapters or verses," as one inspector in the Bureau of Religious Affairs put it to me. This effort formed part of a program to protect the nation from what he called "cults," though which groups would qualify as Christian and Muslim and which as "cults" was still in flux during the time I was there. This propensity of the state to confer recognition on certain religious groups while withholding it from others seems to be a classic case of what Elizabeth Shakman Hurd calls (in her chapter in this volume) the prevailing "foreclosure on religion without belief" by international regimes of religious freedom that "leaves little room" for "dissenters and doubters on the margins of or just outside . . . 'faith communities'" for it "endows hierarchical authorities with the power to represent and pronounce on what is or is not religious belief deserving of special protection or sanction."

I do not wish to come to premature conclusions about what form "religious freedom" will take in South Sudan. I was there in the early days of the formation of this new state and the situation was still very much in flux. The new state of South Sudan promised (and in its early days certainly has achieved) a very different approach to the relationship be-tween religion and state from that in which the Sudan southerners had lived before July 9, 2011, in which the central government in Khartoum had attempted to craft an Islamic state. However, the nature of the par-ticular relationship between religion and state in South Sudan, what its government of referred to as its "secularism," was still up in the air.

Despite the assumption by many that secularism will solve any poten-tial "religion problems" for South Sudan, it is important to reflect on its particular itinerary in the new state. By following it, we become aware that secularism, too, is a mode of governance fraught with difficult con-sequences for the plural practitioners of religions in South Sudan. South Sudanese political actors often present secularism as a means of redeem-ing the nation from decades of religious strife in which the government instrumentally used religion in an attempt to create national unity by force but failed. However, the new government's embrace of secularism as an alternative mode of governing religious diversity has come to be contested by many South Sudanese who claim that it is anything but neu-tral in regard to religion. There is, indeed, a major paradox at the heart of South Sudan's secular project. On the one hand, the category of the secular indicates to South Sudanese political elite a public space in which the state expresses neutrality in regard to the religious confessions of its citizens. This professedly "universalist" definition of the secular draws, in fact, primarily on the American model wherein nonestablishment is said to guarantee a public sphere in which freedom of religion is at least the purported goal. On the other hand, however, South Sudanese political actors understand the secular as a *historically specific* device through which they can erase a painful and violent past in which the political space was forcibly "Islamized" through the actions of conquerors from the north.

In order to clear the ground on which this secular state could be built, the government understood its charge to be the erasure of the marks of past Islamization, acquired during the most recent civil war (1983–2005), that dot the South Sudanese landscape until today. The most visible of these marks are mosques on government properties, built during an era in which the government was trying actively to convert southerners and lay claim to public space as Islamic. Under this revisionist logic, the new state has reclaimed these buildings for "secular pursuits": for ex-ample, the mosques at military installations have been transformed into army barracks, while the mosque at the Malakal Airport has become a restaurant. Such repurposing of these active sites of worship is read by many South Sudanese Muslims to be nothing short of a desecration of sacred space as well as a curtailment of their freedom of worship. Given that large numbers of Muslims serve in the army and make use of public space like the airport, many Muslims read the closure of mosques not as an attack on past Islamization, or a return of public space to neutral ground, but as an attack on Islam, a cleansing of the land of the mark of their identity. Despite assurances of government officials that it is Islamism and not Islam that is the target of secular purges, this variety of the secular is read by many as far from neutral.

The vernacular secularism of South Sudan, caught as it is between the promise of religious neutrality and the de-Islamization of the public sphere, begs the question of whether secularism can guarantee both absolute freedom (of the state) from religion and freedom (for the public) of religion at the same time. The seal of the new Bureau of Religious Affairs expresses graphically what the national ideal may come to be: a large cross at the center, with a smaller *hilal* (representing Islam) and a spear (representing "traditional religions") at either side—indicating, it seems, a Christian-majority state in which other "religions," safely construed as minorities, will be recognized and protected. What exactly will have been freed through this arrangement, and what this freedom will entail for the newfound minorities and majorities, is yet to be determined.

Note

This chapter is an edited version of an Immanent Frame blog posting written in April 2012: that is, prior to the current round of political and communal violence in South Sudan, which began in December 2013. While my fieldwork predates this crisis, I comment on how the crisis is (and is not) related to the contexts I discuss in this chapter in a recent article in the *Journal of Law and Religion*, which is included in the bibliography that follows and which also incorporates and expands upon many of the arguments I make here.

Selected Bibliography

Hutchinson, Sharon. "Spiritual Fragments of an Unfinished War." In *Religion and African Civil Wars*, edited by Niels Kastfelt, 28–53. New York: Palgrave Macmillan, 2005.

Leonardi, Cherry. "Paying 'Buckets of Blood' for the Land: Moral Debates over Economy, War and State in Southern Sudan." *Journal of Modern African Studies* 49, no. 2 (2011): 215–40.

Mahmood, Saba. "Religious Freedom, the Minority Question, and Geopolitics in the Middle East." *Comparative Studies in Society and History* 15, no. 2 (2012): 418–46.

Salomon, Noah. "Religion after the State: Secular Soteriologies at the Birth of South Sudan." *Journal of Law and Religion* 29, no. 3 (2014): 447–69.

Sullivan, Winnifred Fallers. *The Impossibility of Religious Freedom.* Princeton, NJ: Princeton University Press, 2005.

Wani, Abdalla Keri. 2006. *Islam in Southern Sudan: Its Impact, Past, Present and Future* (Khartoum, Sudan: University of Khartoum Press).

CHAPTER TWENTY-FOUR

Is Religion Free?

Michael Lambek

To this stimulating and learned series of commentaries concerning the general effects of submitting questions of religious practice to a particular kind of legal system, I make several comments as an anthropologist.

The first point, as a number of other contributors to the present volume make clear, is that there can be no hard-and-fast definition of religion. Religion is not a natural category; if it is an intrinsic part of the social, as Émile Durkheim thought, this does not mean that it is always abstracted or objectified as a discrete institution or that, when it is, it will always carry the same distinctive features or criteria. "Religions" are not, in the first instance, commensurable tokens of an obvious or pre-existing type. However, as Talal Asad has argued, the very acts of state-based legal systems have constituted such a type, demarcated certain practices and institutions as religious, and recognized specific tokens as religions. Hence both the general nature of "religion" as we have come to conceptualize and encounter it and the recognition of specific "religions" as discrete objects in themselves and as distinct from one another are closely imbricated with the law. Religions in this sense are objects of the legal gaze. But this raises the question of how to talk about what lies outside that gaze.

There is another way to conceptualize religion as unobjectified and immanent to the social that may be invisible to the legal gaze. This is not mutually exclusive of or contradictory to the first conceptualization, but it is quite different. Religion in this second sense is not disembedded from law (nor is law from religion), but it lies at the very constitution of the social. Religion is equivalent in this sense to those aspects of emotional or cognitive function that are virtually inaccessible to the reflective psychological self because they are what constitute the very possibility and grounds for reflective selfhood—which would collapse if fully dissected. Here religion is precisely what the law cannot see; it stands at its own foundations, underlying its legitimacy and even its existence.

In both conceptualizations, albeit for different reasons, religion and law are always already encapsulated in one another; hence it is somewhat paradoxical for the legal system to then grant religion "freedom" as though religion were something discrete and autonomous. Indeed, this suggests that freedom itself, freedom of any kind, is constituted in liberal democratic societies as what lies within the law rather than outside it. Hence there is a difference made (at least implicitly) between legitimate freedom and illegitimate freedom, a distinction that would seem to undermine the very idea of freedom as an absolute ideal or condition. Insofar as this is recognized and conceived as problematic, it may be a factor in the goal of certain right-wing libertarian movements to create a space for freedom entirely outside the state and outside the state's definitions of "freedom." This is not a subject I can pursue further here except to note that "freedom" itself is a concept (or "key symbol") that carries a much heavier symbolic weight in the United States than in other liberal democracies.

A second point concerns features of the anthropological and broader scholarly discourse on or about religion that may be equally relevant for how religion is conceived in the public domain. In their work of description and comparison, anthropologists are forced to fall back on the conceptual language that has emerged within their own tradition. Hence, insofar as "religion" is accepted at face value, we discover "religions" in other societies. This is true of other words in our tool kit as well; among the most salient of these are *belief*, *ritual*, and *experience*. I mention these three terms in particular because it is evident that in trying to offer deeper understandings of religious phenomena, whether with respect to cause or substance or simply to improve description and comparison by means of distinctive or elementary features, anthropologists have tended to draw heavily, and in turn, upon each of these three concepts. They surely enter as well into popular discussions as well as legal deliberation concerning religious freedom, as is illustrated in the commentaries in this volume by Winnifred Fallers Sullivan and Hussein Ali Agrama. Each term also holds particular salience in specific social and religious movements or traditions and indeed in distinguishing neighboring denominations or movements from one another.

Much of the discourse on religion in North American debate has turned on the question of belief. Religion, religions, and the status of an individual's adherence to religion have been articulated in terms of belief. (Religion entails "belief" in god or gods; Christians "believe" that Jesus is their savior; a given person is sincere in his or her "belief" or "beliefs," or is a "true believer.") Belief holds a stubborn presence in the discourse, yet its prominence can be argued to be problematic in a number of respects. As Malcolm Ruel has shown, belief itself has a genealogy and a deeply Christian one; moreover in its contemporary, post-Enlightenment usage, the term *belief* implicitly raises the possibility of doubt, not to mention disbelief or unbelief. Furthermore, it is impossible to ascertain as a particular mental state. It is evident too that its genealogy is not merely Christian in general but that belief became especially salient for Protestantism in the ways that various reform movements distinguished themselves from the Roman Catholic church. Hence, perhaps, its recurrent salience in the field of religious studies, which itself has Protestant foundations. It can be added that the history of the Reformation makes it almost self-evident that the words *freedom* and *belief* belong together. This is linked as well to ideas of individual autonomy and inner reflective life, and thus to conscience and sincerity, as explored by Webb Keane.

A focus on belief rapidly raises the question of "false" beliefs and hence of rationality: how can other people believe what I consider to be patently false? The assumption must be that people of other religions (or of any religion, if one writes as an agnostic scholar or an atheistic rationalist) must be mistaken. From there the discussion leads rapidly into questions of rationalization and interestingly to comparisons of the maintenance of scientific paradigms or commonsense worlds with those of religion and perhaps even how they complement rather than contradict one another.

Such an approach to religion has seemed too "intellectualist" to other scholars. A parallel tradition beginning in France (and developed by scholars steeped in Roman Catholic or Jewish milieux, which themselves by comparison to Protestantism have emphasized ritual observance over abstracted belief) has argued that religion is rooted in ritual—that is, in practice or performance rather than belief, and in practices of a specific, formal kind. This has advantages for empirical scholarship insofar as public ritual acts are considered easier to distinguish and observe than are inner "beliefs" and easier to take as evidence than heard statements. The anthropological study of ritual has made many advances and can be linked to the idea of discipline as derived from Michel Foucault and to social order and political power, but it has seemed too formal or empty, perhaps too "this-worldly," to some scholars to serve as a synecdoche for, or foundation of, religion. Such thinkers understand religion by starting with experience.

At first glance nothing could seem more natural than experience, and indeed certain forms of experience have been used to naturalize and justify religion. Yet "experience" itself has a genealogy, as Martin Jay has illustrated, and is not a self-evident category. Thus the English word *experience* has no German equivalent; in German there is a necessary and obvious distinction between *Erlebnis* (immediate event experience) and *Erfahrung* (cumulative life experience) that is not primary in English. With such a sharp difference between closely related languages, imagine the translation problems between languages from different families. In any case, "experience" has been attractive to a host of Western scholars, who turn their attention to "mysticism," to "Eastern religions," or simply to poetic responses to nature. Of course, experience is also central to both Charismatic Christianity and "new age" practices; in each instance it overrides both ritual and belief. In a competitive religious marketplace, both the Roman Catholic Church and mainstream Protestant traditions have become more open to ways of making their services more experience-rich and hence attractive to a public seeking "experience." There is a parallel emphasis now at my university on something called "experiential learning."

All this is to say that when the law locates religion and deliberates about it or agrees to attribute certain acts or practices in its name, it matters whether it begins with or understands belief, ritual, or experience to be central. I am suggesting that the relevant weighting of criteria is historically informed, inflected though specific religious traditions, and possibly somewhat arbitrary, but that it has immense consequences for what is considered to fall legitimately within the gaze of the law and for the nature of the judgments, discriminations, and decisions that are made. It surely makes a difference whether religion is attributed, or freedom is discerned, with respect to or on the basis of belief, ritual observance, or sheer experience. Furthermore, there is surely a positive feedback loop in which the law produces what it assumes and expects. But there is no doubt of a resistance in the form of new religious movements when one of these three elements appears to be exaggerated at the expense of the others.

Much of what I have been saying pertains specifically to Christianity and to the North Atlantic region. But as the essays in this volume by Noah Salomon, Mathijs Pelkmans, and Robert Hefner—among others—show, it is also useful to step back from the United States, and even from Western Europe, to consider alternative ways of organizing diversity. In northwest Madagascar, where I have conducted ethnographic fieldwork for more than two decades, there has been religious freedom in the sense that the boundaries between practicing Christians and Muslims are fairly open and insofar as it has been perfectly acceptable to be neither Christian nor Muslim without thereby being designated as immoral or "primitive" or subjected to undue missionary activity. As I've written elsewhere, some families might gently direct one of their children toward Islam, another toward Christianity, and a third to "ancestral practices," which are simply referred to as "nonworshipping" (*tsy mivavaka*) rather than by any substantive definition. The implication is that the alternative of not praying together is not a third "religion," a token commensurable to Christianity or Islam, though these two "religions" are viewed as commensurate to each other.

In northwest Madagascar, some people feel "free" to engage in practices drawn from each tradition rather than considering them mutually exclusive. For some, conversion is a matter of adding on a new set of practices without fully relinquishing the practices one has held until then. Although I would not advocate a causal explanation, the pattern fits nicely with the logic of bilateral kinship and wide exogamy that is found in the region. Most people can recognize at least four grandparents and probably eight great-grandparents (and beyond), each of whom may have a distinctive identity with respect to social, political, religious, and geographical affiliation. From among these senior living or deceased relatives people make choices of stronger or weaker identification, influenced by such factors as which grandparent one is sent to stay with on vacations as a child. Diversity is also encouraged by parents, who may call one child by an "ancestral" name, another by a Christian name, and a third by a Muslim name. Or a given individual may have all three names, as is the case of the Antankaraña monarch Isa Alexandre Tsimanamboholahy.

This enables a relatively open society with a good deal of mutual understanding and respect in which no single identification, or the institution behind it, is rendered primary or absolute and in which overlapping sets of practices have more salience than opposed abstract beliefs. In some respects one could say the individual has a good deal of freedom of choice. However, many Malagasy do not experience things in quite this way. In explaining why they live in one place rather than another or carry out a particular set of "religious" or "ancestral" practices they would say they had been called to it by a particular ancestor, who by showing them signs—notably manifest as illness or troubling dreams—subjects them to prohibitions that align them more firmly with that ancestor rather than others. Servants resident at the ancestral shrines were probably forced some generations ago to work there. But today those who remain as their successors cite the wrath of their own ancestors as the reasons for staying on. Religious affiliation is thus a matter of ancestral interpellation before it is a matter of belief, ritual, or explicitly "religious" experience, although obviously all of these come into play.

Interpellation is recognized by means of punishment for doing something that a given ancestor considers forbidden (*fady*, "taboo"). In this there is a logic of the negative. People are defined and define themselves in the first instance by what they don't practice, by the kinds of praying they don't do, the foods they cannot eat, the days they cannot work, the places they cannot live, or the kinds of work or acts of deference they cannot perform rather than by positive attributions or attractions based on belief or experience. This is a kind of freedom by restriction; in clarifying the boundaries of what you cannot or do not do, it leaves wide open what you can do—in large part, but not always, without telling you what you *must* do. And such instruction comes neither from religious authorities nor from the state but largely from one's own predecessors. One could say that this process is immanent to society or sociality rather than under the authority of those somehow transcendent to it.

It is evident that explicit belief and especially mutually exclusive beliefs are not what is salient here. Religion is described with respect to practice, whether one congregates in prayer. Practice is further described in terms of restrictions, as I have just detailed. The most "positive" practice and the one that becomes exclusive, final, and definitive, is where, how, and with whom one is buried. But this comes at the end of life and hence is of more relevance for the orientation of one's descendants than it is for affiliating oneself.

In everyday life and practice pluralism is not unusual. Thus a feature of ancestral practice is spirit possession, in which the living are possessed by specific royal ancestors who develop a long-term personal relationship with them and periodically take over their bodies and speak through them. Spirit possession is in itself neither Christian nor Muslim, but the spirit mediums can be either and, more to the point, so can the spirits. Thus it is possible for a Christian spirit medium to be possessed by a Muslim spirit (i.e., the spirit of someone who was a practicing Muslim when alive) and conversely for a Muslim spirit medium to be possessed by a Christian ancestor. This again is all a matter of practice; the various spirits are distinguished by their style of dress, dietary restrictions, and so forth. One royal ancestor, whose conversion to Islam was marked during his lifetime (in the early nineteenth century), is offered performances of the Maolida (East African odes sung and danced in honor of the Prophet) that the ancestor is said to have enjoyed when alive. Through the body of a medium he is present to observe and appreciate these Muslim performances, generally held in the Islamic month of Maolida, the month of the Prophet's birth. This figure, Ndramañavakarivo, presents the picture of an upright, observant Muslim, though he appears in the form of a Malagasy spirit and his posthumous name is "ancestral," not Muslim. His mediums might be Muslim, Christian, or neither.

Ancestral, Muslim, and Christian calendars proceed alongside each other and try to accommodate one another. In 2012 the scheduling of the annual Great Service, the most important ritual event in the ancestral liturgical year, overlapped with Ramadan. This proved disconcerting for Muslim practitioners, some of whom chose to ignore the fast and participate fully in the Great Service, others to attend while fasting, and others simply to stay away. Someone who is fasting should not be actively possessed by an ancestral spirit, but as this is ultimately the spirit's choice and not the medium's, some mediums did become spontaneously possessed. If Islam here defers or accommodates to ancestral practice, the converse is also the case. Thus, when cattle are sacrificed at the Great Service (in any year), not all are killed in the ancestral manner; some are slaughtered according to Islamic rules so that Muslim participants can partake of the meat.

People in northwest Madagascar look at the practice of staunch Christians and Muslims no less than their own more open and pluralist way of doing things with a certain amount of humor. Thus there are certain spirits, descendants of Ndramañavakarivo, the Muslim monarch mentioned above, who also purport to be Muslims and who, when they appear, sport red fezzes. But these spirits, like many living Malagasy and most non-Muslim ancestors, like to drink alcohol. They carry around bottles of liquor, offering swigs to their admirers. When they come near Ndramañavakarivo, they slip the bottles into their pockets and pretend to be sober abstainers. This play is evident to onlookers, some of whom describe the younger spirits not as Muslim (KiSilamo) but as Muslim-like, or perhaps "Muslim lite" (KoSilimo). Such a frank and friendly acknowledgment of the gradation of religious observance and the layers of ostensibly conflicting practices would be unthinkable in a part of the world in which religious freedom was constituted by the rigorous policing of boundaries. It should be noted that this kind of openness is not unique to Madagascar. Michael Carrithers has depicted religious life in South Asia as "spiritual cosmopolitanism" or "polytropy" with respect to its "eclecticism and fluidity," though admittedly, as scholars like Veena Das have shown, this is increasingly not the case or not always achieved without effort.

I recently encountered a notable American scholar in religious studies who recounted to me his personal history of conversion or movement through a series of Christian denominations. Just as polygamy might be compared to serial monogamy, so one might compare serial or successive religious affiliation with a kind of simultaneous polyreligious practice. These are evidently "freedoms" or contexts of freedom different from one another. The one emphasizes purity, sincerity, and linear transformation; the other heterogeneity, irony, and recursivity. The former is linked up to an ideology of personhood I call forensic, in which relative weight is placed on the irreversibility, accountability for, and consequentiality of one's acts over time. The latter is linked to an ideology of personhood I term mimetic, in which relative weight is placed on contextualized performance and the ability to articulate discontinuous but multiple roles, relationships, or identities. These ideologies presuppose different accounts of freedom and its limits.

As Rosalind I. J. Hackett notes, elsewhere in Africa (and newly reemerging in Madagascar as well) practitioners outside the purview of Christianity and Islam have been vulnerable to the missionizing efforts of the latter persuasions. This process began centuries ago, but in recent years missionization and campaigns for conversion have if anything become more vigorous, sly, or violent. As I have argued in an essay deliberately titled "Provincializing God," the two powerful competing religions are alike in this respect. Moreover, they are alike insofar as they single out an exclusive high god and demand exclusive loyalty to him; in other traditions "god" may be no single or even distinct, independent entity but more akin grammatically to a deictic term (like "home") than a substantive noun with a stable referent. Translation is perilous, but the difficulties extend beyond the simple application of words. Anthropologists of smaller-scale societies have long found themselves in the uncomfortable position of having either to deny that the people they have observed have a god or, indeed, a religion—and thereby rendering them in certain powerful and hegemonic eyes "primitive," "savage," "pagan," "kafir," immoral or amoral, and hence ripe for conversion—or else to traduce their practices in order to make them readable as a commensurable form of divine worship.

We have to be careful that in saving the subject (the practices at hand) we don't destroy it. The problem is that it is readily undermined from either direction. As Asad suggests, the very object of religion may be a creation through law; law transforms what it encompasses, and practices can remain less objectified—more free, in one sense—if they stay outside its purview and are not reproduced according to the dominant image of what "religion" is. We could take a leaf from the northern Malagasy and say that it is clearer if ancestral practices are not considered "religious" or as "a religion," a commensurable token within a type. But from the other direction, such an alternative renders such practices liable to vilification (especially now by Pentecostalism) and renders the practitioners vulnerable to missionary activity, never mind the loss of some benefits, like tax exemptions, in strong states. In many places, practitioners want the respect that comes with being understood as having a commensurate "religion," and in many parts of the world such a depiction is a necessary means for gaining such respect (including self-respect).

In her lucid review herein of discussions concerning religious freedom in Africa, Hackett phrases the dilemma well, arguing that "indigenous religions struggle for public recognition and equal treatment under the law. . . . Moreover, they are hampered by being part of a generalized and heterogeneous category, with no clear designation or centralized leadership." It is evident that the politics of religious life in states like South Africa or Nigeria require some form of protection for what she calls indigenous religions and what I suspect are often heterodox transformations of Christianity that have originated in Africa. But what they are "hampered by" could also be considered their strengths. If such "religions" were identified and regulated by the state, or even by their own "centralized leaders," in what sense would they still be "indigenous" or "traditional"? I am not suggesting that practices have to remain unchanged to retain their integrity, but there is surely something different afoot when a ritual celebrating ancestral powers is transformed into a heritage festival with a UNESCO stamp of approval. As Hackett, drawing on the work of

Ronald Niezen, remarks, "Recent moves to grant institutional, protective space to indigenous expressions of 'spirituality' not only essentialize and objectify traditional forms of belief and practice but also translate and recast them to appeal to cultural outsiders who formally or informally adjudge these rights' claims."

My final comment is that however we want to define religion (and perhaps we could take a leaf from northern Madagascar and leave it open, specifying only what it is not), one of the general features, as the Malagasy ethnography also suggests, is a kind of submission to, or acceptance of, something conceived as larger, higher, or more powerful than oneself. Émile Durkheim called it society; Maurice Bloch calls it deference to authority or to other persons; Roy Rappaport describes it as one of the entailments of engaging in ritual performance. In participating in a ritual, whatever one's state of mind or "belief" at the time, one is accepting the outcome (assuming that the felicity conditions of the performative event are met) and moreover accepting the metaperformativity (i.e., that acts and utterances of this kind, felicitously produced, have the consequences that they do, that baptism, for example, is what it is). Following Rappaport, to perform a ritual is, in the end, to accept a certain liturgical order of which it is part, irrespective of whether this also entails deference to specific officials, like priests. In other words, the freedom to carry out certain kinds of acts is premised on subjection to an order that defines what such acts are, that puts things under a definition and regulates the changes in definition, and that places a value on certain goals, acts, and consequences. As I elaborate in my work on ethics, the process is one of the establishment of criteria, and it is intrinsic to human speech acts. Insofar as what we refer to as specifically "religious" includes the most formal and consequential kinds of performative acts to which we are subjected or subject ourselves, and insofar as practitioners accept both the acts and the definitions, order, and consequences of action, one might say that *what religion is not is freedom.*

Hence, the very idea of freedom of religion is paradoxical; it is the freedom to be unfree in a particular kind of way. Judicial and legislative bodies need to take this point, call it the relativity of freedom or unfreedom, or the deconstruction of freedom, into account. They need to notice Sullivan when she points to "the reinstatement of the rights of religious authority by political authority—in the name of religious freedom." They then need to make informed decisions about which versions of unfreedom to support—and we should all, as Saba Mahmood emphasizes, pay attention to the politics and ideologies that underpin such decisions (a skepticism I share with Lori Beaman concerning federal government initiatives at the present time in Canada). If Muslims were the ones taking the lead in the US courts asking for certain rights and freedoms, would not the self-same justices have argued another way?

This is certainly not to say that we should let everyone be free to do as she or he pleases. Not only is such freedom impossible in the human condition, but there is also the matter of whether my freedom impinges on yours. To emphasize a point in Mahmood's account, the freedom of religion we demand elsewhere (though the point applies internally as well) too often means the freedom to missionize other people. The freedom to practice my religion impinges on the freedom to practice yours in peace.

We need to be careful here. I am not a historian, but I imagine that religious freedom once meant freedom from oppression by the proponents of a stronger religion rather than freedom from interference by the state or the freedom given by the state as a right to specific religions to interfere in other peoples' business. Freedom here too readily comes to mean freedom for the powerful to exercise their power against the vulnerable (as in the free market). Certain proponents of religious freedom in the United States now seem to want to have it both ways: the state is criticized both for being secular and for promoting a "religion" of its own. What is missing in such arguments is attention not to people's own rights or freedoms but the obligation to enable the rights and freedoms of others, as defined by them.

Acknowledgments

I acknowledge long-term support for my research from the Social Sciences and Humanities Research Council of Canada and the Canada Research Chairs program. I thank also my interlocutors in Madagascar and at home.

Selected Bibliography

Asad, Talal. *Genealogies of Religion: Discipline and Reasons of Power in Christianity and Islam*. Baltimore: Johns Hopkins University Press, 1993.

Bloch, Maurice. (2004) "Ritual and Deference." In *Ritual and Memory: Towards a Comparative Anthropology of Religion*, edited by Harvey Whitehouse and James Laidlaw, 65–78. Walnut Creek, CA: Altamira, 2004.

Carrithers, Michael. "On Polytropy: Or the Natural Condition of Spiritual Cosmopolitanism in India: The Digambar Jain Case." *Modern Asian Studies* 34, no. 4 (2000): 831–61.

Das, Veena. "Cohabiting an Interreligious Milieu: Reflections on Religious Diversity." In *A Companion to the Anthropology of Religion*, edited by Janice Boddy and Michael Lambek, 69–84. Malden, MA: Wiley-Blackwell, 2013.

Jay, Martin. *Songs of Experience: Modern American and European Variations on a Universal Theme.* Berkeley and Los Angeles: University of California Press, 2005.

Keane, Webb. *Christian Moderns: Freedom and Fetish in the Mission Encounter.* Berkeley and Los Angeles: University of California Press, 2007.

Lambek, Michael. "Taboo as Cultural Practice among Malagasy Speakers." *Man* 27, no. 2 (1992): 245–66.

———. "Provincializing God? Provocations from an Anthropology of Religion." In *Religion: Beyond a Concept*, edited by Hent de Vries, 120–38. New York: Fordham University Press, 2008.

———. "Towards an Ethics of the Act." In *Ordinary Ethics: Anthropology, Language, and Action*, edited by Michael Lambek, 39–63. New York: Fordham University Press, 2010.

———. "What Is 'Religion' for Anthropology? And What Has Anthropology Brought to 'Religion'?" In *A Companion to the Anthropology of Religion*, edited by Janice Boddy and Michael Lambek, 1–32. Malden, MA: Wiley-Blackwell, 2013.

Rappaport, Roy. *Ritual and Religion in the Making of Humanity.* Cambridge: Cambridge University Press, 1999.

Ruel, Malcolm. "Christians as Believers." In *Religious Organization and Religious Experience*, ed. John Davis, 9–31. London: Academic Press, 1982.

Sullivan, Winnifred Fallers. "The World that *Smith* Made." *The Immanent Frame.* Accessed March 7, 2012 at http://blogs.ssrc.org/tif/2012/03/07/the-world-that-smith-made/.

CHAPTER TWENTY-FIVE

Religious Freedom and the Bind of Suspicion in Contemporary Secularity

Hussein Ali Agrama

In a concise, thoughtful article titled "The Meaning of Secularism," Charles Taylor argues that secularism should not be thought of as primarily an institutional arrangement governed by the principle of the separation of religion and state. That would unduly single out religion from other basic, deeply held forms of belief as a source of especial danger. Secularism is better understood, he argues, as part of the democratic state's response to diversity. This response is ideally guided by three principles: that no one should be coerced with respect to the basic beliefs or position one chooses or finds oneself in; that the state should be neutral between different beliefs; and that everyone should be given a hearing. For Taylor these are the conditions that the state should maintain for religious pluralism—indeed, pluralism of all kinds—to flourish. But in order for this to happen, he argues, there needs to be widespread agreement on a set of basic values within society, else the state would lose its legitimacy. Under the conditions of pluralism, this unity of values can be achieved through an overlapping consensus.

I strongly sympathize with much of Taylor's argument. I agree that religion should not be singled out as a special source of danger, that everyone should be given a hearing, that no one should be coerced on his or her basic beliefs, and that state neutrality is an ideal we cannot do without. Nevertheless I worry that his argument doesn't ultimately work, either as an analysis of or an ideal for secularism. The problem lies in what the argument presupposes for its sense of cogency and seeming plausibility; it embeds a set of historical sensibilities and attitudes that it doesn't fully take into account and that serve to complicate and ultimately undermine it. Nowhere are those sensibilities and attitudes more pronounced than in the confounding way that religious freedom is defined and implemented by a variety of contemporary states. That is what I wish to discuss here.

So I would like to begin with a famous case in Egypt that, though over two decades old, remains salient for thinking about the conundrums of religious freedom. This is the apostasy case of Nasr Abu Zayd, the professor of Arabic and Islamic studies who was declared an apostate by the Egyptian courts and whose marriage was forcibly annulled as a result. The case was raised using a highly controversial principle within Egyptian law, and much of the debate was about whether its use was acceptable within this case. This principle was called *hisba*, and it technically means "the commanding of the good when its practice is manifestly neglected, and the forbidding of the detestable when its practice becomes manifest." If *hisba* were accepted in this court case, it would mean that virtually anyone could subsequently intervene and even dissolve the marriage of anyone else by raising a court case against them. So when the courts affirmed this use of *hisba*, judged Abu Zayd an apostate, and annulled his marriage they set a precedent that, not surprisingly, made many people nervous. For the inviolability of an entire domain of private right seemed to be undermined. Another result of the *hisba* judgment was that a wide range of Islamic practices once considered within the bounds of legitimacy could become suspect, with potentially dire consequences. This was because Abu Zayd's written work, though unorthodox, arguably had antecedents and analogues within Islamic tradition. Yet it was on the basis of his written statements that he was legally declared an apostate and separated from his wife. Partly in response to the ambiguity and anxiety unleashed by the *hisba* decision, the Egyptian parliament passed legislation severely restricting the private uses of *hisba*, vesting it within the office of the general prosecutor instead—an agency with extremely broad investigative authority that stands ambiguously between executive and judiciary power. So the state, instead of reducing the ambiguity of *hisba*, only absorbed its potentially far-reaching power into itself and out of the hands of citizens. Few were pleased by this move, and everyone subsequently looked upon *hisba* with some suspicion.

Many have since written about this case, including myself. In my work, I've detailed how *hisba* is less a deviation from secularism than

an expression of the underlying power that makes secularism possible—
including the state's fundamental right to decide what counts as religious
and the proper place of religion in social life. Here, however, I focus on
something else: how *hisba* became not only an object of general suspicion but also a particular modality of suspicion as a result of court litigation and state legislation. This modality of suspicion, exercised by the
state, is intimately tied to the defense of religious freedom, and I suspect
that it is shared across seemingly very different secular polities. To see
this, consider the following passage from the Abu Zayd judgment:

> The Court notes that there is a difference between apostasy, which is a ma-
> terial action with its basic elements and conditions . . . and belief (i'tiqad).
> Apostasy is necessarily comprised of material acts that have an external be-
> ing. Such acts must make manifest, in a manner undeniable and without dis-
> sent, that one has called God Most High a liar, and the Prophet, peace be
> upon him, a liar by denying what he has brought to Islam. . . . Belief, however,
> differs clearly from apostasy. For apostasy is a crime whose basic material
> elements are presented before a judge to decide whether it exists or not. . . .
> But belief concerns what is in the interior of a human being's self, belong-
> ing to his domain of secrecy. It is neither a matter of judicial probing, nor of
> investigation by people, but is to do with the relationship between the human
> being and his Creator. Apostasy is a breach of the Islamic order, at its highest
> degree and most valued foundations, through manifest, material actions. In
> positive law, it comes close to a breach of the order of the state or high trea-
> son. Apostasy is investigated by the judge or the mufti. However, the punish-
> ment for assaulting religion through [an act of] apostasy does not contradict
> personal freedom. This is because freedom of belief ('aqida) requires that one
> be a believer (mu'minan) in his words and acts, and that he possess a sound
> rationale for his abandonment of belief. But a breach of Islam can only be due
> to corruption in thought or the lure of material, sexual, or other worldly pur-
> poses. To combat this category [of desire] is not considered combat against
> freedom of belief, but rather the protection of belief from such vain, corrupt
> passions.

In distinguishing between apostasy as an "outer" material act and belief that occurs in an "interior" forum, the court defines its jurisdiction
over the determination of apostasy and justifies its approach in making
that determination. On the basis of this distinction, the court took only
Abu Zayd's written work into account without probing into his personal

views—his "interior" relationship with his creator. Taking statements from his written work at face value, the court compared them with statements designated within the sharia as indicating apostasy; finding them to be similar, it pronounced him an apostate.

Many commentaries on the judgment have highlighted how it separates private belief from public act or expression in a distinctively modern way. None, however, have addressed the seeming contradiction it presents just a few lines later, where it reconnects private belief and its public manifestation in the context of a defense of religious freedom. Notably, the court does not see religious freedom as simply a right to believe what one wants. It also includes maintaining the conditions under which religious belief can be sustained and cultivated—that is, the conditions under which it can flourish. For the court this entails that belief be protected from the motives of worldly power that might corrupt it. This, in turn, requires the court to pronounce what those motives are—as it did with Abu Zayd. Acts and expressions of belief are therefore objects of especial suspicion, to be put under particular scrutiny, for potentially harboring ulterior, corrupting motives. Such scrutiny might be seen as a kind of vigilance against power and its potential abuse. (Indeed, part of the court's concern was that Abu Zayd was also teaching his books to university students.) In other words, outer act and inner belief, though initially divided, come to be reunited through a suspicion of motives of material interest or worldly power. In the context of the freedom of religious belief, it becomes imperative to determine whether acts or expressions of belief are genuinely religiously motivated. This presumes the power to pronounce upon, and if necessary probe into, the character of one's private convictions. Here the defense of religious freedom promotes a distinctive form of suspicion.

This suspicion, however, is not exclusive to Egypt. Strikingly similar versions of it are found in seemingly very different secular states. For example, Winnifred Fallers Sullivan has highlighted two central criteria in US jurisprudence on religious freedom. They parallel those of the Abu Zayd case. The first criterion was whether religious acts or expressions were sincerely held to be essential to one's religion. This conflicted with the second, often prevailing, criterion: whether these acts and expressions were authorized and mandated by orthodox religious texts. In US courts there seemed to be a disposition to presume the sincerity of litigants' religious belief—which may be due in part to a traditional American respect for individual belief rooted in a particular Protestant history.

Nevertheless, as legal theorist and jurist Kent Greenawalt writes, "when the state offers exemptions based on people's convictions, it cannot avoid all inquiry into sincerity." The court thus retains the prerogative to determine and investigate this sincerity in the context of defining and defending religious freedoms—a prerogative it has exercised throughout US history. Moreover, this determination and investigation purveys a suspicion of motives of material interests or other worldly purposes. To quote Greenawalt again, "Another category of religious claims that should not count as spiritual are schemes cloaked in religious language in which the incentive to participate is financial self-interest and not spiritual development. . . . A finding that a claimant is sincere should be easy if one cannot discern any secular advantage from a person's engaging in the behavior she asserts is part of her religious exercise." But whether it is preferable for the court to actually investigate sincerity or simply make presumptions about it without an investigation has been historically difficult to decide.

A similar situation is found in France. Anthropologist Mayanthi Fernando describes the dilemma veiled Muslim women faced in opposing the banning of the veil in public schools. If, on the one hand, the veil was deemed an obligation mandated by religious authorities, then it could be construed as potentially coercive and an impingement of religious freedom. The French state was therefore very concerned to ascertain that there was no external coercion or pressure to wear the veil—a concern that entailed knowing about the circumstances of people's private lives and convictions. But if, on the other hand, the veil was construed as a matter of personal belief—a choice—then it was not mandated by orthodox religious texts and therefore inessential to the practice of one's religion. Banning it was therefore not necessarily an impingement on religious freedom.

But even as a personal belief and choice, the veil was still construed by the state as an essentially religious, and fundamentally Islamic, sign. For state officials, it indicated a will and a desire to manifest Islam. Some saw it as potentially indexing a rising Islamism, one that degraded women in ways incompatible with the French republic's fundamental values. It was thus a will and a desire that the state sought not to encourage, lest its values become undermined. Thus, in his analysis of the French state's investigation, Talal Asad notes that "not only [do] government officials decide what sartorial signs mean, but . . . they do so by privileged access to the wearer's motives and will—to her subjectivity—and this is facilitated by resort to a certain kind of semiotics. A governmental commission of inquiry claims to bring private concerns, commitments and sentiments to the public sphere in order to assess their validity for the secular Republic, but it does much more than that. It constitutes meanings by drawing on internal (psychological) signs or external (social) signs, encourages certain desires and emotions at the expense of others." So even though the veil was construed as a choice—indeed, precisely because it was—it could be deemed a suspicious and potentially dangerous act.

That the determination of genuine religiosity in terms of ulterior motives is a practice of suspicion becomes fully evident when it comes to Muslims in Europe and the United States, with the near paranoid quality of the public debates about the building of mosques and minarets, the potential usage of sharia as law, the teaching of Arabic in public schools, the donating to Muslim charities, and the wearing of veils. While there are complicated historical and political reasons for this near paranoia, my point here is to emphasize a central element of the structure it takes: the constant attempt to unmask ulterior motives of material interest and worldly power behind a range of otherwise ordinary (in this case, Muslim) practices and expressions of belief in order to defend those freedoms—including especially religious freedom—that are seen as constitutive of the ways of life the state is supposed to guarantee.

These examples, then, reveal a distinctive structure of legalized suspicion. On the one hand, private belief and public act or expression are made separate, but on the other, they are brought together in order to define and defend religious freedoms. In this case, private belief becomes framed within a complex of motives, will, and desire—one that becomes suspect to the extent it expresses material interests or drives towards worldly power. As such, it can become subject to investigation and disciplining, which means probing into the details of private life and conviction. This structure of suspicion is shared by polities as seemingly different as the United States, France, and Egypt, and it brings together under the pretext of religious freedom two central aspects of liberalism and secularism. The first is a distinctively liberal vigilance against power and its abuse, and the second is a characteristically secular desire to draw a line between religion and material power. But this suspicion is further animated by a contradiction in the very understanding of belief, and which the different cases discussed above demonstrate. On the one hand, the distinction between "inner" belief and "outer" act leads one to see the act as a *sign* of belief. But on the other, there is a recognition of the *causal efficacy* of acts, that they can constitute or powerfully shape belief and thus the values that people hold—a recognition that erodes the divide between "inner" belief and "outer" act. Such an entanglement between *signs* and *causes* of belief lends itself to an ever more pronounced vigilance against the potential power of religious beliefs and acts. What this suggests is that, under a liberal secular legal regime, suspicion of religious belief is the flip side of religious freedom; the one cannot be disentangled from the other.

Here we can return to Charles Taylor's argument about secularism cited at the beginning of this essay. Note that the cases above seem to follow the principles articulated in his argument. In each case, the parties are given a hearing; in each case, the state tries to maintain neutrality between different beliefs even as it tries to promote a unity of basic values; however, in each case, people end up being coerced with respect to their basic beliefs or position. With these less-than-salutary results a seeming aporia opens up: between the aspired-to freedoms and the means by which they are ideally achieved. Taylor's argument does not discern this aporia because it does not fully account for the contradictory structure of suspicion historically rooted in the secular ideal and practice of religious freedom.

Yet one might object that Taylor does indeed account for this suspicion when he argues that religious belief should not be singled out from other kinds of belief and that religious and nonreligious reasoning are not fundamentally different. It is true that he argues this. But by then it is too late; the suspicion he counsels against has already done its undermining work within his argument. This is in two ways. The first is that, despite his blurring of religious and nonreligious reason, his argument construes religion as essentially a species of belief. But such a construal of religion is itself a historical outcome of the suspicion that divides it from and opposes it to knowledge. That is the only way that one can plausibly argue for state neutrality between religion and other kinds of deeply held beliefs. Indeed, it would be difficult to argue that the state should remain neutral between belief and what it sees as knowledge, especially in matters concerning public order and the governance of populations, when that knowledge is considered crucial to such governance. This circumscription of the sphere of religion already articulates the principle that it ought to be separated from material power. Suspicion is thus already embedded in his argument and has done its work to shape it. Yvonne Sherwood, in this volume, insightfully highlights how suspicion of religion promoted its construal as belief secondary to knowledge.

Her work demonstrates an important point: despite liberal secularism's claims to neutrality between beliefs, it is already implicitly concerned with their truth status. That explains why, in the cases cited above, the courts evinced as much a concern for the status of the beliefs in question as of the subjects who ostensibly professed them. More notably, however, is that this concern was typically articulated in terms of the potential threat that these beliefs and the people who held them posed both to material interests and supposedly foundational values.

This leads to the second way that suspicion works in Taylor's argument, which is perhaps even more consequential than the first. It is in his claim about the need to be united on a set of basic values, and that such a unity is indispensable to a democratic state. While this might be a precondition for secular freedoms, it is equally a characteristic manifestation of the secular state's modalities of suspicion. We can see this more clearly if we look at it on a sociological register—that is, if we consider *when* the concern over a unity on basic values typically arises. And it is quite often when an embattled (religious) minority is *already* under suspicion, when its loyalty to the state is *already* in question. Thus, when it comes to Muslims in Europe and the United States, it is not because they've refused to adopt their societies' basic values (if there really are any) or because they are not loyal to the state (however that might be gauged) that they are placed under suspicion; it is because they are already under suspicion that this demand is made of them. That is why no amount of actual assimilation or proof of loyalty will ever quell this demand. It is worth remembering here that the question of secular emancipation was discussed in the late nineteenth and early twentieth centuries in relation to Jews, and it was often in the name of this emancipation that they were placed under an incessant demand to assimilate into the basic values of their societies. Yet no amount of actual assimilation dissipated the suspicion cast upon them; their motives remained continually in question and they were continually construed as a material or moral threat. Historical explanations for this suspicion and discrimination do not therefore cite a lack of proper integration as a cause, even though those were the reasons given then. But we do know that this suspicion helped strengthen the state, increasing its sovereign sway over everyday social life.

This is why I worry that the claim for a need to be united on basic values, the question of how to achieve this unity, and the idea of an overlapping consensus as a potential solution are deeply misguided. We need to more fully understand what such claims and questions do. Here we might make use of the well-known distinction between constatives and performatives. Usually this distinction applies to statements, but we can see them as applying to questions too. The claim for a unity on basic values, the question of how to achieve it, and the presumed consequences that follow if it is not have typically been treated as constatives—as potentially corresponding to social and historical facts and that should be assessed on how well they correspond to those facts. But a consideration of when these claims and questions typically arise urges us to see them as performatives, as performing and purveying an underlying suspicion of those who are seen as not (yet) partaking of foundational values, whatever they are presumed to be. The idea of an overlapping consensus should therefore not be seen as a solution to the question of how to achieve such unity, but as part of the performance of this suspicion, one that sustains it and potentially takes it even further. For example, with respect to Muslims in the United States and Europe, it brings on the further question of whether Islam has the capacity for an overlapping consensus, with the idea that if it does then Muslims could possibly partake of purported foundational values, but if not. . . . Either way, the suspicious scrutiny of Muslim beliefs and practices, in the name of values like religious freedom, continues unabated, with the result that the state's capacity to probe the intimate domains of social life is sustained or further expanded. Hence my worry that such claims, questions, and purported solutions are misguided: they do not fully account for the relation between suspicion and secular emancipation that underlies them. Despite Taylor's counseling against the singling out of religion, his argument about secularism seems to articulate the contradictory structure of suspicion within which secular religious freedom is historically embedded.

The Abu Zayd judgment discussed above poignantly highlights this contradictory structure of suspicion. At one level, the court took Abu Zayd's written statements at face value—to say what they mean—and found them to contradict orthodox doctrines literally construed. The court thus declared him an apostate. But when it came to the question of religious freedom, his words were paid extra attention, taken to mean more than what they said, as having ulterior worldly motives against which the freedom of belief—to cultivate belief and have it flourish—had to be defended. In this case, the court simply presumed and pronounced upon Abu Zayd's motives without investigation. This decision shows that the suspicious attribution of motives does not depend on an investigation, even though it enables one to be done at the discretion of the judiciary.

Hisba, through and under the law, has come to embody this structure of suspicion and the discretionary power that comes with it. It therefore enables the assertion of the state's sovereign power of decision into the intimate domains of everyday life. This becomes clear when we remember that *hisba* was placed in the hands of the general prosecutor, with his ambiguous status between judicial and executive power and his nearly unfettered investigative authority; for now it is the general prosecutor who is responsible for bringing a *hisba* case to court. He must therefore conduct an investigation to decide whether a potential case merits further litigation. He might thus have to scrutinize the motives behind statements of religious belief. If, however, such scrutiny seems to intrude too much into a person's private life or interior forum, the general prosecutor has another option at his discretion: to take these statements at face value, as saying what they mean, as the court did with Abu Zayd. A focus on literal statements, however, may fail to capture the complexity of people's private religious lives. As with the United States and France, it is unclear which is preferable: to investigate how genuine one's religious motives are, or to make presumptions about how genuine they really are.

This tension between intruding into a private, ostensibly protected, domain or taking statements too literally is reminiscent of another tension upon which modern legal legitimacy both rests and continually founders: the enactment and the appearance of justice. The more zealously an official investigates, the more abusive of justice he might seem to be. If, however, he relies solely on procedure, he might be seen as making a mockery of justice. *Hisba* now partakes of this dilemma too.

To conclude, I have cited the Abu Zayd judgments to show how *hisba*, in its contemporary legalized form, embodied a distinctive structure of suspicion. Through the judgments, *hisba* potentially undermined an entire domain of private rights. In restricting *hisba*'s uses, the state transformed it into a modality of suspicion only it could exercise. This modality of suspicion, enabled to defend religious freedoms, nevertheless undermined the crucial distinctions on which they relied. Moreover, it became ensconced within another dynamic of suspicion, the tension between the enactment and the appearance of justice. This tension is even further compounded because, as I show elsewhere, it remains irresolvably indeterminate whether the concept of *hisba* in the court judgments is still an Islamic and thus primarily religious principle, or, as an expression of public order, has become an essentially secular principle. The example of *hisba* therefore not only confirms Sullivan's now famous thesis that religious freedom as a legally enforceable right is impossible to attain, but also shows how such religious freedom will never *appear* to be fully achieved, being entangled in its entirety within the dynamics of law's suspicion and secular/religious ambiguity.

We should not, however, take the impossibility of religious freedom to mean the failure of secularism. That would reduce an analysis of secularism to an assessment of whether it fulfills the promises it makes. Secularism as a historical phenomenon is certainly more than its promises, if only because it so consistently and demonstrably falls short of them. We might consider instead how this sense of a continual failure is built into the historical grammar of secularism and the consequences that follow from it. In this case, the constant disjuncture between religious freedom as a secular aspiration and the secular means of achieving it constitutes a space of a continual striving, one that works to expand and entrench the suspicion and potential for intervention that provoked it in the first place. Within this space, religion is given to continual politicization, political-theological claims acquire plausibility and force, and critique becomes a seemingly indispensible capacity that one must maintain and tirelessly cultivate. And it is also from within this space that the concern for a unity on basic values issues as an incessant demand. As a result, the question of religious freedom, as a central secular stake, remains poignantly alive, drawn into a seemingly unavoidable and incessant cycle of provocation, critique, and intervention. That is, the modalities and dynamics of suspicion outlined here help sustain the *problem-space* of secularism, its constitutive questions and stakes, the critical dispositions it induces, and the propensities toward sovereignty it displays. We remain bound to this problem space through the incessant suspicion it provokes.

Acknowledgment
I thank Talal Asad for his comments and suggestions on a previous draft.

Selected Bibliography
Agrama, Hussein Ali. *Questioning Secularism: Islam, Sovereignty and the Rule of Law in Modern Egypt.* Chicago: University of Chicago Press, 2012.

Asad, Talal. "Reflections on Laïcité and the Public Sphere." *Items and Issues* 5, no. 3 (2005): n.p.

Boltanski, Luc. *Énigmes et complots: Une enquête à propos d'enquêtes.* Paris: Éditions Gallimard, 2012.

Cairo Court of Appeals, case #287, 1995.

Fernando, Mayanthi. "Reconfiguring Freedom: Muslim Piety and the Limits of Secular Law and Public Discourse in France." *American Ethnologist* 37, no. 1 (2010): 19–35.

Greenawalt, Kent. *Religion and the Constitution*. Vol. 1, *Free Exercise and Fairness*. Princeton, NJ: Princeton University Press, 2009.

Schumann, Fredrick, "'The Appearance of Justice': Public Justification in the Legal Relation." *University of Toronto Faculty of Law Review* 66, no. 2 (2008): 189–223.

Sullivan, Winnifred Fallers. "Judging Religion." *Marquette Law Review* 81, no. 2 (1998): 441–60.

———. *The Impossibility of Religious Freedom*. Princeton, NJ: Princeton University Press, 2005.

Taylor, Charles. "The Meaning of Secularism," *Hedgehog Review* 12, no. 3 (2010): 23–34.

Zorza, Richard. "The Disconnect between the Requirements of Judicial Neutrality and Those of the Appearance of Neutrality When Parties Appear *Pro Se*: Causes, Solutions, Recommendations, and Implications." *Georgetown Journal of Legal Ethics* 17 (2004): 423–54.

CHAPTER TWENTY-SIX

Religious Repression and Religious Freedom

An Analysis of Their Contradictions in (Post-)Soviet Contexts

Mathijs Pelkmans

Introduction

Consider an imam in Adjara, Georgia, who longs for the Soviet period when religion was repressed; imagine a state functionary in Kyrgyzstan who complains about the unfairness of religious freedom. This essay uses these and other post-Soviet examples to reveal contradictions in regimes of religious freedom *and* repression.

Recent scholarship on the subject of religious freedom has revealed how the Christian and liberal roots of the modern categories of "religion" and "freedom" have contributed to the emergence of a "political doctrine of freedom" that shapes and restricts the ways in which "religion" can enter the public sphere. The post-Soviet liberalizations of the religious sphere have similarly shown that "freedom" affects religious groups in multiple ways, producing not only opportunities but also new constraints and creating new inequalities. By tracing the (sometimes contradictory) effects of post-Soviet liberalization, this essay contributes to the critical discussion of "religious freedom." However, it argues that this discussion needs to be complemented by attention to its opposites, to "religious unfreedom" or, applied to the politicolegal domain, "religious repression." Such an approach will add a sense of grounding to discussions of freedom and draw attention to the fact that not only "religious freedom projects" but also "religious repression projects" are characterized by multiple contradictions.

The post-Soviet world offers a useful case precisely because it allows us to study religious freedom and repression together. The collapse of the USSR marked the end of seventy years of antireligious policies, a period in which religious expression was severely curtailed, and religious institutions were always controlled, at times co-opted and at other times brutally repressed, with the aim of effecting the demise of religion, an aim which was never fully realized. The post-1991 era was radically different, at least in those newly independent countries such as Kyrgyzstan and Georgia that adopted and implemented liberal laws regarding religious expression and organization. It might be expected that religious leaders and practitioners would have a straightforwardly positive view of this widening scope for religious activities, but this was not always the case. I'll explain using two examples from my own ethnographic research:

> In 2001, the imam of a small town in Adjara, a predominantly Muslim region of Georgia, told me: "During communism we had more freedom; we still had our own lives. Now, we are losing everything."
>
> In 2004, I conversed with a Pentecostal pastor in Kyrgyzstan about the forms of opposition his church encountered in this Muslim-majority context. He remarked: "We pray for [local government] officials to stop hindering us. But this may not be God's way. Our faith thrives when it is being repressed."

These two examples reveal a rather odd longing for religious repression, but they do so in quite distinct ways. The imam's intimation that the new era of religious freedom was less free than the era of repression points to tensions that have accompanied the post-Soviet deprivatization of religion, which can render certain religious tenets more vulnerable or disadvantaged than they previously had been. By contrast the Pentecostal pastor did not so much call "freedom" into question as suggest that freedom is not necessarily beneficial to a church like his own. The unstated logic was that religious movements can only retain their effervescence as long as they provide their members with a sense of exclusivity—that is, when boundaries are maintained with society at large. Neither the imam's nor the pastor's comment should be accepted at face value, but they do require a reevaluation of what is meant by "religious repression" and by "religious freedom." Indirectly they also draw attention to the role of the law, which brings us to two further examples:

> In 2004, a functionary of the state committee of religious affairs in Kyrgyzstan lamented to me: "[These evangelical missionaries] come here and only want to talk about religious freedom. They only talk about rights, rights, rights! For them it is easy. After a few years they leave again, having no idea about the mess they leave behind."
>
> Studying the *Tablighi Jamaat* (a Muslim piety movement) in Kyrgyzstan in 2010, I asked about the impact of a 2009 law prohibiting proselytizing activities by their movement. They were untroubled, in the words of one of them: "people have gotten used to our approach. This law is only intended for Jehovah Witnesses."

These examples point out that the law is only as effective as its implementation is, but they do so in different ways. The first example suggests that the law can become a tool to advance the interests of some religious groups, and in the second example we see a glimpse of the uneven application of the law by power holders. Both examples call attention to the interplay between the law and the social field in which it operates.

These brief ethnographic vignettes raise several important questions. A first set of questions pertains to the possibilities and impossibilities that are (inadvertently) produced by liberal and repressive laws. What forms of "freedom" does religious repression produce? And what constraints and impossibilities are produced through religious freedom? A second set of questions relates to the ways in which religious laws are pushed, applied, ignored, and used. More concretely, who "owns" religious freedom laws and to what effect? And how can religion laws be variously employed?

From Repression to Freedom . . . or Vice Versa?

So what was the freedom in repression that the imam in Adjara alluded to? It is important to point out that he was not referring to the heavy-handed repressions of the 1920s and '30s, decades that were characterized by a rapidly dwindling space for religious institutions and for public religious expression, including the closure of virtually all mosques and madrasas and the imprisonment of religious leaders. Rather, the imam

was referring to the antireligious efforts of the 1960s through the 1980s
that focused on eradicating the so-called backward and harmful traditions by targeting religious holidays and rituals and disseminating atheist
and antireligious ideas through the media and in schools. The combined
effect was that "religion" disappeared from much of public life, but the
resulting status quo also implied that there was room for religious expression in a more "domesticated" fashion.

Notably, Moscow's antireligious line did not always travel intact to local contexts. As is often noted about Muslim regions of the Soviet Union,
even local officials (Communist Party members) would sometimes
participate in religious events such as circumcision feasts and Islamic
funerals. The popular Soviet joke "they pretend to pay us and we pretend
to work" could with some justification be translated into "they pretend to
eradicate religion, and we pretend not to practice religion." Put differently,
there was more room for religious expression in the late Soviet period
than the image of the "totalitarian" USSR tends to project.

Moreover, there is a certain "freedom" in being able to affiliate oneself with a religious tradition *without* conforming to doctrinal demands.
During Soviet times religious affiliation did not always have to be accompanied with other displays of commitment such as fasting, daily prayer,
or abstaining from alcohol. In the words of a villager in Adjara, "we were
Muslims, of course, but we could only pray inside our homes. We didn't
think badly of anyone who drank at work or offered wine to guests, as
those things were simply unavoidable."

Such possibilities were convenient to those who were "not very religious" and tended to think about religion mostly in terms of (family)
tradition and culture, but what about those who cared a great deal about
the doctrinal aspects of their faith? The Pentecostal pastor quoted in the
introduction alluded to the possibility that the intensity of faith-based
communal life may depend on repression. Similar suggestions emerged
from stories of devout elderly men in Adjara, one of whom commented,
with a smile: "We knew exactly, with every neighbor, what you could
and couldn't say. In this way we were able to spread information." The
danger of being reported and restrictions on carrying out religious rituals or circulating forbidden literature produced an intensification of ties
among committed members of religious communities. None of this is to
ignore or downplay the horrific fate of tens of thousands of clergy, the
desperation of those who sent off their deceased in an unholy manner, or
the countless people who lost their positions because their relatives were

linked to religious institutions. But it is important to highlight some of the counterintuitive effects of religious repression: that repression creates opportunities (and some liberties), some of which were lost when the ban on religion was lifted.

These historical reflections may clarify the imam's selective nostalgia informing his statement that "during communism we had more freedom," but it does not clarify the implied indictment of post-Soviet religious "freedom." He elaborated on this further: "You know what the bitter thing is in all this? Finally we are able to freely carry out our beliefs, but now Islam is in decline. Satan is playing his own game." He was indirectly referring to the difficulties he experienced in persuading villagers to attend Friday prayers and the fact that he had been witnessing a steady process of conversion to Orthodox Christianity since the early 1990s.

To understand the context, it is important to remember that Adjara had been part of the Ottoman Empire from the sixteenth to nineteenth centuries and its inhabitants had converted to Islam during that time. When the region became part of Soviet Georgia (as an autonomous republic) its Georgian-speaking inhabitants were classified as Georgians even though their religious affiliation set them apart from other (non-Adjaran) Georgians who were Orthodox Christians. The Soviet domestication of religion proved useful in the sense that it allowed Adjarans to continue to be Muslim at home while increasingly becoming secular (Soviet) Georgians in public. This fragile balance was disrupted when in the 1990s Georgian nationality was framed in Orthodox Christian terms as part of a process to overcome the Soviet ideological legacy and reconnect with the long historical roots of the imagined Georgian nation. Despite this larger national religious framework, the new situation did bring more freedom to practice Islam openly: new mosques were constructed and madrasas were opened, young men studied abroad at Islamic universities, and elderly people went on *hajj* (the pilgrimage to Mecca). However, the return of religion to public life made it problematic to be simultaneously Muslim and Georgian, a conundrum that had the effect of eroding the Muslim community. It is within this context that the imam's nostalgia for religious repression makes perfect sense.

These examples are instructive for other Soviet and post-Soviet settings as well—especially those in which ethnic and religious affiliations have been closely intertwined. Religious freedom tends to increase the expectation that religious affiliation is accompanied by behavior deemed appropriate for that specific faith. During Soviet times, identifying as a Muslim was often a matter of background. If you were Kyrgyz, Uzbek, Azeri, or Adjaran, you were Muslim by default. The repression of religion meant that it was acceptable to drink alcohol, to refrain from participating in Ramadan activities, and to abstain from daily prayers. By contrast religious freedom meant that such behaviors became more controversial—religious affiliation obtained more content. For significant groups of people this created problems. Can a Georgian be Muslim? Is it possible to be a divorced Muslim woman? Can you consider yourself Muslim when you drink alcohol or eat pork? Intriguingly, while during Soviet times antireligious activists would frequently voice their frustration with people who insisted that they were Muslim *because* they were of a specific ethnic background, after 1991 newly trained imams complained about the same attitude. For the former, the amalgamation of ethnic and religious affiliation prevented people from becoming true socialists; for the latter, the problem was that it prevented people from becoming true Muslims.

Moreover, religion became "more free" for some than for others. In Adjara the key asymmetry was that Muslims had to compete against a well-funded Orthodox Christian Church, which was backed by a powerful national discourse that encouraged Georgians to be Christian. Elsewhere in the former Soviet Union, many of the "traditional religions" (a term reserved for religions that existed before the Soviet period) felt that they were up against unfair competition—especially rich foreign evangelical missions. Conversely, representatives of newly active religious groups felt that they were disadvantaged by the distinction made between "traditional" and "nontraditional" religions, a distinction that was enshrined in many religion laws across the former Soviet Union.

It is undeniable that the end of communism dramatically widened the scope for religious activity in the former Soviet states. This has been evidenced by the vibrant construction of mosques and churches, the reappearance of religious symbols in public life, the return of clergy in public positions of various kinds, and the virtual evaporation of atheist ideology. However, the return of religion to the public sphere also brought with it new tensions and new constraints. These vary from social pressure to participate in religious activities to new dynamics of exclusion that accompany the politicization of religion: the entanglement of religious and national identities, the sacralization of secular power, and the impact of the global discourse of (counter)terrorism. These ironies warn against making simple assumptions about either "repression" or "freedom" and draw attention to how possibilities and impossibilities for religious expression graft onto different social realities.

Contradictions of the Law

> The religious freedom guaranteed in the constitution of the Republic of Kyrgyzstan includes the right of every citizen to freely and independently choose his/her relation to religion, to individually or with others profess any religion, or not to profess any, to change one's religious conviction, and also to voice and spread one's conviction as related to religion. — Law of the Republic of Kyrgyzstan on Religious Freedom and Religious Organization

When discussing the contradictions of religious freedom laws, the case of Kyrgyzstan is instructive because of the speed with which the country lifted virtually all restrictions on religious activity after the collapse of communism. Indeed, the Kyrgyz law quoted above was signed only four months after the disintegration of the USSR. Moreover, unlike other central Asian countries such as Uzbekistan and Kazakhstan, which signed liberal religion laws but quickly amended them or restricted religious activity in practice notwithstanding changes to the law, the Kyrgyz government by and large stayed away from strict religious regulation until 2005.

This state of affairs was not, however, seen as an unequivocal blessing by everyone. When a state official pointed out to me in 2004 that "our laws on religion are far more liberal than those held by European countries," he was not boasting about the liberal credentials of his country, but rather bemoaning what he saw as a chaotic situation. This sentiment dovetails with the functionary quoted in the introduction who complained about the law being abused by evangelical missionaries. Both reveal tensions between the law and the state, prompting two questions: Who controls the law? And what are the possibilities for using and manipulating it?

The Kyrgyz government's endorsement of religious freedom was part of a larger "shock therapy" package designed by the International Monetary Fund and the World Bank that was accepted by the Kyrgyz government in the early 1990s. These reforms had unforeseen and often undesired effects. Contradicting all expert knowledge, the dismantling of the planned economy failed to attract hoped-for foreign direct investment.

In the religious sphere, by contrast, the government had assumed that "traditional religions" would resume their activities, but above and beyond that, liberalization triggered significant religious "foreign direct investment" in the form of evangelical missions and Islamic renewal movements such as the Tablighi Jamaat (this now global movement has its origins in 1920s India; it focuses on spiritual reformation at the grassroots level). Such proliferation of religious activity is hardly surprising, but it was not the "religious revival" that the government had desired or anticipated. In Kyrgyzstan, far-reaching religious liberalization was particularly beneficial to religious groups with transnational financial connections that had a strong mission component, focused on the individual, and stressed that faith and culture should be disentangled.

In *The Impossibility of Religious Freedom*, Winnifred Fallers Sullivan draws attention to the fact that law and religion "speak in languages largely opaque to each other." The key problem is that religious freedom laws require religion to be delimited when in fact it is impossible to draw unambiguous lines between religion and culture, especially with regard to everyday life. In the cases she analyzes, the effect is that "lived religion" remains unprotected or even opposed by the law. I agree with Sullivan's argument, but suggest that apart from leaving lived religion unprotected, the impossibility of delimiting religion may also offer opportunities. Indeed, it partly explains why Soviet authorities were unable to eradicate religion. They aimed to eradicate "religion" while promoting "culture," which meant that significant aspects of "lived religion" remained out of sight. Here I make a related argument: the impossibility of delimitation provided room for circumventing the law in post-Soviet Kyrgyzstan. This is so because sometimes the issue is less about having one's religious activities recognized *as* religion and more about having religious activities recognized as *non*religion. Evangelical missionaries were very skilled in producing this blurring effect, and in doing so were not only able to circumvent the law, but also to avoid the various controversies that their presence and activities were likely to produce in a Muslim-majority context.

To appreciate this point, it is important to note that although Kyrgyzstan's liberal laws between 1992 and 2008 did offer opportunities for religious activities originating outside the country, evangelical proselytizing activities among people of Muslim background continued to be controversial. Moreover, foreign "religious workers" had to be registered, and this could be a burdensome and long-winded process. One way to circumvent such requirements and avoid public controversy was to present oneself as a nongovernmental organization (NGO). In the early years of the twentieth century, there were evangelical microloan projects, orphanages and centers for street children, cultural NGOs promoting "mutual understanding," and evangelical cafés offering not only Internet access but also spiritual guidance. Their public appearance was "secular"—and they were registered as such—but evangelization was at least as central to their work. It might be tempting to see this as "abusing" Kyrgyzstan's liberal environment (as the state functionary quoted in the introduction did), but from the point of view of the missionaries, the essence of being a Christian is to share one's faith with others and hence they saw no problem in mixing humanitarian with spiritual aid. Evangelical missions often remained unseen and unopposed precisely because they skillfully adopted the appearance of the aid industry and were associated with the West. Moreover, the strength of their network—including connections with US diplomats—served as a guard against infringements of their rights by the host government.

While evangelical missions were able to pass as (secular) Western NGOs, such a guise was unavailable to the Tablighis for two reasons. First, their dress (long white robes) and beards made them instantly recognizable as religious actors. Second, in the post-9/11 context, Islamic piety movements were far more likely to be seen as a security threat than Christian missions, even in Muslim-majority countries such as Kyrgyzstan. It appears that "religious freedom" is particularly useful to those who fit the freedom image, are able to mobilize market forces, and can manipulate the law.

As mentioned above, Kyrgyz politicians perceived the religious proliferation as a threat to the collective good. They increasingly bemoaned the "excessively" liberal laws, which they (quite realistically) perceived as having been imposed on the country by international organizations. Opposition against these liberal laws eventually resulted in the new Religion Law, adopted in 2008, that outlawed proselytizing and prohibited religious activities that undermined national integrity and was thus clearly aimed at the activities of "nontraditional" religions. Apart from several raids on Jehovah's Witnesses and some closures of evangelical churches, the full effects of the Religion Law are not yet clear because in 2010 the presidential government was ousted from power and replaced with a potentially more liberal but weak parliamentary government. Still, it is useful to refer back to the Tablighi quoted in the introduction, who was unperturbed by the adoption of the new Religion Law despite its making illegal their central practice of *davat*, which refers to regular mission trips that all Tablighis are expected to take part in.

The Tablighis' unworried attitude indicated a realistic view of the fragility of the law, combined with a conviction that God's plan cannot be known. Although it is perhaps overreaching to call it a "benefit," repression of religion may positively contribute to the intensity of religious experience. This idea resonated in comments by Tablighis about the suspicion they encountered in the 1990s, and heroic stories of those who were interrogated or arrested on suspicion of links to terrorism. Equally important, though, is that such stories reveal that the liberal laws of the 1990s offered protection to some groups but not to others. The implementation of the repressive Religion Law of 2008 was equally partial. During the previous ten years, the Tablighis had extended their links to the Muftiate of Kyrgyzstan, and their activities had become familiar, gaining reluctant acceptance by the population at large and the authorities. This meant that they received informal protection from local imams as well as the regional senior imam (*imam khatib*). Their increasingly prominent position and public acceptance was much more significant than a change in the law; hence their relative indifference to a law that was so vehemently contested by religious rights groups.

As the law became more restrictive *and* the political situation became more unstable, possibilities for secular authorities to exercise force randomly increased. The Tablighis were untroubled by the law because they had become integrated into a number of informal orders. However, groups that had not been able to secure such a position—because they were disconnected, disliked, or both—found themselves in an increasingly vulnerable position. The Tablighi quoted in the introduction was correct when asserting that the new law would affect Jehovah's Witnesses, but not the Tablighis.

Conclusion

Religious freedom benefits some religious groups more than others, as seen in my analysis of Adjara and Kyrgyzstan. In the latter case, the government's wish to counteract the "uncontrollable flux" produced by its liberal laws was understandable. As Peter Danchin mentions, the "liberal algebra of rights regimes is unable to resolve such conflicts without considering . . . different conceptions of collective goods in the historical context of particular political communities." This historical context was ignored when religious freedom laws were designed for (and imposed on) Kyrgyzstan, and politicians understandably aimed to counteract the tensions produced by a law perceived to be alien. This does not mean that the repressive turn is in any way desirable—indeed, both religious freedom and the repression of religion are bound to be rife with contradictions and fraught with perils. In Kyrgyzstan, liberal laws were unable to protect the interests of all religious groups evenly, just as more repressive laws of the later years of the first decade of this century did not impact all groups equally. The experience of the Tablighis was particularly instructive in this regard. During the period of religious liberalization they remained unprotected because they did not fit the "freedom" picture, while the subsequent, more restrictive religion laws did directly affect them due to their improved connections with secular and (state-endorsed) religious authorities. The position of Islam in Adjara showed a variation of this dynamic. Here the end of Soviet religious repression increased the public presence of religion, a process that made Muslims more visible and vulnerable as a religious minority within the Georgian national context. Taken together, the examples presented in this essay have not only shown the uneven effects of freedom and repression on different religious groups but also demonstrated that "freedom" and "repression" do not exist as absolutes and may imply each other in a number of ways.

Selected Bibliography

Danchin, Peter. "Who Is the 'Human' in Human Rights? The Claims of Culture and Religion." *Maryland Journal of International Law* 24 (2009): 99–124.

Pelkmans, Mathijs. *Defending the Border: Identity, Religion, and Modernity in the Republic of Georgia*. Ithaca, NY: Cornell University Press, 2006.

———. "The Transparency of Christian Proselytizing in Kyrgyzstan." *Anthropological Quarterly* 82 (2009): 423–46.

Sullivan, Winnifred Fallers. *The Impossibility of Religious Freedom*. Princeton, NJ: Princeton University Press, 2009.

CHAPTER TWENTY-SEVEN

Religious Freedom's Oxymoronic Edge

Wendy Brown

Can religious freedom be understood as itself helping constitute an ethical lifeworld without posing it . . . as liberation from the moralities produced in religion?—Webb Keane, "What Is Religious Freedom Supposed to Be?" (this volume)

. . . the very idea of freedom of religion is paradoxical; it is the freedom to be unfree in a particular kind of way.—Michael Lambek, "Is Religion Free?" (this volume)

The liberty we prize is not America's gift to the world, it is God's gift to humanity. —George W. Bush, State of the Union Address, 2003

Within liberalism, religious liberty has a distinctly oxymoronic edge. Liberty, as John Stuart Mill famously put it, constitutes "the individual [as] sovereign over himself . . . his own body and mind." Liberty's domain is the "inward [one] of conscience . . . thought and feeling . . . opinion and sentiment . . . tastes and pursuits." Its consummate expression is "[p]ursuing our own good in our own way." Within liberalism, liberty is unimpeded individual sovereignty, pursuit, and choice, limited only by the Harm Principle. This is something no religion affirms or advocates. Moreover, such self-sovereignty is strongly tethered to reason rather than faith; hence Mill's exclusion of children and primitives from entitlement to it.

For liberals, liberty requires both having the capacities for self-governance and being unhindered by other people, the state, or other sources of dicta. Put differently, liberty is centered in the individual moral autonomy theorized by Immanuel Kant but also requires leashing or limiting all other sovereign powers to secure a dominion for individual autonomy; that dominion, according to Mill, is the "place where the authority of society ends." This distinctive understanding of liberty is the basis of the antipathy liberals have not only to Thomas Hobbes, but also to Jean-Jacques Rousseau: each of those thinkers attempts to reconcile freedom with submission to authority, in one case the leviathan, in the other popular sovereignty embodied in the general will. Liberals regard as authoritarian or worse such ruses in which we are made to "author" entities that come to have power over and against us. Again, while authority has its place in liberal political orders, we can only be said to be free where and when its domain ends, where and when we authorize ourselves and our actions. Hence, to maximize domains of liberty, both a minimal state and representative government (wherein we retain the capacity to revoke another's actions on our behalf) are required in the political realm. And in the private realm, we must have the widest possible berth for individual choices about ways of life and conduct.

For the rational liberal self, then, liberty rests in choosing one's own values and purposes, one's ends and means. Religion threatens to compromise this. In a world of sovereigns, small and large, if my conscience and soul belong to God, they do not belong to me. Put strongly, as Fyodor Dostoyevsky suggests in *The Grand Inquisitor*, religion may express a desire for a certain escape from freedom, a reprieve and comfort from its extreme burdens—especially those of providing meaning and compass to life, of full accountability for beliefs or choices, and of the contingent discrepancies between motives and effects of action. Put more mildly, for the liberal, liberty and religion pertain to different dimensions and elements of being human—with reason, agency, choice, and responsibility in one part, and faith, authority, submission, and fate in another. Thus, however important religion is to many liberals, and however much Protestantism took its shape to comport with liberty and individualism (including its emphasis on individual interpretation of scripture), submission to religious authority, ritual, or law cannot be squared easily with liberty in the liberal sense of the word. Freedom of worship guarantees citizens the right to choose to be subjected by religious powers and communities; it does not guarantee freedom within religion practice. As it secures the citizen from state interference or coercion in the domain of religion, it guarantees the right to be as religiously unfree as one chooses.

None of this is to say that liberals must eschew religion, only that religion does not emerge as a field of freedom within liberalism; it is thus incoherent to speak of religious freedom without twisting the meaning of freedom away from its liberal predicates. Indeed, the chasm between religion and freedom—sustained by liberalism's binaries of faith and reason, and of authority and liberty—reminds us why accommodation of religious difference in the West is born through the language of toleration rather than freedom. Much has been made of the difference between toleration and equality; far less attention has been paid to its divergence from freedom. So let us now put the matter bluntly: toleration is neither a guarantee of freedom nor freedom's equivalent. Rather, religious toleration licenses difference—different faiths, beliefs, and paths of submission to religious authority and ritual. Toleration as a modus vivendi depends on all three of the following: the separation of religious from state authority, the sequestering of religion in the private sphere, and the public rendering of religion as a matter of faith rather than truth. Hence the novel and strange form that secularism and religious freedom take in the West: as religion becomes personal and private, religious freedom is exercised by the individual to submit to an authority of one's choosing. But as Charles Taylor indirectly reminds us in *A Secular Age*, choice calls the authority into doubt, and authority calls the choice into doubt. Put another way, religious liberty is not freedom in the liberal sense but instead a switch point between submission to political and religious authority, or political and religious communities. Through the liberal formulation of religious freedom, the religious subject secures a public right against state sovereignty in order to submit privately to divine sovereignty. It is unsurprising, then, that Western secular practices feature constant leakages from the private to the public, the individual to the collective, the free mind to the bowed head—leakages that contour everything from the veil debates to judicial decisions to inaugurations of heads of state that begin and end with invocations of God.

One approach to what I am calling the oxymoronic edge of religious liberty is that framing religious toleration as religious freedom entails what philosophers term a category mistake. But we might also understand this edge as productively opening up, even destabilizing, the predicates of secularism and freedom within a liberal schema. It may reveal important slippages in the liberal antimonies of freedom and authority, faith and reason, public and private. In turn, close attention to these slippages in the midst of recent efforts to extend religious freedom to the non-Western world might permit us to rethink religious freedom itself. We might, in other words, parallel the rethinking of secularism occasioned by (imperial) efforts to extend secularism beyond the West with rethinking the relationship of religion to freedom. Such a rethinking would necessarily challenge liberal predicates of both liberty and faith contained in current Western formulations of religious freedom. It might challenge the idea of freedom and authority as opposites and consider instead freedom as a way of negotiating, imbibing, inhabiting, or serving authority—including divine authority. It might formulate reason and faith as related rather than opposed, reason as a certain proclamation of faith, as working on and reflecting on faith. We do not have to go far afield for sources in this work. These kinds of reformulations, and the challenge they offer to conventions of modern liberal religious liberty, can be found at the heart of the Western political tradition itself, notably in the thinking and practices of two of the West's most iconic freedom fighters, Socrates and Martin Luther King Jr. Let us see how this goes.

If liberalism configures freedom as unhindered choice, it does not appear this way within most religions, including Islam, Christianity, and Judaism, where not only messianism but many everyday practices connect freedom with divine truth and authority. Consequently, the work of religiously inspired or motivated political actors, especially but not only in liberal democracies, is often contoured by more than one concept of freedom, for example, civil and religious. For both Socrates and King, freedom materializes through proximity to the divine; it involves serving god and fulfilling god's aims or plan. It also entails setting aside worldly and quotidian matters, care for the self and its interests, in favor of higher concerns, including achieving individual ethical virtue, becoming enlightened, and delivering worldly justice.

Consider Socrates. In Plato's last dialogues (*Crito*, *Apology*, and *Phaedo*) we learn that Socrates regarded his freedom as technically secured by Athenian law but substantially realized by living in accord with god. It is these dual sources of freedom that build the vise yielding both Socrates's death sentence and his willingness to abide by this sentence rather than escape prison and flee Athens. If Socrates's religious piety animated the conduct that threatened the state, his political loyalty governed his obedience to the state's verdict against him. Here Socrates suffered an intensification of a conflict he had navigated throughout his life: on the one hand, he understood his vocation—philosophical inquiry into the nature of the virtuous and the just with his fellow Athenians—to be given to him by his god and as fulfilling his duty to this god. "Avoiding injustice" meant living in accord with his deity. Pursuing justice meant seeking to improve his fellow citizens, and hence Athens, according to divine justice. On the other hand, he remained loyal to Athens, not least because it made possible this vocation along with his very existence. If obedience to divine wisdom sometimes placed him at odds with the justice formulated or practiced by the state, and on several occasions led him to refuse compliance with what he considered corrupt Athenian dictates, he struggled to remain faithful to both Athenian and divine authority, and to do both in the name of freedom.

In the figure of Socrates, then, we encounter a divinely ordained vocation, the pursuit of divine wisdom, and the pursuit of a righteously lived life, all cast as freedom to live according to what we might today call his conscience and which at times positions him against state dictates or practices. Freedom for Socrates is exercised through pursuit of divine truth and living according to divine justice. Yet this does not make freedom purely religious any more than it is purely civil; rather, Socrates finds his freedom in coming close to god in the context of a free Athens, and also in working to bring Athens closer to divine justice and virtue through the improvement of its citizens. Freedom, we might say, materializes in the dialectic between a divinely inspired Socrates and his fellows, between the state and god, between true authority and its discovery. Indeed, freedom can be seen to rest in Socratic dialectic itself—dialectic understood not simply as argument but as a struggle for transformation, improvement, or what Socrates calls the "turning of the soul" toward wisdom and virtue. Dialectic, the uniquely human practice of argument and transformation through speech, may also be seen to express freedom insofar as it emanates from a distinctly human betweenness, from creatures who are neither gods nor beasts but potentially ethical animals who must struggle for knowledge and goodness. Freedom for Socrates is exercised in and through this struggle. It has little to do with self-sovereignty in the liberal sense.

Martin Luther King Jr., in "Letter from a Birmingham Jail," explicitly compares himself to Socrates in his mission of justice. But King takes the religious dimension of his cause up a notch, arguing that freedom itself is God's will, and that he is carrying out a divine purpose in fighting for the universal enjoyment of freedom on earth. King also parts with Socrates on the question of obedience to the laws of the land in which he finds himself. In the "Letter" he argues that he is obligated to obey just but not unjust laws, a distinction drawn according to whether a law accords with divine law or is "out of harmony" with it. Thus King casts good law as the law of God—a law that, among other things, decrees universal equality and freedom.

As is well known, King's distinction between laws that do and do not comport with the divine paves the way for justified civil disobedience. King insists on obeying God's laws when they conflict with earthly human institutions or practices. He is willing to suffer punishment for breaking earthly laws but unwilling to honor them as right. Like Socrates, King identifies an order of justice and righteousness, not found in human convention and practices, that is the source of his own conduct, even as that conduct must reckon with—indeed, negotiate—fealty to a civil state. King's own exercise of freedom in the name of delivering freedom rests in this reckoning or negotiation between God and polity; his aim is to bring them closer together in the cause of freedom.

Matters are complicated here because King says several different things about what makes a law righteous that are not easily squared with one another. Initially he insists that the difference between just and un-just human laws depends on whether or not they align with eternal and natural law. Then he argues that "any law that uplifts human personality is just and any law that degrades human personality is unjust." He shifts the argument yet again to say that an unjust law is one that a majority im-poses on a minority but does not make binding on itself; it is a law of dif-ference and particularity rather than sameness and universality. Finally, he declares a law may be just on its face but unjust in its application; if used tactically for unjust purposes, it becomes unjust. Rhetorically, then, it would seem that King is drawing both on the authority of the divine and the "common sense" of democracy to test any given law's justice or rightness. This, of course, converts God to being a democrat and promul-gating democracy, which is no minor conversion.

These inconsistencies notwithstanding, divine authority remains a rich wellspring of freedom for King. It frees him from submission to ordinary law (which may be terribly unjust), frees him to discern which laws are worthy of obedience and which are not, and frees him to at-tempt to enact justice in accord with that discernment. Interpellation by and alignment with God's authority is in this regard a more fundamental and more radical source of freedom than any secured by a civil order. This interpellation and alignment allow King to act consistently accord-ing to conscience—his interpretation of God's word—rather than accord-ing to external rule or dictate. Paradoxically, divine authority in this way becomes constitutive of individual sovereignty (freedom's fundament in liberalism) as well as a beacon of freedom. Civil law only has the capacity to be such a multi-headed source of freedom to the extent that it aligns with a divine vision.

In the "Letter," King's distinction between religious and civil au-thority, and hence between freedom and subordination, intensifies as he draws on other examples besides Socrates to feature both the justice of disobeying unjust laws and the exercise and promotion of freedom in doing so. His examples include the Christians in Ancient Rome, the new American settlers at the Boston Tea Party, and resistance to "the perfectly legal actions of Nazi Germany" by Germans of that era. According to King, each episode of opposition is itself an act of freedom and is undertaken on behalf of the cause of freedom. In this way he links conscience-inspired dissent, the emancipation of the world, and the divine will. Freedom is God's will unfolding on earth, God's plan being realized.

Like Socrates, King argues that the religiously inspired disobedient enacts his or her freedom in part through submission to earthly consequences, whether being incarcerated (and it is surely significant that both Socrates and King reflect on freedom—and assert their freedom—while sitting in jail, a venue usually considered the epitome of earthly unfreedom) or made to suffer in earthly ways—poverty, humiliation, physical pain, or death. The point is not simply that freedom is costly or dangerous. Rather, both insist that freedom requires and manifests in indifference to earthly deprivations. It is exercised in the choice of virtuous or ethical existence over everyday comforts, satisfactions, and feeding of desires. Again, the point is not asceticism or worldly withdrawal. To the contrary, Socrates and King care about earthly existence and want others to care about making this world in god's image, bringing divine justice down to earth. But freedom arises in living for this aim and according to divine truths, not in satisfying appetites. Those who remain enslaved to concern with comfort or personal desires will neither be free nor set the world free. Of course, Socrates is drawing on a well-known ambivalence toward bodily desire in Greek thought, just as King is drawing on Christian asceticism and Mahatma Gandhi would draw on Hinduism. But all of these also locate freedom in relationship to the divine. We could not be further from liberalism now.

To compress the point, in contrast to the standard secular and liberal presumption that as a domain of authority religion is also a domain of unfreedom, or that the chief bearing of freedom on religion lies in protecting individuals' right to choose their faith, Socrates and King derive their freedom, and their work on behalf of freedom, from attunement to religious authority. Such a nonliberal understanding of freedom establishes it as a stance of resistance to worldly laws or practices that Socrates and King take to be unjust, unholy, or unfree. Freedom is not only the aim of their work but the means: their own freedom pertains to hewing to god's will, indifference to earthly concerns, and seeking to expand the reach of divine wisdom on earth.

Thus, for these two iconic symbols of freedom in the West, religious freedom is not oxymoronic and is not a matter of submitting to the god of one's choosing while keeping the state clear of religious thresholds for justice. Nor does religious freedom take its bearings in opposition to authority or the rule of law. Religion itself is not a matter of private belief sequestered in the private sphere. Instead, religious freedom entails publicly enacting god's will, living in accord with the divine, and challenging the unfreedom of the state through bringing it to the bar of the divine. "Religious freedom" inheres in realizing god's authority, vitalizing it, publicly enacting it. Thus does the thinking and practice of both of these freedom fighters problematize the classic liberal binary between freedom and authority and the secular line between private and public.

I want to conclude with the risky move of linking this discussion of Socrates and King with one (highly contestable) meaning of freedom within Islam. In *The Muslim Concept of Freedom*, Franz Rosenthal suggests that freedom of the soul for a Muslim means "not hankering after bodily matters" and more specifically emancipation from enslavement by desire. This emancipation secures a "natural modesty" of the soul, its nonappetitive, thoughtful, and virtuous bearing. "The soul has more freedom when the intellect is more powerful than bodily desire" Rosenthal writes. Thus, commensurate with Socrates's and King's arguments that quotidian concerns are not the domain of freedom, mastery of desire becomes a prerequisite to acting freely; freedom is not pursuit of desire but mastery over it, ceasing to be its slave. Citing the eighteenth-century Indian scholar at-Tahanawi, Rosenthal adds that, in Sufi usage, freedom comes into partnership with the divine when one achieves "complete relief of the mind from attachment to anything but God. Man arrives at the station of freedom when he no longer has any worldly purpose to follow and does not care for either this world or the hereafter." Freedom lies in becoming slave to the prophet rather than to one's own soul and has as its prerequisite mastery (enslavement) of bodily and worldly cares. Consider this passage from at-Tahanawi's study of Sufi freedom: "Since some heretics say that he who arrives at the station of freedom ceases to be a slave—and this is heresy because no one ever ceases to be a slave of the Prophet—who else (but a heretic) would want to occupy that place? No! When a human being arrives at the station (of freedom), he is no longer a slave of himself, that is, he does not follow the commands of his own soul. Rather *he becomes the owner of his soul.* The soul becomes subservient and obedient to him" (emphasis added).

Ought we to infer, then, that Islam has little appreciation of civil or political freedom, that, as some of its contemporary Western detractors argue, it is a religion "against freedom"? We have prepared another possible reading here, one that foregrounds the extent to which the quest for freedom always carries a self-canceling element of departing one master for another. This is true whether what is being sought is freedom from state sovereignty for individual sovereignty, from a colonial master for local control, from traditional for rational legal authority, from external dicta for conscience, from faith for reason or, as in this case, from worldly for divine authority. Thus the idea of freedom through enslavement or obedience to the divine, rather than being radically at odds with modern Western formulations, highlights a crucial if frequently disavowed feature of them. It reminds us that freedom's imbrication with sovereignty means that freedom is always driven and limned by the desire to be governed by the true authority, whether that authority is self, reason, God, family, revolution, rights, or philosophy. King and Socrates insist forthrightly that freedom is found through subordination to the divine, through replacing a worldly order of justice and truth with a divinely ordered one. Their resistance to unjust civil codes, as both a stance of freedom and on behalf of freedom, is a bow to divine authority no less than Sufism is.

And what of the other side of the liberal religious freedom game, the secular state's commitment to be free of religion, to leave it wholly to the private sphere—is there an oxymoronic edge present here as well? Is there, notwithstanding the establishment clause of the US Constitution, a secret religious life of the free democratic state with which we ought to reckon, as we reckoned with the divinely based freedom of ostensibly secular freedom fighters? This is more familiar territory to recent scholars of secularism. Only the naive continue to believe today that the secular state is the wholly unreligious state, that it has no entwinement with religion, no expression or sanctification of (secular) religious calendars, practices, or rituals. From Carl Schmitt and Saba Mahmood, from Giorgio Agamben and Talal Asad, we know better than to understand the secular state as nontheological and neutral. If theory is not convincing enough, we have been battered by events: the ongoing controversies about whether modest Islamic female dress and perhaps Muslims tout court can and should be banned in Europe; a Germany that, in the name of secularism, seeks to regulate if not abolish infant male circumcision for Jews; publicly circulated media sexually degrading the Prophet Muhammad "tolerated" in Euro-Atlantic nations that would not and have not easily imbibed parallel depictions of Jesus or Moses. And then there is the ongoing self-identification of the Republican Party in the United States with Christian values, an identification overtly animating its positions on policies ranging from charter schools to marriage equality, women's reproductive autonomy to foreign policy. The secular state, we can only conclude, is a distinctive kind of theological state, never "free" of religion.

There is, finally, a more fundamental theoretical paradox in the idea of the religiously free state, one that Hobbes and Rousseau may have theorized most honestly and incisively. Can state authority avoid holding the scepter as well as the sword, even if the scepter is one of civil religion or of a highly secularized and hence disseminated and dissimulated formal religion? Can sovereign state power, however relentlessly and even scrupulously secularized, fully escape a theological dimension? Can state sovereignty itself, whether imitating, joining with, overturning, or displacing that of God, ever fail to invoke divine right or divine succession in its quotidian juridicism as well as in its exceptional words and deeds? Has any state not made its citizens oath-swearers? Has a state ever gone to war without a god on its side? No more than secular subjects, it would seem, can secular states be religiously free.

Selected Bibliography

Agamben, Giorgio. *Homo Sacer: Sovereign Power and Bare Life.* Translated by Daniel Heller-Roazen. Stanford, CA: Stanford University Press, 1998.

———. *The Kingdom and the Glory: For a Theological Genealogy of Economy and Government.* Translated by Lorenzo Chiesa and Matteo Mandarini. Stanford, CA: Stanford University Press, 2011.

Asad, Talal. *Formations of the Secular.* Stanford, CA: Stanford University Press, 2003.

———. "Free Speech, Blasphemy, and Secular Criticism." In *Is Critique Secular? Blasphemy, Injury and Free Speech*, by Talal Asad, Wendy Brown, Judith Butler, and Saba Mahmood, 20–63. Berkeley and Los Angeles: University of California Press, 2009; reprinted, with a new preface, by Fordham University Press, 2012.

Bush, George W. "President Delivers Sate of the Union." White House, Office of the Press Secretary, Washington, DC, 2003. Accessed October 14, 2013 at http://georgewbush-whitehouse.archives.gov/news/releases/2003/01/print/20030128-19.html.

Hobbes, Thomas. *Leviathan.* Edited by Richard Tuck. Cambridge: Cambridge University Press, 1996.

King Martin Luther, Jr. "Letter from the Birmingham Jail." In *Why We Can't Wait.* New York: Harper and Row, 1964.

Mahmood, Saba. "Secularism, Hermeneutics, and Empire: The Politics of Islamic Reformation." *Public Culture* 18, no. 2 (2006): 323–47.

———. "Religious Reason and Secular Affect: An Incommensurable Divide?" In *Is Critique Secular? Blasphemy, Injury and Free Speech*, by Talal Asad, Wendy Brown, Judith Butler, and Saba Mahmood, 64–100. Berkeley and Los Angeles: University of California Press, 2009.

Mill, John Stuart. *On Liberty and Other Writings.* Edited by Stefan Collini. Cambridge: Cambridge University Press, 1989.

Plato. *The Collected Dialogues of Plato, Including the Letters.* Edited by Edith Hamilton and Huntington Cairns. Princeton, NJ: Princeton University Press, 2005.

Rosenthal, Franz. *The Muslim Concept of Freedom.* Leiden, Netherlands: Brill, 1960.

Rousseau, Jean-Jacques. *The Social Contract.* Translated by Maurice Cranston. New York: Penguin, 1968.

Schmitt, Carl. *Political Theology: Four Chapters on the Concept of Sovereignty.* Translated by George Schwab. Chicago: University of Chicago Press, 2005.

Taylor, Charles. *A Secular Age.* Cambridge, MA: Harvard University Press, 1997.

Contributors

HUSSEIN ALI AGRAMA
Department of Anthropology
University of Chicago
Chicago, IL 60637
USA

WAHEEDA AMIEN
Faculty of Law
University of Cape Town
Rondebosch 7701
South Africa

LORI G. BEAMAN
Department of Classics and
    Religious Studies
University of Ottawa
Ottawa ON K1N 6N5
Canada

COURTNEY BENDER
Department of Religion
Columbia University
New York, NY 10027
USA

WENDY BROWN
Department of Political Science
University of California, Berkeley
Berkeley, CA 94720
USA

ELIZABETH A. CASTELLI
Department of Religion
Barnard College at Columbia University
New York, NY 10027
USA

NANDINI CHATTERJEE
Department of History
University of Exeter
Exeter EX4 4RJ
United Kingdom

PETER G. DANCHIN
Francis King Carey School of Law
University of Maryland
Baltimore, MD 21201
USA

ROSALIND I. J. HACKETT
Department of Religious Studies
University of Tennessee, Knoxville
Knoxville, TN 37996-0450
USA

EVAN HAEFELI
Department of History
Texas A&M University
College Station, TX 77843
USA

ROBERT W. HEFNER
Department of Anthropology
Boston University
Boston, MA 02215
USA

ELIZABETH SHAKMAN HURD
Department of Political Science
Northwestern University
Evanston, IL 60208
USA

GREG JOHNSON
Department of Religious Studies
University of Colorado, Boulder
Boulder, CO 80309-0292
USA

WEBB KEANE
Department of Anthropology
University of Michigan
Ann Arbor, MI 48109-1107
USA

CÉCILE LABORDE
Department of Political Science
University College London

London WC1H 9QU
United Kingdom

MICHAEL LAMBEK
Department of Anthropology
University of Toronto, Scarborough
Scarborough, Ontario M1C 1A4
Canada

SABA MAHMOOD
Department of Anthropology
University of California, Berkeley
Berkeley, CA 94720
USA

NADIA MARZOUKI
European University Institute
Florence
Italy
Centre National de la Recherche
    Scientifique
Paris
France

SAMUEL MOYN
Harvard Law School
Harvard University
Cambridge, MA 02138
USA

MATHIJS PELKMANS
Department of Anthropology
London School of Economics
    and Political Science
London WC2A 2AE
United Kingdom

ANN PELLEGRINI
Tish School of the Arts
New York University
New York, NY 10003
USA

NOAH SALOMON
Department of Religion
Carleton College
Northfield, MN 55057
USA

BENJAMIN SCHONTHAL
Department of Theology and Religion
University of Otago
Dunedin
New Zealand

YVONNE SHERWOOD
School of European Culture and
   Languages
University of Kent
Canterbury, Kent CT2 7NF
United Kingdom

DAVID SORKIN
Department of History
Yale University
New Haven, CT 06520
USA

WINNIFRED FALLERS SULLIVAN
Department of Religious Studies
Maurer School of Law
Indiana University, Bloomington
Bloomington, IN 47405
USA

ROBERT YELLE
Wissenschaftstheorie und
   Religionswissenschaft
Ludwig-Maximilians-Universität
   München
Fakultät für Philosophie
D-80539 München
Germany

Index

Printed in Great Britain
by Amazon